D1197252 2

SPECTRUM
MULTIVIEW BOOKS

Justification

FIVE VIEWS

EDITED BY James K. Beilby and Paul Rhodes Eddy

ASSOCIATE EDITOR Steven E. Eenderlein

WITH CONTRIBUTIONS BY Michael F. Bird, James D. G. Dunn, Michael S. Horton, Veli-Matti Kärkkäinen, Gerald O'Collins, S.J., & Oliver Rafferty, S.J.

IVP Academic
An imprint of InterVarsity Press
Downers Grove, Illinois

InterVarsity Press
P.O. Box 1400, Downers Grove, IL 60515-1426
World Wide Web: www.ivpress.com
E-mail: email@ivpress.com

InterVarsity Press® is the book-publishing division of InterVarsity Christian Fellowship/USA®, a movement of
students and faculty active on campus at hundreds of universities, colleges and schools of nursing in the United States
of America, and a member movement of the International Fellowship of Evangelical Students. For information
about local and regional activities, write Public Relations Dept., InterVarsity Christian Fellowship/USA, 6400
Schroeder Rd., P.O. Box 7895, Madison, WI 53707-7895, or visit the IVCF website at <www.intervarsity.org>.

Design: Cindy Kiple
Images: © Carlos Martinez/iStockphoto

ISBN 978-0-8308- 3944-5

Printed in the United States of America ∞

InterVarsity Press is committed to protecting the environment and to the responsible use of natural
resources. As a member of Green Press Initiative we use recycled paper whenever possible. To learn
more about the Green Press Initiative, visit <www.greenpressinitiative.org>.

Library of Congress Cataloging-in-Publication Data

Justification: five views/edited by James Beilby and Paul R.
Eddy.
    p. cm.—(Spectrum multiview book series)
    Includes bibliographical references and index.
    ISBN 978-0-8308-3944-5 (pbk.: alk. paper)
    1. Justification (Christian theology)—History of doctrines. I.
Beilby, James K. II. Eddy, Paul R.
    BT764.3.J88 2011
    234'.7—dc23

2011023117

P	18	17	16	15	14	13	12	11	10	9	8	7	6	5	4	3	2	1
Y	26	25	24	23	22	21	20	19	18	17	16	15	14	13	12	11		

Contents

To our children,

Sierra Beilby, Madeline Beilby, Zachary Beilby, Malia Beilby

Jordan Eddy, Juston Eddy, Rachel Bohn

Abby Enderlein

Abbreviations

AB	Anchor Bible
ABD	*The Anchor Bible Dictionary.* Edited by D. N. Freedman et al. 6 vols. New York: Doubleday, 1992.
ANTC	Abingdon New Testament Commentaries
2 Bar.	*2 Baruch*
Barn.	*Barnabas*
BBR	*Bulletin for Biblical Research*
BDAG	Frederic W. Danker, ed. *The Greek-English Lexicon of the New Testament and Other Early Christian Literature.* 3rd ed. Chicago: University of Chicago Press, 2001.
BECNT	Baker Exegetical Commentary on the New Testament
BJRL	*Bulletin of the John Rylands University Library of Manchester*
COQG	Christian Origins and the Question of God
CR	Corpus Reformatorum
DS	Denzinger-Schönmetzer, *Enchiridion Symbolorum*
D	Denzinger, *Enchiridion Symbolorum*
EDNT	*Exegetical Dictionary of the New Testament.* Edited by H. Balz and G. Schneider. 3 vols. ET. Grand Rapids: Eerdmans, 1990-1993.
ET	English translation
GLAJJ	*Greek and Latin Authors on Jews and Judaism.* Edited, with introductions, translations and commentary, by Menahem Stern. 3 vols. Jerusalem: Israel Academy of Sciences and Hummanities, 1974–1984.
HDT	*Heidelberg Disputation*
HTR	*Harvard Theological Review*
JETS	*Journal of the Evangelical Theological Society*
JTI	*Journal of theological Interpretation*
Jub.	*Jubilees*
ICC	International Critical Commentary
Institutes	John Calvin. *Institutes of the Christian Religion.* Edited by J. T.

	McNeill. Translated by F. L. Battles. Philadelphia: The Westminster Press, 1960.
LSJ	*A Greek-English Lexicon,* compiled by Henry George Liddell and Robert Scott, revised and augmented by Sir Henry Stuart Jones. New York: Oxford University Press, 1996.
LW	*Luther's Works.* American Edition. Edited by Jaroslav Pelikan and Helmut T. Lehman. 55 vols. St. Louis: Concordia, 1955-1986.
NSBT	New Studies in Biblical Theology
NTS	*New Testament Studies*
PBM	Paternoster Biblical Monographs
PL	Patrologia latina. Edited by J.-P. Migne. 217 vols. Paris, 1844-1864.
Pss. Sol.	*Psalms of Solomon*
R&R	*Reformation and Revival*
SBET	*Scottish Bulletin of Evangelical Theology*
SNTSMS	Society for New Testament Studies Monograph Series
TDOT	*Theological Dictionary of the Old Testament*
ThTo	*Theology Today*
WA	*Weimar Ausgabe*
WBC	Word Biblical Commentary
WCF	Westminster Confession of Faith
WTJ	*Westminster Theological Journal*
WUNT	Wissenschaftliche Untersuchungen zum Neuen Testament
ZNW	*Zeitschrift für die neutestamentliche Wissenschaft*

Preface

The formula for a good "multiple views" book is relatively straightforward. First, the book must address an important biblical or theological issue; ideally, a topic on which there is currently substantial discussion and debate. Second, the issue or debate itself must be capable of some degree of clear definition. Some topics are inherently poor candidates for this sort of book because of their conceptual complexity. In such a case, it is never clear which of the literally dozens of embedded questions is being addressed at any particular moment, and it is enormously difficult to avoid having conversations in which the interlocutors talk past each other. Third, the conversants must represent positions that are: (1) identifiably distinct from each other and (2) reasonably expressive of the range of views in the contemporary debate.

The reader will have to decide whether or how well this book meets the aforementioned criteria, but we take it for granted that few if any would question the theological importance of and current interest in the topic of justification. Stimulated by various ecumenical conversations and vigorous debates over the "new perspective" on Paul, the debate over the nature and implications of justification language in Scripture has reached a fever pitch. And, for most Christians, a lot is riding on this conversation; at stake is nothing less than the understanding of the nature of sin, the atonement, conversion and salvation itself. Of course, it is this very fact that makes this topic difficult for a multiple views book—there are many historical, biblical and theological issues that are intertwined with the justification debate. Consequently, we have asked our contributors to engage in a herculean task—namely, address a wide range of important biblical and theological issues as they present their views.

The selection of which perspectives to include in a multiple-views book is perhaps the most difficult of editorial tasks. There are always more views than can be included in a single volume, and almost every view has various subviews—each of which can lay claim to being the best representative of the broader perspective. When we selected contributors, we looked not only for people that could ably represent the primary views on this subject, but for people that could engage the justification question on multiple levels: biblically, historically and theologically. Our contributors are Michael Horton, defending the traditional Reformed view; Michael Bird, defending the progressive Reformed view; James Dunn, defending the "new perspective" view; Veli-Matti Kärkkäinen, defending the deification view; and Gerald O'Collins, S.J., and Oliver Rafferty, S.J., defending the Roman Catholic view. We take it for granted that the inclusion of these views needs no explanation. There is, however, an omission that needs some explaining. Readers might be surprised to see the Lutheran view missing from the list. Our response is that Horton's traditional Reformed view is functionally identical in all the significant theological aspects to the traditional Lutheran view. Moreover, Kärkkäinen's deification view represents a less traditional Lutheran view. There are, of course, many other possible views of justification, and some of them are genuinely interesting and important. We only hope that readers will understand the necessity of drawing the line someplace: this "five views" book is already long enough.

We would like to thank each of our contributors for their willingness to participate in this project. Working with them was a joy. Many others have given valuable advice or assistance along the way, including David Clark, Mike Holmes, Brendan Lorentz and Laine Gebhardt. Special mention, however, goes to two people. First, our IVP Academic editor, Dan Reid, has been a model of encouragement and tireless support. Second, our colleague, Steve Enderlein, provided us with such a degree of assistance, including coauthoring the introductory chapters, that it seemed only fair to acknowledge his efforts by making him an associate editor. Our greatest debt, however, is owed to our families and, particularly, to our children, to whom this book is dedicated. In all honesty, you make academic work more difficult—for we would rather be spending time with you. Nevertheless, you provide us with a daily reminder of the reality and depth of God's sacrificial love for us. Our prayer is that each of you will be able to say, with the apostle Paul, "For I am convinced that neither death nor life, neither angels nor demons, neither the present nor the future, nor any powers, neither height nor depth, nor anything else in all creation will be able to separate us from the love of God that is in Christ Jesus our Lord" (Rom 8:38-39).

1

Justification in Historical Perspective

Theological debates within scholarly quarters of the church are nothing new for the Christian faith. Occasionally, however, one of these debates spills over from the academic world and begins to ignite controversy within and among churches and parachurch ministries, between pastors and friends. This was certainly the case with the "openness of God" debate that rocked the evangelical Christian world in the 1990s.[1] At the opening of the second decade of the twenty-first century, it appears that another debate has reached similar proportions in evangelical circles and beyond, namely, the debate on the nature of *justification* and its proper place within Christian theology.

In an important sense, the church was handed the justification debate within the very texts that constitute its authoritative canon. There, the apostle Paul writes concerning the nature of grace, faith and works: "For by grace you have been saved through faith, and this is not your own doing; it is the gift of God—not the result of works, so that no one may boast" (Eph 2:8-9 NRSV). And concerning justification:

> Because by works of the law no flesh will be justified in his sight, for through law comes the knowledge of sin. But now, apart from the law, the righteousness of God has been manifested, although it is testified to by the law; the righteousness of God *has been manifested* through faith of Jesus Christ to all those who believe. For there is no distinction, for all sinned

[1]On which see James K. Beilby and Paul R. Eddy, eds., *Divine Foreknowledge: Four Views* (Downers Grove, Ill.: InterVarsity Press, 2001).

and are lacking the glory of God; they are justified freely by his grace, through the redemption that is in Christ Jesus. (Rom 3:20-24, authors' translation[2])

And then there is James:

But someone will say, "You have faith and I have works." Show me your faith apart from your works, and I by my works will show you my faith. You believe that God is one; you do well. Even the demons believe—and shudder. Do you want to be shown, you senseless person, that faith apart from works is barren? Was not our ancestor Abraham justified by works when he offered his son Isaac on the altar? You see that faith was active along with his works, and faith was brought to completion by the works. Thus the scripture was fulfilled that says, "Abraham believed God, and it was reckoned to him as righteousness," and he was called the friend of God. You see that a person is justified by works and not by faith alone. . . . For just as the body without the spirit is dead, so faith without works is also dead. (Jas 2:18-24, 26 NRSV)

Sixteen centuries later, the Protestant Reformers would seize upon Paul's expression of justification as constituting the very essence of the gospel itself. Similar to traditional Lutherans, many Reformed evangelicals today view the doctrine of justification by faith as "the heart of the Gospel," as "the article by which the church stands or falls."[3] And so, it is not surprising to find a number of Reformed evangelicals making strong statements in defense of the centrality of justification over the last several decades.[4] However, more recently the debate has intensified among evangelicals in that challenges to the traditional Reformed understanding of justification are increasingly arising from within the broader evangelical camp itself. From academic monographs to the popular pages of *Christianity Today* magazine,[5] from the high-profile engagement of renowned

---

[2]In some cases the authors have provided their own translation to preserve some of the ambiguities in the text, in order not to privilege any single interpretive option.

[3]E.g., J. I. Packer, "Justification in Protestant Theology," in *Here We Stand: Justification by Faith Today*, by J. I. Packer et al. (London: Hodder & Stoughton, 1986), p. 84; James R. White, *The God Who Justifies* (Minneapolis: Bethany House, 2001), pp. 17-32.

[4]E.g., Packer et al., *Here We Stand: Justification by Faith Today* (London: Hodder & Stoughton, 1986); D. A. Carson, ed., *Right with God: Justification in the Bible and the World* (Grand Rapids: Baker, 1992).

[5]E.g., see Simon Gathercole, "What Did Paul Really Mean?" *Christianity Today*, August 10, 2007, pp. 22-28; Trevin Wax and Ted Olsen, "The Justification Debate: A Primer," *Christian-*

pastor-scholars John Piper and N. T. Wright to controversy within campus parachurch ministries,[6] the justification debate is being felt throughout the evangelical world.

Unlike the "openness of God" debate, however, contemporary ferment related to justification ranges far beyond evangelical circles. For example, in the eyes of many, the 1999 "Joint Declaration on the Doctrine of Justification" has served largely to reverse the five-hundred-year split between the Roman Catholic and Lutheran churches on justification.[7] In academic New Testament studies today, the "new perspective on Paul" has embroiled scholars of many stripes in both exegetical debates about justification and historical disagreements about the nature of Second Temple Judaism(s). In fact, as one begins to canvas the various issues related to justification today, it quickly becomes apparent that almost every question is a contested one. Debate piles upon debate, layer upon layer. And like most theological controversies of magnitude, the intensity of the contemporary justification debate(s) is in large part due to the fact that it is inherently tied to a number of other issues of significant import—issues exegetical and hermeneutical, soteriological and ecclesiological, methodological and historical, ethical and practical.[8] This chapter offers a historical survey of the development of, and debates concerning, the doctrine of justification in its many permutations throughout church history.

THE EARLY CHURCH

The seemingly straightforward question of the status of the doctrine of justification in the early church is, in fact, a significant point of debate

---

ity Today, June 2009, pp. 34-37; Collin Hansen, "Not All Evangelicals and Catholics Together: Protestant Debate on Justification is Reigniting Questions about Rome," *Christianity Today,* November 2009, pp. 19-22.

[6]John Piper, *The Future of Justification: A Response to N. T. Wright* (Wheaton, Ill.: Crossway, 2007); N. T. Wright, *Justification: God's Plan and Paul's Vision* (Downers Grove, Ill.: InterVarsity Press, 2009). On the split over justification within the InterVarsity Christian Fellowship chapter at George Washington University, see Hansen, "Not All Evangelicals and Catholics Together."

[7]Lutheran World Federation and the Roman Catholic Church, *Joint Declaration on the Doctrine of Justification* (Grand Rapids: Eerdmans, 2000).

[8]The ethical and practical often appear to fade from view in this discussion. For words of caution in this regard see James B. Martin-Schramm, "Justification and the Center of Paul's Ethics," *Dialog* 33 (1994): 106-10; Andrea Bieler and Hans-Martin Gutmann, *Embodying Grace: Proclaiming Justification in the Real World,* trans. Linda A. Maloney (Minneapolis: Fortress, 2010).

today. No one doubts that Pauline-like statements on justification are scattered throughout the early church writings. For instance, near the end of the first century, we find Clement of Rome professing:

> And so we, having been called through his will in Christ Jesus, are not justified through ourselves or through our own wisdom or understanding or piety, or works that we have done in holiness of heart, but through faith, by which the Almighty God has justified all who have existed from the beginning; to whom be the glory for ever and ever. Amen. (1 Clem. 32.4)[9]

Similar statements throughout the next several centuries are common.[10] But the question is: What is to be made of such statements? For some, despite statements such as these, the pre-Augustinian fathers show an unfortunate lack of truly independent interest in, or reflection upon, Pauline doctrines of original sin, grace and justification by faith alone.[11] According to Alister McGrath, the limited amount of attention given to the topic in patristic literature is characterized by "inexactitude and occasional apparent naivety," and reflects a "works-righteousness approach to justification."[12] For others, early Christian statements on justification reflect a significant continuity not only between the patristic writers and Paul, but between patristic writers and the Reformers themselves. No one has argued this point more forcefully than Thomas Oden, who claims that "there is a full-orbed patristic consensus on justification that is virtually indistinguishable from the Reformer's teaching."[13]

Between these two views, one finds a range of scholars who conclude for some form of a via media. Most emphasize that serious account must be taken of the historical, polemical and rhetorical particularities of the early church, that the richly textured images of salvation are many and varied within patristic literature, and that what Reformation-sensitive ears could easily hear as "justification by works" is better interpreted as

---

[9]Michael W. Holmes, trans. and ed., *The Apostolic Fathers in English*, 3rd ed. (Grand Rapids: Baker Academic, 2006), p. 57.

[10]As documented by Thomas C. Oden, *The Justification Reader* (Grand Rapids: Eerdmans, 2002).

[11]E.g., Thomas F. Torrance, *The Doctrine of Grace in the Apostolic Fathers* (Edinburgh: Oliver & Boyd, 1948).

[12]Alister E. McGrath, *Iustitia Dei: A History of the Christian Doctrine of Justification*, 3rd ed. (New York: Cambridge University Press, 2005 [1986]), p. 38.

[13]Oden, *Justification Reader*, p. 49.

an early Christian defense of the biblical notions of human freedom, moral responsibility and the goodness of God against the competing perspectives of astrology/fatalism, stoicism and Gnosticism.[14] While concern with Paul broadly, and justification by faith specifically, can be found in the early church, we cannot thereby conclude that they meant by these statements what the later Reformers would mean.[15] What does seem clear is that when the pre-Augustinian fathers wrote of the gracious, works-free nature of salvation/justification, many of them indexed this to *initial justification*, which itself was connected to conversion and/ or baptism.[16] Once initial justification had taken place, believers were expected to be caught up in a transformative process of growth in grace, virtue and good works.

Assessments of the distance between patristic and later Protestant conceptions of justification vary. Again, Oden argues that a robust patristic "consensus" on justification existed and is in substantial continuity with the later Reformers. For others, certain early writers stand out as significantly "more Protestant," whether Clement of Rome, Marius Victorinus, Augustine of course, or even—in terms of an emphasis on "faith alone"— Pelagius himself![17] And then there is Origen.

Origen
Much of the debate about the fate of Paul's doctrine of justification by faith in the pre-Augustinian church has centered on Origen and his *Commentary on Romans*. Here, Origen expounds on Paul's teaching on justification:

---

[14]On the varied images of salvation in Pauline and early church literature, respectively, see Gordon D. Fee, "Paul and the Metaphors for Salvation: Some Reflections on Pauline Soteriology," in *The Redemption: An Interdisciplinary Symposium on Christ as Redeemer*, ed. Stephen T. Davis, Daniel Kendall and Gerald O'Collins (New York: Oxford University Press, 2004), pp. 43-67; Brian Daley, "'He Himself Is Our Peace' (Ephesians 2:14): Early Christian Views of Redemption in Christ," in *Redemption*, ed. Davis, Kendall and O'Collins, pp. 149-76. On the ubiquitous patristic defense of the goodness of God and human freedom, see Robert L. Wilken, "Justification by Works: Fate and the Gospel in the Roman Empire," *Concordia Theological Monthly* 40 (1969): 379-92; Eric Osborn, "Origen and Justification: The Good Is One, There Is None Good but God (Matt. 19.17 et par.)," *Australian Biblical Review* 24 (1976): 18.

[15]Riemer Roukema, "Salvation *Sola Fide* and *Sola Gratia* in Early Christianity," in *Passion of Protestants*, ed. P. N. Holtrop et al. (Kampen: Kok, 2004), pp. 27-48.

[16]Ibid., pp. 47-48; Robert B. Eno, "Some Patristic Views on the Relationship of Faith and Works in Justification," *Recherches Augustiniennes* 19 (1984): 3-27.

[17]Eno, "Patristic Views," pp. 10-11.

A human being is justified through faith; the works of the law contribute nothing to his being justified. But where there is no faith which justifies the believer, even if one possesses works from the law, nevertheless because they have not been built upon the foundation of faith, although they appear to be good things, nevertheless they are not able to justify the one doing them, because from them faith is absent, which is the sign of those who are justified by God.[18]

And yet, despite such statements, Origen's view of justification has not infrequently come under strong suspicion. Owing in no small part to Melanchthon, many within the Reformation tradition have come to see Origen as an early corrupter of the Pauline doctrine of justification by faith—even as something of a pre-Pelagian "Pelagian."[19] From this perspective, it is only with Augustine that we finally arrive at the "fountainhead" of the doctrine of justification in the post–New Testament church.[20] Others, however, offer more complex assessments of Origen and the import of his doctrine of justification—including his influence upon Augustine's later formulation. Rowan Williams, for example, proposes that Origen is "very close to Pauline thinking in his commentary on Romans," while Eric Osborn concludes that the "gospel of justification by grace was still [Origen's] chief concern."[21] Mark Reasoner has argued for a significant conceptual continuity between Origen's understanding of Paul's thought in Romans and the new perspective on Paul.[22]

In the most comprehensive study of Origen's doctrine of justification to date, Thomas Scheck argues that Origen's commentary was not simply motivated by anti-Gnostic, anti-Marcionite concerns, but also by a real desire to understand Paul. This being said, Scheck reveals the importance of the anti-Marcionite factor. Given that Marcion was the first Christian to claim that the "works" of the believer will not be weighed by God in the final judgment, it is not surprising to find Origen (and not only Origen) argu-

---

[18]Thomas P. Scheck, *Origen: Commentary on the Epistle to the Romans*, 2 vols. (Washington, D.C.: Catholic University of America Press, 2001, 2002), 1:228.
[19]Thomas P. Scheck, *Origen and the History of Justification: The Legacy of Origen's Commentary on Romans* (Notre Dame, Ind.: University of Notre Dame Press, 2008), chap. 6.
[20]McGrath, *Iustitia Dei*, p. 38.
[21]Rowan Williams, "Justification," in *Encyclopedia of Christian Theology*, ed. Jean-Yves Lacoste, 3 vols. (New York: Routledge, 2005), 2:844; Osborn, "Origen and Justification," p. 26.
[22]Mark Reasoner, *Romans in Full Circle: A History of Interpretation* (Louisville: Westminster John Knox, 2005), pp. xxvi-vii.

ing—in defense of the orthodox Rule of Faith, against Marcion—that faith and good works are "two complementary conditions of salvation that must not be separated."[23] Scheck concludes that "on the theme of justification, faith, and works, Augustine does not differ substantially from Origen."[24]

Augustine

In turning to Augustine, there is wide agreement that his mature understanding of justification is indebted to a significant theological shift that came with a letter written in 396 to his former mentor, Simplicianus. In the years leading up to this, Augustine had wrestled with key Pauline texts from Romans concerning the nature of grace, election and salvation.[25] Prior to his *Letter to Simplicianus,* his conclusions on these questions reflected the wide-ranging patristic consensus—that is, he maintained a strong doctrine of human freedom, and explained God's election as predicated upon divine foreknowledge of future human choices, as opposed to divine predeterminism.[26] However, with his 396 response to Simplicianus's questions on these matters, Augustine essentially rejects his earlier approach—and with it the patristic consensus—and instead locates the reason for the divide between the elect and the reprobate as, ultimately, residing within God's own mysterious will. Decades later, Augustine would explain this 396 reversal: "I, indeed, labored in defense of the free choice of the human will; but the grace of God conquered, and finally I was able to understand, with full clarity, the meaning of the Apostle: '. . . what hast thou that thou hast not received?'"[27]

---

[23]Scheck, *Origen and the History of Justification,* p. 11.

[24]Ibid., p. 12. Similarly, Prosper Grech, "Justification by Faith in Origen's Commentary on Romans," *Augustinianum* 36 (1996): 354.

[25]W. S. Babcock, "Augustine's Interpretation of Romans (A.D. 394-396)," *Augustinian Studies* 10 (1979): 55-74.

[26]On this pre-Augustinian consensus, see Peter Gorday, *Principles of Patristic Exegesis: Romans 9–11 in Origen, John Chrysostom, and Augustine* (New York: Mellen, 1983); Rowan A. Greer, "Augustine's Transformation of the Free Will Defense," *Faith and Philosophy* 13 (1996): 471-86; Mark Nispel, "*De servo arbitrio* and the Patristic Discussion of Freedom, Fate, and Grace," *Logia* 7 (1998): 13-22. Occasionally, the claim has been made that Augustine's post-396 views reflect the earlier patristic tradition; e.g., John Gill, *The Cause of God and Truth,* reprint ed. (London: Collingridge, 1855 [1735-1738]), pp. 220-328; R. K. McGregor Wright, *No Place for Sovereignty* (Downers Grove, Ill.: InterVarsity Press, 1996), pp. 18-20. However, most within the Augustinian-Reformed tradition join the wide-ranging consensus of scholars who conclude otherwise. For a particularly candid example, see Torrance, *Doctrine of Grace,* pp. 133-41.

[27]Augustine, *Retractions* 2.1.3; cited in Joseph T. Leinhard, "Augustine on Grace: The Early Years," in *Saint Augustine the Bishop: A Book of Essays,* ed. Fannie LeMoine and Christopher

It is important to consider Augustine's series of reflections on Pauline themes such as grace, election and justification in the context of the wider fourth-century renaissance in the study of Paul's letters. Some scholars see Augustine's study of Paul in the 390s as born of a "non-polemical context," and motivated primarily by a straightforward interest in Paul.[28] Increasingly however, the fourth-century renewal of interest in Paul—Augustine's own interest included and perhaps especially—is seen as directly tied to the spread of Manichaeism. The Manichees had made tireless use of Paul, particularly the very texts (Rom 7 and 9) with which Augustine wrestled—texts that could easily be read as supporting a robust anthropological dualism and predestinarian election that characterized Manichaean theology.[29] In fact, it has been argued that Augustine's 396 shift was very likely directly—if unconsciously—related to his previous public polemical engagement with the Manichaean apologist, Fortunatus, in 392.[30]

In any case, Augustine's post-396 perspective on the workings of grace led him to a conception of salvation—including justification—that is solely indebted to God's sovereign grace and particular election, and in this sense Augustine can be seen as pre-shadowing the Reformation doctrine of justification. In Augustine's words:

> "What have you that you did not receive?" (I Cor. 4:7). If, therefore, faith entreats and receives justification, according as God has apportioned to each in the measure of his faith (Rom. 12:3), nothing of human merit precedes the grace of God, but grace itself merits increase . . . with the will accompanying but not leading, following along but not going in advance.[31]

On the other hand, in contrast to what would emerge as the standard Reformation doctrine, Augustine often states that justification includes the idea of "making righteous," not simply "declaring/reckoning as righteous." This has led to a debate concerning just how closely Augustine's

---

Kleinhenz (New York: Garland, 1994), p. 190. On Augustine's 396 shift, see J. Patout Burns, *The Development of Augustine's Doctrine of Operative Grace* (Paris: Études Augustiniennes, 1980), pp. 30-44.

[28]McGrath, *Iustitia Dei*, p. 39.

[29]W. H. C. Frend, "The Gnostic-Manichaean Tradition in Roman North Africa," *Journal of Ecclesiastical Studies* 4 (1953): 21-22.

[30]Paul Rhodes Eddy, "*Can* a Leopard Change Its Spots? Augustine and the Crypto-Manichaeism Question," *Scottish Journal of Theology* 62 (2009): 342-46.

[31]From Augustine's letter (186, 3, 10) to Paulinus of Nola; cited in Oden, *Justification Reader*, p. 46.

view of justification anticipates that of Martin Luther's. While some propose a close affinity, others, such as McGrath, emphasize an important distinction:

> Augustine has an all-embracing transformative understanding of justification, which includes both the event of justification (brought about by operative grace) and the process of justification (brought about by cooperative grace). Augustine himself does not, in fact, see any need to distinguish between these two aspects of justification; the distinction dates from the sixteenth century.[32]

THE LATIN MIDDLE AGES

"All medieval theology is 'Augustinian' to a greater or lesser extent," notes McGrath.[33] And such is the case with the doctrine of justification in the Western/Latin context. Reflecting the thought of Augustine, the standard view of the medieval Catholic Church is that "justification refers not merely to the beginning of the Christian life, but also to its continuation and ultimate perfection, in which Christians are made righteous in the sight of God and of humanity through a fundamental change in their nature, and not merely in their status."[34] It is not surprising to find the concept of justification taking on a new importance during this period of the Western church. In the eleventh century, Anselm of Canterbury constructed a critique of the Christus Victor model of the atonement, which had dominated the church throughout its first millennium.[35] In its place, Anselm offered his satisfaction theory in his work *Cur Deus Homo? (Why God Became Human)*. The attractiveness of Anselm's theory in the Middle Ages is connected to the fact that it capitalized on an idea that was tied both to the Catholic practice of penance and to the recently arisen feudal system—the idea of *satisfaction*. This theory had the advantages of avoiding some of the eccentricities of the Christus Victor model (i.e., the ran-

---

[32]McGrath, *Iustitia Dei,* p. 47; similarly, see G. R. Evans, "Augustine on Justification," *Studia Ephemeridis Augustinianum* 26 (1987): 280-81, 284. For a contrasting view that emphasizes the affinity between Augustine and Luther on justification, see Mark Ellingsen, "Augustinian Origins of the Reformation Reconsidered," *Scottish Journal of Theology* 64 (2011): 13-28.

[33]McGrath, *Iustitia Dei,* p. 38.

[34]Ibid., p. 59. See also Oliver Rafferty's insightful section on this historical period in his essay contained in this present volume (below, pp. 271-78).

[35]Gustav Aulén, *Christus Victor: An Historical Study of the Three Main Types of the Idea of the Atonement* (New York: Macmillan, 1969 [1931]).

som theory with its "bait and switch" images), while providing an explication of the work of Christ that takes human sin seriously and offers a
reasonable explanation of how Jesus' death satisfies the demands of God's
honor. With Anselm's new approach to the atonement came a turn from
the "Satanward" paradigm of the Christus Victor model (i.e., atonement as
Jesus' victory over Satan via cosmic battle) to an "objective" paradigm
wherein *legal and moral* categories now took center stage.[36] Within this
theological context, the concept of "justification" and its juridical entail-
ments found a natural home.

Taking Augustine's concept of God's indwelling presence in justified
persons as a starting point, much of medieval theology's reflection on justification can be seen, broadly speaking, as exploring the question of the
"effect produced by that presence."[37] With Thomas Aquinas, we find a
classic medieval expression of the four-stage process of justification in the
life of the Christian: (1) the infusion of grace, (2) the movement of the free
will directed toward God through faith, (3) the movement of the free will
directed against sin, and finally (4) the remission of sin.[38] Aquinas continues to reflect Augustine when he insists that justification includes both
forgiveness of sins and the actual transformation of the sinner's life: "in
justification of souls, two things occur together, namely, the remission of
guilt and the newness of life through grace."[39]

With High Scholasticism (e.g., the mid-thirteenth-century *Summa
Fratris Alexandri*) came the idea that the unique presence of God within
the justified sinner necessarily brings with it "created grace," that is, grace
that produces an *ontological* change in the soul of the Christian that con-
forms them to God.[40] While God is seen as the sole author of this internal
change of the soul, the change itself is real and transformative.

Later medieval theology saw the rise of the *via moderna* (i.e., "Nominalism") in the fourteenth and fifteenth centuries, associated with such
scholars as William of Ockham and Gabriel Biel. Following the prior

---

[36]For a survey of the three major atonement paradigms through church history, see Paul Rhodes
Eddy and James K. Beilby, "Atonement," in *Global Dictionary of Theology*, ed. William A. Dyrness and Veli-Matti Kärkkäinen (Downers Grove, Ill.: InterVarsity Press, 2008), pp. 84-92.
[37]Williams, "Justification," p. 845.
[38]*Summa Theologiae* IaIIae, q. 113, a. 8. For discussion, see McGrath, *Iustitia Dei*, pp. 64-65;
John Riches, *Galatians Through the Centuries* (Malden, Mass.: Blackwell, 2008), pp. 118-21.
[39]*Summa* IIIa, q. 56, a. 2 ad. 4.
[40]McGrath, *Iustitia Dei*, p. 68; Williams, "Justification," p. 845.

work of Duns Scotus, a strong emphasis on the absolute freedom of God's gracious initiative characterizes this approach, one designed to make it abundantly clear that no human moral achievement of any sort ever *obligates* God to any particular response. In regard to justification, this emphasis on God's absolute, nonobligatory freedom in the salvation process eventually manifested itself in the concept of God's "two powers"—that is, his "absolute power" to do whatever he pleases, on the one hand, and the power of his radically contingent, self-imposed decision to (in this case) graciously produce the effects of justification in the Christian's life, on the other.[41] Nonetheless, in his comprehensive survey of the doctrine of justification in the Latin Middle Ages, McGrath concludes that "the entire medieval discussion of justification proceeds upon the assumption that a *real* change in the sinner is effected thereby. This observation is as true of the *via moderna* as it is for the earlier period."[42] Among the various ways of expressing justification on the eve of the Reformation, the broad common ground held that justification was *a process,* one that began at baptism and continued on, and one that involved *actual intrinsic righteousness,* made possible by God's initiating grace and subsequent *human cooperation* with that grace.

THE PROTESTANT REFORMATION AND ITS AFTERMATH

When it comes to the question of "forerunners" of the Protestant doctrine of justification, once again debate ensues. Heiko Oberman has argued that just such "forerunners" did exist in the context of the fourteenth-century Augustinian renaissance, with its strongly anti-Pelagian sentiments (e.g., Gregory of Rimini).[43] In contrast, McGrath argues that, with respect to the real Protestant distinctives, there really is no medieval "forerunner."[44] For McGrath: "The doctrines of justification associated with the Lutheran and Reformed Confessions may be concluded to constitute genuine theological *nova.*"[45] And yet, while "forerunner" may be too strong a term, it

---

[41]McGrath, *Iustitia Dei,* pp. 69-71, 50-58; Williams, "Justification," pp. 845-46.

[42]McGrath, *Iustitia Dei,* p. 71.

[43]Heiko A. Oberman, *Forerunners of the Reformation: The Shape of Late Medieval Thought* (New York: Holt, Rinehart & Winston, 1966).

[44]Alister McGrath, "Forerunners of the Reformation? A Critical Examination of the Evidence for Precursors of the Reformation Doctrines of Justification," *HTR* 75 (1982): 219-42; idem, *Iustitia Dei,* pp. 210-17.

[45]McGrath, "Forerunners," p. 241.

has been pointed out that Luther and Melanchthon were both indebted to Erasmus—not least for his 1516 Greek New Testament, including his annotations and later paraphrases—for elements of what would become their breakthrough doctrine of justification.[46]

Martin Luther

Whatever the case, all can agree that Martin Luther's prioritization and articulation of the doctrine of justification marks a seismic shift in the conversation. In Luther's words:

> [I]f we lose the doctrine of justification, we lose simply everything. Hence the most necessary and important thing is that we teach and repeat this doctrine daily, as Moses says about his Law (Deut. 6:7). For it cannot be grasped or held enough or too much. In fact, though we may urge and inculcate it vigorously, no one grasps it perfectly or believes it with all his heart. So frail is our flesh and so disobedient to the Spirit![47]

With Luther, the doctrine of justification is presented as "the article by which the church stands or falls."[48]

As Luther himself reports, a key interpretive moment came when he happened upon a new understanding of Paul's words in Romans 1:16-17:

> For I am not ashamed of the gospel; for, it is the power of God for salvation to everyone who believes, to the Jew, first, and to the Greek. For, in it the righteousness of God is revealed by faith to faith, just as it is written, "The righteous one by faith will live." (authors' translation)

In his famous "tower experience" (recounted years later in the 1545 preface to his Latin writings), Luther shifted from understanding the "righteousness of God" in this passage as God's *terrifying* righteousness by which he justly judges and punishes sinners, to the *gracious* righteousness that God imputes to sinners and by which they are now counted as "righteous" in his sight. And this righteousness by which sinners are justified in God's sight is appropriated by *faith alone*.

But what, exactly, did this mean for Luther, and how should we inter-

---

[46]Lowell C. Green, "The Influence of Erasmus upon Melanchthon, Luther and the Formula of Concord in the Doctrine of Justification," *Church History* 43 (1974): 183-200.

[47]"Lectures on Galatians—1535," in *LW* 26:26.

[48]Although Luther did not coin this famous formula himself, it is widely acknowledged that it nicely captures his sentiments concerning justification.

pret his many subsequent statements on justification over the years? With these and other questions we are brought to another point of significant debate today: How best to understand Luther's own doctrine of justification?

McGrath has helpfully noted three points that distinguish the mature Protestant doctrine of justification: (1) Justification involves a *forensic declaration* of righteousness that effects a change in *legal status before God*, as opposed to a process that actually makes one righteous. (2) There is a clear conceptual difference between justification ("the act by which God declares the sinner to be righteous") and either regeneration or sanctification (the actual "internal process of renewal by the Holy Spirit"). (3) Justifying righteousness is understood as an external, "alien" righteousness, graciously *imputed* to the Christian through the act of faith.[49] But where does the "historical Luther" fit with regard to these distinctives?

In scholarship today, the answer is anything but uniform. For some, the traditional Protestant story line of Luther's view remains valid—while Luther's own views clearly underwent development, with his mature view of justification we find remarkable consistency between Luther, Melanchthon and the Protestant orthodoxy that followed them.[50] For others, Luther shared some but not all of what would become the classical Protestant distinctives. According to McGrath, while Luther clearly defended the "alien" nature of justifying righteousness, he "did not teach a doctrine of forensic justification in the strict sense. . . . Indeed, Luther can be regarded as remaining faithful to the Augustinian understanding of justification as both event and process."[51] By McGrath's lights, it is only with Melanchthon and later Protestant orthodoxy that an *unambiguously forensic* view of justification is reached, and with it an equally clear distinction between justification and sanctification. The idea of a decisive cleft between Luther and the later Melanchthon is a staple of this perspective, one that has characterized readings of Luther such as those of Albrecht Ritschl, Adolf

---

[49]McGrath, "Forerunners," p. 223.

[50]Twentieth-century exponents of this perspective drew inspiration from a 1927 reissue of Theodosius Harnack, *Luther's Theologie mit besonderer Beziehung auf seine Versöhnungs- und Erlösungslehre*, 2 vols. (Erlangen: Blaesing, 1862, 1885). More recently, see R. Scott Clark, "*Iustitia Imputata Christi:* Alien or Proper to Luther's Doctrine of Justification?" *Concordia Theological Quarterly* 70 (2006): 307.

[51]"Forerunners," p. 225.

von Harnack and the twentieth-century "Luther renaissance" initiated by the work of Karl Holl.[52] Finally, in recent years the "Finnish school" of Luther interpretation has emerged (on which, more below), and with it the claim that Luther's approach to justification has far more in common with the Eastern Orthodox view of *theosis* than has generally been recognized. One's take on Luther here will, in part, depend upon one's sense of the development—or essential lack thereof—of his doctrine of justification over the course of his lifetime.

THE TRADITIONAL REFORMATION DOCTRINE OF JUSTIFICATION: LUTHERAN AND REFORMED

Whatever one makes of the particulars of Luther, the traditional Protestant Reformed doctrine of justification emerged and, in its essentials, came to characterize both the traditional Lutheran and Calvinist-Reformed perspectives on the matter. John Calvin was no less clear than Martin Luther that justification was "the primary article of the Christian religion."[53] From the Lutheran Book of Concord to the Heidelberg Catechism to the Westminster Confession, one finds the same general proclamation of justification by faith as a forensic declaration of God in which Christ's righteousness is graciously imputed to the believer through faith alone.[54]

There are, of course, nuances that have distinguished Lutheran and Reformed articulations of justification over the years. Another matter of debate today is the nature and significance of these differences. One issue here involves the question of how Luther and Calvin approached the *ordo salutis* (i.e., the "order of salvation") regarding justification and union with Christ. Some argue that, while Calvin emphasized that union with Christ is the ground from which flow the distinct but unprioritized benefits of

---

[52]Albrecht Ritschl, *A Critical History of the Christian Doctrine of Justification and Reconciliation*, trans. John S. Black (Edinburgh: Edmonston & Douglas, 1872), pp. 167-69; Adolph von Harnack, *History of Dogma*, trans. Neil Buchanan, 7 vols. (New York: Dover, 1961), 7:256. On Holl and the "Luther Renaissance," see Karl Kupisch, "The 'Luther Renaissance,'" *Journal of Contemporary History* 2, no. 4 (1967): 39-49.

[53]*Institutes* 3.2.1. On Calvin's doctrine of justification, see David Steinmetz, *Calvin in Context*, 2nd ed. (New York: Oxford University Press, 2010 [1995]), pp. 65-73; Karla Wübbenhorst, "Calvin's Doctrine of Justification: Variations on a Lutheran Theme," in *Justification in Perspective: Historical Developments and Contemporary Challenges*, ed. Bruce L. McCormack (Grand Rapids: Baker Academic, 2006), pp. 99-118.

[54]Book of Concord, "Defense of the Augsburg Confession": Article IV (II): Of Justification; Heidelberg Catechism, q. 60-64; Westminster Confession of Faith, chap. 13.

justification and sanctification, Luther, in contrast, believed that justification gives rise to union with Christ.[55] Others have challenged this interpretation of Luther, proposing instead that, while Luther may lack the terminological precision of Calvin and the subsequent Reformed tradition, his own view is quite close to that of Calvin, and perhaps helped to shape Calvin's own idea of union with Christ.[56] In any case, these sorts of nuances aside, major voices from both Lutheran and Reformed groups have continued to articulate and defend the same basic contours of the Reformation doctrine of justification.[57] This traditional Reformation perspective is well represented by Michael Horton in this present volume.[58]

Anglicanism

Due to the influence of Luther and especially Melanchthon on Archbishop of Canterbury Thomas Cranmer, the Anglican Church came to hold a view on justification largely in line with the traditional Reforma-

---

[55]E.g., see Richard B. Gaffin Jr., *By Faith, Not by Sight: Paul and the Order of Salvation* (Colorado Springs: Paternoster, 2006).

[56]E.g., see J. V. Fesko, "Luther on Union with Christ," *Scottish Bulletin of Evangelical Theology* 28 (2010): 161-76.

[57]On the Reformed side, a remarkably consistent trajectory can be found through the centuries as evidenced by such landmarks as the Belgic Confession (1561); the Heidelberg Confession (1563); the Westminster Confession (1647); and the individual works of Reformed thinkers such as John Owen (seventeenth century), Jonathan Edwards (eighteenth century) and Charles Hodge (nineteenth century). More recently, this traditional Reformed view has been presented in an impressive number of books, including Carson, *Right with God;* J. V. Fesko, *Justification: Understanding the Classic Reformed Doctrine* (Phillipsburg, N.J.: Presbyterian & Reformed, 2008); Ryan Glomsrud and Michael Horton, eds., *Justified: Modern Reformation Essays on the Doctrine of Justification* (n.p.: CreateSpace, 2010); Michael Horton, *Covenant and Salvation: Union with Christ* (Louisville: Westminster John Knox, 2007); Alister McGrath, *Justification by Faith: What It Means for Us Today* (Grand Rapids: Acadamie/Zondervan, 1988); K. Scott Oliphint, ed., *Justified in Christ: God's Plan for Us in Justification* (Ross-shire, U.K.: Mentor, 2007); R. C. Sproul, *Faith Alone: The Evangelical Doctrine of Justification* (Grand Rapids: Baker, 1995); White, *God Who Justifies.*

In the Lutheran context, a similar trajectory can be traced from the confessions within the Book of Concord, through various voices within the "Lutheran orthodoxy" from the late sixteenth to the early eighteenth centuries—although Carl Braaten (*Justification: The Article by which the Church Stands or Falls* [Minneapolis: Fortress, 1990], p. 28) alerts us to its "steady deterioration" in Lutheran contexts throughout this period. More recently, see Gerhard O. Forde, *Justification by Faith: A Matter of Death and Life* (Mifflintown, Penn.: Sigler, 1990); Robert Preus, *Justification and Rome* (St. Louis: Concordia Academic, 1997).

[58]Among Horton's works that touch on justification and related topics, see *Covenant and Salvation;* idem, *The Christian Faith: A Systematic Theology for Pilgrims on the Way* (Grand Rapids: Zondervan Academic, 2011), pp. 620-47; idem, *Putting Amazing Back into Grace: Embracing the Heart of the Gospel,* 2nd ed. (Grand Rapids: Baker, 2002); Glomsrud and Horton, *Justified.*

tion view (expressed in article 4 of *The Thirteen Articles*).[59] There has been a long-standing debate as to whether or not the influential sixteenth-century Anglican Richard Hooker wandered from the Reformation view, but it appears that he maintained its essence.[60] John Wesley, an Anglican until his death, deviated from the Reformed theological tradition by embracing the "Arminian" notion of a Christologically grounded universal prevenient grace that afforded all people the ability to exercise saving faith.[61] Nonetheless, his "heart warming" experience on Aldersgate Street in 1738, while listening to Luther's *Preface to Romans* being read aloud, left its mark on his doctrine of justification. Wesley aligned himself with a significant tenet of the Reformation view by affirming that justification does *not* entail being *made* righteous; justification and sanctification must be distinguished. However, contrary to traditional Protestantism, Wesley did not emphasize the *imputation* of Christ's righteousness to the Christian.[62]

In the early nineteenth century, John Henry Newman presented his famous *Lectures on Justification*, originally offered as an Anglican "middle-way" between Rome and Protestantism. Decades later, having converted from the Anglican Church to Roman Catholicism (in fact, just a few years before being made a cardinal), he reissued the original text with virtually no change of substance, saying that he was still able fully to embrace its essence. And so, this same text has been influential in both Anglican and Roman Catholic contexts. In it, he writes:

> It appears that justification is an announcement or fiat of Almighty God breaking upon the gloom of our natural state as the Creative word upon chaos; that it *declares* the soul righteous, and in that declaration, on one

---

[59]For a helpful summary of the Anglican approach to justification, see Peter Toon, *Justification and Sanctification* (Westchester, Ill.: Crossway, 1983), pp. 89-101.

[60]So argues Corneliu C. Simut, *Richard Hooker and His Early Doctrine of Justification: A Study of his Discourse of Justification* (Burlington, Vt.: Ashgate, 2005); Williams, "Justification," p. 847.

[61]On Wesley's doctrine of prevenient grace, see J. Gregory Crofford. *Streams of Mercy: Prevenient Grace in the Theology of John and Charles Wesley* (Lexington, Ky.: Emeth, 2010); Robert V. Rakestraw, "John Wesley as a Theologian of Grace," *JETS* 27 (1984): 193-203 (esp. pp. 196-97).

[62]On Wesley's doctrine of justification, see Kenneth J. Collins, "The Doctrine of Justification: Historic Wesleyan and Contemporary Understandings," in *Justification: What's at Stake in the Current Debates*, ed. Mark Husbands and Daniel J. Treier (Downers Grove, Ill.: InterVarsity Press, 2004), pp. 177-202; Rakestraw, "John Wesley," pp. 197-99.

hand, conveys *pardon* for its past sins, and on the other *makes* it actually *righteous*.[63]

COUNTER REFORMATION AND BEYOND: THE ROMAN CATHOLIC RESPONSE

The official Roman Catholic response to Luther and the Protestant Reformation, including its doctrine of justification, came with the Council of Trent, which met for twenty-five sessions between 1545 and 1563.[64] As Oliver Rafferty wisely notes in his essay in this present volume: "It would be wrong . . . to think that the sophisticated and subtle theology expounded by Trent can easily be summarized."[65] (Rafferty himself does a remarkable job at this, and so we encourage the reader to turn to his discussion of Trent below for a more extended and nuanced summary than we are able to provide here.) For our purposes, it suffices to say that Trent's primary intentions concerning justification were to present the Catholic position, while making clear the errors of the Protestants. As many have pointed out, the language of Trent avoids much of the technical phrasing associated with the medieval Catholic debates, frequently making use of biblical terminology. In fact, by Rowan Williams's assessment, Trent's decree on justification "is actually much closer to Luther and Calvin than to the medieval debate."[66] Nonetheless, contrary to the Protestant view, one of the chief emphases of Trent regarding justification is that it involves not only the forgiveness of sins but also the internal transformation of the believer in terms of holiness.

Avery Cardinal Dulles, S.J., helpfully summarizes the essential continuity on justification in the Catholic Church from Trent down to the twentieth century:

> The theology of justification in Roman Catholic teaching has undergone no dramatic changes since the Council of Trent. . . . Justification is

---

[63]Newman, *Lectures on Justification* (London: Rivingtons, 1838), p. 90. On Newman, see Toon, *Justification and Sanctification*, pp. 113-19.

[64]For Trent's statement on Justification, see *The Canons and Decrees of the Council of Trent*, trans. H. J. Schroeder (Rockford, Ill.: Tan, 1978), pp. 29-45. On Trent's understanding of justification, see McGrath, *Iustitia Dei*, pp. 308-57; and Oliver Rafferty's discussion of Trent in this present volume (pp. 278-81 below).

[65]Gerald O'Collins, S.J., and Oliver Rafferty, S.J., "Roman Catholic View," p. 278 below.

[66]Williams, "Justification," p. 846.

rarely discussed at length except in polemics against, or dialogue with, Protestants. . . . From the time of Trent until the early twentieth century, justification was studied primarily with the conceptual tools of late Scholasticism. It was accordingly understood as an efficacious divine intervention whereby a supernatural accident was infused into the human soul as a kind of ornament rendering it pleasing in God's sight. This accident ("sanctifying grace") made its possessor inherently righteous and able to perform meritorious actions, thus earning a strict title to eternal rewards.[67]

This basic continuity from Trent down to today is apparent from the official statement contained in the current *Catechism of the Catholic Church:* "justification is not only the remission of sins, but also the sanctification and renewal of the interior man."[68] It should be noted that, contrary to Luther and Calvin—but quite in line with Erasmus, Eastern Orthodoxy, the Anabaptists, the Arminian-Wesleyan tradition and most Pentecostals—the post-Tridentine Catholic Church has tended to maintain a role for some form of libertarian human freedom within the salvation process. Ever since Augustine, lurking behind many of the twists and turns of the justification debate lay the issue of the nature of human freedom and its role in the salvific process.

Along with these fundamental continuities, the twentieth century did bring a change in tone in the articulation of justification among a number of leading Catholic theologians. Scholastic modes of expression were increasingly modified. The combined forces of the Thomistic revival, personalist phenomenology and renewed interest in biblical and patristic theology led a variety of Roman Catholic scholars to explore new ways of thinking about traditional theological categories, including justification. The most influential twentieth-century Catholic theologian, Karl Rahner, is a case in point.[69] For Rahner, "while admitting that the objective

---

[67]Avery Cardinal Dulles, S.J., "Justification in Contemporary Catholic Theology," in *Justification by Faith: Lutherans and Catholics in Dialogue VII,* ed. H. George Anderson et al. (Minneapolis: Augsburg, 1985), pp. 256-57.

[68]*The Catechism of the Catholic Church* (New York: USCCB, 1995), p. 492.

[69]Rahner's reflections on justification include "Some Implications of the Scholastic Concept of Uncreated Grace," in *Theological Investigations,* 23 vols. (Baltimore: Helicon, 1961-1992), 1:319-46; "Questions of Controversial Theology on Justification," in *Theological Investigations,* 5:199-205; "Justified and Sinner at the Same Time," in *Theological Investigations,* 6:218-30. On Rahner's understanding of justification and its gracious context, see Avery Cardinal Dulles,

event of God's act in Christ is causally prior to any change in the redeemed," he continues to maintain the traditional Catholic view by affirming that "the *subjective justification of the individual is really identical
with that individual's sanctification.*"[70] Yet, aided by the resources of tran-
scendental Thomism and the categories of mystery and symbol, Rahner is
able to articulate the basic Catholic convictions about justification "in
terms of uncreated grace and symbolic actuation," and in doing so has
provided many contemporary Roman Catholics with a new means of moving beyond traditional scholastic language and of entering more fruitfully
into dialogue about justification with other Christian traditions.[71] In this
present volume, Gerald O'Collins, S.J., and Oliver Rafferty, S.J., together
provide a contemporary Roman Catholic perspective on the doctrine of
justification.[72]

NOTABLE MOMENTS IN THE MODERN
PROTESTANT CONVERSATION

With the rise of the Enlightenment, the broadly shared understanding of
the basic human spiritual plight that characterized the Reformation-era
debates came under attack. For all of their differences, the various view-
points represented in the medieval and Reformation periods agreed that
the fundamental human problem was the dire state of sinfulness and the
desperate need for a gracious God. Within the Enlightenment vision, this

---

"Justification and the Unity of the Church," in *The Gospel of Justification: Where Does the Church
Stand Today?* ed. Wayne C. Stumme (Grand Rapids: Eerdmans, 2006), pp. 125-40; Paul D.
Molnar, "The Theology of Justification in Dogmatic Context," in *Justification: What's at Stake
in the Current Debates*, ed. Mark Husbands and Daniel J. Treier (Downers Grove, Ill.: Inter-
Varsity Press, 2004), pp. 224-48.

[70]Dulles, "Justification in Contemporary Catholic Theology," p. 257 (emphasis added).

[71]Ibid., p. 277. For a range of contemporary Roman Catholic expressions of justification, see
Dulles, "Justification in Contemporary Catholic Theology"; R. A. Sungenis, *Not by Faith
Alone: The Biblical Evidence for the Catholic Doctrine of Justification* (Santa Barbara, Calif.:
Queenship, 1997); George H. Tavard, *Justification: An Ecumenical Study* (New York: Paulist,
1983).

[72]Prior work of O'Collins that touches on justification and/or related topics includes *Jesus Our
Redeemer: A Christian Approach to Salvation* (New York: Oxford University Press, 2007); idem,
"Redemption: Some Crucial Issues," in *The Redemption: An Interdisciplinary Symposium on
Christ as Redeemer*, ed. Stephen T. Davis, Daniel Kendall and Gerald O'Collins (New York:
Oxford University Press, 2004), pp. 1-24; idem, "Salvation," in *ABD*, 5:907-13; O'Collins and
Edward G. Farrugia, "Justification," in *A Concise Dictionary of Theology* (New York: Paulist,
1991), p. 115; Gerald O'Collins and Mario Farrugia, *Catholicism: The Story of Catholic Christi-
anity* (New York: Oxford University Press, 2003), pp. 209-11.

problem, and therefore its solution, appeared less and less plausible. Though stated several centuries later, this statement from a 1963 meeting of the Lutheran World Federation succinctly captures a sentiment that came to characterize the Enlightenment mindset:

> The man of today no longer asks, "How can I find a gracious God?" He suffers not from God's wrath, but from the impression of his absence; not from sin, but from the meaninglessness of his own existence; he asks not about a gracious God, but whether God really exists.[73]

Rather than spiritual justification, it was the here-and-now quest for human autonomy and fulfillment that progressively took center stage in the modern "enlightened" world. With Deism came a stream of critiques of particular Christian doctrines—the Trinity, the deity of Christ, original sin, substitutionary atonement—each of which played a significant role in more traditional views of justification. In such a context, the traditional doctrine of justification itself was sure to suffer in certain quarters.[74]

Pietism

During the modern period there are, of course, those like Whitefield and Wesley, like Jonathan Edwards and Charles Hodge—those who staunchly maintained traditional elements of the Reformation view of justification, despite the modernist tides. And then there is Pietism.

Reacting against the perceived "dead orthodoxy" of Protestant scholasticism, the Pietist movement, originally centered in the University of Halle, has been assessed variously with regard to its embrace of justification by faith. On one hand, many scholars point out that the Pietist emphasis on a living faith that results in personal holiness and heart devotion naturally leads to a critique of the standard Reformation view of a purely forensic justification.[75] On the other hand, there are those who see the early Pietists, with their commitment to biblical authority, as defending the traditional doctrine, even while warning of the damaging effects of its common misunderstanding.[76] In any case, as Carl Braaten notes, after years of steady ne-

---

[73]*Proceedings of the Fourth Assembly of the Lutheran World Federation, Helsinki, July 30–August 11, 1963* (Berlin/Hamburg: Lutherisches Verlagshaus, 1965), p. 57.

[74]McGrath, *Iustitia Dei*, pp. 358-81; Williams, "Justification," pp. 847-48.

[75]Ritschl, *Critical History*, p. 515; McGrath, *Iustitia Dei*, pp. 292-95; Carter Lindberg, *The Third Reformation?* (Macon: Mercer University Press, 1983).

[76]Gary DeLashmutt, "Early German Lutheran Pietism's Understanding of Justification," Xenos

glect and decline, it was with the nineteenth-century University of Halle theologian and Pietist Martin Kähler that the doctrine of justification made a "dramatic comeback"—and in "a fashion resembling the form and function it possessed in the thought of the Reformers."[77]

The Liberal Protestant Response

As the Enlightenment mood spread, it fostered a rationalist sense of morality, one based in the commonsense workings of nature, which deeply affected certain European sensibilities about "justification." Essential to this moral vision was the presupposition that whatever was expected of humanity, ethically speaking, was well within its autonomous capacity to achieve. Immanuel Kant, in his own unique (if internally tensive) way, brought a moral challenge to this modernist approach.[78]

As the eighteenth gave way to the nineteenth century, bringing with it the growing sentiments of Romanticism, Friedrich Schleiermacher offered a religious critique of the Enlightenment rooted in the fundamental idea of human "feeling" (a never entirely adequate translation of the German term *Gefühl*), particularly the sense of being *absolutely dependent upon God* (i.e., "God-consciousness"). Schleiermacher's attempt to find a mediating path between Enlightenment religion and Protestant orthodoxy would, of course, deeply impact his concept of salvation: Christ's superlative God-consciousness is mediated to humanity, though always through natural means. With regard to justification specifically, Schleiermacher clearly strives to maintain a line of continuity with the Reformation tradition.[79] And yet his proclivities, Pietist and otherwise, led him to resist emphasizing a purely imputed, forensic righteousness. He adamantly rejects the idea that justification is about appeasing God's wrath and avoiding divine punishment. While he distances himself from the Catholic Church, since it holds that justification "takes place [after faith is exercised] by means of good works," he also has critical words for the traditional Reformation doctrine. He writes: "There is only one eternal and universal decree justifying men for Christ's sake." And yet this decree is

Christian Fellowship website (copyright 2010) www.xenos.org/essays/pietism.htm.
[77]Braaten, *Justification*, p. 28.
[78]McGrath, *Iustitia Dei*, pp. 371-76.
[79]Friedrich Schleiermacher, *The Christian Faith*, ed. H. R. Mackintosh and J. S. Stewart, 2 vols. (New York: Harper & Row, 1963 [1928]), 2:496-505.

never simply a "declaratory act" alone.[80]

As the nineteenth century progressed under the continued pressure of modernism and Hegel's increasing influence, attitudes toward traditional, objective notions of justification steadily declined within liberal Christian circles. However, after the mid-century faltering of Hegelianism, a new reconsideration of the doctrine of justification presented itself in the form of Albrecht Ritschl's three-volume study, *A Critical History of the Christian Doctrine of Justification and Reconciliation* (1870, 1874). Like a number of other left-leaning Christians of the modern age, Ritschl believed the pristine faith of the early church had been progressively corrupted by Hellenistic metaphysics, an unfortunate effect that informed a number of classical Christian dogmas. Nonetheless, Ritschl's study of justification, while critiquing aspects of the Reformation view, retains a central place for this longstanding Christian concept.

Ritschl saw himself as recovering the original kernel of insight that Luther had stumbled upon centuries earlier, an insight that, with Melanchthon and Reformation orthodoxy, had progressively degenerated. It is not surprising therefore that "Ritschl regards the justification of humanity as the fundamental datum from which all theological discussion must proceed, and upon which it is ultimately grounded."[81] Ritschl even returns an objective component to justification—justification involves the forgiveness of sins and the acceptance of sinful people by God back into relationship with him. However, Ritschl's reformulation of the doctrine of justification remains decidedly "modern" in its essence. In his attempt to render it understandable, let alone palatable, to the modern Christian mind, Ritschl makes it clear that justification is ultimately a means to an end—namely, "the communal striving for the kingdom of God."[82] And in this sense, Ritschl's theology can be seen as "a reformulation and reinterpretation of Kant's philosophy of religion."[83]

Existentialist Reinterpretations

Reinterpretation and reformulation of the Reformation doctrine of justifi-

---

[80]Ibid., pp. 501, 502.
[81]McGrath, *Iustitia Dei,* p. 384; see pp. 381-92 for McGrath's helpful discussion of Ritschl's approach to justification.
[82]Christophe Chalamet, "Reassessing Albrecht Ritschl's Theology: A Survey of Recent Literature," *Religion Compass* 2, no. 4 (2008): 628.
[83]Ibid.

cation continued unabated into the twentieth century. Existentialist interpretations of justification were made popular by two German Lutherans,
Paul Tillich and Rudolf Bultmann.[84] From Kähler, his former teacher at
Halle, Tillich appropriated the conviction of the centrality of justification
to the Christian faith, even identifying its essence with "the Protestant
principle."[85] Tillich's reformulation, however, brought some interesting
developments. For example, in Tillich's words:

> The step I myself made . . . was the insight that the principle of justification
> through faith refers not only to the religious-ethical but also to the reli-
> gious-intellectual life. Not only he who is in sin but he who is in doubt is
> justified through faith. The situation of doubt, even doubt about God, need
> not separate us from God. . . . So the paradox got hold of me that he who
> seriously denies God, affirms him. Without it I could not have remained a
> theologian.[86]

Bultmann, the son of a Lutheran minister, when engaged in descriptive
exegetical tasks, echoes many Reformation themes. Thus, he regards the
issue of justification—and self-justification—as important from early on.
In a 1924 essay, he writes: *"Man's fundamental sin is his will to justify himself
as man, for thereby he makes himself God."*[87] Later, he defined sin as "man's
self-powered striving . . . to procure salvation by his own strength"; then,
he claims that the heart of Paul's gospel, Romans 3:21–7:6, establishes
"that 'righteousness' is bestowed upon the faith which appropriates the
grace of God and not upon the works of the Law."[88] Furthermore, he considers justification (or being "rightwised," as he prefers) to be a forensic
term—not being innocent, but acknowledged as innocent—and stresses
that it is God's eschatological judgment made real in the present.[89]

However, Bultmann's existentialist hermeneutic and his program of

---

[84]McGrath, *Iustitia Dei*, pp. 409-13; Peter Sedgwick, "'Justification by Faith': One Doctrine,
Many Debates," *Theology* 93 (1990): 5-13.

[85]Braaten, *Justification*, pp. 41-62; Toon, *Justification and Sanctification*, pp. 127-33.

[86]Paul Tillich, *The Protestant Era*, trans. James L. Adams, abridged ed. (Chicago: University of
Chicago Press, 1957 [1948]), pp. x-xi.

[87]Rudolf Bultmann, "Liberal Theology and the Latest Theological Movement," in *Faith and
Understanding*, trans. L. P. Smith (New York: Harper & Row, 1969), pp. 46-47 (emphasis in
text).

[88]Rudolf Bultmann, *Theology of the New Testament*, trans. Kendrick Grobel, 2 vols. (New York:
Charles Scribner's Sons, 1951-1955), 1:264.

[89]Ibid., 1:272.

"demythologizing"—translating the mythological language of the New
Testament into existentialist language relevant for contemporary humanity—lead him to reconfigure traditional Protestant thinking. In this re-
configuration, anthropology dominates. For instance, he determines that
Pauline theology "deals with God not as He is in Himself but only with
God as He is significant for man" and that "every assertion about God is
simultaneously an assertion about man and vice versa. For this reason and
in this sense Paul's theology is, at the same time, anthropology."[90] As
Richard Hays points out, this "inevitably tends to shift the weight of emphasis away from God's action and onto the human-faith decision."[91] For
justification this entails that the subjective side is magnified, while the
objective grounding is minimized. Thus, once demythologized from its
Jewish-cultic and Hellenistic-Gnostic redeemer myth elements, *"the salvation occurrence is nowhere present except in the proclaiming, accosting, demand-
ing, and promising word of preaching . . .* which accosts the hearer and com-
pels him to decide for or against it."[92] Here, the historical reality of the
death of Christ, while accepted by Bultmann, recedes into the background,
and, in the process concedes the foreground to the existentially critical
decision of faith in the present and, with it, the subjective appropriation of
justification.[93] Accordingly, Bultmann marginalizes the traditional connection between atonement theology and justification.[94] In the final analysis, because Bultmann's concerns were overridingly anthropological, his
understanding of justification placed primary emphasis on the anthropological dimension. This magnified a tendency, already present in the dominant Lutheran understanding, to read justification texts as concerned
principally with—myopically so, in the view of some—how humans appropriate justification. The surprising fact is that Bultmann's elevation of
the subjective side of justification over its objective basis exhibits such cu-

---

[90]Ibid., 1:190-91.

[91]*The Faith of Jesus Christ: The Narrative Substructure of Galatians 3:1–4:11*, 2nd ed. (Grand Rapids: Eerdmans, 2002), p. 51.

[92]Bultmann, *Theology of the New Testament*, 1:302.

[93]Of course, reaction to Bultmann's historical skepticism was a prime cause for the second quest
for the historical Jesus.

[94]Note, for instance, his claim that "all pagan notions that men must do something to reconcile
(propitiate) God, are far from Paul's thought. It never occurs to him that *God* needed to be
reconciled; it is *men* who receive the reconciliation which God has conferred" (*Theology of the
New Testament*, 1:287). He also contends that passages like Rom 3:25 "do not contain Paul's
characteristic view" (p. 296).

rious affinities with traditions, like popular evangelicalism, which have overtly rejected his hermeneutical paradigm.

Karl Barth

Despite critique of the traditional Reformation doctrine of justification from classical liberal and existentialist Christian quarters, other twentieth-century forces served to revive important elements of it, if in modified forms. Karl Holl and the "Luther renaissance" is one key factor here. So is the massive influence of the single most influential theologian of the twentieth century, Karl Barth. As with virtually any topic related to Barth today, there is ample discussion and debate about his doctrine of justification.[95] For some, Barth's emphasis on the radical, transcendent "otherness" of God and his "righteousness" is something of a recovery of Luther's similar sentiments. For others, Barth is still too beholden to the modern mind, granting it far too much power to define things, even as he critiques it. Here, we will avoid most of the debate about Barth, and simply note several of the provocative statements from Barth himself that have energized that debate.[96]

In his monumental *Church Dogmatics*, Barth writes: "There never was and there never can be any true Christian church without the doctrine of justification. In this sense, it is indeed the *articulus stantis et cadentis ecclesiae*" (i.e., "the article by which the church stands or falls").[97] And yet, for Barth, this is not the final word on the matter. Within a few pages, Barth picks up the same topic, with noticeably different results:

> The *articulus stantis et cadentis ecclesiae* is not the doctrine of justification as such, but its basis and culmination: the confession of Jesus Christ, . . .

---

[95] E.g., Braaten, *Justification*, pp. 63-79; Hans Küng, *Justification: The Doctrine of Karl Barth and a Catholic Reflection*, trans. Thomas Collins et al. (Philadelphia: Westminster Press, 1983 [1957]); Bruce L. McCormack, *"Justitia aliena:* Karl Barth in Conversation with the Evangelical Doctrine of Imputed Righteousness," in *Justification in Perspective: Historical Developments and Contemporary Challenges*, ed. Bruce L. McCormack (Grand Rapids: Baker Academic, 2006), pp. 167-96; Molnar, "Theology of Justification."

[96] Even so, perhaps it says something about the current state of Barth studies that this is the only section of this historical survey about which the authors are nervous to say *anything* for fear of being shown not just wrong, but *pitifully wrong*. Then again, we find a small bit of comfort in the fact that no matter what we say here, most likely *someone* in the Barthian world will come to our defense!

[97] Karl Barth, *Church Dogmatics* 4/1, trans. G. W. Bromiley (Edinburgh: T & T Clark, 1956), p. 523.

the knowledge of his being and activity for us and to us and with us. It could probably be shown that this was also the opinion of Luther. If here, as everywhere, we allow Christ to be the centre, the starting-point and the finishing point, we have no reason to fear that there will be any lack of unity and cohesion, and therefore of systematics in the best sense of the word.[98]

No one familiar with Barth will be surprised by this qualification. For, as Braaten has memorably put it, "Barth put all his methodological eggs in a Christological basket."[99] *Everything* in Christian theology—including the all-important doctrine of justification—must ultimately be seen through the lens of Christology. And so, in *Church Dogmatics*, justification finds its place as one of three aspects of the wider doctrine of reconciliation—justification, sanctification and vocation (i.e., calling).

But what, for Barth, constitutes the doctrine of justification? Again, the key is found in Jesus Christ—*literally*. Justification takes place, first and foremost, *within Jesus Christ*, specifically in his death and resurrection. The objective reconciliation—including the justification—of God and sinful humanity takes place within the very person of the God-man, Jesus Christ. And so, as Bruce McCormack succinctly puts it, for Barth, *"what Jesus Christ accomplishes is not merely the possibility of reconciliation but the reality of it."*[100] But this does not mean that the subjective experience of justification is lost for the rest of humanity. As Barth states:

> There is no room for any fears that in the justification of man we are dealing only with a verbal action, with a kind of bracketed "as if," as though what is pronounced were not the whole truth about man. Certainly we have to do with a declaring righteous, but it is a declaration about man which is fulfilled and therefore effective in this event, which corresponds to actuality because it creates and therefore reveals the actuality. It is a declaring righteous which without any reserve can be called a making righteous.[101]

And so, with the range of complex and provocative language about justification in his work, it is not surprising that Barth's view has been variously interpreted as, on one hand, in "fundamental agreement" with that of the

[98]Ibid., pp. 527-28.
[99]Braaten, *Justification*, pp. 76-77.
[100]McCormack, *"Justitia aliena,"* p. 179.
[101]*Church Dogmatics* 4/1, p. 95.

Roman Catholic Church, and, on the other, as "an extension and radicalization of the Reformation doctrine."[102]

VOICES FROM THE MARGINS: JUSTIFICATION IN ANABAPTIST, LIBERATION, FEMINIST AND PENTECOSTAL THEOLOGIES

It is not uncommon to find Western-based historical surveys on justification skipping over a number of traditions and perspectives that deserve a voice in the conversation. Frequently, little to no mention is made of approaches to justification in Anabaptism, liberation and feminist theologies, Pentecostal thought, and Eastern Orthodoxy. In this section we will canvas the first four, saving Orthodoxy for a later section.

Anabaptist Theology

For some, there is good reason for the general neglect of the "Radical Reformers" when considering the doctrine of justification by faith: from such early Anabaptist founders as Denck, Grebel, Hoffman, Hubmaier, Marpeck, Philips, Riedemann and Menno Simons, on down through the centuries, it appears that the notion of a "forensic view of grace, in which the sinner is . . . undeservedly justified . . . [is] simply unacceptable" to the Anabaptists.[103] Similar to Wesley, despite their appreciation of certain aspects of the magisterial Reformation, the Anabaptists soundly rejected the ideas of the utter bondage of the human will and God's unconditional election of only a portion of humanity to salvation.[104] They also feared that the traditional Reformed doctrine of justification led logically to "cheap grace" and the possibility of a Christian life that looked nothing like that of Jesus' own example. And so, for most Anabaptists, there has been much to be concerned about with a doctrine of justification that amounts to a forensic declaration, an alien, imputed righteousness and a decisive separation of justification from sanctification.[105]

---

[102]See, respectively, Küng, *Justification,* p. 277; McCormack, *"Justitia aliena,"* p. 196.

[103]Robert Friedmann, *The Theology of Anabaptism* (Scottdale, Penn.: Herald, 1973), p. 91.

[104]Alvin J. Beachy, *The Concept of Grace in the Radical Reformation* (Nieuwkoop: De Graaf, 1977), esp. pp. 33-34, 46-55; T. N. Finger, "Grace," in *The Mennonite Encyclopedia,* ed. Cornelius J. Dyck and Dennis D. Martin, 5 vols. (Scottdale, Penn.: Herald, 1990), 5:352-53.

[105]Beachy, *Concept of Grace,* pp. 29-32; Mennonite Church and the General Conference Mennonite Church, *Confession of Faith in a Mennonite Perspective* (Scottdale, Penn.: Herald, 1995), p. 37.

Then again, things may not be that simple. With his landmark 1943 presidential address before the American Society of Church History, Harold Bender offered a new lens by which to understand Anabaptism. In Bender's words, "Anabaptism is the culmination of the Reformation, the fulfillment of the original vision of Luther and Zwingli"; so much so that it deserves to be recognized as "consistent evangelical Protestantism."[106] From this perspective, the general neglect of justification language in such a historic Anabaptist statement as the 1527 Schleitheim Confession can largely be explained in ways that leave connections with the traditional Reformers intact. For instance, regarding the Schleitheim Confession, Guy Hershberger writes:

> It is first of all striking that these articles say nothing about God, Jesus Christ, and justification by faith. The central truths of the Christian faith are not mentioned. Why? Because the men who adopted this confession were in agreement with Luther and Zwingli concerning all of these central truths. Zwingli himself emphasized repeatedly that nothing involving belief in God, Christ, and grace separated the Anabaptists from him. The Schleitheim Confession deals only with those points in which Anabaptism and the Reformation differ.[107]

Just such an interpretation explains how J. C. Wenger, in what can be considered the first real Anabaptist systematic theology text to be produced in over four hundred years, offers a discussion of justification that falls within the lines of what Mennonite theologian Thomas Finger describes as "Protestant orthodox fashion with little development."[108]

In his own recent exploration of justification in the Anabaptist tradition—one of the most thorough to date—Finger sheds much illumination on this contentious question.[109] He reveals the points at which early Ana-

---

[106]Harold Bender, "The Anabaptist Vision," *Mennonite Quarterly Review* 18 (1944): 74.

[107]Guy Hershberger, *The Recovery of the Anabaptist Vision* (Scottdale, Penn.: Herald, 1957), p. 65.

[108]J. C. Wenger, *Introduction to Theology* (Scottdale, Penn.: Herald, 1954), pp. 284-90; T. N. Finger, *A Contemporary Anabaptist Theology: Biblical, Historical, Constructive* (Downers Grove, Ill.: InterVarsity Press, 2004), p. 132.

[109]*Contemporary Anabaptist Theology*, pp. 109-56. See also T. N. Finger, "An Anabaptist Perspective on Justification," in *Justification and Sanctification in the Traditions of the Reformation*, ed. Milan Opocensky and Paraic Reamonn (Geneva: World Alliance of Reformed Churches, 1999), pp. 44-86.

baptists—particularly Phillips, Hubmaier, Marpeck and even Menno Simons himself—seemed quite comfortable with justification language.[110] And so: "Like Protestants, all Anabaptists affirmed that salvation originates from God's initiative and is basically apprehended through faith."[111] And yet, at the same time, Finger's study reveals the significant discontinuities between Anabaptists and the traditional Reformation view:

> Like Catholics, however, Anabaptists were most concerned about salvation's goal (righteous character) and the process leading to it. They sought to conceive faith as an activity that intrinsically produced works. To this end, many stressed that faith unites people directly with the risen Christ. Yet such a union involved ontological transformation. At this point the faith-works question, raised within the justification framework, led beyond it to Anabaptism's primary soteriological notion: divinization.[112]

Liberation and Feminist Theologies

Similar to Anabaptism, justification by faith has not played a dominant role in most forms of liberation and feminist theology. When the concept does appear, it is often in the context of interrogating and critiquing the traditional Reformation doctrine. For some, the traditional Reformation emphasis on the passive reception of justification by faith represents a threat to the hope of active—and actual—salvific liberation in the historical here-and-now. Juan Segundo sounds this concern when he notes that the Lutheran doctrine of justification by faith "turns faith into the confident but essentially passive acceptance of God's fixed plan for human destiny and the construction of his eschatological kingdom."[113] The Brazilian Roman Catholic liberation theologian, Leonardo Boff, proposes an adjustment of terminology: "Instead of using the term 'justification' (a key word in the theology of Paul and the Council [of Trent]), I shall use the term 'liberation.' It is the same reality, but now elaborated in terms of its

---

[110]Finger, *Contemporary Anabaptist Theology*, pp. 115-16, 124, 129.

[111]Ibid., p. 131.

[112]Ibid. Beachy's earlier work (*Concept of Grace*, pp. 229-30) served to highlight the importance of salvation as "divinization" in Anabaptist thought. See also T. N. Finger, "Anabaptism and Eastern Orthodoxy: Some Unexpected Similarities," *Journal of Ecumenical Studies* 31 (1994): 67-91.

[113]Juan Segundo, *Liberation of Theology*, trans. John Drury (Maryknoll, N.Y.: Orbis, 1976 [1975]), p. 143 (see pp. 138-51 for his interaction with justification).

dynamic, historical dimensions."[114] For liberationist theologies, "God's righteousness is manifested in liberative deeds."[115] And so, it is not justification, but rather concrete, here-and-now justice and liberation that characterize the central soteriological concerns of liberationist theologies.[116] Where justification language is taken up, reformulation is common. There is a promise of "liberation by grace alone," and the call to solidarity with the poor and oppressed in their struggle for justice can, itself, be seen as "a reception of grace, a social justification by faith (not by work or achievement) and certainly not a privilege nor a right."[117]

For a variety of feminist thinkers, the Reformation notion of justification, and the constellation of doctrines and images surrounding it, can be especially problematic.[118] For example, Serene Jones asks what happens when most women are placed "in the position of the sinner before God in Luther's courtroom drama?" Her conclusion: One of two things. Either they cannot relate to this male-inspired scene at all, or, even worse, they embrace Luther's scenario and take upon themselves a pride-centered role in a foreign soteriological script, one designed by and for males with their own particular manifestations of sin.[119] In either case, the end result is unhelpful at best, damaging at worst. Given women's very different experience, Jones suggests that, for women, the traditional Reformed order of justification followed by sanctification needs to be reversed, "starting with sanctification and its rhetoric of building up instead of with justification and its initial language of undoing." This makes sense in light of the fact that "God desires to empower and liberate women rather than to break

---

[114]Leonardo Boff, *Liberating Grace*, trans. John Drury (Maryknoll, N.Y.: Orbis, 1979 [1976]), pp. 151-52.

[115]Allan Boesak, *Black and Reformed: Apartheid, Liberation and the Calvinist Tradition* (Maryknoll, N.Y.: Orbis, 1984), p. 8.

[116]E.g., James H. Evans Jr., *We Have Been Believers: An African-American Systematic Theology* (Minneapolis: Fortress, 1992), pp. 16-18; Mercy Amba Oduyoye, *Introducing African Women's Theology* (Cleveland: Pilgrim, 2001), p. 64.

[117]Respectively, John W. de Gruchy, *Liberating Reformed Theology: A South African Contribution to an Ecumenical Debate* (Grand Rapids: Eerdmans, 1991), p. 156; Feliciano V. Carino, "Biblical and Theological Reflections on Current Economic Life," *Reformed Life* 42 (1992): 100.

[118]Feminist engagements with the doctrine of justification include Serene Jones, *Feminist Theory and Christian Theology: Cartographies of Grace* (Minneapolis: Augsburg Fortress, 2000), pp. 49-68; Elsa Tamez, *The Amnesty of Grace: Justification by Faith from a Latin American Perspective*, trans. Sharon H. Ringe (Nashville: Abingdon, 1993 [1991]); Kathryn Tanner, "Justification and Justice in a Theology of Grace," *ThTo* 55 (1999): 510-23.

[119]Jones, *Feminist Theory*, pp. 62-63.

what little self-confidence they have."[120] For Jones then:

> To be sanctified is to be a coherent self in the space of divine grace. In justi-
> fication, by a divine decree of forgiveness, woman is pronounced a newly born
> agent and is called to live in just relation with others. To be justified means to
> be a self renewed and enabled for continued life in community.[121]

One of the most thorough engagements of justification by a feminist
thinker is that of Latina theologian Elsa Tamez.[122] Central for Tamez is a
strong correlation between justice and justification:

> Justification has been understood, and correctly so, as a synonym for hu-
> manization. . . . A Third World theological reading of justification in a
> context in which the poor are discriminated against and threatened in
> their existence demands that the accent be placed on the justice and grace
> of God, who raises the excluded to the dignity of being son or daughter of
> God. Rather than speaking of "reconciliation with the sinner," it speaks
> of God's solidarity with the excluded.[123]

For Tamez, human beings can hope to bring about world transformation
"because they have been justified (made and declared just) by grace and
faith."[124]

Pentecostal Theologies

"Without any doubt, the mystery of our religion is great: He was revealed
in the flesh, justified by the Spirit." First Timothy 3:16 is so rendered by a
number of Pentecostal scholars. With these words, apparently drawn from
an earlier creedal hymn, a Pauline text introduces a curious phrase to the
average Western Christian ear—"justified by the Spirit." And yet it is just
such a phrase that resonates deeply with Pentecostal sensibilities. The
Western church has always emphasized the holistic soteriological roles of
the Father and, especially, the Son. However, "both Catholic and Protestant traditions have been ambivalent about the role of the Spirit in justification," in essence, keeping the Holy Spirit "at arm's length from the sub-

---

[120]Ibid., p. 63.
[121]Ibid., p. 112.
[122]See her *Amnesty of Grace.*
[123]Elsa Tamez, "Justification" (trans. Phillip Berryman), in *Dictionary of Third World Theologies*,
ed. Virginia Fabella and R. S. Sugirtharajah (Maryknoll, N.Y.: Orbis, 2000), pp. 116-17.
[124]Tamez, *Amnesty of Grace*, p. 112.

stance of justification."[125] In the last two decades, pneumatologically minded scholars have set out to address this imbalance, and in the process have begun to articulate what they consider to be a more authentically "Trinitarian theology of justification."[126]

To date, the most extensive Pentecostal exploration of a pneumatologically oriented approach to justification is the collective work of Frank Macchia.[127] Within his work, one quickly notices a number of themes reminiscent of similar concerns within Anabaptist, Eastern Orthodox, liberationist and certain new perspective approaches to justification: wariness of merely forensic/legal categories, an emphasis on participation in the divine life of the indwelling Spirit, righteousness as covenant faithfulness, and justifying faith as, from the outset, always to be expressed in tandem with the concretely liberating powers of hope and love.[128] Making use of the "crown jewel of the Pentecostal message"—namely, "the baptism in the Holy Spirit"—Macchia offers a vision of justification that is more than simply

> adding a charismatic experience onto a mainstream Protestant understanding of forensic justification. Justification . . . is rather the pardon and liberation experienced in the embrace of the Spirit, which leads to empowered witness, healing, and divine vindication through signs and wonders and, ultimately, resurrection. . . . There is implicit potential here for a theology of justification that involves both the justice of divine communion (mutual indwelling) and the witness of the Spirit to the victory of God's faithfulness in the world to embrace all flesh. Justification can [be] regenerative without being anthropocentric.[129]

Pentecostal theologian Amos Yong has proposed a similar vision, wherein justification is understood as

> a pneumatologically accomplished reality that includes, but is not limited to, the forgiveness of sins (understood in forensic terms). This means . . .

---

[125]Frank D. Macchia, *Justified in the Spirit: Creation, Redemption, and the Triune God* (Grand Rapids: Eerdmans, 2010), p. 5.

[126]Ibid., pp. 293-312. Inspiration came from Jürgen Moltmann's *The Spirit of Life: A Universal Affirmation*, trans. M. Kohl (Minneapolis: Fortress, 2001 [1991]). An influential article (originally a 1998 AAR conference paper) came from Lyle Dabney, "'Justified by the Spirit': Soteriological Reflections on the Resurrection," *International Journal of Systematic Theology* 3 (2001): 46-68.

[127]See especially his *Justified in the Spirit*.

[128]Ibid., pp. 4-6, 75-85, 105-14, 214-18, 254-57, 311-12.

[129]Ibid., p. 85.

that baptism in the Holy Spirit understands justification as intimately related to sanctification, not in order to advocate any kind of works righteousness but in order to see that God both declares sinners righteous through Jesus Christ and makes sinners righteous through the purifying fire of the Holy Spirit, restoring them to the full image of God as revealed in the life of Jesus.[130]

Finally, the Finnish theologian Veli-Matti Kärkkäinen—a contributor to this present volume—has added another dimension to the Pentecostal conversation.[131] Kärkkäinen is a proponent of the Finnish school's approach to Luther interpretation (on which, see below). From this background, Kärkkäinen has explored a pneumatologically oriented doctrine of justification that makes substantial use of the Eastern Orthodox concept of *theosis*.[132] He explains:

[I]mplied in the integration of justification and theosis is the role of the Spirit in salvation. Deification is a pneumatologically loaded image of salvation. . . . Participation in God is possible through the Spirit of Christ, the Spirit of adoption. "There is not [sic] justification by faith without the Holy Spirit. Justifying faith is itself the experience that the love of God has been poured into our hearts 'through the Holy Spirit' (Rom 5:5)."[133]

THE TURN TO DIALOGUE: JUSTIFICATION IN CONTEMPORARY ECUMENICAL CONTEXTS

Over the last several decades, ecumenical concerns have led to a number of intra-Christian dialogues on the question of justification. Hans Küng's 1957 book, *Justification: The Doctrine of Karl Barth and a Catholic Response*, supplied a crucial impetus on the Roman Catholic side. In it, Küng comes

---

[130]Amos Yong, *The Spirit Poured Out on All Flesh: Pentecostalism and the Possibility of Global Theology* (Grand Rapids: Baker Academic, 2005), p. 102.

[131]Kärkkäinen's prior work on justification includes *One with God: Salvation as Deification and Justification* (Collegeville, Minn.: Liturgical, 2005); idem, "Justification," in *Global Dictionary of Theology*, ed. William A. Dyrness and Veli-Matti Kärkkäinen (Downers Grove, Ill.: InterVarsity Press, 2008), pp. 447-52; idem, "Justification as Forgiveness of Sins and Making Righteous: The Ecumenical Promise of a New Interpretation of Luther," *One in Christ* 37 (2002): 32-45; idem, "The Holy Spirit and Justification: The Ecumenical Significance of Luther's Doctrine of Salvation," *Pneuma* 24 (2002): 26-39; idem, "Salvation as Justification and Theosis: The Contribution of the New Finnish Luther Interpretation to Our Ecumenical Future," *Dialog* 45 (2006): 74-82.

[132]See especially Kärkkäinen, *One with God.*

[133]Kärkkäinen, "Holy Spirit and Justification," pp. 30, 34; here Kärkkäinen is quoting K. L. Bakken, "Holy Spirit and Theosis," *St. Vladimir's Theological Quarterly* 38 (1994): 410.

to the startling conclusion that there is a "fundamental agreement between Karl Barth's position and that of the Catholic Church in regard to the theology of justification seen in its totality."[134] With Küng's work came new hopes of rapprochement between Catholics and Protestants concerning the centuries-old divide on justification.

Roman Catholic–Lutheran Dialogue

In the wake of the Second Vatican Council (1962-1965) and its encouragement toward ecumenical dialogue, the Catholic Church has entered into a number of discussions on justification with other ecclesial traditions. Not surprisingly, the most high-profile of these has been its dialogue with Lutheranism. The stage was set for this dialogue on the Lutheran side by the 1963 Helsinki meeting of the Lutheran World Federation (LWF). The first major statement, coissued by the LWF and the Vatican Secretariat for Promoting Christian Unity, was the 1972 "Malta Report," which concluded that an important consensus was developing between the two groups. The landmark 1983 common statement on "Justification by Faith" marked the next major advance.[135] Through the 1980s and 1990s, the question was faced of whether or not the sixteenth-century Roman Catholic and Reformation condemnations regarding justification continue to apply to each other today in the context of dialogue.[136] From 1994 to 1998, various drafts of a joint statement on justification between the LWF and the Pontifical Council for Promoting Christian Unity (PCPCU) were drawn up, analyzed and modified, all working toward a joint declaration.

On Reformation Day, October 31, 1999, at Augsburg, Germany, the historic "Joint Declaration on the Doctrine of Justification" was signed. It instantly made international headlines. The "Joint Declaration" explains that it "does encompass a consensus on basic truths of the doctrine of justification and shows that the remaining differences in its explication are no longer the occasion for doctrinal condemnations."[137] Though acknowl-

---

[134]Küng, *Justification*, p. 277-78. On Küng's book and its influence in Catholic circles, see Anthony N. S. Lane, *Justification by Faith in Catholic-Protestant Dialogue: An Evangelical Assessment* (New York: T & T Clark, 2002), pp. 87-96.

[135]H. George Anderson et al., eds., *Justification by Faith: Lutherans and Catholics in Dialogue VII* (Minneapolis: Augsburg, 1985), pp. 13-74.

[136]E.g., Karl Lehmann, Michael Root and William G. Rusch, eds., *Justification by Faith: Do the Sixteenth-Century Condemnations Still Apply?* (New York: Continuum, 1997).

[137]*Joint Declaration*, p. 11.

edging that differences remain, the "Joint Declaration" affirms that the consensus is "substantial," and that the differences are not sufficient to prevent fellowship between the two churches. It is important to note that, while the joint declaration is seen as a historic accord, it is not officially binding on the faithful of either church body. Reactions to the joint declaration have been mixed, with supporters and critics emerging from within both Catholic and Lutheran circles and beyond.[138]

Lutheran-Orthodox Dialogue and the "Finnish School"

A number of other intra-Christian dialogues (some official, others more informal) involving justification have also taken place, including those between Lutherans and the Eastern Orthodox.[139] Unlike the Western Church, Eastern Orthodoxy has never seen justification as a central category by which to express the soteriological process. Instead, Orthodoxy has prioritized the notion of *theosis* ("divinization," "deification"), which envisions salvation in Christ as being graced to participate in the very nature of God (e.g., 2 Pet 1:3-4),[140] This difference between the Eastern and Western churches is due, in large part, to the fact that they are characterized by two "significantly different explanations of the economy of creation and salvation."[141] Given the dominance of this category in the West, most Orthodox statements on justification today come in the context of discussing East-West differences, and so, not surprisingly, can be tinged

---

[138]See, e.g., Gerhard O. Forde, "The Critical Response of German Theological Professors to the *Joint Declaration on the Doctrine of Justification,*" *Dialog* 38 (1999): 71-72; Lane, *Justification by Faith;* Christopher J. Malloy, *Engrafted into Christ: A Critique of the Joint Declaration* (New York: Lang, 2005); William G. Rusch, ed., *Justification and the Future of the Ecumenical Movement: The Joint Declaration on the Doctrine of Justification* (Collegeville, Minn.: Liturgical, 2003); Reinhard Stenczka, "Agreement and Disagreement about Justification: Ten Years after the *Joint Declaration on the Doctrine of Justification,*" *Concordia Theological Quarterly* 73 (2009): 291-316.

[139]E.g., John Meyendorff and Robert Tobias, eds., *Salvation in Christ: A Lutheran-Orthodox Dialogue* (Minneapolis: Augsburg, 1992).

[140]On the Eastern Orthodox doctrine of *theosis,* see Michael J. Christensen and Jeffery A. Wittung, eds., *Partakers of the Divine Nature: The History and Development of Deification in the Christian Tradition* (Madison, N.J.: Fairleigh Dickson University Press, 2007); Vladimir Lossky, *The Vision of God,* trans. Asheleigh Moorhouse (Crestwood, N.Y.: St. Vladimir's Seminary Press, 1983); Norman Russell, *The Doctrine of Deification in the Greek Patristic Tradition* (New York: Oxford University Press, 2005). On the biblical grounding of this concept, see Stephen Thomas, *Deification in the Eastern Orthodox Tradition: A Biblical Perspective* (Piscataway, N.J.: Gorgias, 2008).

[141]J. Patout Burns, "The Economy of Salvation: Two Patristic Traditions," *Theological Studies* 37 (1976): 599.

with polemical undertones. For example: "Humanity's justification through forgiveness of sins is not a mere covering over man's sins, but a real destruction of them. It is not a mere external decision but a reality. . . . God does not declare someone to be justified if he [or she] is not really free."[142] As Eastern Orthodox Christians listen in to the ongoing discussions and disputes about justification in the Western Church, at one level they cannot help but wonder "what all the fuss [is] about."[143]

In recent years, the Eastern Orthodox concept of *theosis* has been receiving a stunning amount of attention in contemporary Western discussions of soteriology.[144] Increasingly, Western theologians from a wide variety of backgrounds are coming to agree with F. W. Norris that "deification should be viewed by Protestants not as an oddity of Orthodox theology but as an ecumenical consensus, a catholic teaching of the Church, best preserved and developed by the Orthodox."[145] In light of this growing Western interest in *theosis*, one of the most fascinating phenomena to emerge from intra-Christian dialogues on justification is the previously mentioned "Finnish school" of Luther interpretation that was inspired by a series of dialogues between Finnish Lutherans and the Russian Orthodox (1970-1995).[146] Centered around Tuomo Mannermaa (professor emeritus of ecumenical theology at the University of Helsinki), and thus alternately known

---

[142]Constantine Dratsellas, cited in Maximos Aghiorgoussis, "Orthodox Soteriology," in Meyendorff and Tobias, eds., *Salvation in Christ*, p. 49.

[143]Valerie A. Karras, "Beyond Justification: An Orthodox Perspective," St. Paul's Greek Orthodox Church website, p. 1, www.stpaulsirvine.org/html/Justification.htm.

[144]As noted by Gösta Hallonsten, "*Theosis* in Recent Research: A Renewal of Interest and a Need for Clarity," in Christensen and Wittung, eds., *Partakers*, pp. 281-93. See, e.g., Boff, *Liberating Grace*, pp. 175-83; Gannon Murphy, "Reformed Theosis?" *ThTo* 65 (2008): 191-212; Finger, "Anabaptism and Eastern Orthodoxy," pp. 76-83; Avery Cardinal Dulles, "Justification and the Unity of the Church," in *The Gospel of Justification: Where Does the Church Stand Today?* ed. Wayne C. Stumme (Grand Rapids: Eerdmans, 2006), pp. 139-40; Kärkkäinen, *One with God;* Clark H. Pinnock, "Spirit and Union," in *The Flame of Love: A Theology of the Holy Spirit* (Downers Grove, Ill.: InterVarsity Press, 1996), pp. 149-83; Michael J. Gorman, *Inhabiting the Cruciform God: Kenosis, Justification, and Theosis in Paul's Narrative Soteriology* (Grand Rapids: Eerdmans, 2009).

[145]F. W. Norris, "Deification: Consensual and Cogent," *Scottish Journal of Theology* 49 (1996): 422. On some of the complexities involved with regard to Western attempts to quickly and easily appropriate the Orthodox *theosis* concept, see Paul R. Hinlicky, "Theological Anthropology: Toward Integrating *Theosis* and Justification by Faith," *Journal of Ecumenical Studies* 34 (1997): 38-73.

[146]For a survey of Lutheran-Orthodox dialogues (from a member of the Finnish school), see Risto Saarinen, *Faith and Holiness: Lutheran-Orthodox Dialogue 1959-1994* (Göttingen: Vandenhoeck & Ruprecht, 1997).

as the "Mannermaa school," this approach sees in Luther an understanding of *faith* that involves

> a real participation in Christ, that in faith a believer receives the righteousness of God in Christ, not only in a nominal and external way, but really and inwardly. . . . [W]e participate in the whole of Christ, who in his divine person communicates the righteousness of God. Here lies the bridge to the Orthodox idea of salvation as deification or *theosis*.[147]

A key idea for Mannermaa's reading of Luther is that, in faith itself, Christ is really present. While this theme has been recognized before, Mannermaa and his followers argue that, due to mistaken philosophical (e.g., neo-Kantian) assumptions, this theme has never been given its due in a robust way within modern Luther research.[148] The Finnish school has made a noticeable impact in North America ever since it was given a favorable reception by leading Lutheran theologians Carl Braaten and Robert Jensen.[149] It has also been warmly embraced by some within (particularly Lutheran) Pentecostal/charismatic spheres.[150] The effects of this school are reaching to Pauline studies, specifically as one source of challenge to the way in which the "Lutheran Paul" has often been vilified in recent years.[151] Again, the Finnish school perspective is represented by Kärkkäinen in this present volume.

Responses to the Ecumenical Conversation

Strong reactions to the fruit of some of the ecumenical dialogues—particularly the conclusions on Luther and *theosis* of the Finnish school—have come from more traditional quarters of Luther interpretation, including those who have been identified with the "radical Lutheran" approach.[152]

---

[147]Carl E. Braaten and Robert W. Jensen, "Preface: The Finnish Breakthrough in Luther Research," in *Union with Christ: The New Finnish Interpretation of Luther*, ed. Carl E. Braaten and Robert W. Jensen (Grand Rapids: Eerdmans, 1998), p. viii.

[148]See Tuomo Mannermaa, *Christ Present in Faith: Luther's View of Justification* (Minneapolis: Augsburg Fortress, 2005).

[149]Braaten and Jensen, eds., *Union with Christ;* Robert W. Jensen, "Justification as a Triune Event," *Modern Theology* 11 (1995): 425.

[150]Kärkkäinen, *One with God;* Markku Antola, *The Experience of Christ's Real Presence in Faith: An Analysis on the Christ-Presence-Motif in the Lutheran Charismatic Renewal* (Helsinki: Luther Agricola Society, 1998).

[151]Risto Saarinen, "The Pauline Luther and the Law: Lutheran Theology Reengages the Study of Paul," in *The Nordic Paul: Finnish Approaches to Pauline Theology*, ed. Lars Aejmeleus and Antti Mustakallio (New York: T & T Clark, 2008), pp. 90-113.

[152]On "radical Lutheranism," see Gerhard O. Forde, "Radical Lutheranism," *Lutheran Quarterly*

Some of the critique is historical/exegetical in nature. For example, there is the counterclaim that *theosis*-like concepts are only found in Luther's early writings, and do not characterize his mature views. Other critiques are more theological in orientation. At the forefront of this type of response is the charge that the Finnish school and other ecumenical modifications among Lutherans regarding justification have served to threaten the centrality of this doctrine as the "article by which the church stands or falls." For these more "radically" traditional Lutherans, justification is not simply one of the central doctrines of the Christian faith. Rather, it is *the center*, the single criterion of the gospel—the gospel just is "the gospel of the justification of the ungodly."[153]

At the end of the nineteenth century, Martin Kähler had made justification by faith something of a practical center of his theology. Into the twentieth century, some Lutheran theologians such as Ernst Wolf, Joachim Iwand and Gerhard Gloege came to identify justification as the theological center in an increasingly strong sense. They drew, of course, from some of Luther's more provocative statements about justification, such as, "The article of justification is the master and prince, the lord, the ruler, and the judge over all kinds of doctrines; it preserves and governs all church doctrine and raises up our consciences before God. Without this article the world is utter darkness and death."[154] Today, one increasingly finds among more traditional and "radical" Lutherans the claim that justification by faith is "the one and only criterion for all theological statements."[155] As such, it functions as a meta-criterion—as "the *discrimen* by which all theological loci are to be evaluated."[156] For

---

1 (1987): 1-16; Robert Kolb, "Contemporary Lutheran Understandings of the Doctrine of Justification: A Select Glimpse," in *Justification: What's at Stake in the Current Debates*, ed. Mark Husbands and Daniel J. Treier (Downers Grove, Ill.: InterVarsity Press, 2004), pp. 153-76. For Lutheran critiques of the Finnish school, see Kolb, "Contemporary Lutheran Understandings," pp. 153-56; Mark C. Mattes, *The Role of Justification in Contemporary Theology* (Grand Rapids: Eerdmans, 2004), pp. 126-32.

[153]Eberhard Jüngel, "On the Doctrine of Justification," *International Journal of Systematic Theology* 1 (1999): 25.

[154]Martin Kähler, *What Luther Says: An Anthology*, ed. Ewald M. Plass, 3 vols. (St. Louis: Concordia, 1959), 2:703.

[155]Jüngel, "Doctrine of Justification," p. 51. See also idem, *Justification: The Heart of the Christian Faith* (New York: T & T Clark, 2001).

[156]Mattes, *Role of Justification*, p. 15.

Oswald Bayer, justification is the "basis and boundary of theology."[157] And for Eric Gritsch and Robert Jensen, justification is "a metalinguistic stipulation" about the "*kind* of talking" that can properly count as "proclamation and word of the church."[158] From the perspective of "radical Lutheranism," most strongly championed in North America by Gerhard Forde and his students, even those who agree that justification by faith is the single and central criterion can come under criticism for including elements—methodological or otherwise—that serve effectively to undercut the undiluted force of this claim.[159]

In response to this radical centering of justification, other Lutheran theologians offer a warning. Wolfhart Pannenberg reminds his fellow Lutherans: "Even for Paul himself [justification] is not the only center of his theology that controls all else. For Paul this center is Jesus Christ."[160] Carl Braaten offers a warning as well: "Why cannot there be more than one indispensible criterion . . . ? The tyranny of a single principle is more the legacy of German Idealism than of the Lutheran *Confessions*." According to Braaten, "exalting justification as the only criterion of Christian truth . . . borders on denominational ideology."[161] Interestingly, both Braaten and Pannenberg are favorable to Mannermaa and the Finnish school.[162]

Critical reactions to the treatment of justification within ecumenical contexts can be found outside Lutheran circles as well. As noted above, the number of evangelical publications that come to the defense of the traditional Reformation doctrine of justification is growing at a remarkable rate year by year, with many of them registering concern that, in pursuit of the laudable goal of ecumenical consensus, the historic Reformation perspec-

---

[157]Oswald Bayer, "Justification: Basis and Boundary of Theology," in *By Faith Alone: Essays on Justification in Honor of Gerhard O. Forde*, ed. Joseph A. Burgess and Marc Kolden (Grand Rapids: Eerdmans, 2004), pp. 67-85.

[158]Eric Gritsch and Robert Jensen, *Lutheranism: The Theological Movement and Its Confessional Writings* (Philadelphia: Fortress, 1976), p. 42.

[159]E.g., by Mattes' *(Role of Justification)* assessment, Jüngel, Pannenberg, Moltmann and even Robert Jensen all fall short in this respect. For Forde's approach to justification, see his *Justification by Faith*.

[160]Wolfhart Pannenberg, *Systematic Theology*, trans. Geoffrey W. Bromiley, 3 vols. (Grand Rapids: Eerdmans, 1991-1998), 3:213. For Pannenberg's extended discussion of justification, see pp. 58-96.

[161]Carl Braaten, *That All May Believe* (Grand Rapids: Eerdmans, 2008), p. 5.

[162]Braaten and Jensen, "Preface"; Pannenberg, *Systematic Theology*, 3:215 n. 368.

tive itself has been placed in jeopardy.[163] In addition, the British evangelical Alister McGrath (in the relatively short section on ecumenical dialogues within his magisterial study of justification) concludes that "ecumenical interests" have been "an important contributing factor to the quiet marginalization" of the doctrine of justification.[164] McGrath's sentiment reflects a broad consensus of concern among evangelical Reformed thinkers regarding the growing marginalization and/or misunderstanding of justification within the wider church today. At stake, they claim, is the heart of the gospel—the forensic declaration of God by which sinners are justified through the imputation of an alien righteousness found only in Jesus Christ.

There is, in fact, an interesting conceptual connection between one's appraisal of the necessity and prospects of the ecumenical conversation on justification and one's appraisal of the viability of traditional forensic accounts of justification. On the one hand, even Reformed traditionalists who value ecumenical conversation may have a degree of uneasiness with the trajectory or conclusions of the ecumenical conversation. On the other hand, those committed to not just the value but the necessity of the ecumenical conversation typically are fully willing to modify traditional categories to achieve other theological or ecclesiological ends deemed to be valuable.

---

[163]E.g., Henri A. Blocher, "The Lutheran-Catholic Declaration on Justification," in Husbands and Treier, eds., *Justification*, pp. 197-217; Fesko, *Justification;* Gary L. W. Johnson and Guy P. Waters, eds., *By Faith Alone: Answering the Challenges to the Doctrine of Justification* (Wheaton, Ill.: Crossway, 2006); Horton, *Covenant and Salvation;* Oliphint, *Justified in Christ.*

[164]McGrath, *Iustitia Dei,* p. 418. On the other hand, A. C. Ogoko Nkwume, for instance, has recently proposed ecumenical dialogue on justification as the very thing that may prove effective at revitalizing and unifying the churches of Nigeria. See A. C. Ogoko Nkwume, *Dialogue on Justification: A Model for Ecumenical Dialogue Among the Churches in Nigeria?* (Berlin: LIT, 2007).

2

Justification in Contemporary Debate

Over the last three decades, the discussion surrounding justification has increasingly centered around what has come to be known as the "new perspective" on the apostle Paul.[1] With the new perspective has come not simply challenges to the Reformation interpretation of Paul's concept of justification itself, but also to related Pauline matters (e.g., the nature of Paul's "conversion"—if it even should be termed such, the origin and "center" of Paul's theology, Paul's view of the "law," etc.), and to the traditional Reformation understanding of the nature of first-century Judaism. But some of these questions were already being pressed years before the rise of the new perspective.

By the end of the nineteenth century, it was common for Protestant biblical scholars to disparage Second Temple Judaism as a legalistic, particularistic religion that focused upon externals—a religion diametrically opposite that of the Christianity espoused by Jesus and Paul. The earlier work of F. C. Baur helped to foster this image when he counterposed Judaism's nationalistic particularism with Christianity's "new universal principle of consciousness."[2] This negative caricature of ancient Judaism was

---

[1]For introductory discussions of the new perspective on Paul—some affirmative, some critical—see Michael B. Thompson, *The New Perspective on Paul* (Cambridge: Grove, 2002); Guy Prentiss Waters, *Justification and the New Perspective on Paul: A Review and Response* (Phillipsburg, N.J.: Presbyterian & Reformed, 2004); Stephen Westerholm, *Perspectives Old and New on Paul: The "Lutheran" Paul and His Critics* (Grand Rapids: Eerdmans, 2004); Kent L. Yinger, *The New Perspective on Paul: An Introduction* (Eugene, Ore.: Cascade, 2011).
[2]John Riches, *Galatians Through the Centuries* (Malden, Mass.: Blackwell, 2008), p. 131.

epitomized in the work of Ferdinand Wilhelm Weber. Weber's image of Judaism influenced Wilhelm Bousett and the (Old) History of Religions School, and, from there, eventually touched the thought of Bultmann. In this scholarly context, a "Hellenized" Pauline Christianity was easily played off against an insular "Palestinian Judaism." And so, at the turn of the century and beyond, it was not uncommon to find liberal Protestantism maintaining a generally negative aura around Judaism reminiscent of the earlier Reformers in their polemic against Roman Catholicism. Not infrequently, Paul's doctrine of justification by faith was presented as the diametrically opposed alternative to the legalism and works-righteousness of Judaism.[3]

PRECURSORS TO THE NEW PERSPECTIVE

And yet a few voices arose in the late nineteenth and early twentieth centuries to challenge these negative portrayals of ancient Judaism, and in this regard functioned as forerunners to the new perspective. Notable here are the works of Claude Montefiore and George Foote Moore, both of whom challenge the negative caricatures of Judaism that had become standard fare in the post-Reformation Protestant church.[4] Contrasting with the common opposition of the apostle Paul to the Palestinian Judaism of his day, a few New Testament scholars—for example, William Wrede, Albert Schweitzer, W. D. Davies and Richard Longenecker, each in their own way—offered a more positive assessment of this relationship.[5] Not surprisingly, with this reassessment came a departure from the Reformation perspective regarding the nature and importance of justification in Paul's thought. Wrede and Schweitzer argued that the notion of justification was born out of the early Christian polemical encounter with Judaism—and thus is a historically conditioned, situation-specific category. For neither of them was justification by faith anything like the center of Paul's thought.

---

[3]E.g., Rudolf Bultmann, *Theology of the New Testament*, trans. Kendrick Grobel, 2 vols. (New York: Charles Scribner's Sons, 1951-1955), 1:262-64.

[4]E.g., Claude Montefiore, *Judaism and St. Paul: Two Essays* (London: Goschen, 1914); George Foote Moore, "Christian Writers on Judaism," *HTR* 14 (1921): 197-254.

[5]William Wrede, *Paul*, trans. Edward Lummis, reprint ed. (Lexington, Ky.: American Theological Library Association, 1962); Albert Schweitzer, *The Mysticism of Paul the Apostle*, trans. William Montgomery (New York: Holt, 1931); W. D. Davies, *Paul and Rabbinic Judaism: Some Rabbinic Elements in Pauline Thought*, rev. ed. (London: SPCK, 1955 [1948]); Richard Longenecker, *Paul: Apostle of Liberty* (New York: Harper & Row, 1964), pp. 65-85.

In fact, for Schweitzer, justification is but a "subsidiary crater" of Paul's theology, the true heart of which is the notion of mystical participation in Christ.[6]

A clear foreshadowing of the new perspective came with Krister Stendahl's 1963 essay, "The Apostle Paul and the Introspective Conscience of the West."[7] Here, Stendahl argues that a psychologically introspective sensibility, one plagued by a perpetually guilty conscience, has characterized important moments in Western Christianity from Augustine, through Luther, on up to today. And this introspective anthropology has read itself back into Paul's letters with a distorting effect. Actually, Paul shows no such tendency, but rather reports a robust conscience during his days as a Pharisee (i.e., Phil 3:6). Those texts in Paul that have been used as evidence for his own introspective conscience are, in fact, arguments about the relationship of Jewish and Gentile Christians and the place of the Law therein. For Paul, the key problem he had to deal with was the claim by Jewish believers that Gentiles, in effect, had to become Jews (i.e., Torah observant) to become Christians. And to this, Paul says "No!" According to Stendahl, this is the point at which Paul's understanding of justification by faith makes its appearance. Paul uses his justification by faith argument not to describe the universal experience of guilt-ridden individual humans before God, but rather to safeguard Gentile converts from being forced to adopt circumcision, sabbath keeping and dietary laws in order to be seen as full-fledged members of the early church. From this perspective, justification becomes not the center of Paul's gospel, but a temporally conditioned response to a sociological conflict (Jew-Gentile) within the early church. From this perspective, for example, Romans 9–11 becomes not a secondary parenthesis in Paul's argument (as has often been the case in articulations of the standard Reformation view), but rather the very point and climax of the letter.

In a memorable response to Stendahl's essay, Ernst Käsemann acknowledges his agreement that it is "impossible to overstress the polemical character of Paul's doctrine of justification."[8] He also aligns himself with Sten-

---

[6]Schweitzer, *Mysticism of Paul*, p. 225. See also Wrede, *Paul*, pp. 122-23.

[7]Krister Stendahl, "The Apostle Paul and the Introspective Conscience of the West," *HTR* 56 (1963): 199-215 (originally published in Swedish in 1960).

[8]Ernst Käsemann, "Justification and Salvation History in the Epistle to the Romans," in *Perspectives on Paul*, trans. Margaret Kohl (Philadelphia: Fortress, 1971 [1969]), pp. 60-78 (here p. 71).

dahl—and ostensively distances himself from Bultmann, or at least one common interpretation of Bultmann—when he rejects the "individualist curtailment of the Christian message."[9] For Käsemann:

> To be justified means that the creator remains faithful to the creature . . . ; it means that he changes the fallen and apostate into new creatures. . . . This means that in justification it is simply the kingdom of God proclaimed by Jesus which is at stake.[10]

Such language noticeably breaks out of the dominant forensic categories of the traditional Lutheran perspective. Käsemann's previous investigation of Paul's notion of the righteousness of God in its apocalyptic context as both gift *and power* also serves to put pressure on the traditional Reformation view.[11] And yet, against Stendahl and his category of "salvation history," Käsemann ends by defending justification as the central concept by which Paul's thought is to be understood: "salvation history must not take precedence over justification. It is its sphere. But justification remains the centre, the beginning and end of salvation history."[12]

In a 1968 article, Markus Barth (the son of Karl Barth) picks up on the social/ecclesial context of Paul's vision of justification by faith articulated by Stendahl and develops it further.[13] Barth warns of "the danger of a crass individualism, of a religiously or ecclesiastically embellished egoism" tied to the traditional Reformation view of justification.[14] He goes on to express the inherently social nature of justification in Paul:

> No man is ever made righteous for himself; justification by faith is a reality only in community with those fellow-men whom God elected for common justification. . . . There is no personal justification by God without justification of fellow-men by God. . . . Briefly: where there is no love there is no faith and no justice. . . . Justification by works is, correspondingly, to be identified with anti-social behavior. Indeed, those works of law which cannot justify, are present wherever an arbitrary selection is made from the law,

---

[9]Ibid., p. 74.
[10]Ibid., pp. 74-75.
[11]Ernst Käsemann, "'The Righteousness of God' in Paul," in *New Testament Questions of Today*, trans. W. J. Montague (London: SCM, 1969 [1965]), pp. 168-82.
[12]Ibid., p. 76.
[13]Markus Barth, "Jews and Gentiles: The Social Character of Justification in Paul," *Journal of Ecumenical Studies* 5 (1968): 241-67.
[14]Ibid., p. 243.

. . . and where selected items are employed for the purpose of separating man from fellow-man, or of supporting the right of one group to dominate another.[15]

THE "NEW PERSPECTIVE ON PAUL" AND JUSTIFICATION

The "old perspective," to which the new perspective is juxtaposed, is, of course, the traditional Reformation—particularly "Lutheran"—interpretation of Paul and first-century Palestinian Judaism. By the lights of its new perspective critics, the old perspective fails when it paints first-century Judaism as a religion of merit wherein one "earns" salvation by doing the "works of the law." In this old perspective scenario, Paul emerged guilt ridden (thus anticipating the experiences of Augustine and Luther) from Judaism to step into the new and liberating experience of justification by grace through faith alone—*Christian grace* has replaced *Jewish law; Christian faith* has replaced *Jewish works,* as the way in which God reconciles sinful, guilty individuals to himself. It is over and against this "old perspective" that the new perspective offers what it presents as a return to an even "older perspective"—Paul's real perspective. And it turns out that what actually unites advocates of the new perspective is not so much a single "perspective" on Paul (here significant diversity emerges), but rather a broadly shared perspective on first-century Judaism.

James Dunn has frequently been credited with coining the phrase "New Perspective on Paul."[16] But according to Dunn, N. T. Wright used the phrase earlier in a 1978 paper.[17] The new perspective to which they refer is that expressed in E. P. Sanders's 1977 landmark study, *Paul and Palestinian Judaism,* the publication of which typically marks the birth of the new perspective.[18] At the heart of Sanders's work is a new perspective on ancient Judaism, one that directly challenges the traditional Protestant portrait of Judaism as a works-based religion where salvation is earned through

---

[15]Ibid., pp. 244-45, 251.

[16]Reference is typically made to his article, "The New Perspective on Paul," *BJRL* 65 (1983): 95-122, and the 1982 conference paper on which it was based.

[17]James D. G. Dunn, "The New Perspective: Whence, What and Wither?" in *The New Perspective on Paul,* rev. ed. (Grand Rapids: Eerdmans, 2008 [2005]), p. 7 n. 24. See N. T. Wright, "The Paul of History and the Apostle of Faith," *Tyndale Bulletin* 29 (1978): 61, 64, 77-84.

[18]E. P. Sanders, *Paul and Palestinian Judaism: A Comparison of Patterns of Religion* (Philadelphia: Fortress, 1977).

law keeping. By canvassing a wide range of Jewish literature from 200
B.C.E. to 200 C.E., Sanders detects a broadly shared "pattern of religion"
within the Judaism of this period. He terms this pattern "covenantal nomism." Sanders explains:

> Covenantal nomism is the view that one's place in God's plan is established
> on the basis of the covenant and that the covenant requires as the proper
> response of man his obedience to its commandments, while providing
> means of atonement for transgression. . . . Obedience maintains one's posi-
> tion in the covenant, but it does not earn God's grace as such.[19]

Crucial to Sanders's thesis is the difference between "getting in" and
"staying in." Sanders argues that the normative pattern of Second Temple
and Rabbinic Judaism is that the Jews are graciously granted by God the
saving status of elect covenant people, apart from works or merit—"getting
in" is all about the gracious election of God. However, once in this gracious relationship, the Jews are now called to *maintain* that relationship
through obedience to God's commandments—"staying in," therefore, is
tied to keeping of the law. Simply put: *"salvation is by grace . . . ; works are
the condition of remaining 'in,' but they do not earn salvation."*[20]

But if Judaism was essentially a religion of grace, then why did Paul
reject it? According to Sanders, the answer is simple: for Paul, the problem
with Judaism is that it does not recognize Jesus the Christ as the sole path
of salvation. In Sanders's memorable words: *"This is what Paul finds wrong
in Judaism: it is not Christianity."*[21] In Sanders's estimation, Paul does not
actually begin with a religious "plight" derived from Judaism (i.e., a guilt-
ridden conscience) and arrive at a "solution" (i.e., Jesus Christ). Rather, he
begins with a paradoxical solution—the crucified Messiah Jesus as the
path to salvation—and then retrospectively articulates a plight that would
make sense of such a solution.[22]

Sanders's new perspective was rapidly engaged, critiqued and developed
by a number of scholars, most notably James Dunn and N. T. Wright. As
David Aune notes, together, Sanders, Dunn and Wright "constitute the
triumvirate chiefly responsible for formulating and marketing the New

---

[19]Ibid., pp. 75, 420.
[20]Ibid., p. 543 (emphasis in original).
[21]Ibid., p. 552 (emphasis in original).
[22]Ibid., pp. 482, 484.

Perspective."[23] Dunn and Wright—along with all proponents of the new perspective—agree with Sanders that ancient Judaism was not a legalistic religion of earned salvation. Dunn has further developed this insight by investigating Paul's concept of the "works of the law." According to Dunn, this phrase refers not to Jewish striving to keep the moral laws of God in order to earn salvation (i.e., as in the Reformation view). Rather, "works of the law" refer primarily to particular laws—circumcision, sabbath-keeping, dietary laws—that serve as ethnic "badges" or boundary markers that separate Jews from Gentiles. Paul's problem with these "works" is that if they are allowed into the church, they serve to separate believers along ethnic lines, thus privileging one ethnicity over another, and needlessly dividing the body of Christ. For Paul, the single identity marker of the new covenant people of God is faith in Jesus Christ.[24] Regarding Paul and the Judaism of his day, Dunn recognizes more continuity than does Sanders. With Stendahl, he sees Paul's embrace of Messiah Jesus more in terms of a "calling" than a "conversion" from one religion to another. As a leading voice of the new perspective, Dunn has continued to develop and refine his own approach over the last several decades.[25] Dunn ably represents the new perspective in this present volume.[26]

N. T. Wright entered into the discussion with an important article published in 1978.[27] Reflecting the shared conviction of the new perspective, Wright states that traditional Pauline interpretation "has manufactured a false Paul by manufacturing a false Judaism for him to oppose."[28] Wright sees Israel's "meta-sin" as an ethnic-based boasting in her graciously given vocation—an attempt to "confine grace to one race," wherein the symbols

---

[23]David E. Aune, "Recent Readings of Paul Relating to Justification by Faith," in *Rereading Paul Together: Protestant and Catholic Perspectives on Justification*, ed. D. E. Aune (Grand Rapids: Baker Academic, 2006), p. 205.

[24]Dunn, "New Perspective on Paul," pp. 194-98.

[25]See, e.g., James Dunn, *Jesus, Paul, and the Law: Studies in Mark and Galatians* (Louisville: Westminster John Knox, 1990); idem, *The Theology of Paul the Apostle* (Grand Rapids: Eerdmans, 1998); idem, *New Perspective*.

[26]Beyond the publications cited in the notes above, Dunn's prior work on justification and/or the new perspective includes: Dunn, "The Justice of God: A Renewed Perspective on Justification by Faith," *Journal of Theological Studies* 43 (1992): 1-22; idem, "Yet Once More—'The Works of the Law': A Response," *Journal for the Study of the New Testament* 46 (1992): 99-117; Dunn and Alan M. Suggate, *The Justice of God: A Fresh Look at the Old Doctrine of Justification by Faith* (Grand Rapids: Eerdmans, 1994).

[27]Wright, "Paul of History."

[28]Ibid., p. 78.

that mark her as distinctive from other peoples (circumcision, sabbath, dietary laws) are turned into "badges of superiority."[29] Over the last few decades, Wright has continued to develop and defend his own unique take on the new perspective in a wide range of publications.[30] More recently, both Dunn and Wright have emphasized that their views are not antithetical to the concerns and perspective of the Reformers, but rather that they provide additions and correctives that can be seen as complementary to more traditional, particularly Reformed, Protestant views.[31]

But what does all of this imply for understanding Paul's teachings on justification? To begin, Don Garlington reminds us that the "issue of justification, as such, was not on the original agenda of the NPP [New Perspective on Paul]. . . . [I]t has to be clarified that there is no such thing as 'the NPP position on justification.' That is a misnomer."[32] And yet, while it is true that there is no single view of justification commonly held by its proponents, the fundamental intuitions that drive the new perspective naturally lead to a de-centering of justification in Paul. For the new perspective, the concern that Paul's concept of justification by faith addresses is not a universal human self-righteousness instantiated in a Pelagian-like, works-driven Judaism. Rather, it is a problem specific to the setting of the early church, where a dominant Jewish majority was attempting to force the Gentile minority into adopting the Torah-based symbols of the (Jewish) people of God in order to gain access to the (Jewish) Messiah Jesus. As such, Paul's teaching on justification is nothing like the "center" of his theology—let alone the "article by which the church stands or falls." Thus, for Sanders for example, it is not justification but rather an active participation in Christ that is of central concern for Paul.[33]

For Dunn, the concept of justification by faith will only be fully grasped when its originating context is clearly kept in view: Paul's mission to the Gentiles. It is intrinsically bound up with "Paul's fundamental objection to

---

[29]N. T. Wright, *The Climax of the Covenant: Christ and the Law in Pauline Theology* (Minneapolis: Fortress, 1991), pp. 240, 243.

[30]E.g., N. T. Wright, *What Saint Paul Really Said: Was Paul of Tarsus the Real Founder of Christianity?* (Grand Rapids: Eerdmans, 1997); idem, *Paul: In Fresh Perspective* (Minneapolis: Fortress, 2005).

[31]E.g., Dunn, "New Perspective: Whence," p. 96; Wright, *Justification,* pp. 72-73, 252.

[32]Don Garlington, "The New Perspective on Paul: Two Decades On," in *In Defense of the New Perspective on Paul: Essays and Reviews* (Eugene, Ore.: Wipf & Stock, 2005), p. 4.

[33]Sanders, *Paul,* pp. 502-8; see also pp. 434-42.

the idea that God has limited his saving goodness to a particular people."[34]
More specifically:

> Justification by faith is a banner raised by Paul against any and all such
> presumption of privileged status before God by virtue of race, culture or
> nationality, against any and all attempts to preserve such spurious distinc-
> tions by practices that exclude and divide.[35]

Contrary to some criticisms of his view, Dunn is clear that Paul's doctrine
of justification is not restricted merely to sociological or ecclesiological concerns. It also involves the issue of individual salvation. Again, Dunn has no
desire to reject the Reformation view—he can even support the idea of an
"alien righteousness"—but simply to supplement its missing dimensions.[36]
In challenge to the traditional Reformation view, Dunn argues for the importance of first an "initial" justification and then a "final" justification on
the Day of Judgment. And on that Day, the latter, active obedience ("works")
is seen to be not merely evidence that, but rather part of the basis upon
which, the believer is finally justified. In Dunn's words: "Paul's theology of
justification by faith alone has to be qualified as final justification by faith
and by works accomplished by the believer in the power of the Spirit."[37] And
yet, Dunn himself warns that false and dangerous "works" of many kinds
constantly threaten to erode justification by faith, some of them ironic:
"Even the insistence on a particular formulation of the doctrine of 'justification by faith alone' can become one of the 'works' by which a self-perceived
orthodoxy clouds the truth of the gospel!"[38] (For further exposition of
Dunn's view of justification, see his essay in this present volume.)

Unlike some within new perspective circles, Wright is convinced that
Paul's justification metaphor, drawn from the realm of the law court, "does
not denote *an action which transforms someone* so much as *a declaration which
grants them a status*," namely, "*the status that someone has when the court has
found in their favor.*"[39] Here, Wright seems solidly in line with the Reformation view over against Augustine and the Roman Catholic tradition.

---

[34]Dunn and Suggate, *Justice of God*, p. 28.
[35]Dunn, *New Perspective*, p. 205.
[36]Dunn, "New Perspective: Whence," p. 85.
[37]Ibid., p. 88.
[38]Ibid., p. 96.
[39]Wright, *Justification*, pp. 91, 90 (emphases in original).

But Wright goes on to point out that serious interpretive problems arise when we take the justification image—simply one among many soteriological images for Paul—and force it to "do duty for *the entire picture of God's reconciling action toward the human race.*"[40] Additionally, Wright argues that Paul's view of justification will be seriously distorted if it is removed from the tripartite conceptual context in which it always functioned for Paul—namely, a "law-court" conditioned by "covenant" (i.e., shorthand for Paul's understanding of God's single plan to save the world from its plight through Abraham and his family, Israel) and "eschatology" (i.e., Paul's conviction that, through Messiah Jesus, God had inaugurated the messianic "age to come").[41] In this conceptual matrix, the rich texture of Paul's Christology emerges. Through the corporate inclusion of God's people in Messiah, Jesus' faithful life of obedience becomes their life; his sin-condemning death becomes their death; and with his vindicating resurrection comes "the beginning of the entire new creation" and the anticipation of the final victory over "all enemies, including death itself."[42]

Again, the covenantal dimensions of Paul's sense of the biblical narrative is crucial for Wright. For example (and similar to Dunn) Wright sees Paul's notion of the "righteousness of God" as primarily referring *to God's covenant faithfulness.*[43] Furthermore, Paul's notion of justification cannot be divorced from the precious gift of the new covenant: God's own Holy Spirit. Simply put, a faithful articulation of Paul's understanding of justification will always be "trinitarian in shape."[44] In Wright's words, the

> lawcourt verdict [of justification], implementing God's covenant plan, and all based on Jesus Christ himself, is announced both in the *present*, with the verdict issued on the basis of faith and faith alone, and also in the *future*, on the day when God raises from the dead all those who are already indwelt by the Spirit. The present verdict gives the *assurance that* the future verdict will match it; the Spirit gives the *power through which* that future verdict, when given, will be seen to be in accordance with the life that the believer has then lived.[45]

---

[40]Ibid., p. 86.
[41]Ibid., pp. 92-102.
[42]Ibid., p. 106.
[43]Ibid., p. 99. See Dunn, "New Perspective on Paul," p. 190.
[44]Wright, *Justification,* p. 107.
[45]Ibid., p. 251 (emphasis in original).

Wright adds further clarification to his view when he notes that "[j]ustification is not 'how someone becomes a Christian.' It is God's declaration about the person who has just become a Christian."[46]

RESPONSES TO THE NEW PERSPECTIVE

Reactions to the new perspective have varied widely. Many scholars view the new perspective as having breathed "fresh" biblical life into an old Protestant doctrine. Among those generally sympathetic with the new perspective, some embrace the descriptor itself quite comfortably.[47] Others, while holding views similar to professed new perspective proponents, either make little to nothing of the phrase itself or even explicitly distance themselves from it. Douglas Campbell, for example, agrees wholeheartedly with the new perspective that the old perspective—which he refers to as the "Justification theory"—is "a paradigm with multiple flaws." Yet he also stresses that the "interpretive difficulties" we face today "are more fundamental and comprehensive than the new perspective generally suggests—and much more so!" Consequently, in Campbell's estimation, the current discussion is "rapidly moving beyond both old and new perspectives on Paul, as we must."[48] Likewise, Francis Watson, although expressing similar concerns about the old perspective as do new perspective advocates, in the recent revision of his 1986 book, *Paul, Judaism, and the Gentiles*, has changed the subtitle from "*A Sociological Approach*" to "*Beyond the New Perspective*."[49] And so, it is not surprising that the call has gone out for the move to a "Post–New Perspective Perspective."[50] Much of this seems to be little more than haggling over semantics. Wright himself points out that "the most important thing about the new perspective" is the fact that

---

[46]N. T. Wright, "New Perspectives on Paul," in *Justification in Perspective: Historical Developments and Contemporary Challenges*, ed. Bruce L. McCormack (Grand Rapids: Baker Academic, 2006), p. 260.

[47]E.g., Brenda B. Colijn, "Justification by Faith(fulness)," in *Images of Salvation in the New Testament* (Downers Grove, Ill.: InterVarsity Press, 2010), pp. 196-218; Garlington, *Defense*; Thompson, *New Perspective*; Yinger, *New Perspective*.

[48]Douglas A. Campbell, *The Deliverance of God: An Apocalyptic Rereading of Justification in Paul* (Grand Rapids: Eerdmans, 2009), pp. 202-3.

[49]Francis Watson, *Paul, Judaism, and the Gentiles: Beyond the New Perspective*, 2nd ed. (Grand Rapids: Eerdmans, 2007 [1986]). Watson articulates four points at which his view moves beyond the new perspective, see pp. 12-26.

[50]Brendan Byrne, "Interpreting Romans Theologically in a Post-'New Perspective' Perspective," *HTR* 94 (2001): 227-41; Michael F. Bird, "When the Dust Finally Settles: Reaching a Post–New Perspective Perspective," *Criswell Theological Review* n.s. 2 (2005): 57-69.

"there is no such thing as *the* new perspective. . . . There is only a disparate family of perspectives, some with more, some with less family likeness, and with fierce squabbles and sibling rivalries going on inside."[51] Then again, if the phrase "new perspective" comes to mean nothing more than a new way to read Paul in light of our own current topic of passion, drawn from "contemporary contexts, crises and moral values," it will come, ultimately, to mean nothing in particular at all.[52]

Despite the contentions of both new perspective and post–new perspective advocates, one of the prominent reactions to the new perspective, especially among evangelicals, has been a reaffirmation of the essence of the older Reformation paradigm, albeit in nuanced form.[53] These scholars—usually from more traditional Lutheran and Reformed persuasions—generally grant Sanders's contention that Palestinian Judaism did not hold a crass scorecard-legalism, in which good deeds were weighed against bad ones. However, like Schreiner, they are "still convinced that the Reformers understood Paul better than those who are espousing new approaches,"[54] and that first-century Judaism is still liable to a nuanced charge of legalism. Thus, they tend to agree with McGrath that the new perspective represents just one more force serving to "eclipse" and "marginalize" the doctrine of justification by faith today.[55]

As previously described, the new perspective provided a persuasive argument that ancient Judaism was not the legalistic, salvation-by-works religious system as portrayed by the old (Reformation) perspective—an anachronistic characterization generally attributed to the projection of medieval Catholicism back onto ancient Judaism. Most New Testament scholars, even detractors to the new perspective, have come to agree with this new perspective assessment.[56] Nonetheless, the de-

[51]Wright, *Justification*, p. 28 (emphasis in text).

[52]David G. Horrell, "A New Perspective on Paul? Rereading Paul in a Time of Ecological Crisis," *Journal for the Study of the New Testament* 33 (2010): 3.

[53]Stephen Westerholm, who provides a helpful survey of this position in *Perspectives Old and New on Paul*, pp. 201-25, characterizes these reactions as "'Lutheran Responses," regardless of the traditional affiliation of the advocate.

[54]Thomas R. Schreiner, *The Law and Its Fulfillment: A Pauline Theology of the Law* (Grand Rapids: Baker, 1993), p.11.

[55]Alister E. McGrath, *Iustitia Dei: A History of the Christian Doctrine of Justification*, 3rd ed. (New York: Cambridge University Press, 2005 [1986]), pp. 418-20.

[56]E.g., D. A. Carson, "Summaries and Conclusion," in *Justification and Variegated Nomism*, ed. D. A. Carson, Peter T. O'Brien and Mark A. Seifrid, 2 vols. (Grand Rapids: Baker Academic, 2001, 2004), 1:505.

tractors remain unconvinced of the overall conclusions of the new perspective. One of the most sustained cases against Sanders's claim that covenantal nomism characterizes the common Judaism of the first century is the two-volume work *Justification and Variegated Nomism,* the first volume of which is devoted to testing Sanders's claim. In the conclusion to the volume, D. A. Carson states that "[o]ne conclusion to be drawn, then, is not that Sanders is wrong everywhere, but he is wrong when he tries to establish that his category [of covenantal nomism] is right everywhere."[57] Instead of a ubiquitous, monolithic "covenantal nomism," Carson discerns a "variegated nomism" within ancient Judaism. For Carson, Sanders's broad rubric of "covenantal nomism" hides within it "huge tracks of works-righteousness or merit theology."[58] With Carson, a number of other scholars continue to defend the traditional Reformation interpretation of ancient Judaism as widely infected with a legalistic works-righteousness.[59]

Several of the contributors to the second volume of *Justification and Variegated Nomism* have also provided expanded critiques of the new perspective in other venues. Mark Seifrid, both an editor and contributor, has criticized aspects of the new perspective extensively, both in what it affirms and in what it denies. He contends that new perspective advocates have misunderstood Luther's doctrine of justification and, in turn, that "Luther's theology of the cross and justification . . . more closely accords with Paul than recent attempts to understand him."[60] Moreover, he maintains that the notion that covenantal nomism provides an overarching synthesis for Judaism is misleading, because in segments of Judaism "covenantalism" and "nomism" stand side-by-side in unintegrated fashion.[61] Finally, even granting the accuracy of covenantal nomism as a descriptor of Judaism, Seifrid highlights the similarity between this pattern of reli-

---

[57]Ibid., 1:543.

[58]Ibid., 1:545.

[59]E.g., John Piper, *The Future of Justification: A Response to N. T. Wright* (Wheaton, Ill.: Crossway, 2007), pp. 145-61; Cornelius P. Venema, *The Gospel of Free Acceptance in Christ: An Assessment of the Reformation and 'New Perspective' on Paul* (Carlisle, Penn.: Banner of Truth Trust, 2006), pp. 299-301.

[60]Mark A. Seifrid, "Blind Alleys in the Controversy over the Paul of History," *Tyndale Bulletin* 45 (1994): p. 74.

[61]Mark A. Seifrid, *Christ, Our Righteousness: Paul's Theology of Justification* (Downers Grove, Ill.: InterVarsity Press, 2000), pp. 15-16.

gion and that of the medieval theology to which Luther was reacting.[62]

Another contributor, Simon Gathercole, has examined early Jewish soteriology carefully and determines that "to understand Second-Temple Judaism as 'covenantal-nomism' downplays, ignores, or denies the role of obedience as a decisive criterion for final vindication in the Jewish texts." Instead, he finds, "alongside the emphasis on God's gracious election in Second-Temple Jewish literature (argued for powerfully by Sanders), there is nevertheless a firm belief in final vindication on the basis of works. Obedience leads to final justification."[63] In addition, Gathercole ascertains that works also play a decisive role in final justification for Paul. However, the continuity ceases at this point, because these decisive works remain the ongoing product of God's grace through the empowering work of the Spirit. Thus, he contends that "the attempts of some new perspective scholars to draw attention to the similarity between Jewish and Pauline soteriological patterns run aground on the rocks of Paul's pneumatology."[64] Finally, Gathercole concludes that Paul does, in fact, criticize Judaism for its confidence or boasting in its ability to obey, not simply for its exclusion of Gentiles on the basis of proprietary identity markers, as misconstrued by new perspective advocates.

In addition to the contributors to the second volume of *Justification and Variegated Nomism*, there have also been other full-scale challenges mounted to the conclusions of the new perspective. For instance, Tom Schreiner argues that the myopic focus on laws, which one encounters in the Mishnah, establishes a practical legalism, even if justification was theoretically grounded on grace in Judaism.[65] Moreover, he contends that Paul—and in this respect read rightly by Luther—would have regarded the notion of "staying in" by works, which is of the essence of Sanders's portrayal of Judaism, as itself synergistic, and therefore inherently legalistic.[66] Andrew Das has similarly challenged the conclusions of the new perspective. Like Schreiner and against Sanders, Das concludes that Paul

---

[62]Seifrid, "Blind Alleys," p. 92.

[63]Simon J. Gathercole, "After the New Perspective: Works, Justification and Boasting in Early Judaism and Romans 1–5," *Tyndale Bulletin* 52 (2001): 304.

[64]Gathercole, *Where Is the Boasting? Early Jewish Soteriology and Paul's Response in Romans 1–5* (Grand Rapids: Eerdmans, 2002), p. 134.

[65]Schreiner, *Law and Its Fulfillment*, p. 115.

[66]Ibid., p. 94.

believed that the law requires perfect obedience for justification.[67] Furthermore, he finds that for Paul the conviction that Christ is the sole means of mediation for God's grace collapses any gracious covenantal framework in Judaism and accentuates the rigorous demands of the law, so that "the Jew who disobeys the law has no effective path to resolve the situation caused by sin, since its resolution can be found only in Christ."[68]

SOME CURRENT EXEGETICAL FLASH POINTS IN THE JUSTIFICATION DEBATE

Labels aside, a number of other points of exegetical contention surrounding the justification debate are clear today. We will end this survey with a brief mention of five of the more commonly considered issues.

Paul's Attitude Toward Judaism

When the focus turns specifically to Paul's own attitude toward Judaism, things become complex. Generally, both the old and new perspectives agree that Paul's primary concern with the Judaism of his day (or any other religious system for that matter) would be the fact that Jesus Christ alone is the way of salvation. But beyond this, what concerned Paul about Judaism particularly in relation to the justification passages in his letters? Central to this debate is the question of Paul's attitude toward the Torah, and what, precisely, he meant by "works of the law."[69] For those who defend something like the traditional Reformation view, a fundamental problem of Paul's regarding Judaism remains, in one sense or another, its legalistic orientation to salvation.[70] On the other hand, as noted above, new perspective proponents typically identify Paul's main problem with Judaism not as legalism, but rather *ethnocentrism*. Finally, at the far end of the spectrum is an approach that some are now terming the "new view" of Paul.[71]

---

[67]A. Andrew Das, *Paul, the Law, and the Covenant* (Peabody, Mass.: Hendrickson, 2001), pp. 145-70.

[68]Ibid., p. 144; see also pp. 70-94, 113-44.

[69]For a range of perspectives, see Dunn, *Jesus, Paul, and the Law;* Lloyd Gaston, "Paul and the Torah," in *Antisemitism and the Foundations of Christianity,* ed. A. T. Davies (New York: Paulist, 1979), pp. 48-71; Das, *Paul, the Law, and the Covenant;* Schreiner, *Law and Its Fulfillment.*

[70]The "sense" in which this is the case is often quite nuanced today. For a range of expressions, see Das, *Paul, the Law, and the Covenant;* Gathercole, *Where Is the Boasting?;* Piper, *Future of Justification,* pp. 145-61; Schreiner, *Law and Its Fulfillment.*

[71]John G. Gager, *Reinventing Paul* (New York: Oxford University Press, 2000), p. 50; Aune,

For this new view, Paul in fact *had no problem* with Judaism *per se*. Inspired by Lloyd Gaston's work, scholars such as John Gager and Stanley Stowers have, each in their own way, argued that Paul's actual view of Judaism has suffered distortion at the hands of Christian interpreters for centuries due to polemical uses of Paul in quite foreign socioreligious contexts, and/or in conjunction with anti-Semitic tendencies.[72] In Gager's eyes, Paul held to a form of the "two-covenant" model of salvation wherein the Jews were to adhere to the Torah and Gentiles to Christ. Thus, for Gager, faith in Christ was not a soteriological necessity—therefore justification by faith was intended for Gentiles alone.

The Role of Works in Final Justification/Judgment

A further complexity in the relationship of Paul to Judaism involves the fact that each appears to affirm some sort of role for works in final justification or judgment, which has raised questions as to whether works function similarly or distinctly in their respective patterns of religion. In addition, the growing perception that deeds do play some role for Paul in final judgment raises a further question regarding the congruence between this recognition and his affirmation of justification by faith. With regard to this last assessment, some see an irresolvable tension in Paul's thinking at this point—an incoherence created by a vestige of his Jewish thinking (i.e., judgment according to works) and his Christian conviction about justification by faith. Nonetheless, the majority of commentators on Paul have sought a resolution for the apparent tension between justification and works. Classical Protestant attempts to synthesize Paul's statements about justification and judgment according to works typically accentuated the discontinuity between Paul and Judaism. Of course, expressions of the Reformation perspective did this by indicting Judaism as a legalistic religion, in which works played a meritorious role, in contrast to Paul who championed *sola fide*. From this point of view, works in Paul were only regarded as either the basis for degrees of reward among the redeemed or as of evidentiary value at the final judgment—although not contingent for a positive verdict, or even as entirely immaterial.[73]

"Recent Readings," pp. 219-23.

[72]Gaston, "Paul and the Torah"; Gager, *Reinventing Paul;* Stanley K. Stowers, *A Rereading of Romans: Justice, Jews, and Gentiles* (New Haven: Yale University Press, 1994).

[73]For instance, the Protestant Orthodoxy of the seventeenth century, to which Spener and the

On the other hand, contemporary attempts to integrate Paul's statements about works and justification have had to reckon with the impact of the new perspective. Subsequently, scholars have sought to reconcile Paul's affirmations about justification by faith and judgment according to works by emphasizing in various ways the extent of the continuity/discontinuity between Paul and Judaism and by their assessment of the validity of covenantal nomism as an appropriate delineation of Palestinian Judaism. For example, Kent Yinger contends that Paul is in essential continuity with Judaism in that he is a covenantal nomist who affirms a similar connection between grace and obedience. In other words, initial incorporation in the [new] covenant people is by grace, but remaining in requires obedience. He concludes that Paul's view "is the standard Jewish expectation that one's outward behavior (one's *work* or *way*) will correspond to, and be a visible manifestation of, inward reality. The eschatological recompense according to deeds *confirms*, on the basis of deeds, one's justification."[74] At the same time, Yinger finds that there is also a discontinuity between Paul and Judaism that consists of Paul's substitution of faith in Christ for the identity markers of Judaism to demarcate the people of God and of Paul situating his view of judgment according to works within his confidence in the new covenant activity of the Spirit.[75]

By way of contrast, Robert Gundry sees much greater discontinuity between Paul and Judaism. In his estimation, for Palestinian Judaism, works are both a sign of and a condition for staying in; whereas for Paul, works are only evidential of, not instrumental for, staying in, with "faith being the necessary and sufficient condition of staying in as well as getting in."[76] A novel solution to the relationship has been advanced by Chris Van Landingham. He rejects covenantal nomism as an accurate description of the religious pattern of Palestinian Judaism, instead advancing the case that this Judaism does, in fact, regard deeds as meritorious, and, thus, determinative of individual destiny. The really surprising feature of his

---

other Pietists reacted, excessively minimized the role of holy actions in the life of one who had been justified by faith.

[74]Kent L. Yinger, *Paul, Judaism, and Judgment According to Deeds* (New York: Cambridge University Press, 1999), pp. 15-16, 290.

[75]Ibid., pp. 15-16, 202.

[76]Robert Gundry, "Grace, Works, and Staying Saved in Paul," *Biblica* 66 (1985): 35; see also pp. 11-12.

thesis is that he contends that Paul is in continuity with Judaism at this point, and so likewise considers individual works as meriting either justification or condemnation at the last judgment.[77] Initial justification simply provides forgiveness for previous sins and the possibility of obedience, but then people determine their own fate at the final judgment by the moral quality of their deeds. Most significantly, unlike Yinger, who roots the good deeds of the Christian in the activity of the indwelling Spirit, Van Landingham holds that following initial justification the human volition itself can produce vindicating works.[78]

Particularly in evangelical circles, the current deliberation over the role of works in justification has frequently been distilled down to an exegetical debate over the meaning of several key New Testament texts. The first of these texts is Romans 2 and, in particular, Paul's statement that "the doers of the law will be justified" (Rom 2:13), along with his definition of the true circumcision to include the uncircumcised person who "keeps the requirements [dikaiōmata] of the law" (Rom 2:26-29; cf. Rom 8:4, in which Paul claims that the person walking according to the Spirit fulfills the "requirement [dikaiōma] of the law"). The traditional reading of Romans 2 holds that Paul affirmed, in principle, that one could be justified by doing the law, but that he denied, in fact, that anyone actually accomplished this.[79] Paul would then be using this position to prosecute his indictment against those who compromise his understanding of *sola gratia*. However, an increasing number of scholars advocate interpreting these texts as references to Christian Gentiles, who are enabled to fulfill the law through the empowering activity of the Spirit. These interpreters hold that what becomes explicit in Romans 8:3-4 is already in play in Romans 2. Even here though, there are important nuances. Some are highly concerned to emphasize that works are exclusively of evidentiary value at the final judgment, testifying to the genuine faith that is the actual grounding of justification; whereas others seem to allow that these

---

[77]Chris Van Landingham, *Judgment and Justification in Early Judaism and the Apostle Paul* (Peabody, Mass.: Hendrickson, 2006), pp. 5-15.

[78]Evangelicals opposed to the new perspective may be attracted to Van Landingham's conclusions concerning Judaism, while remaining highly skeptical of his reading of Paul. For an excellent review essay that contests his conclusions, see Michael Bird, "Judgment and Justification in Paul: A Review Article," *BBR* 18 (2008): 299-313.

[79]E.g., Douglas Moo, *The Epistle to the Romans* (Grand Rapids: Eerdmans, 1996), pp. 142-43, 147-48.

Spirit-produced deeds are the actual basis for final justification.

N. T. Wright, a chief proponent of this "Christian" reading of Romans 2, is often thought to be an example of the latter. He is convinced that Paul is speaking here of Spirit-enlivened Christian Gentiles, because of the links forward to Romans 8[80] and backwards to the great new covenant texts of the Old Testament—seeing the description "the work of the law written on their hearts" (Rom 2:15) as an echo of Jeremiah 31:33, and the depiction of "keeping the requirements of the law" (Rom 2:26) as a deliberate allusion to Ezekiel 36:27.[81] Prior to questions being raised about his understanding of justification, Wright could claim: "Present justification declares, on the basis of faith, what future justification will affirm publicly . . . *on the basis* of the entire life."[82] However, subsequently Wright has been more careful to say that the verdict of future justification "will be seen to be *in accordance with* the life that the believer has then lived."[83]

In various ways, Wright's evangelical critics have found his emphases deficient and are intent on highlighting the purely evidentiary nature of works in relation to final justification. Thus, John Piper is concerned that interpreters "treat the necessity of obedience not as any part of the basis for justification, but strictly as the evidence and confirmation of our faith in Christ whose blood and righteousness is the sole basis of justification."[84] Michael Bird is sympathetic to Wright's position and explicitly attests that "Paul's anthropological pessimism about the human inability to keep the law is matched only by his pneumatological optimism that Spirit-empowered persons will be able to fulfill the requirements of the law when they walk by the Spirit (Rom. 8.4; Gal. 5.25)."[85] However, he too is concerned that "it shifts the material cause of eschatological justification from chris-

---

[80]Wright, *Justification*, p. 190.

[81]N. T. Wright, "The Law in Romans 2," in *Paul and the Mosaic Law*, ed. James D. G. Dunn (Grand Rapids: Eerdmans, 1996), pp. 146-47 and pp. 135-36, respectively. See also his commentary, "The Letter to the Romans," in *The New Interpreter's Bible*, vol. 10, ed. Leander E. Keck et al. (Nashville: Abingdon, 2002), pp. 442, 448.

[82]Wright, *What Saint Paul Really Said*, p. 129.

[83]Wright, *Justification*, p. 251 (emphasis added). John Piper identified the failure to distinguish precisely enough between justification *in accordance with* works and *on the basis of* works as a chief difficulty in Wright's understanding of justification; see Piper's *Future of Justification*, pp. 118-19.

[84]Piper, *Future of Justification*, p. 110.

[85]Michael Bird, *The Saving Righteousness of God: Studies on Paul, Justification and the New Perspective* (Colorado Springs: Paternoster, 2007), p. 173.

tology to pneumatology,"[86] and wants to safeguard the conclusion that "the final grounds of acquittal and vindication remains [*sic*] in the death and resurrection of Jesus Christ."[87]

The other New Testament text that has figured prominently in this aspect of the discussion of justification is James 2:14-26, especially as it relates to the apparent intra-canonical tension it creates with Paul's perspective on justification. The tension appears acute in that James claims that "a person is justified by works and not by faith alone" (Jas 2:24); and yet, like Paul in Romans and Galatians, he cites Genesis 15:6 and utilizes Abraham as an example of his point. However, reasonable explanations for resolving the tension have been advanced. The classic explanation posits that James is responding to a misconstrued Paulinism—which Paul himself would likewise have rejected—but that he uses vocabulary that, while happening to overlap with Paul's, connotes an entirely different meaning. Specifically, he uses "works" to refer to genuine morally good deeds, not to the "works of the law" which Paul rejects. He regards unproductive "faith" as simply an orthodoxy that fails to transform the one who holds it. And, finally, he employs "justification" language in congruence with the LXX, in the sense of demonstrating one to be righteous. Paul uses these same terms differently, which "results in an artificial conflict between James and Paul."[88] Thus, Peter Davids concludes: "In reality, both James and Paul had similar ideas on the role of good works in the Christian life, but since they ministered in different spheres socially and geographically, they addressed different concerns and used their overlapping terminology differently."[89]

Recent considerations generally concur with, but nuance, the traditional conclusion. They see congruence between the perspectives of James and Paul on justification, provided that the relationship between justification and works is understood a certain way in Paul. Alexander Stewart, who attempts to consider James independently from Paul, describes "faith" and

---

[86]Ibid., p. 173.
[87]Ibid., p. 174.
[88]Peter Davids, "James and Paul," in *Dictionary of Paul and His Letters,* ed. G. F. Hawthorne, R. P. Martin and D. G. Reid (Downers Grove, Ill.: InterVarsity Press, 1993), p. 459. This article is a lucid presentation of the classic resolution of the tension between James and Paul, as outlined above.
[89]Ibid., p. 460.

"works" in much the same fashion as the traditional explanation (described above); however, he rejects the conclusion that James uses justification language in simply a demonstrative sense. Instead, he finds that "justification in James primarily represents the vindicating verdict from the eschatological judge (4:12; 5:7-9) resulting in eschatological salvation."[90] This leads him to the conclusion that "according to James, believers are not finally saved until the final judgment and what they 'do' between the present and that future day actually carries weight and will affect the outcome of the verdict."[91]

Timo Laato, in a very detailed and penetrating analysis, paints a similar picture. He especially highlights James's description of the faith-derived "implanted word" (Jas 1:21), which he regards as a fulfillment of Jeremiah's new covenant promises concerning the internalization of God's law.[92] Consequently, the works that are necessary for justification must be regarded as Spirit-produced works and equate to Paul's fruit of the Spirit (Gal 5:22-23). Both Paul and James then affirm a living faith that produces Spirit-empowered works. For Laato, this establishes that "James and Paul differ from one another terminologically, but not theologically."[93] Thus, he affirms that "James and Paul agree with one another also in their estimation of the eschatological character of the Christian pattern of life. Both teach that a judgment according to works shall take place."[94] It is worth noting that these latter assessments bear similarities to the way that Yinger and Wright understand the relationship between works and final justification in Paul—wherein works, while not playing a role in initial justification, do play a role at the final judgment, establishing the new covenant activity of God through the Spirit in the believer's life and, hence, the reality of faith.[95]

---

[90]Alexander Stewart, "James, Soteriology and Synergism," *Tyndale Bulletin* 61 (2010): 301.
[91]Ibid., pp. 309-10.
[92]Timo Laato, "Justification According to James: A Comparison with Paul," *Trinity Journal* 18 (1997): 53.
[93]Ibid., p. 77.
[94]Ibid., pp. 75-76.
[95]Mention should be made at this point of a related intra-evangelical disagreement on the nature of *saving faith*—namely, the "Lordship salvation" debate. In its most popular terms, the debate boils down to the question of whether Jesus must be one's "Lord" (i.e., one to whom a believer demonstrates actual obedience) in order to be one's "Savior." The "free grace" position says "clearly no"; the "Lordship" position says "clearly yes"; and various mediating views have sought for a via media. The first famous exchange on this topic came with the Everett F.

Justification/Righteousness in the Old Testament

Another point of debate today is the question of the Old Testament concept of justification/righteousness and its illumination of the New Testament use of these ideas. The Hebrew root *ṣdq* grounds the various Old
Testament terms associated with justice/righteousness. One of the central
points of debate is the question of just what conceptual context Old Testament justification/righteousness language should be read within. One
common answer to this question has been a *relational* context. From the
catalyzing thought of Hermann Cremer at the turn of the twentieth century, through the influential work of Gerhard Von Rad and on up to today,
numerous scholars have understood the Old Testament concept of righteousness fundamentally as a relational term, grounded in Yahweh's *covenant with Israel*. Here "righteousness" is primarily seen in terms of "faithful adherence to the structure of obligations established by the covenant."[96]
This is so for God as well as humanity. Thus God's righteousness refers
primarily to God's "covenant faithfulness"—that is, his faithfulness to the
covenant promises he has made, particularly the promises of salvation and
"restorative justice."[97]

In reaction to this approach, others have emphasized the *creational* context of Old Testament justification/righteousness language. Key here is
the work of H. H. Schmid, which connects God's righteousness to God's
determination to "secure the good and beneficial order of creation."[98] Taking inspiration from Schmid, Mark Seifrid has pushed to distance Old

---

Harrison–John R. W. Stott debate, "Must Christ be Lord to be Savior?" *Eternity* 10 (September 1959): 13-16, 36, 37, 48. The issue reached heated proportions again in the late 1980s and
early 1990s. See S. Lewis Johnson, "How Faith Works," *Christianity Today*, September 22,
1989, pp. 21-25. The "free grace" position is championed most famously by Zane Hodges,
Absolutely Free! A Biblical Reply to Lordship Salvation (Grand Rapids: Zondervan, 1989). The
"Lordship" view's most well-known defender is John MacArthur, *The Gospel According to Jesus*
(Grand Rapids: Zondervan, 1988). For a set of essays offering a middle path, see Michael S.
Horton, ed., *Christ the Lord: The Reformation and Lordship Salvation* (Grand Rapids: Baker,
1992).
[96]Richard B. Hays, "Justification," in *ABD*, 3:1129. Similarly, see Elizabeth R. Achtemeier,
"Righteousness in the Old Testament," in *Interpreter's Dictionary of the Bible*, ed. G. A. But-
trick, 4 vols. (Nashville: Abingdon, 1962), 4:80-85.
[97]Christopher D. Marshall, *Beyond Retribution: A New Testament Vision for Justice, Crime, and
Punishment* (Grand Rapids: Eerdmans, 2001), pp. 53-59.
[98]Mark A. Seifrid, "Righteousness Language in the Hebrew Scriptures and Early Judaism," in
Justification and Variegated Nomism, ed. D. A. Carson, Peter T. O'Brien and Mark A. Seifrid,
2 vols. (Grand Rapids: Baker Academic, 2001, 2004), 1:426. Hans H. Schmid, *Gerechtigkeit
als Weltordnung* (Tübingen: Mohr Siebeck, 1968).

Testament righteousness language from a covenant context and relocate it primarily in a wider, creational context. In distancing God's righteousness from an interpretive matrix dominated by God's faithfulness to his covenant promises of salvation to Israel, Seifrid is also able to find new impetus for a retributive/punitive side to divine righteousness.[99]

Still others argue that there is no reason to pit creational and covenantal/relational contexts against each other. Yahweh certainly is Creator and King over creation, and as such is responsible to maintain its cosmic order. And so Schmid and others are right to point out how this theme was sorely neglected in much twentieth-century biblical theology. But this fact does not diminish the unique (vis-à-vis other ancient Near Eastern religions) *covenantal* dimensions of Yahweh's righteousness as expressed in the biblical narrative.[100] From the early chapters of Genesis onward, creation and covenant are bound together in a unique fashion, mutually shaping much of the rest of the Old Testament's theological concepts.[101] With regard to righteousness/justification, this inherently involves God's covenant promises to deliver Israel from her enemies and, through her, to restore the glory of the original human vice-regency over the earth.[102]

Justifying Righteousness: Imputation, Transformation or Incorporation?
Within evangelical circles, one of the most intense debates related to justification involves the question of the nature and effect of the righteousness by which believers are justified. In recent years, a significant chorus of voices has come to the defense of the traditional Protestant notion of the *imputation* of Christ's righteousness to the believer.[103] In Protestant ortho-

---

[99]Seifrid, "Righteousness Language," pp. 425-29. Prior to Seifrid, John Piper made use of Schmid in a similar fashion; see *The Justification of God: An Exegetical and Theological Study of Romans 9:1-23*, 2nd ed. (Grand Rapids: Baker Academic, 1993 [1983]), pp. 103-19.

[100]See esp. Mary Sylvia Chinyere Nwachukwu, *Creation-Covenant Scheme and Justification by Faith* (Rome: Editrice Pontifica Universita Gregoriana, 2002). See also Brevard S. Childs, *Biblical Theology of the Old and New Testaments* (Minneapolis: Fortress, 1992), pp. 487-91; John Goldingay, "Justice and Salvation for Israel and Canaan," in *Reading the Hebrew Bible for a New Millennium*, vol. 1: *Theological and Hermeneutical Studies*, ed. Wonil Kim et al. (Harrisburg, Penn.: Trinity Press International, 2000), pp. 169-87.

[101]William Dumbrell, *Covenant and Creation* (Nashville: Thomas Nelson, 1984). See also idem, "Justification and the New Covenant," *Churchman* 112 (1998): 17-29.

[102]E.g., see respectively, Peter J. Leithart, "Justification as Verdict and Deliverance: A Biblical Perspective," *Pro Ecclesia* 16, no. 1 (2007): 56-72; Jonathan Moo, "Romans 8:19-22 and Isaiah's Cosmic Covenant," *NTS* 54 (2008): 74-89.

[103]E.g., John Piper, *Counted Righteous in Christ: Should We Abandon the Imputation of Christ's Righteousness?* (Wheaton, Ill.: Crossway, 2002); Brian Vickers, *Jesus' Blood and Righteousness:*

doxy, justification is commonly described in terms of the "non-imputation" (or remission) of sins and the "imputation" of the perfect obedience of Christ to the believer.[104] In the words of John Piper:

> God counts us as having his righteousness in Christ because we are united to Christ by faith alone. That is, we are counted as perfectly honoring and displaying the glory of God, which is the essence of God's righteousness, and which is also a perfect fulfilling of the law. That is what God imputes to us and counts to us as having because we are in Christ who perfectly honored God in his sinless life.[105]

Among other things, the imputation doctrine clarifies and safeguards the *alien nature* of God's justifying righteousness *reckoned* to the believer in Christ.

In recent years, a host of Pauline scholars has reacted against this traditional Protestant doctrine of imputation, among them a number of evangelicals.[106] Chief among their concerns is that the Protestant notion of imputation is simply missing in Paul's letters. This point has been argued by as diverse a range of evangelical Pauline scholars as Robert Gundry, Mark Seifrid and N. T. Wright.[107] Wright, for example, proposes that once one grasps Paul's notion of corporate solidarity in Christ and the consequent effects for the believer, one gains the heart of what the imputation doctrine was designed to achieve, but without its unhelpful baggage and un-Pauline language.[108] Proponents of imputation argue that, while the *term* itself may be missing in Paul, the *concept* is expressed or implied in a number of Pauline texts (e.g., Rom 4:3-8; 2 Cor 5:21; Phil 3:9).

Paul's Theology of Imputation (Wheaton, Ill.: Crossway, 2006).

[104]McGrath, *Iustitia Dei*, pp. 270-71. Noteworthy here is the dispute concerning the "active obedience of Christ" between more traditional Reformed thinkers and those who align with the "Federal Vision" perspective. See David VanDrunen, "To Obey Is Better Than Sacrifice: A Defense of the Active Obedience of Christ in the Light of Recent Criticism," in *By Faith Alone: Answering the Challenges to the Doctrine of Justification*, ed. Gary L. W. Johnson and Guy P. Waters (Wheaton, Ill.: Crossway, 2006), pp. 127-46.

[105]Piper, *Future of Justification*, p. 165.

[106]E.g., Craig Keener, *Romans* (Eugene, Ore.: Cascade, 2009), p. 29.

[107]Robert H. Gundry, "The Nonimputation of Christ's Righteousness," in *Justification: What's at Stake in the Current Debates*, ed. Mark Husbands and Daniel J. Treier (Downers Grove, Ill.: InterVarsity Press, 2004), pp. 17-45; Mark A. Seifrid, "Luther, Melanchthon, and Paul on the Question of Imputation," in *Justification: What's at Stake in the Current Debates*, ed. Mark Husbands and Daniel J. Treier (Downers Grove, Ill.: InterVarsity Press, 2004), pp. 137-52; Wright, *Justification*, p. 46, 105, 135, 157-58, 206.

[108]Wright, *Justification*, p. 105.

For many, the notion of imputed righteousness is not only exegetically flawed—it is also ethically bankrupt. Here, the classic imputation doctrine is often charged with turning the Christian's righteousness into a mere "legal fiction." Marcus Borg and John Dominic Crossan have put it bluntly:

> If you misread the justice of Paul's God as retributive, the only good news might be that God would pretend, as it were, that we were just, that God would impute to us a justice we did not have. Such an "as if" treatment would have horrified Paul. There is nothing, for example, about fictional imputation of justice, but everything about factual transformation by justice in these claims from [Paul].[109]

In his book *The Saving Righteousness of God*, Michael Bird proposes the idea of "incorporated righteousness" as a via media position that both covers essential concerns of imputational proponents while remaining faithful to Paul's actual linguistic/conceptual world.[110] In this and other issues related to Paul's concept of justification, the work of Bird reflects that of a growing number of evangelical scholars who are searching for a middle path between "older" Protestant interpretations and new perspective approaches. In this sense, Bird offers a Progressive Reformed view, a perspective that he represents in this present volume.[111]

Finally, some might be tempted to suppose that the imputation vs. non-imputation debate breaks down neatly along "Arminian" and "Calvinist" lines.[112] However, things are not that simple. For example, Seifrid—a soteriological "Calvinist" rejects imputation (as noted above), while Roger Olson, one of "Arminianism's" most ardent defenders today, staunchly embraces the imputation doctrine—as, apparently, Arminius himself did.[113]

---

[109]Marcus J. Borg and John Dominic Crossan, *The First Paul: Reclaiming the Radical Visionary Behind the Church's Conservative Icon* (San Francisco: HarperOne, 2009), p. 165.

[110]Bird, *Saving Righteousness*, pp. 60-87.

[111]Bird's prior work on justification and related topics includes *The Saving Righteousness of God;* idem, "Justification as Forensic Declaration and Covenant Membership: A *Via Media* Between Reformed and Revisionist Readings of Paul," *Tyndale Bulletin* 57 (2006): 109-30; idem, "Judgment and Justification in Paul"; idem, "When the Dust Finally Settles"; idem, *Introducing Paul: The Man, His Mission and His Message* (Downers Grove, Ill.: InterVarsity Press, 2009).

[112]A claim made by Richard D. Phillips, "A Justification of Imputed Righteousness," in Johnson and Waters, eds., *By Faith Alone*, pp. 75-83.

[113]Roger Olson, *Arminian Theology: Myths and Realities* (Downers Grove, Ill.: InterVarsity Press, 2006), p. 220. Olson surveys Arminian views on the issue on pp. 200-220.

The Meaning of Pistis

The phrase *pistis Christou* (or slight variations)—which occurs seven times in the Pauline letters (Rom 3:22, 26; Gal 2:16 [twice]; 3:22; Eph 3:12; Phil 3:9), typically in contexts related to justification—is grammatically ambiguous and open to being understood as an objective genitive (i.e., "faith in Christ") or a subjective genitive (i.e., "faith/fulness of Christ") or possibly even as another type of genitive, such as source (i.e., "the faith which comes from Christ").[114] Despite this ambiguity, for almost 450 years after Luther translated *pistis Christou* into the vernacular as *Glauben an Christus* ("faith in Christ") the objective reading, also known as the anthropological reading, dominated Protestant interpretation and was seen to be an indispensable component of the doctrine of justification by faith alone. In recent decades, this dominant position has been challenged by proponents of the subjective reading, also known as the Christological reading, who have argued that the phrase is better understood as a reference to Jesus' own faith and/or faithfulness, rather than as a reference to the human means of appropriating justification.[115] While there were prior early adopters,[116] the Christological interpretation sprang into prominence with the publication of Richard B. Hays's dissertation, *The Faith of Jesus Christ: An Investigation of the Narrative Substructure of Galatians 3:1–4:11*, in 1983.[117] The central aim of Hays's work is actually to demonstrate that Paul's argument and theological reflections in Galatians presuppose a story; that is, they have a narrative substructure.[118] However, his contention that the faithful death of Jesus, to which Paul alludes with the phrase *pistis Christou*, plays a pivotal role in this story actually garnered the majority of attention.

---

[114]With regard to *pistis* and its cognates, Wright summarizes four broad trajectories of meaning; see "Faith, Virtue, Justification, and the Journey to Freedom," in *The Word Leaps the Gap: Essays on Scripture and Theology in Honor of Richard B. Hays*, ed. J. Ross Wagner, C. Kavin Rowe and A. Katherine Grieb (Grand Rapids: Eerdmans, 2008), pp. 472-97 (esp. pp. 482-89).

[115]On the widespread understanding within Second Temple Judaism of *pistis* as both "faith" and "faithfulness," see Maureen W. Yeung, *Faith in Jesus and Paul* (Tübingen: Mohr Siebeck, 2002), p. 297. See also Colijn, "Justification by Faith(fulness)," pp. 196-218.

[116]Such as Markus Barth, "The Faith of the Messiah," *Heythrop Journal* 10 (1969): 363-70; George Howard, "Notes and Observations on the 'Faith of Christ,'" *HTR* 60 (1967): 459-65.

[117]Now republished as Hays, *The Faith of Jesus Christ: The Narrative Substructure of Galatians 3:1–4:11*, 2nd ed. (Grand Rapids: Eerdmans, 2002).

[118]Hays, *Faith of Jesus*, p. xxiv.

The debate over the objective and subjective understandings of *pistis Christou* initially focused on lexical and syntactical arguments.[119] Contentions and rebuttals have been made regarding a number of features of possible relevance: the lexical meaning of *pistis* (trust, faith and/or faithfulness); the significance of the semantic domains of *pistis* and its cognate verb *pisteuō;* the presence or absence of the article in the *pistis Christou* construction; other uses of *pistis* with a genitive personal noun (e.g., Rom 4:16, "the faith of Abraham"); the import of the collocation of *pistis* with "obedience" language (e.g., Rom 1:5); and the presence of repetition as an acceptable means of emphasis versus its presence as unacceptable redundancy.[120] While various scholars still find certain grammatical points persuasive, it is generally conceded that such arguments have led to no definitive conclusion.[121] Consequently, the arguments have since broadened out to ones focused on issues of exegetical and canonical context and theological coherence.

As the conversation has progressed into these issues, a different set of questions has moved to the forefront. Discussion has focused on Paul's contrast between *pistis Christou* and works of the law. Is this contrast one of two human responses, one of works and one of faith, which would support the objective reading; or is the contrast between a human response and a divine response, which would buttress the subjective interpretation? Another point of discussion concerns the relationship between *pistis Christou* and the righteousness of God. Paul claims that *pistis Christou* is the means of unveiling God's righteousness (Rom 3:21-22). Is it more coherent to follow the Christological interpretation and to understand this to mean that the faithfulness of the Messiah discloses God's righteousness; or is it still possible to hold the anthropological interpretation and posit

---

[119]On the current state of the debate, see Michael F. Bird and Preston M. Sprinkle, eds., *The Faith of Jesus Christ: Exegetical, Biblical, and Theological Studies* (Peabody, Mass.: Hendrickson, 2009). For helpful surveys of the history and nature of the debate, see Matthew C. Easter, "The *Pistis Christou* Debate: Main Arguments and Responses in Summary," *Currents in Biblical Research* 9 (2010): 33-47; Debbie Hunn, "Debating the Faithfulness of Jesus Christ in Twentieth-Century Scholarship," in Bird and Sprinkle, eds., *Faith of Jesus Christ*, pp. 15-31.

[120]For instance, does Paul claim that "we believed in Christ Jesus, in order that we might be justified by faith in Christ [*pistis Christou*]," use repetition as an acceptable means of emphasizing the significance of human faith; or is this rendering unacceptably redundant, and should instead be rendered "we believed in(to) Christ Jesus, in order that we might be justified by Christ's faithfulness" (Gal 2:16)?

[121]So, for instance, Hunn, "Debating," p. 26.

that our faith in Christ reveals God's righteousness, provided that human faith itself is rightly seen as a divine act?

An additional topic of deliberation has centered on the significance of Paul's use of Habakkuk 2:4 and, in particular, on the identity of the "righteous one" described therein. Is this to be understood as a generic reference to believers, which would be congruent with the anthropological reading; or is this a Christological title, which would strongly support reading *pistis Christou* subjectively as a reference to the Messiah's own faithfulness?[122] A last area of contention concerning the Pauline evidence has focused on the eschatological arrival of *pistis*, which terminates the custodial role of the law, as delineated in Galatians 3:23-29. Since human faith was present prior to this point, as the example of Abraham testifies, and since Christ as Abraham's seed is likewise described as "coming" (Gal 3:19), should *pistis* not be understood Christologically? Or is it possible to understand the coming of *pistis* to refer simply to the inauguration of the new age, which is characterized by the appropriate human response of faith to what Christ has accomplished, as Dunn contends?[123] Finally, at this point the debate has broadened out to consider the congruence of either the objective or subjective readings of *pistis Christou* with the evidence of the remainder of the New Testament canon. Exegetes in both camps have suggested that evidence outside of the Pauline epistles—such as the Synoptics, the fourth Gospel, James or Revelation—augments the case for one or the other of the readings.[124]

An additional ancillary aspect of the *pistis Christou* debate merits mention. It is often perceived that the Christological reading is a direct product of the new perspective. This is not entirely accurate. Hays, the primary popularizer of the subjective reading, has not overtly advocated for a new perspective reading of Paul. Conversely, Dunn, one of the

---

[122]The Christological reading was brought to prominence by Richard B. Hays, "'The Righteous One' as Eschatological Deliverer: Hermeneutics at the Turn of the Ages," in *The New Testament and Apocalyptic*, ed. J. Marcus and M. L. Soards (Sheffield: JSOT Press, 1988), pp. 191-215. Recently, it has cautiously been affirmed by Desta Heliso, *Pistis and the Righteous One* (Tübingen: Mohr Siebeck, 2007).

[123]James Dunn, "ΕΚ ΠΙΣΤΕΩΣ: A Key to the Meaning of ΠΙΣΤΙΣ ΧΡΙΣΤΟΥ," in *The Word Leaps the Gap: Essays on Scripture and Theology in Honor of Richard B. Hays*, ed. J. Ross Wagner, C. K. Rowe and A. Katherine Grieb (Grand Rapids: Eerdmans, 2008), p. 364.

[124]See especially the contributions in part 4, "The Witness of the Wider New Testament," in Bird and Sprinkle, eds., *Faith of Jesus Christ*, pp. 209-74.

leading proponents of the new perspective, affirms the objective reading. To the extent that there is a relationship between the new perspective and the subjective reading of *pistis Christou,* it lies in the fact that the new perspective led to a reevaluation of Paul and to what was most essential in his thinking. Its general skepticism toward a Lutheran reading of Paul created space to consider means or metaphors other than justification by faith as foundational.

Rather than the centrality of this doctrine, a number of scholars proceeded to identify narrative or story as fundamental for Paul. Advocates of this position hold that a grand Story or meta-narrative—sweeping from a world gone wrong in Adam through God's initial solution in choosing Abraham to its climax in the faithful death and resurrection of God's obedient Son, who is also Abraham's seed, Israel's Messiah, and humanity's second Adam—is foundational to Paul's thought. This conviction has generated not only a reconsideration of the importance of justification by faith, but also its very meaning. Accordingly, those who advocate a narrative reading of Paul's thought have also championed reading *pistis Christou* as a reference to Christ's own faithfulness since it is seen to be so coherent with and to play such a climactic role in the reconstructed Pauline narrative.[125]

A further effect of this has been different estimations of the connection between justification and participation. Advocates of the traditional objective reading of *pistis Christou* tend to consider participation in Christ to be secondary to justification by faith alone.[126] Conversely, proponents of the subjective reading are inclined to elevate the importance of participation, and to associate it intimately with justification, in that it is the person "in Christ" who benefits from his faithfulness. In fact, on this side of the debate, participation plays the role that imputation does in the traditional reading.

---

[125]Notable examples, in addition to Hays, are A. Katherine Grieb, *The Story of Romans: A Narrative Defense of God's Righteousness* (Louisville: Westminster John Knox, 2002), pp. 37-38; and Ben Witherington III, *Paul's Narrative Thought World: The Tapestry of Tragedy and Triumph* (Louisville: Westminster John Knox, 1994), pp. 268-70.

[126]While he believes it need not be the case, in the foreword to Bird and Sprinkle, *Faith of Jesus Christ,* James Dunn acknowledges that "the Reformation tradition has found it difficult to integrate Paul's participation in Christ ("in Christ") emphasis with 'justification by faith' as the article by which the church stands or falls" (p. xvii).

CONCLUSION: EXEGESIS, HERMENEUTICS
AND *AGAPE*-LOVE

It will be clear by now that the doctrine of justification is a contested one at virtually every turn. At stake for many is the defining conviction of the Protestant Reformation. At stake for all concerned is a proper understanding of Scripture and, particularly, the thought of Paul. One might hope that the scriptural question could be settled by proper exegesis, which could then provide a basis for movement toward a common Christian rapprochement on the theological front. But most are aware today that things are just not that hermeneutically simple. Behind the centuries of debate about justification lies a host of methodological and disciplinary fractures which, in turn, inform and are informed by an array of divergent theological, epistemological, sociocultural and experiential presuppositions and assumptions. The move from Scripture to doctrine is never easy—even when it seems so. And even within the same broad tradition, say contemporary Protestant evangelicalism, the divergent exegetical and theological paradigms at work can lead scholars who are equally committed to the authority of Scripture and the guidance of historic orthodoxy to amazingly different conclusions.[127]

Still, a commitment to scriptural authority, diligent and methodologically nuanced exegesis, a self-conscious and broadly informed theological method, and a commitment to humble dialogue with those whom we disagree on the matter—a dialogue wherein "speaking the truth [as we currently apprehend it] in *agape*-love" (Eph 4:15) is the norm—these are the lights by which our collective path to a better understanding of justification must be lit. It is toward this end that we, as editors of this volume together with Dan Reid and Andy Le Peau of InterVarsity Press, originally conceived of this project. And it is due to the fact that our amazing team of contributors exemplifies just such a truth-seeking and grace-filled dialogue that we now turn the conversation over to them with appreciation and confidence.

---

[127]E.g., the Piper-Wright debate on justification. For an interesting exchange that reveals how hermeneutical traditions and assumptions can shape the move from Scripture to dogma in regard to justification, see Leithart, "Justification as Verdict"; and R. Michael Allen and Daniel J. Treier, "Dogmatic Theology and Biblical Perspectives on Justification: A Reply to Leithart," *WTJ* 70 (2008): 105-10. On the role of theological presuppositions in the new perspective debate, see Kent Yinger, "Reformation *Redivivus:* Synergism and the New Perspective," *Journal of Theological Interpretation* 3 (2009): 89-106.

3

Traditional Reformed View

Michael Horton

It may not be an overstatement to suggest that the doctrine of justification is as widely discussed and challenged today as it was in the sixteenth century, within Protestantism as well as outside of it. Particularly in view of the diverse criticism of this view from various quarters, I am cautious about the framing of this chapter in terms of "traditional Reformed" versus "progressive Reformed" positions. Since Reformed views are defined by our confessions, especially on such a crucial doctrine, positioning departures as progress might convey the impression that defenders of the confessional view are merely repristinating a tradition rather than confessing a faith that is as exegetically defensible today as it was in the sixteenth century. My goal in this essay is not simply to repeat the relevant paragraphs in our confessions and catechisms, but to argue that their view of justification is even more firmly established by recent investigations.

I begin by offering a simple summary of the view that I will be defending. In fulfillment of his promise to Abraham, Yahweh has acted in and through his people, Israel, to redeem a worldwide family of sinners. Like Adam, Israel was God's servant, entrusted with the commission to cleanse God's garden of sin and to expand his righteous reign to the ends of the earth. However, "Like Adam, Israel sinned and broke my covenant" (Hos 6:7).[1] Yet God promised through the prophets that on the basis of another covenant (in continuity with the promise made to Abraham), God himself

---

[1] Biblical quotations in this essay are taken from the NRSV.

would transfer the guilt of his people to the Suffering Servant and transfer to them this obedient son's righteousness (Is 53). In his own commissioning vision, Isaiah, beholding God's holiness, realized that even he was condemned, yet the prophet is forgiven (Is 6). Zechariah 3 records the prophecy of Joshua the high priest in the heavenly courtroom, with Satan as the prosecuting attorney and the Angel of the LORD as Joshua's defender. Although condemned in himself, Joshua has his filthy clothes removed by the Angel of the LORD and is arrayed in a spotless robe. All of these passages flood the imagination of the apostles as they testify to Jesus Christ as "the LORD Our Righteousness" (Jer 23:5-6; 33:16, with 1 Cor 1:30-31; 2 Cor 5:21).

God justifies the wicked (Rom 4:5). As counterintuitive as it is simple, that claim lies at the heart of the good news. Not only the nations, but Israel too is swept into the category of "the ungodly," under the condemnation of the law. And now, together with a remnant from the nations, Israel has seen the salvation of its Covenant Lord. It was this simple claim that caused the apostle Paul to look back on all of his zealous obedience as "a Pharisee of Pharisees" and call it "dung," "in order that I may gain Christ and be found in him, not having a righteousness that is of my own that comes from the law, but one that comes through faith in Christ, the righteousness from God that depends on faith" (Phil 3:8-9).

As the revelation of the righteousness *of* God, the law condemns and leaves no one standing. Yet the gospel is the revelation of the righteousness *from* God, the good news that sinners "are justified by his grace as a gift, through the redemption that is in Christ Jesus, whom God put forward as a propitiation by his blood, to be received by faith" (Rom 3:24-25). "And to the one who does not work but trusts him who justifies the ungodly, his faith is counted as righteousness, just as David also speaks of the blessing of the one to whom God counts righteousness apart from works" (Rom 4:5-6). "Therefore, since we have been justified by faith, we have peace with God through our Lord Jesus Christ" (Rom 5:1). Paul considered this doctrine to be so central that he regarded its explicit denial as "anathema"—that is, an act of heresy that the Galatian church was on the verge of committing (Gal 1:8-9). For Paul, a denial of justification was tantamount to a denial of grace and even to a denial of Christ, "for if justification were through the law, then Christ died for no purpose" (Gal 2:21).

THE STATE OF THE CONTROVERSY

This claim that God justifies the wicked brought enormous controversy to the apostolic church as it has to this day.[2] And in spite of the heroic efforts of representatives on both sides during the sixteenth century, the Council of Trent (1545-1563) in no uncertain terms condemned the Reformation's understanding of justification.

The Reformation Debate

It remains the official Roman Catholic position that "justification is not only the remission of sins, but also the sanctification and renewal of the interior man."[3] Justification is therefore regarded as a process of becoming actually and intrinsically righteous. The first justification occurs at baptism, which eradicates both the guilt and corruption of original sin.[4] Due entirely to God's grace, this initial justification infuses the habit (or principle) of grace into the recipient. By cooperating with this inherent grace, one merits an increase of grace and, one hopes, final justification.[5] So while initial justification is by grace alone, final justification depends also on the works of the believer, which God graciously accepts as meritorious.[6] Since the believer's progress in holiness is never adequate to cancel the guilt of actual sins, he or she must be refined in purgatory before being welcomed into heaven.

By contrast, the Reformers taught and evangelicals teach that justification is distinct from sanctification. Although both are inseparable gifts of union with Christ through faith, justification is a verdict that declares sinners to be righteous even while they are inherently unrighteous, simply on the basis of Christ's righteousness imputed to them. Where Rome teaches that one is finally justified by being sanctified, the Reformed conviction is that one is being sanctified because one has already been justified. Rather than working toward the verdict of divine vindication,

---

[2]The teaching of the ancient church is ambiguous with respect to justification. On one hand, there are marvelous testimonies to God's justification of sinners, as Thomas Oden observes in *The Justification Reader* (Grand Rapids: Eerdmans, 2002). On the other hand, there are many threads of synergism that later Eastern Orthodoxy developed in Byzantine theology in a manner that parallels Western (medieval) developments.

[3]*The Catechism of the Catholic Church* (New York: USCCB, 1995), p. 492, quoting the Council of Trent (1574): DS 1528.

[4]Ibid., p. 482.

[5]Ibid., p. 483.

[6]Ibid., pp. 486-87.

the believer leaves the court justified in the joy that bears the fruit of faith: namely, good works.

In Scripture, especially in Paul, Luther discovered that the righteousness that God is, which condemns us, is the same righteousness that God gives, freely, as a gift, through faith in Jesus Christ (Rom 3:19-31). This "marvelous exchange" of Christ's righteousness for the sinner's guilt was beautifully articulated by some medieval theologians, such as Bernard of Clairvaux (1090-1153). However, it was in the Reformation that the understanding of justification as an exclusively forensic (legal) declaration, based on the imputation of Christ's righteousness through faith alone, was most fully articulated.

Although Luther felt the inextricable connection between doctrine and experience, he did not arrive at his conclusions simply out of his own "tortured subjectivity," as some modern interpreters suggest.[7] Jacques Lefèvre d'Étaples (1455-1536), an eminent French humanist and biblical scholar (who made the first French translation of the Bible from the Latin Vulgate) arrived at some of Luther's principal insights a decade earlier. Erasmus also had made important textual contributions that paved the way for the Reformers. Luther's own mentor and head of Germany's Augustinian Order, Johann von Staupitz, also played a crucial role in the reformer's developing insights, and he recommended Luther as a professor of Bible in the university. Like Luther, Calvin and the other magisterial Reformers were humanists, steeped in the original languages and guided by the Renaissance cry, *Ad fontes*, "Back to the sources!" Regardless of one's verdict concerning their conclusions, the Reformers were biblical exegetes of the first rank.

All of the magisterial Reformers were at one in concluding that justification is a judicial verdict consisting in the gift of an "alien righteousness" through faith alone because of Christ alone. Calvin regarded justification as "the primary article of the Christian religion," "the main hinge on which religion turns," "the principal article of the whole doctrine of salvation and

---

[7]Attempts to psychoanalyze Luther to explain his "evangelical breakthrough" reached its hagiographical limits in Erik H. Erikson's, *Young Man Luther: A Study in Psychoanalysis and History* (New York: W. W. Norton, 1962). Krister Stendahl's *Paul Among Jews and Gentiles* (Minneapolis: Fortress, 1976) followed this thesis, which has become a largely unexamined assumption among advocates of the new perspective(s) on Paul (especially James D. G. Dunn and N. T. Wright).

the foundation of all religion."[8] In fact, Melanchthon and Calvin influenced each other in working out the refinements of this common evangelical position.[9] This righteousness "consists in the remission of sins, and in this: that the righteousness of Jesus Christ is imputed to us."[10] According to this evangelical interpretation, justification is not a process of transformation from a condition of sinfulness to a state of justice. Believers are *simultaneously* justified and sinful.[11] Sin's dominion has been toppled, but sin still indwells believers.[12] Consequently, whatever works believers perform will always fall short of that righteousness that God's law requires; nevertheless, they are accepted as fully righteous already through faith in Christ.

This orientation stood in sharp contrast not only with Rome, but with the radical Protestants.[13] Though more radical in other ways, Anabaptist views on justification were similar to Rome's.[14] In either case, justification was understood as a process of inner transformation, rather than as God's free acquittal of sinners for the sake of Christ and his imputation of Christ's righteousness to their account.

Of course, we recognize a wide diversity of moral character, ranging from reprehensible to praiseworthy, but Calvin reminds us (repeating Luther's contrast), that righteousness before humanity *(coram hominibus)* is

---

[8]*Institutes* 3.2.1, 3.11.1, and Sermon on Luke 1:5-10 in CR 46:23.

[9]See, for example, Richard Muller, *The Unaccommodated Calvin: Studies in the Foundations of a Theological Tradition* (New York: Oxford University Press, 2001), pp. 126-27. Calvin, however, sharply criticized Melanchthon's later synergistic turn, which the orthodox (Gnesio) Lutherans also rejected.

[10]Calvin, *Institutes* 3.11.2.

[11]Ibid., 3.3.10.

[12]Ibid., 3.3.11.

[13]Ibid., 3.3.14: "Certain Anabaptists of our day conjure some sort of frenzied excess instead of spiritual regeneration," Calvin relates, thinking that they can attain perfection in this life.

[14]Thomas A. Finger, *A Contemporary Anabaptist Theology: Biblical, Historical, Constructive* (Downers Grove, Ill.: InterVarsity Press, 2004), p. 109. Contemporary Anabaptist theologian Thomas Finger observes, "Robert Friedmann found 'A forensic view of grace, in which the sinner is . . . undeservedly justified . . . simply unacceptable' to Anabaptists. A more nuanced scholar like Arnold Snyder can assert that historic Anabaptists 'never talked about being "justified by faith."'" Finger believes that Anabaptist soteriological emphases (especially on divinization) can bring greater unity especially between marginalized Protestant groups (Pentecostals and Quakers) and Orthodox and Roman Catholic theologies of salvation (p. 110). Finger observes that recent Anabaptist reflection is no more marked in its interest in this topic than its antecedents, with discipleship ("following Jesus") and the inner transformation of the believer as central (pp. 132-33).

not the same as righteousness before God *(coram deo)*.[15] Calvin rejects the view that Christ's sacrifice remits the guilt but not the punishment of sins.[16] "Therefore," he states, "we explain justification simply as the acceptance with which God receives us into his favor as righteous. And we say that it consists in the remission of sins and the imputation of Christ's righteousness."[17] In book 3 of the *Institutes*, Calvin argues that this righteousness is alien to us, merited by the life, death and resurrection of the incarnate Son.[18] Yet Christ is not only given *for* us, but *to* us.[19] Through faith we receive not only Christ's gifts but Christ himself.[20] Yet faith is merely the instrument, not the ground, of our justification.[21]

After all, "if faith in itself justified one by its own virtue, then, seeing that it is always weak and imperfect, it would be only partly effectual and give us only a part of salvation."[22]

One of the clearest summaries of the evangelical doctrine of justification is found in chapter 13 of the Westminster Confession:

> Those whom God effectually calls, he also freely justifies: not by infusing righteousness into them, but by pardoning their sins and by accounting and accepting their persons as righteous; not for anything wrought in them or done by them, but for Christ's sake alone; not by imputing faith itself, the act of believing, or any other evangelical obedience to them as their righteousness; but by imputing the obedience and satisfaction of Christ unto them, they receiving and resting on him and his righteousness by faith; which faith they have not of themselves, it is the gift of God. Faith, thus receiving and resting on Christ and his righteousness, is the sole instrument of justification; yet it is not alone in the person justified, but is ever accompanied with all other saving graces, and is no dead faith, but works by love.

The justified may fall into grave sin and "fall under God's Fatherly displeasure," but they "can never fall from the state of justification."[23]

---

[15]Ibid., 3.12.2.
[16]Ibid., 3.4.30.
[17]Ibid., 3.11.2.
[18]Ibid., 3.2.15-17; 3.11.2.
[19]Ibid., 3.1.1.
[20]Ibid., 3.1.1; 3.1.4; 3.2.24; 4:17.11.
[21]Ibid., 3.11.7; 3.18.8.
[22]Ibid., 3.11.7.
[23]The Westminster Confession of Faith, chap. 13, in *The Book of Confessions* (Louisville, Ky.: PCUSA, 1991).

The Heidelberg Catechism also emphasizes that this divine verdict has Christ's righteousness, not ours, as its basis, so that through faith alone we who "have grievously sinned against all the commandments of God and have not kept any one of them" are nevertheless regarded as though we had never sinned and had perfectly kept the commands. Not even the gift of faith itself can be considered the ground of justification, but simply the empty hand that receives it. This teaching cannot be used to justify moral carelessness, however, "for it is impossible for those who are engrafted into Christ by true faith not to bring forth the fruit of gratitude."[24] Similar summaries can be found, of course, in the Lutheran Book of Concord, the Anglican Thirty-Nine Articles, and the London/Philadelphia (Baptist) Confession.

It was this understanding that Rome officially anathematized at the Council of Trent in its longest decree, which included the following:

Canon 9. If anyone says that the sinner is justified by faith alone, . . . let him be anathema.

Canon 11. If anyone says that men are justified either by the sole imputation of the righteousness of Christ or by the sole remission of sins, . . . let him be anathema.

Canon 12. If anyone says that justifying faith is nothing else than confidence in divine mercy, which remits sins for Christ's sake, or that it is this confidence alone that justifies us, let him be anathema.

Canon 24. If anyone says that the justice [righteousness] received is not preserved and also not increased before God through good works, but that those works are merely the fruits and signs of justification obtained, but not the cause of the increase, let him be anathema.

Canon 30. If anyone says that after the reception of the grace of justification the guilt is so remitted and the debt of eternal punishment so blotted out to every repentant sinner that no debt of temporal punishment remains to be discharged either in this world or in purgatory before the gates of heaven can be opened, let him be anathema.

Canon 32. If anyone says that the good works of the one justified are in such manner the gifts of God that they are not also the good merits of him

---

[24]The Heidelberg Catechism, Q. 60-64 in *The Book of Confessions* (Louisville, Ky.: PCUSA, 1991).

justified; or that the one justified by the good works that he performs by the grace of God and the merit of Jesus Christ, whose living member he is, does not truly merit an increase of grace, eternal life, and in case he dies in grace the attainment of eternal life itself and also an increase of glory, let him be anathema.[25]

Although there have been fruitful conversations since the Second Vatican Council, Trent remains binding dogma and any significant convergence between Protestants and Roman Catholics on justification has come at the expense of the former's testimony to the Reformation's consensus. Not even in the "Joint Declaration on Justification" between the Lutheran World Federation and the Vatican (whose status is not confirmed, much less binding, on the Roman Catholic side) is the Reformation's formulation of justification affirmed.[26] Furthermore, the Vatican's Pontifical Council for the Promotion of Christian Unity issued a caution when the "Joint Declaration" was released. While applauding the consensus reached by both sides, the statement added, "The Catholic Church is, however, of the opinion that we cannot yet speak of a consensus such as would eliminate every difference between Catholics and Lutherans in the understanding of justification."[27] Citing the Council of Trent, the official statement reminded Roman Catholics that they must hold as dogma that "eternal life is, at one and the same time, grace and the reward given by God for good works and merits."[28]

The Roman Catholic Church has never denied the necessity of grace—indeed, even its priority. In fact, the Council of Trent expressly repeated

---

[25] *Canons and Decrees of the Council of Trent: Original Text with English Translation,* trans. H. J. Schroeder, O.P. (St. Louis: B. Herder, 1960), pp. 43, 45-46.

[26] *Joint Declaration on the Doctrine of Justification: The Lutheran World Federation and the Roman Catholic Church* (Grand Rapids: Eerdmans, 2000). Among other problems, the Declaration teaches, "The justification of sinners is forgiveness *and being made righteous*" (4.3.27, emphasis added); particular acts of sin require the sacrament of penance (4.3.30). Thus, the Roman Catholic position is not altered on this fundamental point; it is the evangelical view that is surrendered. Only in this way can the agreement conclude that the condemnations of the sixteenth century no longer apply to the respective partner. It should be noted that the Lutheran World Federation, like the World Alliance of Reformed Churches, represents the more liberal wing of Lutheranism. Their confessional rivals (including the Lutheran Church Missouri Synod) rejected the "Joint Declaration," because they still hold the views condemned by the Council of Trent and all subsequent reaffirmations by the magisterium.

[27] Reported in the official Vatican newspaper, *L'Osservatore Romano,* weekly edition in English, July 8, 1998, p. 2.

[28] Ibid.

the condemnations of Pelagianism. However, the addition of works to faith as the instrument of justification is as strongly affirmed today as it was in the sixteenth century. From the evangelical perspective, the strongest affirmation of the importance of God's grace does not mitigate the corruption of the gospel by including our own merits. For evangelicals (in the original sense of that term), the apostolic gospel is not upheld simply by praising grace above and before all of our merits, but by insisting upon Christ's merits alone as the basis, grace alone as the source and faith alone as the divinely given means of justification before God: "But if it is by grace, it is no longer on the basis of works, otherwise grace would no longer be grace" (Rom 11:6).

Defining Justification Exegetically

"And those whom he called he also justified" (Rom 8:30). Understanding what Paul meant by justification depends on whether we can come to terms with his anthropology (universal human depravity)[29] and therefore his compelling interest in, as Peter Stuhlmacher puts it, "whether Jews and Gentiles will or will not survive before God's throne of judgment."[30] The gospel is not simply that Jesus was crucified and raised, or that these events demonstrate his lordship, but that he "was crucified *for our sins* and was raised *for our justification*" (Rom 4:25, emphasis added).

1. Declarative (judicial) meaning. Even advocates of the new perspective on Paul recognize that the verb "to justify" (in Hebrew as well as Greek) is a forensic, courtroom term. "In the *qal*," notes E. P. Sanders, "the verb [*tsadaq*] usually means 'to be cleared in court' and is not really distinguishable from the use of the *zakah* root to mean 'innocent.'"[31] "It may also mean to make something correct, as in the phrase 'make the scales just.' The hif'il, 'to justify,' also has a forensic connotation. When the passage in Ex. 23.7 says 'I will not justify the wicked,' it is clearly understood to mean 'hold innocent.'"[32] In the Hebrew Scriptures the verb *hitsdik* (along with the piel form *tsiddek*) is generally used for a judicial declaration that one is in the right according to the law (Ex 23:7; Deut 25:1; Prov 17:15; Is 5:23;

---

[29]See Timo Laato, *Paul and Judaism: An Anthropological Approach* (Atlanta: Scholars Press, 1995).
[30]Peter Stuhlmacher, *Revisiting Paul's Doctrine of Justification: A Challenge to the New Perspective* (Downers Grove, Ill.: InterVarsity Press, 2001), p. 43.
[31]E. P. Sanders, *Paul and Palestinian Judaism* (Minneapolis: Fortress, 1977), p. 198.
[32]Ibid., p. 199.

Jer 3:11). Similarly, the Greek verb *dikaioō*, "to declare just," is unmistakably judicial in character.

However, this meaning of the original text was lost through the faulty Latin Vulgate translation. Just as the medieval system of penance was founded exegetically on the Vulgate's mistranslation of *metanoeō* (to change one's mind) as *poenitentium agite* (do penance), *dikaioō* (to declare just) was erroneously rendered *iustificare* (to make righteous).[33] Though hardly motivated by doctrinal concerns, Erasmus had pointed out these lexical inconsistencies even before Luther. Obviously, it is quite a different thing to be *made* righteous than to be *declared* righteous. By itself, the latter term itself does not require the evangelical doctrine of justification, but it does render erroneous the Vulgate's translation and therefore the interpretation of justification as moral transformation.

A number of Roman Catholic New Testament scholars have pointed out in recent years that *dikaioō* has to do with a legal vindication and not with an infused habit or inner transformation.[34] The lexical definition of justification is "to be cleared in court."[35] As noted above, even Sanders affirms that this is the same meaning as in the Old Testament (*ṣdq* and cognates), and N. T. Wright is of the same mind, insisting repeatedly that justification is a legal, courtroom verdict. That significant consensus can be reached on this point even among those who stand in some critical relation to the Reformation interpretation demonstrates that we are quite far from witnessing the destruction of a forensic definition of justification. If Roman Catholic and Protestant exegetes can agree on this lexical meaning of the term—the very heart of the Reformation debate—then it would seem that any remaining controversy at least on this point concerns the authority of the canon vis-à-vis ecclesiastical dogmas.

The opposite of justification is condemnation *(katakrima)*, which is quite evidently a judicial concept as well (Jn 3:17-18; Rom 5:16-17; 8:1, 33-34). Justification cannot therefore mean gradual transformation, recogni-

---

[33]Alister E. McGrath, *Iustitia Dei: A History of the Christian Doctrine of Justification* (Cambridge: Cambridge University Press, 1986), pp. 11-14.

[34]See, for instance, Joseph Fitzmyer, "The Letter to the Romans," and "The Letter to the Galatians," in *The Jerome Biblical Commentary*, ed. Raymond S. Brown, Joseph A. Fitzmyer and Roland E. Murphy (Englewood Cliffs, N.J.: Prentice-Hall, 1968), esp. pp. 241-44 and 303-15, respectively.

[35]See BDAG, pp. 246-50.

tion of membership in the people of God, or anything else other than the courtroom declaration that someone is righteous before God. This fact by itself does not indicate the basis on which or the means by which one is justified before God. It simply stipulates that *the demands of the law have been fully met* (Acts 13:39; Rom 5:1, 9; 8:30-33; 1 Cor 6:11; Gal 2:16; 3:11).

2. The righteousness of God. Justification is a declarative, judicial verdict, not a process: this scholarly consensus is considerable. Nevertheless, the further question concerns the nature of the phrase "the righteousness of God" and whether it can be credited or imputed to believers. According to Wright, God's righteousness can only refer to his own faithfulness to the covenant.[36] Though certainly "a forensic term, that is, taken from the law court," righteousness is not something that can be transferred from God to us. Nor can it mean that the defendant is inherently righteous and therefore deserving of acquittal. Rather, "for the plaintiff or defendant to be 'righteous' in the biblical sense *within the law-court setting* is for them to have that status *as a result of the decision of the court*."[37] However, this courtroom verdict cannot involve an imputation of righteousness. It makes no sense to say that the judge somehow gives his own righteousness to the defendant.[38] God's people will be "justified." "*But the righteousness they have will not be God's own righteousness.* That makes no sense at all. God's own righteousness is his covenant faithfulness" (emphasis original).[39]

By way of response, it is crucial to point out that the Reformation position has never been that *God's righteousness* is imputed. First, this assumes that righteousness is a substance or a commodity that is transferred from one person to another, rather than a legal status. Although Rome holds that justifying grace is a spiritual substance infused into the soul from God, it was precisely this view that the Reformers rejected, which makes it all the more remarkable that Wright would characterize this as their position.[40]

---

[36]N. T. Wright, *What Saint Paul Really Said: Was Paul of Tarsus the Real Founder of Christianity?* (Grand Rapids: Eerdmans, 1997), p. 96.

[37]Ibid., pp. 97-98.

[38]Ibid., p. 98.

[39]Ibid., p. 99.

[40]Ibid., p. 98: "If we use the language of the law court, it makes no sense whatever to say that the judge imputes, imparts, bequeaths, conveys or otherwise transfers his righteousness to either the plaintiff or the defendant. Righteousness is not an object, a substance or a gas which can be

Second, missing from Wright's courtroom setting is the third party: the mediator who, as representative head, fulfills the law and merits for himself and his covenant heirs the verdict of "righteous" or "just" before God. Although the one who fulfilled the terms of the law-covenant as the human servant is also the divine Lord, it is his active and passive obedience rather than the essential divine attribute of righteousness that is credited to believers. (In fact, Calvin offered a lengthy rebuttal of Andreas Osiander's view that justification consists in a supposed impartation of Christ's essential righteousness as divine.) In this covenantal interpretation, Christ becomes the believer's righteousness both in justification (by imputation) and in sanctification (by impartation), just as Adam's federal headship yielded both condemnation and corruption.

Third, Wright's view of justification amounts (ironically) to a legal fiction when he rejects the imputation of Christ's obedience. One of many examples of false antitheses, Wright claims, "It is not the 'righteousness' of Jesus Christ which is 'reckoned' to the believer. It is his death and resurrection."[41] If "the righteousness of God" refers to God's courtroom verdict concerning his covenant partners, they must have the moral status that allows God justly to accept them. It is not an infused quality or substance that is transferred, but the record of having fulfilled the law. Wright discounts the idea of justification involving moral achievement, yet this is precisely how God justifies and condemns. The Reformers and their heirs labored the point that it is Christ's successful fulfillment of the trial of the covenantal representative that is imputed or credited to all who believe. This is what keeps justification from being abstract or a legal fiction, since the justified do in fact possess "in Christ" the status of those who have perfectly fulfilled all righteousness. In addition, "in Christ" their transgressions of the covenant have been borne away at the cross, and their public vindication has been realized in his resurrection. Thus, Christ's

---

passed across the courtroom." Wright seems unaware of the Reformers' view that Christ himself—his person as well as his work—is the gift of righteousness. Calvin explicitly criticized the medieval view for teaching that grace is something (i.e., a substance) rather than Christ's act of clothing his people with himself (see, for example, *Institutes* 3.1.1; 3.1.4; 3.2.24; 4.17.11). In fact, the mature Reformation doctrine of justification was articulated against both Rome's understanding of justification as an infused quality of righteousness and Andreas Osiander's notion of the believer's participation in the essential righteousness of Christ's deity.

[41]N. T. Wright, *Justification: God's Plan and Paul's Vision* (Downers Grove, Ill.: IVP Academic, 2009), p. 232.

whole life shares in winning our redemption, culminating in his death and resurrection. There is no reason to cut the former off from the latter, as Wright's false antithesis suggests.

The Adam-Christ and Israel-Christ typology evident in the Gospels (particularly, Jesus' recapitulation of Israel's trial, "fulfilling all righteousness") and the Epistles (especially in Romans 5) suggests that Christ's obedient life is the basis of justification, along with his death and resurrection. To build on Paul's banking analogy, for one to have not only one's debts cancelled but a full account by a transfer of funds from someone else renders that wealth no more a fiction than if it were the fruit of one's own labors. As Paul looks over his ledger in Philippians 3, he places all of his own righteousness in the liabilities column and all of Christ's righteousness in his assets column. Wright's account so far does not seem to allow for an inheritance to actually be given to anyone in particular. Justification may be forensic (that is, judicial), but there can be no transfer of assets, if you will, from a faithful representative to the ungodly.

Therefore, imputation—at least the imputation of guilt to Christ—is involved in the sacrificial-substitutionary nature of Christ's work on the cross. It would seem that Wright is willing to affirm this point.[42] If *guilt* can be imputed from one person to another, then why not *righteousness*? The sin of Adam was imputed to the human race as a covenantal entity in solidarity because it was imputed to each member (Rom 5:12). This notion of imputing the sin of one person to each Israelite—and thus to the nation generally—is found elsewhere, as in Achan's theft (Josh 7:10-26), not to mention in Isaiah 53.

Interpreting "the righteousness of/from God" *(dikaiosynē tou theou)* as a subjective genitive, Wright paraphrases Romans 1:17: "The gospel, he says, reveals or unveils God's own righteousness, his covenant faithfulness, which operates through the faithfulness of Jesus Christ for the benefit of all those who in turn are faithful ('from faith to faith')."[43] However, does

---

[42]N. T. Wright, *Jesus and the Victory of God* (Minneapolis: Fortress, 1998), pp. 604-10.

[43]Wright, *What Saint Paul Really Said*, p. 109. Related to this debate over the righteousness of God is the question as to whether "faith in Christ" should also be given the subjective genitive construction (as "the faith of Christ"). This does not seem to make sense of the ordinary way Paul describes the relation of faith and justification, however. For example, Paul speaks of "the righteousness of God through faith in Jesus Christ for all who believe" (Rom 3:22), the last clause repeating the same idea as the middle *(dia pisteōs Iesou Christou)* and in verse 25 adds that his propitiatory death is "to be received by faith." This debate is beyond our scope here,

this make adequate sense of the rest of the verse: "as it is written, 'The one who is righteous will live by faith'"? Paul's citation of Habakkuk 2:4 refers to the human partner in the covenant rather than to God. It seems more consistent with Paul's wider argument in Romans 1–3 to say, in agreement with Luther, that the law reveals God's essential righteousness (his justice that condemns us), while the gospel reveals God's gift of righteousness that saves us. After establishing the point that everyone, Jew and Gentile, is condemned by the law and will never be justified by it because of their sin, Paul adds, "But now, apart from law, the righteousness of God has been disclosed, and is attested by the law and the prophets, the righteousness of God through faith in Jesus Christ for all who believe" (Rom 3:21-22). They are "now justified by his grace as a gift, through the redemption that is in Christ Jesus, whom God put forward as a propitiation by his blood, effective through faith" (Rom 3:24-25). According to this view, God indeed reveals his covenant faithfulness, but by itself this is not good news—unless God reveals that the righteousness that he is and that his law requires has been given to us as a gift in Jesus Christ.

The Reformation distinguished the essential righteousness of God (which condemns all) from the gift of righteousness from God (which justifies everyone who believes). In fact, Luther's "breakthrough" occurred when he recognized this distinction in Romans 1–3. So Wright's repeated assertion that in the Reformation view God's essential righteousness is transferred to the believer forms a significant misunderstanding in his polemic. Where the Reformation interpretation recognizes that Paul speaks of the righteousness of God as his essential justice and faithfulness to the covenant *and* as the gift of righteousness (i.e., God as "just and the justifier of those who have faith in Christ Jesus" [Rom 3:26]), Wright reduces all references to the former. Yet the dialectical play between these two seems to lie at the heart of Paul's argument, especially in Romans 1–3: the righteousness that God *is* (as revealed in the law) condemns everyone, Jew and Gentile alike. "But now, apart from law, the

---

but for a defense of the subjective genitive construction, see Bruce W. Longenecker, "Contours of Covenant Theology in the Post-Conversion Paul," in *The Road from Damascus: The Impact of Paul's Conversion on His Life, Thought, and Ministry,* ed. Richard N. Longenecker (Grand Rapids: Eerdmans, 1997), p. 133; cf. Richard Hays, *The Faith of Jesus Christ: An Investigation of the Narrative Substructure of Galatians 3:1–4:11* (Chico, Calif.: Scholars Press, 1983); Richard Hays, "Justification," in *ABD,* 3:1129-33.

righteousness of/from God has been disclosed, and is attested by the law and the prophets, the righteousness of God through faith in Jesus Christ for all who believe" (Rom 3:21).

It makes little sense, especially in the sweep of Paul's argument, to say that *God's* covenant faithfulness is disclosed through *our faith* in Christ. Rather, Paul argues that the righteousness that God is (i.e., his essential righteousness) actually *condemns* everyone—Jew and Gentile alike, because no one has fulfilled it; the gospel, however, discloses the gift of righteousness that is received through faith. The revelation of God's righteousness that is revealed by the law, "so that every mouth may be silenced, and the whole world may be held accountable to God" (Rom 3:19), is different from the revelation of God's righteousness that is revealed in the gospel "apart from law," through faith in Christ (Rom 3:21). The law reveals that God is just (and therefore must condemn all transgressors), but the gospel reveals that God is just and justifier (Rom 3:26).

There is no place for a transfer of Christ's covenantal obedience to the believer in Wright's interpretation, but for Paul, in this passage, "the righteousness of God through faith in Jesus Christ" is a "justification" that is "a gift" given to "all who believe." The closest that Wright comes to allowing for justification as a gift of right-standing given to individuals is in the statement that believers "are declared, in the present, to be what they will be seen to be in the future, namely the true people of God. Present justification declares, on the basis of faith, what future justification will affirm publicly (according to 2:14-16 and 8:9-11) *on the basis of the entire life.*"[44] Not only do we meet the distinction in Roman Catholic theology between present and future justification; the basis of the latter is one's own covenant faithfulness. Where for Paul the verdict of the last day has already been rendered in favor of those who have faith in Christ—through faith alone—according to Wright this future verdict is merely anticipated in faith but on the basis of the believer's faithfulness.

According to Wright, faith is not how one is "saved," but "is the badge of the sin-forgiven family."[45] "The emphasis of the chapter [Rom 4] is

---

[44]Wright, *What Saint Paul Really Said*, p. 129, emphasis added.
[45]Ibid. For a good critique of Wright's argument on this point see Mark A. Seifrid, *Christ, Our Righteousness: Paul's Theology of Justification* (Downers Grove, Ill.: IVP Academic, 2001), p. 176 n. 13.

therefore that covenant membership is defined, not by circumcision (4:9-
12), nor by race, but by faith."[46] However, this faith is now also redefined
as faithfulness—our own covenantal obedience, which is the basis for
the final justification.[47] Crucially absent from his list is Paul's clause,
"nor by works," or the apostle's statement that this justification comes to
the one (notice the individual-personal reference) "who does not work
but trusts in the one who justifies the ungodly" (Rom 4:5). Paul's contrast is between working and trusting, not between circumcision and our
Spirit-led obedience. Basically, Wright's claim is tantamount to saying
that we are justified by some works (our covenant faithfulness), but not
by others (ethnic purity).

Eastern Orthodox theologians remind us of the importance of Christ's
victory over the powers of death and hell. His work is not only penal.
However, this legal aspect is so central that without it the other facets,
such as cosmic conquest, are left hanging in midair. Christ's fulfillment of
the law's demands and his bearing of its sanctions against us provides the
basis for a cosmic and eschatological victory of Yahweh over the powers
that hold us in bondage. Similarly, far from excluding personal and cosmic
renewal, the justification of the ungodly is the source of the abundant and
varied fruit of Christ's conquest. In Colossians 2:13-15, Christ's conquest
of the powers is based on his having borne our debt for violation of the law,
just as in 1 Corinthians 15:53-56 the gift of immortality is attributed to
Christ's having taken away the legal basis for death's dominion: "The sting
of death is sin, and the power of sin is the law. But thanks be to God who
gives us the victory through our Lord Jesus Christ" (1 Cor 15:56-57).[48]

3. Imputed righteousness? The Reformation view of justification rests on
the declarative character of the verb and the twofold meaning of the righteousness of God as that justice that God is, which condemns us, and the
justice that God gives, which saves us. Yet it requires a further point:
namely, *imputation* as the way in which God gives this righteousness or
justice to the ungodly through faith.

Only a crude biblicism would make the doctrine of imputation to de-

---

[46]Wright, *What Saint Paul Really Said,* p. 129.
[47]Ibid., p. 160.
[48]I explore this cosmic-eschatological aspect in *Covenant and Salvation: Union with Christ*
  (Louisville: Westminster John Knox, 2007), pp. 289-302.

pend on the prominence of the term itself. The New Testament offers a broad range of images, such as clothing, transferring debts and assets, a last will and testament, a gift of righteousness, and other metaphors for imputation. The verb "to impute" *(logizomai)* is used explicitly in Romans, especially in chapter 4, where Paul refers to Abraham, quoting Genesis 15:6: "Abraham believed God, and it was counted to him as righteousness" (Rom 4:3). Notice how imputation fits in Paul's argument: "Now to the one who works, his wages are not counted [imputed] as a gift but as his due. And to the one who does not work but trusts him who justifies the ungodly, his faith is counted as righteousness" (Rom 4:4-5). Clearly something is being transferred or given from one person (employer) to another (employee): namely, wages. But in this case it is different: God does not justify those who work for it but only imputes righteousness to those who trust in the justifier of the ungodly. David is another example of one "against whom the Lord will not count his sin" (Rom 4:8). Abraham could not even count his circumcision as the instrument of his justification before God (Rom 4:9-12). "But the words, 'it was counted to him' were not written for his sake alone, but for ours also. It will be counted to us who believe in him who raised from the dead Jesus our Lord, who was delivered up for our trespasses and raised for our justification" (Rom 4:23-25).

In Galatians 3, with the contrast between "the works of the law" and "hearing with faith," Paul repeats the quotation from Genesis 15:6. "Counting as" or "being counted as," *logizomai eis,* is also found in Romans 2:26; 9:8; and 2 Corinthians 12:6, as well as Acts 19:27 and James 2:23. Although the term does not appear in Romans 5, the idea is evident throughout Paul's comparison and contrast between Adam and Christ. Under Adam's headship, the whole race is guilty and corrupt; under Christ's headship, many are justified and made alive. These passages unmistakably teach that the righteousness by which the believer stands worthy before God's judgment is *alien:* that is, belonging properly to someone else. It is Christ's righteousness imputed, not the believer's inherent righteousness—even if produced by the gracious work of the Spirit.

As we have seen, N. T. Wright holds that God's final justification is a declaration that believers are righteous based on their whole life lived. While generally eschewing talk of the *ordo salutis* ("how individuals 'get saved'"), he does make regeneration the basis for the verdict that one is at present a member of this community that will be justified on the last day. Therefore, whatever other differences there might be on other points, he shares Rome's view of justification as an analytic verdict. They are "in the right" before God because they belong to the people of God and therefore have good reason to believe that they will be justified finally by their faithful lives. It is precisely this sort of position that the quotation above from the Westminster Confession has in view when it says that it is not only works "done by us" but even works "wrought in us"—by the Holy Spirit— that are excluded from justification. Far from denying the Spirit's work within us, the Confession is simply saying that this is not justification.

The notion of one person's righteousness being imputed to another is already present in Second Temple Judaism (the "merit of the fathers").[49] Furthermore, we have already seen that Wright strongly affirms that our sins were transferred or credited to Christ, so his rejection of an imputation of righteousness from Christ to the believer seems arbitrary.

Criticisms of imputation are not restricted to new perspective advocates. For example, Mark Seifrid remains unconvinced that the language of "imputation" is necessary. Justification grants forgiveness of sins; what need is there for an imputation of righteousness on the basis of Christ's active obedience, which Seifrid considers "unnecessary and misleading"?[50] "In reducing 'justification' to a present possession of 'Christ's imputed righteousness,' Protestant divines inadvertently bruised the nerve which runs between justification and obedience. It is not so much *wrong* to use the expression 'the imputed righteousness of Christ' as it is *deficient*."[51]

However, this is a theological rather than exegetical point. The first

---

[49]Hermann Lichtenberger, "The Understanding of the Torah in the Judaism of Paul's Day," in *Paul and the Mosaic Law: The Third Durham-Tübingen Research Symposium on Earliest Christianity and Judaism*, ed. James D. G. Dunn (Grand Rapids: Eerdmans, 2001), p. 16. He refers to a prayer in the rabbinical sources that God will keep petitioners from sin "so that you may find joy at the end of the age, . . . this being *counted to you for righteousness* if you do what is true and good before God for the salvation of yourself and of Israel," pp. 25-32). See also E. P. Sanders' interpretation of the Jewish belief in "the merit of the fathers" in *Paul and Palestinian Judaism*, pp. 180-89. I interact with Sanders' summary in *Covenant and Salvation*, pp. 37-52. The fact that early Judaism held that the merit of the patriarchs could be imputed does not require us to conclude that Paul held that Christ's merit could be imputed, but it undermines the argument that such thinking is a foreign incursion of medieval and Reformation categories and questions.
[50]Seifrid, *Christ, Our Righteousness*, 175.
[51]Ibid.

question is whether Scripture teaches imputation, not whether one considers it unnecessary or as endangering sanctification. Furthermore, the Reformed interpretation cannot be reductive or deficient if it actually says *more* than Seifrid allows.[52] More critically, the question arises, how does forgiveness by itself establish rectitude? It is not *forgiveness* (negation of guilt) that withstands the last judgment, but *righteousness* (positive standing). Without the latter, the goal of the covenant as well as its conditions are left unfulfilled. Seifrid concludes: "Justification" cannot be "reduced to an event which takes place for the individual at the beginning of the Christian life" within "an 'order of salvation' *(ordo salutis)*."[53] Yet does not Paul place it in an *ordo salutis* in Romans 8:30? Apart from the positive imputation of righteousness, based on Christ's active obedience (fulfilling the law in our place), justification truly is a "legal fiction," as its critics allege. On the other hand, because the obedience of Christ is actually imputed or credited to us, we are legally just before God.

Robert Gundry also objects to the doctrine of imputation. First, he highlights the texts that refer to imputation of righteousness explicitly. "But none of these texts says that Christ's righteousness was counted," writes Gundry, "so that righteousness comes into view not as what is counted but as what God counts faith to be."[54] What God counts or imputes is faith, not Christ's righteousness, Gundry argues.[55] To be sure, "Paul rejects the Jewish tradition that God counted Abraham's faith as righteousness because it was a work (a good one, of course)."[56] Yet if faith is the ground of justification rather than the instrument, one wonders how that Jewish interpretation could be faulted. Gundry clearly states that "the righteousness that comes 'from' *(ek)* faith (Rom 9:30; 10:6) and from God 'through' *(dia)* faith and 'on the basis of' *(epi)* faith (Phil 3:9) is the faith

---

[52]In an intriguing remark, Herman Bavinck judges, "The rationalistic school is rooted basically in Piscator's teaching, according to which the righteousness we need is accomplished not by the active but solely by the passive obedience of Christ!" (*Reformed Dogmatics,* ed. John Bold, trans. John Vriend [Grand Rapids: Baker Academic, 2006], 3:531).

[53]Seifrid, *Christ, Our Righteousness,* p. 176.

[54]Robert Gundry, "The Nonimputation of Christ's Righteousness," in *Justification: What's at Stake in the Current Debates,* ed. Mark Husbands and Daniel J. Treier (Downers Grove, Ill.: IVP Academic, 2004), p. 18.

[55]Ibid., p. 22.

[56]Ibid. Gundry notes J. A. Ziesler's survey of the Jewish literature, *The Meaning of Righteousness in Paul: A Linguistic and Theological Inquiry,* SNTSMS 20 (Cambridge: Cambridge University Press, 1972), pp. 43, 103-4, 109, 123, 125-26, 175, 182-83.

that God counts as righteousness. Paul's language is supple: faith is the *origin*, the means, and the *basis* of righteousness in that God counts it as righteousness."[57]

However, *epi* has a much broader lexical range than Gundry allows.[58] While in technical theological jargon, the basis (or formal cause) of something is distinguished from the means (or instrumental cause), *epi* and *dia* both are used with greater range and flexibility in Scripture, as their English equivalents are in common use. In fact, *epi* appears as a basis ("on account of"/"because of"), a marker of basis for a state of being, an action or a result, in numerous places.[59] In other words, *epi* ("on account of") is interchangeable with *dia* ("through").

In the light of various challenges to the Reformation understanding of justification from Protestant as well as Roman Catholic quarters, the terminology became more refined: justification by grace, through faith, because of Christ. However, it would be anachronistic to impose the more refined distinctions of scholasticism on the New Testament. Even Luther can say, in his exegesis of Galatians, that we are justified "for the sake of our faith in Christ or for the sake of Christ," as if the two phrases are interchangeable.[60] It all depends on what one is contrasting: faith and works or faith as an inherently worthy basis versus passive instrument. In Gundry's formulation, however, one would say that we are justified by faith, through faith, on the basis of faith.

Rejecting the imputation of Adam's sin, since the people's sinning (before the law) was "not after the likeness of Adam's transgression," Gundry denies imputation in relation to justification.[61] Yet this verse (Rom 5:14) seems to make the opposite point: namely, that even though they did not commit the *same* sin, they were still sinners in Adam. Further, Gundry speaks of "the failure of Paul, despite his extensive discussion of law and writing that Christ was 'born under the law' (Gal 4:4), ever to make a point of Christ's keeping the law perfectly on our behalf (not even his sinlessness in 2 Cor 5:21 being put in relation to law-keeping)."[62]

---

[57]Ibid., p. 25, emphasis added.
[58]There are no fewer than eighteen possible renderings, according to BDAG, pp. 363-67.
[59]Ibid., esp. p. 366.
[60]Martin Luther's 1535 Galatians commentary in *LW* 26:233.
[61]Gundry, "Nonimputation of Christ's Righteousness," p. 28.
[62]Ibid., p. 32.

Yet what other import might the phrase "born under the law" have served? And how else would a Jew have understood sinlessness other than "in relation to law-keeping"? And why does Paul contrast Adam's one act of disobedience and Christ's one act of obedience? Does this not suggest that Christ's obedience, rather than our faith, is imputed? Gundry argues, "To be sure, *dikaiōma,* translated 'act of righteousness' in Romans 5:18 and 'righteous requirement' in Romans 8:4 (also in Rom 1:32), may be collective in Romans 8:4 for all the requirements of the law. But that collective meaning is unsure, even unlikely, for Paul writes in Galatians 5:14 that 'the whole law is fulfilled in one command, "You shall love your neighbor as yourself.""[63]

Yet even such an interpretation of Galatians 5:14 seems strained. Paul was merely summarizing "the whole law" (i.e., all the requirements of the law collectively comprehended). Surely loving one's neighbor does not consist in one act. And in the context of his running polemic in Galatians, would it not be legitimate to assume here that Paul is simply repeating the claim in 3:10 that to offend at one point (failing to love God and neighbor perfectly) is to be "under the curse" of the law? Although he has argued that faith is not a work, Gundry says, "The righteousness of faith is *the moral accomplishment* that God counts faith to be even though it is not *intrinsically* such an accomplishment."[64] Christ's "obediently righteous act of propitiation made it right for God to count faith as righteousness."[65]

Gundry's view is not new; it was advanced by some of Arminius's disciples.[66] However, aside from historical parallels, is Gundry's position exe-

---

[63]Ibid., p. 34.

[64]Ibid., p. 36, emphasis added.

[65]Ibid., p. 39.

[66]Although Arminius held simultaneously that the meritorious ground of justification was Christ's imputed righteousness, his followers (Simon Episcopius and Hugo Grotius) taught that faith itself (and repentance) becomes the ground of justification. The Puritan Richard Baxter made a similar argument, treating faith and evangelical obedience as the "new law" that replaces the "old law" as the basis for justification. Chapter 13 of the Westminster Confession targets this error when it states that believers are justified "not by imputing faith itself, the act of believing, or any other evangelical obedience to them as their righteousness; but by imputing the obedience and satisfaction of Christ unto them, they receiving and resting on him and his righteousness by faith; which faith they have not of themselves, it is the gift of God." In fact, it is possible to recognize parallels with the covenant (or better, contractual) theology of late medieval nominalism, according to which justification is granted on the basis of one's imperfect obedience. No one merits final justification according to strict merit *(de condigno),* but only according to God's gracious decision to accept it as if it were meritorious *(de congruo).*

getically plausible? D. A. Carson responds, first, by offering a salutary reminder that systematic and biblical (or exegetical) theology represent different fields of discourse that should serve each other's ends, but often speak past each other, failing to take each other's fields and research into account.[67] "In Jewish exegesis," Carson points out, "Genesis 15:6 was not quoted to prove that Abraham was justified by faith and not by works," but rather as meritorious obedience (Rabbi Shemaiah, 50 B.C.E.; *Mekilta* on Ex 14:15 [35b]; 40b). "What this means, for our purposes, is that Paul, who certainly knew of these traditions, was explicitly interpreting Genesis 15:6 in a way quite different from that found in his own tradition, and he was convinced that this new way was the correct way to understand the text."[68]

More specifically, Carson draws our attention to the parallelism in Romans 4:5-6:

4:5 God justifies the ungodly.
4:6 God credits righteousness apart from works.

"In other words, 'justifies' is parallel to 'credits righteousness'; or, to put the matter in nominal terms, justification is parallel to the imputation of righteousness."[69] And it has to be an "alien" righteousness, since "God justifies *the ungodly* (Rom 4:5); he credits righteousness *apart from works* (Rom 4:6)."[70] Carson reasons, "If God has counted or imputed our faith to us as righteousness, then, once he has so counted or imputed it, does he then count or impute the righteousness to us, a kind of second imputation?"[71] In Philippians 3, it is clearly not an inherent righteousness.[72] "In 2 Corinthians 5:19-21, we are told that God made Christ who had no sin to be sin for us, so that *in him* we might become the *righteousness* of God. It is because of God that we are in Christ Jesus, who has become for us *righteousness* (and other things: 1 Cor 1:30). Passage after passage in Paul runs down the same track."[73] Faith—even if it is faith in Christ—is not the

---

[67]D. A. Carson, "The Vindication of Imputation," in *Justification: What's at Stake in the Current Debates,* ed. Mark Husbands and Daniel J. Treier (Downers Grove, Ill.: IVP Academic, 2004), p. 49.
[68]Ibid., p. 56.
[69]Ibid., p. 61.
[70]Ibid.
[71]Ibid., p. 64.
[72]Ibid., p. 69.
[73]Ibid., p. 72.

same as having a righteousness that is "not of my own." In Grundry's construction, faith, not Christ, becomes the basis for the transfer from unrighteous to righteous.[74]

CONCLUSION: THEOLOGICAL PRESUPPOSITIONS AND EXEGESIS REGARDING JUSTIFICATION

In spite of an often professed independence, biblical scholars are as indebted as others to particular dogmatic presuppositions and ecclesiastical traditions. Many Protestants today share the Roman Catholic suspicion that a purely forensic doctrine of justification *(sola gratia, sola fide, solo Christo)* affords no basis for moral action. The repeated insistence of the Reformers and their heirs that one cannot receive Christ for justification without also receiving him for sanctification and that justification is given apart from works but never without the fruit of good works often goes unheard. The churches of the Reformation confess not only their faith in the imputed righteousness of Christ in justification but also its inseparable connection to the renewal of believers in sanctification.

Precisely because "There is therefore now no condemnation for those who are in Christ Jesus" (Rom 8:1), believers are free from the dominion of sin over their lives. This connection seems obvious enough in Paul's argument from Romans 3–5 to Romans 6–8. Long ago, Albert Schweitzer judged, "But those who subsequently made his doctrine of justification by faith the centre of Christian belief, have had the tragic experience of finding that they were dealing with a conception of redemption, from which no ethic could logically be derived."[75] Yet this conclusion, which swept the apostle himself into its critique, completely misses the quite natural transition in Paul's logic even in Galatians , where, as in his other epistles, ethical imperatives are drawn from rather than in antithesis to judicial indicatives. The gospel of free justification gives rise to a spontaneous embrace of the very law that once condemned us. This spontaneous life Paul calls "life in the Spirit," yielding "the fruit of the Spirit" (Gal 5:16-26). When we were "in Adam," that law yielded death and condemnation; "in Christ," the law approves us—hence, Calvin's view that the so-called third use (guiding believ-

---

[74]Ibid.
[75]Albert Schweitzer, *The Mysticism of the Apostle Paul* (New York: Seabury, 1968), p. 225.

ers in the way of gratitude) is, for the Christian, "the primary use" of the law.[76] Every Lutheran and Reformed catechism includes an application of the Ten Commandments to the Christian life.

Proponents of covenantal nomism (synergism) have from time immemorial insisted that a gospel of free grace can only lead logically to license. E. P. Sanders, who pioneered the new perspective, assumes that an unconditional election is arbitrary: there must be *something* in the chosen that explains the gift.[77] To be sure, "getting in" depends on obedience, but this does not constitute "works-righteousness," since there are things that we can do to make up for our mistakes. These theological presuppositions guide Sanders' verdicts on Second Temple Judaism and Paul.

James D. G. Dunn concedes that his interpretation of Paul is consistent with his Arminian theological commitments.[78] N. T. Wright pleads, "If Christians could only get this [doctrine of justification] right, they would find that not only would they be believing the gospel, they would be practicing it; and that is the best basis for proclaiming it."[79] Thus, the gospel is something to be done by us, not simply an astonishing and disruptive announcement of what has already been achieved once and for all on our behalf.[80] Faith and holiness belong together, Wright properly insists, but the only way to keep them together, he seems to suggest, is to conflate them. "Indeed, very often the word 'faith' itself could properly be translated as 'faithfulness,' which makes the point just as well," although he reminds us that "faith" is not the way one gets in but is the badge indicating who is in.[81]

Gundry appeals to Mark Seifrid's far from novel charge that "in reducing 'justification' to a present possession of 'Christ's imputed righteousness,' Protestant divines inadvertently bruised the nerve which runs between justification and obedience." He appeals also to Wesley's criticism on the same

---

[76] *Institutes* 2.7.12.

[77] Sanders, *Paul and Palestinian Judaism*, pp. 101-6.

[78] "An Evening Conversation on Jesus and Paul with James D. G. Dunn and N. T. Wright" (2007), p. 20, www.NTWrightpage.com.

[79] Wright, *What Saint Paul Really Said*, p. 159.

[80] Even where Paul speaks of "obeying" the gospel, what he has in mind is believing: "But not all have obeyed the good news; for Isaiah says, 'Lord, who has *believed* our message?' So faith comes from what is heard, and what is heard comes through the word of Christ" (Rom 10:16-17).

[81] Wright, *What Saint Paul Really Said*, p. 160.

ground: it leads to antinomianism.[82] Gundry sees his treatment as going "a long way toward satisfying the legitimate concerns not only of Roman Catholics but also of pietists in the Lutheran tradition, in the Anabaptist and Baptist tradition, in the Keswick movement, in the Holiness movement and in Pentecostalism."[83] No less than the Reformers and their heirs, therefore, are such criticisms of the evangelical doctrine of justification shaped by systematic-theological categories and assumptions.

Even when engaging new perspective writers somewhat critically, I have also discovered many profound insights from scholars like N. T. Wright.[84] However, to put it bluntly, Wright does not think that the Reformers understood Paul very well, and I don't think that Wright understands the Reformers very well. Much of the tension in this debate among Reformed believers at least is due, I believe, to caricatures—particularly, one-sided interpretations—that reveal a glaring lack of familiarity with the nuances especially in Calvin and other Reformed theologians, as well as the covenant theologians who followed in their wake.[85] More often than not, for me at least, it is not what new perspective scholars see in Paul but what they leave out that disappoints.

As in any discipline, the test of a good theory is its capacity for accounting for the widest available data. Exegetically and theologically, all versions of covenantal nomism (identified historically as synergism) are reductionistic, fatally excluding crucial data. Where the basic lines of Reformation exegesis affirm both the free justification of sinners in Christ alone through faith alone as well as their renewal, sanctification and glorification, nomism denies the former and therefore cannot provide an adequate basis for the transformative effects of union with Christ.

Especially when we see justification in its connection with adoption, we recognize that a new status creates a new relationship. We do not have to

---

[82]Gundry, "Nonimputation of Christ's Righteousness," p. 44, citing Seifrid, *Christ, Our Righteousness*, p. 175.
[83]Gundry, "Nonimputation of Christ's Righteousness," 44-45.
[84]See my *Lord and Servant: A Covenant Christology* (Louisville: Westminster John Knox, 2005), and especially *Covenant and Salvation*.
[85]I recognize that New Testament specialists are rarely specialists also in historical theology. However, much of the new perspective rests on the claim (attended often by sweeping representations) that the Reformation misunderstood Paul. Therefore, one would expect more scholarly responsibility in interpreting original and secondary sources in Reformation exegesis of the relevant topics.

choose between judicial and relational categories. Adapting the Ancient Near Eastern treaties to God's covenantal purposes, Scripture indicates that to be adopted by the Great King, the vassal "puts on" the identity of the suzerain, including its regal glory. It is this lost glory that is recovered—and, because it is no less than the glory of the God-Man, it is greater than the original glory of "the first man . . . from the earth, a man of dust" (1 Cor 15:47). "Just as we have borne the image of the man of dust, we will also bear the image of the man of heaven" (1 Cor 15:49).[86] "To be the image of God is to be the son of God."[87]

To "put on Christ" is to derive all of one's righteousness from him, both for justification and sanctification. That is the case not only because he is the eternal Son, but because he is the justified covenant head of his people, "and was declared to be Son of God with power according to the Spirit of holiness by resurrection from the dead" (Rom 1:4; see text note). In Christ, our rags are exchanged for robes of regal splendor, and we are seated at the same table with Abraham, Isaac, and Jacob.

The clothing analogy is not original to Pauline theology. It occurs first with God's clothing of Adam and Eve after the Fall, the vision of Joshua the high priest having his filthy clothes exchanged for a robe of righteousness in Zechariah 3, and a host of other passages. In Isaiah 61:10-11, we read, "I will greatly rejoice in the LORD, my whole being shall exult in my God; for he has clothed me with the garments of salvation, he has covered me with the robe of righteousness, as a bridegroom decks himself with a garland, and as a bride adorns herself with her jewels" (cf. Rev 21:2, which paraphrases this verse). The guests at the wedding feast in Jesus' parable are adorned in festive garments (Mt 22:1-14), and the prodigal son is decked out by the father in the best clothes upon his return (Lk 15:11-32). So when Paul says that Christ is "our righteousness, holiness, and redemption" (1 Cor 1:30) and refers repeatedly to our being "clothed with Christ," "having put on Jesus Christ," and calls us on that basis to "put on Christ" in our daily conduct, this same connection

---

[86]Appealing to the research of Phyllis Bird, I pointed out in *Lord and Servant* (chap. 4) that Genesis 1–2 exploits Egyptian mythology for polemical purposes. While the Pharaoh was thought to be the son of the gods, in Genesis this royal sonship extends beyond the king, and not only to all sons but to all human beings: "male and female" created in God's *image*, the language of sonship.

[87]M. G. Kline, *Images of the Spirit* (Eugene, Ore.: Wipf and Stock, 1999), p. 35.

between justification and sanctification is being drawn.

In common with the practices of its neighbors, Israel's law made the firstborn son heir of the estate, which was also the inheritance law of the Greco-Roman world. Yet in the new covenant (fulfilling the promise to Adam and Eve as well as the covenant with Abraham and Sarah), with Christ as the head, "There is no longer Jew or Greek, there is no longer slave or free, there is no longer male and female; for all of you are one in Christ Jesus. And if you belong to Christ, then you are Abraham's off-spring, heirs according to promise" (Gal 3:28-29). Everyone who is in Christ is a "firstborn son," co-heir of the entire estate (Gal 4:1-7, 27). These "sons" who are legally entitled to the inheritance include females as well as males, Gentiles as well as Jews, slaves as well as free citizens, without distinction (Gal 3:28-29).

Furthermore, these brothers and sisters are not only heirs of whatever is left over from the spoils of the firstborn son's inheritance. In fact, the very passage we are using for the structure of the *ordo salutis* (Rom 8:30) begins first with the statement, "For those whom he foreknew he also predestined to be conformed to the image of his Son, in order that he might be the firstborn within a large family" (Rom 8:29). Jews and Gentiles alike are "fellow heirs, members of the same body, and sharers in the promise in Christ Jesus through the gospel" (Eph 3:6). Properly speaking, it is Christ who is the "heir of all things" (Heb 1:2; cf. Lk 20:14), but precisely because he possesses all things not only as a private but as a public person, his inheritance is a public trust. Believers hold all things in common with Christ and therefore with each other.

In the economy of the Sinai covenant, Moses is a servant in God's house, while Jesus Christ is the firstborn son (Heb 3:1-6). So even Moses' justification and adoption are dependent not on the condition of his personal fulfillment of the law-covenant made at Sinai but on Christ's personal fulfillment of that covenant by which he has won the inheritance for his brothers and sisters in the covenant of grace: "For the one who sanctifies and those who are sanctified all have one Father. For this reason Jesus is not ashamed to call them brothers and sisters, saying, 'I will proclaim your name to my brothers and sisters, in the midst of the congregation I will praise you.' And again, 'I will put my trust in him.' And again, 'Here am I and the children whom God has given me'" (Heb 2:11-18). As with justification, this adoption is not a legal fiction, since the law is fulfilled: the firstborn Son has won the entire estate by his victorious service to the crown, but, as established in the mutuality of the covenant of redemption (i.e., election), every adopted child has an equal share.

The children need not worry about their future or jockey for their Father's favor (as did Jacob and Esau). After all, "He who did not withhold his own Son, but gave him up for all of us, will he not with him also give us everything else?" (Rom 8:32). If union with Christ in the covenant of grace is the matrix for Paul's *ordo,* justification remains its source, even for adoption. We do not move from the topic of justification to other (more interesting) ones, but are always relating the riches of our inheritance to this decisive gift. In William Ames's words, "Adoption of its own nature requires and presupposes the reconciliation found in justification. . . . The first fruit of adoption is that Christian liberty by which all believers are freed from the bondage of the law, sin, and the world."[88]

Adoption, like justification, is simultaneously legal and relational, as is the obverse: alienation and condemnation. Adoption is not a goal held out to children who successfully imitate their parents; nor is it the result of an infusion of familial characteristics or genes. Rather, it is a change in legal status that issues in a relationship that is gradually reflected in the child's identity, characteristics and actions. From the courtroom, with the legal status and inheritance unalterably established, the child moves into the security of a growing and thriving future.

Just as there is no opposition between forensic and relational categories here, we are not forced to choose between forensic and effective categories either. God's Word declares us to be righteous heirs of the kingdom, and this same Word immediately begins to conform us existentially, morally, and socially to this new-creation reality, with the firstborn Son as its archetype. Justification is distinct from regeneration, yet both are the effect of union with Christ, which the Spirit effects by his Word. This is why Paul compares justification and its effects to God's creation of the world *ex nihilo* by his Word (Rom 4:17, with Ps 33:6). As Oswald Bayer expresses this point, interpreting Luther, "What God says, God does. . . . God's work is God's speech. God's speech is no fleeting breath. It is a most ef-

---

[88]William Ames, *The Marrow of Theology,* ed. John Dykstra Eusden (Grand Rapids: Baker Academic, 1997), p. 165.

fective breath that creates life, that summons into life."[89]

Far from denying the subjective transformation of the new birth and sanctification, the classic evangelical view points to its only possible source. As with all sound teaching in the Scriptures, the goal of the doctrine is to bring us to doxology, giving all praise to God with nothing left for ourselves. "What then are we to say about these things? If God is for us, who is against us? . . . Who will bring any charge against God's elect? It is God who justifies. Who is to condemn? . . . Who will separate us from the love of Christ?" (Rom 8:31-35).

It is the outcasts—the ungodly—whom God justifies through faith in his Son. It is they who will be seated at the wedding feast clothed in the wedding garment, said Jesus, while those who enter in their own attire will be cast out (Mt 22:1-14). It is the prodigal who, expecting to be no more than a servant upon his return from squandering his inheritance, is welcomed with the best robe and a celebratory feast.

Perhaps the best image in the New Testament for justification comes from Jesus' parable of the tax collector and the Pharisee. "The Pharisee, standing by himself, prayed thus: 'God, I thank you that I am not like other men, extortioners, unjust, adulterers, or even like this tax collector. I fast twice a week; I give tithes of all that I get.' But the tax collector, standing far off, would not even lift up his eyes to heaven, but beat his breast, saying, 'God, be merciful to me, a sinner!'" (Lk 18:11-13). Luke introduces this parable as intended by Jesus for "some who trusted in themselves that they were righteous, and treated others with contempt" (Lk 18:9). Clearly, Jesus sees the problem of the religious leaders as self-righteousness, which bore fruit of course in exclusionary practices. Furthermore, the Pharisee and tax collector both "went up to the temple to pray" (Lk 18:10), so the contrast was not between some works (circumcision and dietary laws) rather than others. Finally, the Pharisee even thanked God for his righteousness, tipping his hat to grace (Lk 18:11). Nevertheless, the tax collector asked for mercy rather than for an approval of his righteousness. "I tell you," Jesus concluded, "this man went down to his house justified, rather than the other" (Lk 18:14).

---

[89]Oswald Bayer, *Living by Grace: Justification and Sanctification*, trans. Geoffrey W. Bromiley (Grand Rapids: Eerdmans, 2003), p. 43.

■

Progressive Reformed Response

Michael F. Bird

I CONSIDER IT A PLEASURE TO BE ABLE TO engage Michael Horton in this book. Horton is one of the leading lights among Reformed evangelical theologians in North America. I have benefited immensely from his treatments on covenant theology. Both of us claim the mantle of being "Reformed." However, my "Progressive Reformed" position can be differentiated from his "Traditional Reformed" perspective by virtue of my willingness to incorporate insights from fields beyond the Reformed confessions and out of my readiness to modify some of the confessional claims where I think that they need correction or clarification. I find myself agreeing with Horton on aspects like the forensic nature of justification and affirming that God justifies the ungodly. However, there are several areas I would bid him to reconsider. I will focus on four areas: justification and sanctification, justification and forgiveness, justification and imputation, and justification and social context.

1. *Justification and sanctification.* I concur with Horton that for Paul justification (being declared legally righteous before God) is *generally* distinct from sanctification (becoming morally righteous as empowered by God). Though I prefer the term "transformation" over "sanctification" since words associated with "sanctification" in the New Testament (e.g., *hagiazō*) are mostly about positional holiness, that is, they pertain to possessing the status of consecration to God. The justification/transformation distinction is defensible because (1) justification is the opposite of condemnation (Rom 5:1, 18; 8:1, 33-34; 2 Cor 3:9) and justification is properly conceived of as a legal status and not a process of becoming just; and (2) the charge that Paul is antinomian (Rom 3:7-8; 6:1-2; Acts 21:21) would not have emerged if Paul was treating justification as something based on moral transformation. I believe, with Calvin (and Horton), that justification and transformation are both rooted in the same reality of union with Christ so that God's declarative word of acquittal and God's effective work of new creation cannot be divorced. Thus, justification and

transformation are linked logically and even Christologically, but the latter cannot be subsumed under the former conceptually.

However—and this is the problem of comparing exegesis and systematic theology—sometimes the divide between justification and transformation gets a little fuzzy. Let me give several examples.

In Galatians 5:5 Paul says that through the Spirit and by faith we eagerly await the "hope of righteousness" (*elpida dikaiosynēs*). Does that mean we look forward to the day when the verdict of justification will finally be implemented at the consummation? Or does the hope of righteousness refer to a longing that by the Spirit we will actually become morally righteous? While I lean toward the forensic view, I have to admit that here "righteousness" could be ethical too!

In 1 Corinthians 1:30, Paul refers to Christ Jesus, who became for us "wisdom from God, righteousness, and holiness, and redemption." Christ is obviously the source of the believer's righteousness, but is this our righteous status or our power for living righteously? It could be either; it could be both!

In Romans 5:19, Paul states: "For just as through the disobedience of the one man the many were *made sinners,* so also through the obedience of the one man the many *will be made* righteous." The verb *kathistēmi* ("made-appointed-constituted") is used to describe how humanity was made sinners and in parallel how believers will be made as righteous. The debate is whether *kathistēmi* means to make righteous or to declare righteous. For some commentators, Adam's disobedience is imputed to sinners and then believers have Jesus' obedience imputed to them for justification. The problem is—and I have a little rhyme about this—no matter how much people may try, *kathistēmi* does not mean *logizomai* (*logizomai* being the word from which we get "impute" or "reckon"). The word *kathistēmi* refers to an actual state of affairs and not to transactions. To say that believers will be made righteous is to posit a rectification in both their legal status and in their moral state. As Tom Schreiner comments, "This is powerful evidence that righteousness in Paul, although forensic, cannot be confined in every instance to forensic categories."[1]

In Romans 6:7, Paul says, "for one who has died has been set free from

[1]Thomas R. Schreiner, *Romans,* BECNT (Grand Rapids: Baker, 1998), p. 288.

sin." The words "set free" are based on the verb *dikaioō*, which we normally translate as "justify." So Paul says literally that the one who has died to sin has been "justified from sin." Taken at face value, *dikaioō* is used here in the sense of liberation from the power of sin, that is, transformatively. The deployment of the verb *dikaioō* with the preposition *apo* may be idiomatic for "free from" (see Acts 13:38-39). That is plausible given the parallel of Romans 6:7 with Romans 6:18 where Paul says explicitly that believers have been freed from sin *(eleutherōthentes apo tēs harmatias)*. Still, to quote Schreiner again, "Those who are in a right relation to God have also been dramatically changed; they have also been made righteous."[2]

So theologically I agree that justification and transformation are distinct. Yet exegetically, I have to concede that such a distinction is not absolute at the level of the biblical text.

2. Justification and forgiveness. According to Horton, the forgiveness of sins is insufficient to constitute the grounds of justification. Horton affirms the standard Reformed position that justification is the forgiveness of sins supplemented by the imputation of Jesus' righteousness. The logic is that forgiveness clears the slate so to speak and negates guilt. Then after that believers still need an imputation of righteous law-keeping in order to have a positive legal status before God. That is certainly logical, but it is not biblical. The fact is that the biblical writers use justification and forgiveness interchangeably. That is not to say that justification and forgiveness mean the same thing, but they are not construed as two legs in a journey. Rather they are more like two sides of the same coin. Consider the following:

First, note how Paul in Romans 4:7-8 proves that God counts righteousness (i.e., God justifies) apart from works of law by way of reference to Psalms 32:2: "Blessed are those whose lawless deeds are *forgiven,* and whose sins are covered; blessed is the one against whom the Lord *will not count his sin.*" Here God's justifying verdict is correlated with forgiveness and the nonimputation of sin. According to Brian Vickers, "Paul's emphasis in Romans 4, the thing he wants to make explicit by his citation of Psalm 32, is that the imputation of righteousness has primarily to do with the forgiveness of sins."[3]

---

[2]Ibid., p. 319.
[3]Brian Vickers, *Jesus' Blood and Righteousness: Paul's Theology of Imputation* (Wheaton, Ill.:

Second, Paul's speech in Pisidian Antioch includes the remark: "Let it be known to you therefore, brothers and sisters, that through this man *forgiveness of sins* is proclaimed to you, and by him everyone who believes is *justified* from everything from which you could not be *justified* by the law of Moses" (Acts 13:38-39). The forgiveness of sins stands in direct relation to justification understood as liberation from the condemnation of the Mosaic Law.

Elsewhere in Romans justification is linked to redemption (Rom 3:24), peace (Rom 5:1), reconciliation (Rom 5:9-11) and salvation (Rom 10:10). The reason why Paul can switch between these images so freely is because no single image for salvation is hegemonic. They are all different ways of expressing the one reality of God's acceptance of persons because of their faith in Jesus Christ. The various images of salvation are the contingent metaphors that attest to the coherent reality that God has acted dramatically in Christ for the deliverance of his people.[4] Evidently justification is not the positive status that tops up the forgiveness of sins. Forgiveness itself provides a positive status as it does in the Old Testament (e.g., Lev 4:20; 5:10; Num 15:25-26, 28). I don't know what that observation does for Horton's theological system, but I suspect that it might require a serious rethink.

3. *Justification and imputation.* I found myself somewhat confused by Horton's remarks on imputation. On the one hand he says that the righteousness that is imputed is not "a substance or a commodity" but a "legal status"—Amen I say! Then later he says that imputed righteousness is Christ's "passive and active obedience" and even something that Christ "merits" for others. Now I can handle the notion of a status of righteousness being conferred on believers when they are incorporated into the righteousness of Christ. Yet I categorically reject the concept of merits for two reasons:

First, the problem humanity has is not a lack of moral merits. The problem is a broken relationship. What is needed is not merit but reconciliation to fix that problem. Jesus takes us from alienation to restoration through his messianic ministry, by his atoning death and his vindicating resurrec-

---

Crossway, 2006), p. 108 (see esp. pp. 100-109).
[4]Cf. J. Christiaan Beker, *Paul the Apostle: The Triumph of God in Life and Thought* (Philadelphia: Fortress, 1980), pp. 364-77.

tion, so that God's verdict against us becomes God's verdict for us. Believers escape the punishment of their sin when Christ's takes the penalty for them and they experience justification when they participate in the justification of the Messiah who has fulfilled the role God gave to Adam and Israel as representatives of humanity.

Second, Horton appeals to the rabbinic teaching of the "merit of the fathers" as proving that the concept of merits is congruent with the world of Paul. However, first, the rabbinic teaching on the merits of the fathers belongs to the post-135 C.E. period and cannot be read back into first-century Judaism. Second, what the rabbis meant by the merits of the fathers is vastly different from the medieval Catholic notion of a treasury of merits dispensed by the pope. As George Moore said, "That God, having regard to the character of the patriarchs, his relations to them and his promises to them in his good pleasure shows special favor or undeserved leniency to their posterity, is a wholly different matter [Roman Catholicism]. Men may seek of God the forgiveness of sins 'for the sake of the fathers'; but they cannot claim to have their demerit offset by the merits of the fathers."[5]

I believe that imputation is a theological implicate of the biblical teaching. Yet rather than tie this to some kind of merit theology (and then haggle over whether merit is imputed or imparted), I think we are better off following N. T. Wright when he says that one of the "great truths of the gospel" is that "the accomplishments of Jesus Christ is *reckoned* to all those who are 'in him.'"[6] Yet the accomplishment is the fulfillment of a role, not the acquisition of merit. Believers are justified because they participate in the faithfulness, death and resurrection of the Messiah so that what is true of the Messiah is true of his people.

4. *Justification and social context.* Probably my biggest gripe with Horton's treatment is what he does not say. Horton does a fine job of demonstrating that Paul's teaching on justification by faith rules out any kind of works righteousness. Paul's letters amply demonstrate one cannot earn salvation by good works (see Rom 3:20; 4:4-5; Gal 3:1-5; Eph 2:8-9; Tit 3:5,

---

[5]G. F. Moore, *Judaism in the First Centuries of the Christian Era: The Age of the Tannaim*, 3 vols. (Cambridge, Mass.: Harvard University Press, 1927), 1:544-45.

[6]N. T. Wright, "Paul in Different Perspective: Lecture 1: Starting Points and Opening Reflections," unpublished lecture delivered at Auburn Avenue Presbyterian Church, Monroe, Louisiana (January 3, 2005) <www.ntwrightpage.com/Wright_Auburn_Paul.htm>.

etc.). However, Paul's primary concern in Galatians and Romans was not with refuting salvation by works according to the Council of Trent. Paul argued that Gentiles do not have to become Jews in order to become Christians. Horton mostly ignores what Paul so painstakingly emphasizes: justification by faith means that God creates one people around Jesus Christ.[7] For Paul the opposite of justification by faith is not legalism, but ethnocentrism (Rom 3:29). Christ was cursed on the cross for the purpose of redemption and bringing Gentiles into the family of Abraham (Gal 3:13-14). The wonderful text about salvation by grace through faith with good works planned for believers in Ephesians 2:9-10 is followed immediately with Paul's lengthy discourse about the unity of Jews and Gentiles in the commonwealth of a restored Israel (Eph 2:11–3:12). If you talk about justification by faith and never get around to talking about the unity of Jews and Gentiles in one church, then you are not talking about the stuff that Paul talked about on justification. Horton shows in his introduction how the promise to "redeem a worldwide family of sinners" is the background story of Paul. But he needs to relate that to the local story of house churches in Rome, Antioch and Galatia who struggled with issues of their identity and status vis-à-vis the Law of Moses in the social context of the Jewish Diaspora.

---

[7]To be fair, Horton does mention Jews and Gentiles at a few points, but they remain peripheral to his overall treatment of the subject.

■

New Perspective Response

James D. G. Dunn

THIS IS AS CLEAR AND AS VIGOROUS AN exposition and defense of the classic Reformed theology of justification in terms of imputation as one could have wished for. Despite my Calvinist background in Scotland, I am not a close student of the Genevan master (or of his elder Wittenberg contemporary). And I find little or nothing to quarrel with in Michael Horton's exposition of the Reformation debates and the opposition of Trent. And when he turns to exegesis, the agreement extends still further. "Justification" is certainly a forensic metaphor. Nor does it mean "transformation" or signify a process.

However, as soon as Horton turns to the exegesis of Paul, questions begin to arise. And they all focus round the growing suspicion that Horton is forcing all the biblical material examined to fit with his conviction of the centrality of forensic imputation, to fit into the quite narrow grid of his exposition of the legal metaphor. For example, one would find it hard to recognize in his treatment of "the righteousness of God" the fact that Paul in Romans 1:17 and elsewhere was drawing primarily on the Old Testament usage where God's "righteousness" is well translated as "vindication" or "deliverance."[1] The background of course is the commitment (do we really want to say "legal commitment"?) that God made in entering into covenant with Israel—his righteousness was the deliverance to which he had committed himself in choosing Israel. But to narrow the focus to a legal obligation undermines the gracious initiative of God, precisely in going beyond what could be legally expected/required of him.

Horton's criticism of Tom Wright for identifying "God's righteousness" with "the covenant faithfulness of God" is not unfair. But only a brash disregard of Romans 3:3-7 would allow anyone to ignore the fact that God's righteousness and covenant faithfulness are closely integrated and overlapping concepts. The argument of Romans, not just chapters 1–4 but also chapters 9–11, falls apart without the recognition that a major concern of Paul was to defend God's faithfulness.

To take *logizesthai* as "impute" = "reckon" is plausible enough. But I do find highly implausible an exposition of Romans 4 that insists that Paul intended the recipients of his letter to understand that it was not Abraham's (or their) *faith* that was being reckoned to him/them as righteousness, but *Christ's righteousness* (Horton's critique of Bob Gundry). Paul is about as clear as he could be: "Abraham believed God and it was

---

[1] I have made such points often, but apparently to deaf ears, since references to my *The Theology of Paul the Apostle* (Grand Rapids: Eerdmans, 1998), pp. 340-46; *The New Perspective on Paul*, rev. ed. (Grand Rapids: Eerdmans, 2008), pp. 2-4; *Beginning from Jerusalem* (Grand Rapids: Eerdmans, 2009), pp. 879-80, seem to be lacking in this debate.

reckoned to him for/as righteousness" (Rom 4:3); "faith was reckoned to Abraham for/as righteousness" (Rom 4:9); "the righteousness of the faith which he had while still uncircumcised, in order that he might be the ancestor of all who believe without being circumcised, in order that righteousness might be reckoned to them also" (Rom 4:11); "It was not written for his sake alone that 'it was reckoned to him,' but for us also, to whom it is to be reckoned, who believe in him who raised Jesus our Lord from the dead" (Rom 4:23-24). The logic of dogma should always bow the knee to exegesis.

I also find it difficult to read Romans 5 as suggesting "that Christ's obedient life is the basis of justification, along with his death and resurrection." I would have thought that once again it was about as plain as it could be that two single acts as well as two single individuals are being contrasted: Adam's act of disobedience, and Christ's act of obedience (Rom 5:19; as in Phil 2:8). And the argument that the imputation of Christ's righteousness is paralleled by the imputation of Adam's sin leaves me rather breathless. "The sin of Adam was imputed to the human race as a covenantal entity in solidarity because it was imputed to each member (Rom 5:12)." Not only do we seem to be back into the most offensive (and unfounded) "original sin" interpretations of Romans 5:12, but an important element in Paul's argument in the passage is being ignored. For Paul makes a point of restricting guilt to the conscious act of breaching the law: "sin is not reckoned [*ellogeitai* is a near synonym to *logizetai*] when there is no law" (Rom 5:13). Sin is not "imputed" where there is no active disobedience. So if there is indeed a parallel here with the imputation of righteousness, then it would follow that the imputation is consequential upon acts of obedience! A more careful exegesis of Romans 5:19 surely has to be made: "Just as through the disobedience of one man the many were made sinners, so also though the obedience of one man the many shall be made righteous."

I am a little more miffed by Horton's criticism of "the new perspective" that it challenges the doctrine of justification and claims "that the Reformation misunderstood Paul." That criticism might have had validity in the 1980s or 1990s. But I had hoped that it was now more apparent that "the new perspective" (certainly that which attaches to my name) is primarily an attempt to highlight a *missing dimension* of Paul's doctrine of justification—missing despite its being of prime importance for Paul himself. So far as I was concerned this was never a criticism of the Reformed doctrine itself, especially if that was detached from an unjustified denigration of Judaism. It was rather an attempt to bring back on to center stage, where Paul had placed it, his concern that Gentile believers should be fully accepted as members of the church of God as were Jewish believers. This involved the breaking down of the historic barrier (of law) separating Israel from the (other) nations/Gentiles. Horton unfortunately ignores this aspect of why Paul formulated his doctrine of justification in the way he did (he only alludes to it), which simply reinforces any "new perspective" protest that this dimension (not the whole) of Paul's doctrine has been lost to sight.

What most caught me unawares was the countercharge that "the new perspective" leaves out important aspects of Paul's teaching on the subject and fails to account "for the widest available data." For that is precisely the criticism leveled at "the old perspective"—and Horton himself is a good example of what the criticism was getting at. For he simply fits such other "data" that he reviews into his imputation interpretation. He does not ask whether it can or should be so fitted. His repeated denial that justification means "transformation" pays no attention to the fact that Paul himself was more than happy to use the language of transformation (Rom 12:2; 2 Cor 3:18). So if that language cannot be contained within a tight doctrine of justification, where is it to go? Here is important data that should be at least related to the doctrine of justification since it was evidently of importance for Paul that his converts should be "transformed."

Similarly, Horton seems to read the "in Christ" motif in Paul as simply another way of affirming that the righteousness of Christ has been imputed to believers.[2] But "in Christ" is a far more varied motif and gives more substance to the participationist way of reading Paul than Horton seems able to envisage. It is here I would again press for the relational dimension of the righteousness that is at the center of Paul's gospel. When the forensic imagery is stressed too much or given the sole role in understanding Paul's gospel, then it leaves itself too much open to the criticism of "legal fiction." Whereas a righteousness that does not count sin, em-

---

[2]Does Horton really mean it when he says, "Justification is distinct from regeneration, yet both are the effect of union with Christ, which the Spirit effects by his Word"?

braces the lawless, gives the Spirit of adoption to those who simply trust, moves beyond the limitations of the legal metaphor. We should never forget that Paul uses the forensic imagery to highlight how much the mercy of God upsets the legal process (he justifies the ungodly!) and transcends its logic.

The problem with pushing all of Paul through the narrow gauge of a strict forensic reading of justification is that it strips off so much of the fuller richness of the diversity of images and metaphors on which Paul draws to expound his gospel—including the "in Christ" language, the gift of the Spirit theme, and all that is involved in them. I am really quite alarmed at Horton's unwillingness to take seriously Paul's understanding of final judgment, to give his exhortations and warnings the seriousness that Paul evidently intended. In attempting to refute Tom Wright's insistence that for Paul final judgment will take account of the believer's life, he simply assumes that "for Paul the verdict of the last day has already been rendered in favor of those who have faith in Christ," and reaffirms that "the justified . . . 'can never fall from the state of justification.'"

> The repeated insistence of the Reformers and their heirs that one cannot receive Christ for justification without also receiving him for sanctification and that justification is given apart from works but never without the fruit of good works often goes unheard. The churches of the Reformation not only confess their faith in the imputed righteousness of Christ in justification, but also its inseparable connection to the renewal of believers in sanctification.

So, Paul, why did you worry so much about your churches? Why were you so anxious to present them blameless on the day of Christ? Why did you warn them that various behaviors could cause them to fail and die? Why no reference to a passage like Romans 2:6-16? Significant perhaps is Horton's dismissal of "covenantal nomism" as "synergism," to be abbreviated simply to "nomism." For at least "covenantal nomism" was an attempt to chart a proper balance between the divine initiative of covenant (election and promise) and the chosen nation's responsibility to obey the law, both emphases so clearly present in the Old Testament and the literature of the period. And the phrase, if it can be used to describe Paul's soteriology, has an equivalent emphasis—both grace through faith, and the obedience of faith.[3] I am uneasy, then, at the bold (or do I mean crass?) dismissal of attempts to take Paul's exhortations, warnings and concepts of transformation and final judgment according to works seriously. But I would rather see an attempt to take these Pauline "data" seriously than wrap them up in a glib reassurance that all good works to be acknowledged by God will have been done by the Spirit, or in the power of the Spirit. That will no doubt be how the faithful believer looks back on a life commended by God. But Paul's exhortations and warnings are for the believer in the midst of the process of salvation. If Paul was right, some believers need reassurance, but more need to take his warnings seriously.

---

[3]Which is why I find unacceptably baffling Horton's comment that "exegetically and theologically, all versions of covenantal nomism (identified historically as synergism) are reductionistic, fatally excluding crucial data," since it is precisely the phrase's attempt to do justice to *both* strands of Paul's teaching ("the *obedience* of *faith*") which I find to be wholly lacking in Horton's essay.

■

Deification Response

Veli-Matti Kärkkäinen

AS A EUROPEAN—AND PARTICULARLY Scandinavian—theologian, I am sensitive to differences in theological ethos and themes between the two theological worlds on opposite sides of the Atlantic Ocean. This compilation of essays tells me something about the importance of Reformed tradition in there being no essays assigned to Lutheran writers—even when the topic is *the* Lutheran one!—and instead, three writers (Horton, Bird and Dunn) come from Reformed perspectives. My own essay, written by a non-Lutheran and from a "revisionist" perspective, is the only one that directly engages the Lutheran tradition.

Professor Horton sets out to describe and defend what he names the traditional confessional Reformed understanding. Even though that is not my view, I highly appreciate his candor in defining his intention carefully and irenically in the beginning of the essay: "Since Reformed views are defined by our confessions, especially on such a crucial doctrine, positioning departures as progress might convey the impression that defenders of the confessional view are merely repristinating a tradition rather than confessing a faith that is as exegetically defensible today as it was in the sixteenth century." The obvious challenges for such a task, however, are many, such as who is to tell us which particular Reformed confession is the "canonical" one and even if such an agreement exists, whether all who subscribe to that definition interpret it in a similar way. The Catholic writers in this book honestly tell the reader that even the Council of Trent's sixth session does not have only one "official" reading!

I understand why the author, in defense of the "traditional" Reformed view of justification, juxtaposes radically the Roman Catholic view at Trent and the prevailing Reformation confessional view (both in Reformed and Lutheran traditions). There are two main reasons, in my understanding. First, behind the opposition to the Roman Catholic linking of justification with sanctification, unlike traditional Protestant theology that makes a categorical distinction between the two, is the fear of "works-righteousness" and denial of salvation by "faith" alone. Second, coupled with this concern are some key Roman Catholic formulae and doctrines that are part of the matrix of the Tridentian soteriology and doctrine of grace, most prominently the notion of merit and teaching of purgatory. Those fears and suspicions are real and should not be easily dismissed.

However, as I seek to argue in my essay—and it seems to me is also basically argued by Dunn on the basis of the new perspective in New Testament studies and by our Roman Catholic colleagues in light of the wider Catholic tradition—after the five hundred years of impasse, new ways of negotiating these centuries-long debates are on the horizon. Let me state my point briefly here and just refer to my own essay for further elucidation. First, with regard to the fear of "works-righteousness," I mention the fact that in Luther's own theology, the presence of Christ-in-faith through the Holy Spirit in the believer *(in ipsa fide Christus adest)* helped him move beyond the mere forensic declaration. Even when he speaks of an "alien faith" in terms of its origin being outside the human being, he is not thereby denying the fact that this alien righteousness also becomes "our righteousness" as a gift. Christ's presence in the Christian by default begins to renovate and change the person toward Christlikeness. A forensic understanding, as I mention in my response to the Catholic O'Collins's most helpful explanation, can be attached to this "effective" understanding without making the legal framework exclusive.

Second, as a Protestant I do not feel comfortable speaking of "merits," even though, as I mention in the context of Professor O'Collins's nuanced remarks, the way he speaks of the matter as a Catholic theologian is less problematic to me than the way Trent puts it. Nor do I believe in purgatory. That said, neither one of those problematic formulae has to be part of the common confession between Roman Catholics and Protestants regarding an understanding of justification both as declaring and making us righteous. The "Joint Declaration" between Catholics and Lutherans (again, see my own essay) shows the way to do this in a manner that does not negate traditional and denominational differences and yet formulates enough common basis.

To make my point more nuanced: With the advocacy of the view of justification that combines both declarative and effective aspects, I am not thereby wanting to downplay, and certainly not to deny, the validity of a forensic framework. What I do oppose—in sync with some leading Lutheran theologians such as Pannenberg and Reformed theologians such as Moltmann—is the biblically, historically, dogmatically and ecumenically unfounded and counterproductive tendency in some conservative Protestant traditions to make the forensic framework not only the dominant one but also the exclusive one. Just a cursory look at Pauline theology—let alone the rest of the New Testament—tells us that there are a number of diverse metaphors, symbols, images of salvation, and that even one particular metaphor such as "justification" in different contexts may display different nuances. It seems to me that whatever one thinks of the new perspective at large, it has been able to show convincing evidence of the legitimate multiplicity of metaphors of salvation and soteriology. Hence, as I mention in my essay and both Dunn and the Roman Catholic authors similarly do, there is no biblical, historical or dogmatic reason to make one metaphor the dominant and only one, not even justification.

The attempt to make Luther an unambiguous advocate of the exclusively forensic, judicial view of justification is a failing enterprise historically and theologically. (For a fuller argumentation on the basis of Luther's own writings, see my *One with God: Salvation as Deification and Justification.*[1]) Where I am in agreement with Professor Horton, though, is that however one understands Luther's own theology of salvation, it cannot be made primarily a function of his existential *Angst.* A number of biographical, historical, ecclesiastical, cultural, biblical and dogmatic influences played into his "tower experience" in the wider sense of the word.

Going back to the need to speak of justification both in terms of a declarative pronouncement and an effective making-just, to speak of both does not oppose the two key claims of traditional Reformation doctrine, as presented by Professor Horton: "Believers are *simultaneously* justified and sinful," and "Sin's dominion has been toppled, but sin still indwells believers." As I explain in my essay, Luther never gave up his great discovery of *simul iustus et peccator,* even when he also insisted on the fact that by his forgiveness and presence in the believer, Christ "absorbs" all sin in a moment. Daily repentance and return to the grace of baptism was for Luther the key to walk the Christian life, not in terms of earning merits but in terms of letting the Christ-as-present renovate our lives from the inside out, as it were.

It is quite true that the Radical Reformation, with its great concern over the complacency of many mainline Protestant Christians and with its robust following of the "way of Jesus," often stood closer to the Roman understanding of an integral link between faith and works, or declaring and making just. That observation, however, I do not take as a criticism of Anabaptists and others but rather as a testimony to their "biblical" faith. Indeed, the traditional Reformation doctrine as expressed in the confessions—both among the Lutheran and Reformed families of churches—may too easily lead to a lack of attention to the Christian walk, discipleship and cultivation of Christian virtues. In that respect, Luther's own linking of the two aspects of justification materially quite similarly to that of the best of Roman Catholic theology, the Radical Reformers' call to take one's faith seriously (cf. James of the New Testament) and Eastern churches' "synergistic" orientations, rightly understood and rightly interpreted, may help Protestants come into a more balanced understanding of the Christian life and walk.

In the second footnote in his essay, Professor Horton makes a statement

---

[1]Collegeville, Minn.: Liturgical Press, 2004.

about the patristic views of justification that is in need of some comment: "The teaching of the ancient church is ambiguous with respect to justification. On one hand, there are marvelous testimonies to God's justification of sinners. . . . On the other hand, there are many threads of synergism that later Eastern Orthodoxy developed in Byzantine theology in a manner that parallels Western (medieval) developments." With regard to the first statement, it certainly is true that no clearly formulated doctrine of justification can be found among the Fathers. To call it "ambiguous," however, sounds to me like the patristic soteriological formulae are assessed in light of the later Reformation doctrines. In other words: patristic testimonies to justification are ambiguous because they do not stick with the "pure gospel" of Reformation doctrine. That, however, means nothing less than putting the cart before the horse. Shouldn't we rather—or at least as much—evaluate the correctness of later formulations in light of the former? To be historically more accurate, one should say what Professor Rafferty mentions in his essay, namely, that prior to Augustine, not much debate about the doctrine of justification took place—not even frequent mention of the term itself! It simply is a historical fact that the Fathers by and large spoke of soteriology using other metaphors than justification by faith (let alone, that they would have had a "semi-technical" developed doctrine after the manner of the Reformation). If so, then the exclusive clinging to one historically fairly late formulation should be put in perspective rather than made a measuring stick for all soteriological formulae.

With regard to the rest of the statement in the footnote, I take it Professor Horton equates Orthodox synergism with medieval "works-righteousness." Although in medieval theology—and certainly in folk doctrine and practice—"synergistic" tendencies were rampant, to lump Orthodox tradition's distinctive, grace-based doctrine of divine-human *synergia* under the same category is a hasty "guilt by association."

■

Roman Catholic Response

Gerald O'Collins, S.J.

BEFORE RESPONDING TO MICHAEL Horton's chapter, let me say how much working on this joint study of justification has meant to me. It has been a privilege to share with some old friends (Jim Beilby, James Dunn, Paul Eddy and Oliver Rafferty) and with some new colleagues. Horton sides with Dunn on the question of the correct way to interpret the Pauline language of "the faith of Christ," but considers the debate to be "beyond our scope" (n. 43). In my response to Dunn, I followed those exegetes who understand Paul to be speaking of Christ's own faith/faithfulness in which we can share. Setting this question aside, let me take up six other issues.

First, Horton happily remarks that the "new status" of the justified "creates a new relationship. We do not have to choose between judicial and relational categories." What then are we to make of justification as an "exclusively forensic (legal) declaration" that should be understood in a "judicial" fashion and belongs to a courtroom setting? If "to be cleared in court" accurately renders *dikaioō* (a lexical definition proposed by Horton), we might recall that, if a jury says at the end of a trial, "we find the accused not guilty," that statement *does* things and *transforms* the situation: the accused is free to walk away. Clearing someone in court is, to use the speech act theory of John Langshaw Austin, a performative utterance, an utterance that effectively does something. Toward the end of his chapter, Horton quotes Oswald Bayer's interpretation of Luther: "what God says, God does. . . . God's speech is no fleeting breath. It is a most effective breath that creates." One might gloss this remark and say: forensic justification *is* effective justification. As Kärkkäinen observes in his essay in this volume, in Luther's view justification means both declaring righteous and making righteous. Hence it is insufficient to say that "justification is a verdict that *declares* sinners to be righteous." As Paul boldly says, God has acted so that "we might *become* the righteousness of God" (2 Cor 5:21).

Second, while recognizing how in the mind of Luther and other Reformers justification and sanctification are "inseparable gifts of union with Christ through faith," Horton insists that they are distinct. Kärkkäinen, however, claims that such a distinction between justification and sanctification is foreign to Luther's thought. But I leave this issue to the judgment of those who are truly experts in the Reformer's work.

Third, Horton and Kärkkäinen obviously differ sharply in their assessment of the *Joint Declaration on Justification,* signed in 1999 by representatives of the Lutheran World Federation and the Roman Catholic Church.[1] Certainly this declaration did not embody a full consensus, and in fact it explicitly acknowledges differences that still remain. Yet as a Roman Catholic theologian, I am grateful for this joint declaration. While not "binding" me in the sense that the Scriptures or such major confessions as the Nicene-Constantinopolitan Creed do, nevertheless, I would find myself seriously at fault if I refused to let this declaration guide my thinking in the area of justification and in the choice of appropriate ways to express our common Christian faith about God's justifying action in Christ.

Fourth, Kärkkäinen put the case for "deification," "divinization" or *theōsis* being integral to Luther's thinking, and found here a valuable link to be developed with Eastern Christianity's version of what salvation brings. It could also be useful to introduce some of the language that Horton takes from Calvin's *Institutes:* "Christ is not only given *for* us, but *to* us. Through faith we receive not only Christ's gifts but Christ himself." Christ himself "is the gift of righteousness."

Fifth, let me again raise my voice against the notion of the *personal guilt* of men and women being literally transferred to the obedient and innocent Son of God and opening the way to his being condemned and punished by the Father. Can *personal guilt* be "imputed" from one person to another, as Horton and innumerable others (including many notable Roman Catholics like Bishop Jacques-Bénigne Bossuet) have held? But if I insist that our individual, personal guilt cannot be transferred to another person,[2] what

---

[1]The Vatican "caution" apropos of the "Joint Declaration" was issued "by common agreement" between the Congregation for the Doctrine of the Faith [a notoriously cautious and even negative body] and the Pontifical Council for Promoting Christian Unity, and not, as Horton states, by the Council alone.

[2]I emphasize *personal guilt* to make it clear that I am not taking a position here on "original sin." The inherited "sinfulness" of original sin does not refer to personal guilt but to the sinful condition in which and into which human beings are born.

do I make of the language of God "laying on" the servant "the iniquity of us all" and punishing him (Is 53:4-6)?

The Greek version of the Hebrew Scriptures (LXX) shows some sensitivity to this issue and translates the Hebrew ("the LORD has laid on him the iniquity of us all") as "the Lord has handed him over to our sins" (Is 53:6). The same Greek verb *(paradidōmi)* is later picked up by Paul: "he [Christ] was handed over [by God] for our sins" (Rom 4:25); "God did not spare his only Son but handed him over for us all" (Rom 8:31-32). The LXX and Paul should dissuade us from interpreting the intensely dramatic language of Isaiah's fourth servant song in a way that seems theologically and (one should add) philosophically questionable. But to say this is not to put into doubt that the self-sacrifice of Christ representatively expiated the sins of the world

What then of the language of punishment and talk about "the will of God to crush him [the servant] with pain" (Is 53:10). Deutero-Isaiah (40–55) at times pictures God as inflicting punishment on a people who have ignored or offended their divine Lord (e.g., Is 42:18-22, 24-25; 43:24, 27-28). Through the discipline of such "punishment," they can be turned from their evil ways and healed. This could lead us to interpret in a collective sense "the servant" and his sufferings, even in the fourth "Servant Song." But, if we insist here on an individual meaning and one that prefigures Christ, we should also remember that in the sixth century B.C. no distinction had yet been drawn between the "absolute" will of God and the "permissive" will of God. Such a distinction allows us to understand how God may allow even his totally innocent Son to be "handed over" to suffering and to being cruelly punished by human beings.

The fourth "Servant Song" should be treasured as a uniquely brilliant statement on the value of expiatory suffering for others, and to be applied (as the New Testament did) to the passion of Christ. But the meaning of this vivid poem should not be pushed beyond what it actually says or misread as if it were a precise theological treatise about the transfer of personal guilt.[3]

Other scriptural texts have been repeatedly cited in support of the thesis of penal substitution. Theologians, preachers and exegetes of various Christian denominations, including Roman Catholics, have appealed, for instance, to Psalm 22 and its opening cry of abandonment to support their

---

[3]See further G. O'Collins, *Jesus Our Redeemer: A Christian Approach to Salvation* (Oxford: Oxford University Press, 2007), pp. 148-52.

view that God carried on war against his Son hanging on the cross. The crucified Jesus was understood to be the object of the divine anger, a substitute for sinful human beings, treated by God as the worst sinner of all times, and even punished with the pains undergone by those condemned to the eternal sufferings of hell. I set myself elsewhere to rebut at length this use (or rather misuse) of Psalm 22 to support the notion of Jesus as our penal substitute who suffered the divine anger on the cross.[4]

Sixth, let me conclude with several points that bear on the history of doctrine. It was never Roman Catholic belief that *all* must be "refined in purgatory before being welcomed into heaven." Those who suffered death through martyrdom were understood to "go straight to heaven." Then, unfortunately Horton did not quote in full canons 9 and 11 from the Council of Trent's decree on justification; the full text gives a more nuanced and sophisticated account than is suggested by the partial quotations. Finally, in responding to N. T. Wright, Horton points out that "the Reformation position has never been that *God's righteousness* is imputed." To be sure, John Calvin explains justification as consisting in "the remission of sin and *the imputation of Christ's righteousness.*"[5] So where does Christ's righteousness that is imputed to us come from? Does it come, as Horton argues, simply in virtue of the active and passive obedience of Christ, the human servant who has fulfilled the law-covenant? Does this imply that justification comes from within humanity and not from God? Calvin wants to protect the idea that righteousness has been acquired for us by the obedience and sacrificial death of Christ and not simply through the union of divinity and humanity in him. I leave to the Calvin experts the details of his lengthy rebuttal of Andreas Osiander's view that "justification consists in a supposed impartation of Christ's essential righteousness as divine."[6]

---

[4]Ibid., pp. 140-48.
[5]*Institutes* 3.11.2, emphasis added.
[6]Ibid., 3.11.5.

4

Progressive Reformed View

Michael F. Bird

INTRODUCTION

My goal in this essay[1] is to provide a "progressive" Reformed view of justification. The designation "progressive Reformed" needs some unpacking.[2] I consider myself "Reformed" in the sense that I believe in the supremacy of Scripture in the life of the church, I hold to a Calvinistic scheme of salvation, I have a theological framework that is broadly covenantal, and I regard the Reformed confessions as good though clearly fallible summaries of Scripture. I can be called "progressive" for several reasons: (1) If the church is to be "always reforming" then it is no good to simply restate the veracity of your tradition in the face of exegetical and theological challenges to it, but we have to "test all things" (1 Thess 5:21) and be willing to modify our tradition if it is shown not to line up with Scripture. (2) I think that Reformed theologians in general have read Scripture while wearing a theological straight jacket and have read Paul through the lens of an *ordo salutis* (order of salvation) to the neglect of a *historia salutis* (his-

---

[1]My appreciation goes to Brian Vickers, Joe Mock, Jason Hood and Steven Coxhead for reading an earlier draft of this essay.
[2]To define my position bibliographically, I would stand somewhere between Francis Watson, *Paul, Judaism, and the Gentiles: Beyond the New Perspective,* 2nd ed. (Grand Rapids: Eerdmans, 2007); and D. A. Carson et al., eds., *Justification and Variegated Nomism,* 2 vols. (Grand Rapids: Baker, 2001-2004).

tory of salvation). (3) Much Reformed interpretation of Paul simply lacks
social realism and often glosses over the specific historical context of Paul's
letters in favor of using the Pauline corpus to forge interecclesial weapons
for theological polemics against perceived foes. That said, I think there are
some good resources in the Reformed tradition for reading Paul: the works
of Calvin and Luther are pervaded by a genuine *Paulinism;* the reformed
catch-cry *sola gratia* announces the *leitmotif* of Paul's theology; the Reformers also recognized the anthropological pessimism of Paul who sees
human creatures in desperate need of an efficacious grace; the Reformed
tradition follows Paul to the tee when it declares that God justifies the
ungodly, not the righteous; it was the Reformed tradition that gave us the
discipline of biblical theology; and the Reformed dogmatics rightly emphasizes the unity of God's plan of salvation and the continuity between
Israel and the church.

In light of this framework, I intend to expound Paul's teachings about
justification in Galatians and Romans 1–4 (due to space limitations), offer
some remarks about imputation, and comment on Paul and James concerning faith and works.[3] What I hope to show is that justification is the
act whereby God creates a new people, with a new status, in a new covenant, as part of the first installment of the new age. This occurs through
the apocalyptic revelation of God's saving righteousness in the gospel of
the crucified and risen savior. Justification, then, is Paul's contingent juridical expression of how deliverance is wrought in Jesus Christ, the Righteous One, whose atoning death and powerful resurrection avails for the
salvation of the covenant family.[4]

RIGHTEOUSNESS BY FAITH IN GALATIANS AND ROMANS
Paul and the Deliverance of God (Galatians)
Galatians is Paul's most polemical epistle, and he is responding to Jewish
Christian visitors to Galatia who are trying to either supplant or complete

---

[3]For fuller treatments of Paul and justification see Michael F. Bird, *The Saving Righteousness of God: Studies in Paul, Justification and the New Perspective*, PBM (Carlisle, U.K.: Paternoster, 2007); idem, *A Bird's-Eye View of Paul: The Man, His Mission and His Message* (Nottingham, U.K.: Inter-Varsity Press, 2008), pp. 93-98; idem, "Judgment and Justification in Paul: A Review Article," *BBR* 18 (2008): 299-313; idem, "What if Martin Luther Had Read the Dead Sea Scrolls? Historical Particularity and Theological Interpretation in Pauline Theology: Galatians as a Test Case," *JTI* 3 (2009): 107-25.
[4]Cf. Richard Hays, "Justification," *ABD* 3:1130.

his gospel by compelling Gentile Christian converts to be circumcised. I am ordinarily critical of those who refer to a "gospel of justification." Besides the fact that the phrase never appears in Scripture, it privileges justification over other equally important images like redemption, reconciliation and adoption. What is more, referring to a "gospel of justification" can also create the false impression that one is justified by believing in justification by faith whereas justification is Paul's preferred way of describing how the gospel saves Gentiles and brings them into the heritage of Israel. Even so, in Galatians when Paul defends the gospel, he does this by defending his thesis of justification by faith without works of law.

In his opening prescript, Paul refers to the Lord Jesus as "the one giving himself for our sins and in this way he delivered us from the present evil age according to the will of God our Father" (Gal 1:4).[5] Paul is using imagery that is apocalyptic and comports with similar language used by other Judean groups like those associated with the Dead Sea Scrolls. This perspective presents the world as riddled with supernatural evil, condemned, and it envisions Israel's God acting dramatically to save the elect from the power of an evil age. The language of righteousness in Galatians must be subordinated to this apocalyptic framework of God's dramatic intervention to rescue his people.

The heart of the epistle is Galatians 2:1–3:29, which contains the bulk of the materials about justification by faith. In Galatians 2:1-10 Paul recounts the Jerusalem council, which he attended with Barnabas and Titus on account of certain "false brothers" who wanted to enslave them to a message that required Gentiles to observe the law. Paul reports that during that meeting nothing was added to his message, and the legitimacy of his gospel to the uncircumcised was ratified by the pillar apostles (testified by the fact that Titus was not circumcised).

Just when Paul thought that everybody was singing off the same sheet of gospel music, Peter visited Antioch and participated in the mixed fellowship, but later when "certain men from James" arrived, Peter withdrew and separated from table fellowship with Gentiles (Gal 2:11-14). This incident is complex and requires some unpacking. As I see it, we have to appreciate what was happening in Judea in the 40s of the first century. It

---

[5]Biblical quotations in this essay are my translation.

was during this decade that Caligula attempted to have a statue of himself erected in the Jerusalem temple, there was a series of incompetent Roman governors, a swelling of brigandage and revolutionary fervor, and an increasing anti-Gentile sentiment that resulted in pressure being placed on the Jerusalem church to avoid fraternizing with Gentiles or else risk persecution (see Gal 6:12; 1 Thess 2:16). James sent a delegation to Peter informing him not to fellowship with Gentiles unless they were circumcised because it was creating hardship for believers in Jerusalem. Peter and Barnabas complied and withdrew from table fellowship. Paul, however, was livid at this hypocrisy because Peter's actions were implying that Gentile Christians were not full and equal members of the church, and yet both he and Peter had been living openly among them until recently. Paul envisions Peter trying to save his own skin by forcing Gentiles to part with a small piece of theirs!

Paul's argumentation becomes much more intense in Galatians 2:15-21, where he provides a fuller rationale for his objections against Peter, and his remarks also inform his response to the situation in Galatia. Paul states: "We who are by nature Jews and not Gentile sinners know that a person is not justified by works of law, but through the faith of Jesus Christ, and we have believed in Christ Jesus in order that we might be justified by the faith of Christ and not from works of law, because by works of law no flesh will be justified" (Gal 2:15-16). Note the following:

1. The "we" is Jewish Christians, and the notion that faith and not works of law is the instrument of justification was part of the Jewish Christian tradition from the beginning and not something that Paul invented.

2. The "works of law" simply means works that the law requires, though in some contexts the laws that distinguish Jews from Gentiles were at the forefront (e.g., monotheism, food laws, sabbath) or laws that marked "rites of entry" were in view (e.g., circumcision).

3. Although "faith of Christ" could mean the "faithfulness of Christ" or "faith in Christ," I prefer a more mediating position, namely, that it refers to entrusting oneself to God's action in Jesus Christ including, in particular, Jesus' act of self-giving obedience on the cross (see Gal 1:4; 2:19b-20).

4. While the presenting issue is the symbolic boundary of food and fel-

lowship separating Jews and Gentiles, the problem is more extensive than Gentile exclusion from the meals of the believing community. Rather, works of law are unable to justify because of a universal condition, that is, "no flesh [= no one at all] will be justified by works of law," which is also why, "if righteousness came through the law then Christ died for no reason" (Gal 2:21). Paul unreservedly propounds the singularity of the gospel to effect salvation and the complete impotence of the law to do the same.[6]

5. When discoursing on justification by faith, Paul immediately switches to participationist categories of "seeking to be justified *in* Christ," having been "crucified *with* Christ," and "Christ lives *in* me" (Gal 2:17, 19b-20). That is because justification, dying to the law and living to God are realities that one apprehends only in union with Christ.

In Galatians 2:11-21, Paul stood for the truth of the gospel when Peter's actions in Antioch implied that Gentiles could only be treated as equal members of the community provided that they first became Jews through circumcision (i.e., proselytes). Paul's response was, in effect, that one does not have to become a Jew in order to become a Christian. Paul appealed to a shared tradition among Jewish Christians that it is by faith in Christ and not through works of law that one is justified. To insist on any further requirement compromises the sole demand for "faith in Christ" and negates the central claim of the gospel that God accepts those who trust in him.

Speaking out of his own experience, Paul declared that, by seeking to be justified in Christ, Jewish Christians like himself and Peter may be found to be operating outside the sphere of the law by living among and living like Gentiles. But it does not necessarily follow that Christ is thereby promoting Jews to become lawless-Gentile-sinners. On the contrary, anyone who attempts to reerect the law either as a means of separation (from

---

[6]We have to get beyond the false dichotomy that Paul was refuting *either* legalism *or* ethnocentrism. The law was an expression of the Mosaic covenant, and Paul is saying that the law-covenant belongs to a bygone era superseded by the revelation of Christ (see Gal 3:24-25; 4:4-5). The law was bound up with a particular period of redemptive-history that cocooned God's promises around Israel and revealed what God expected of his people at that time. Yet it was never the final word, nor was it designed to be the instrument that actualized the Abrahamic promises. The scope of salvation was always meant to be wider than ethnic Israel, and thus the means of salvation (i.e., faith) was always going to be broader than the unique strictures of the Mosaic covenant.

sinners) or as a mode of righteousness (from sin), proves oneself a transgressor by rejecting the central claim of the gospel: faith in Christ and nothing else saves. In other words, attempting to rebuild the law as the basis for Christian community is to sin against the finished work of Christ because it implies that the cross was insufficient to justify and define a people. While fraternizing with Gentiles might not seem kosher, it pales into insignificance compared to the transgression of denying the work of Christ.

Thus, Paul asserted that to retreat to the law to deal with sin/sinners is to set aside God's grace manifested in the gospel. That is singularly inappropriate because Christ's death was purposed on the grounds that righteousness does not come through the law.[7] What is needed, instead, is the experience of passing from death to life. By being crucified with Christ, Paul says that he died to the law and he thereafter lives to God. Evidently Christ does not quicken believers in the law-covenant so that they can apprehend righteousness there. Rather, one must die with Christ that Christ may *live in them* and Christ may *enliven them*. The only life to be found is found in the faithfulness of the Son of God who loved Paul and gave himself up for Paul.

Paul's own experience of dying with Christ to the law is confirmed by the Galatians' experience of receiving the Spirit. They received the Spirit through the gospel as opposed to receiving it through the law in Galatians 3:1-5. The law did not impart the Spirit to them, but the Spirit was received through faith in the crucified Jesus (and the Spirit enables them to fulfil the law; see Rom 8:4; Gal 6:2). Paul's next move is to demonstrate the conformity of his gospel to the pattern of Scripture in Galatians 3:6-14. Most likely these are texts that the teachers in Galatia were themselves using. Paul cites Genesis 15:6 to show that faith and not works are the grounds for God's acceptance of Gentiles. Unlike other Jewish contemporaries, Paul does not think that Abraham had a private revelation of the law (e.g., Sir 44:19-21; *Jub.* 23.10; *2 Bar.* 57.1-2) or that God credited him righteousness based on his foreknowledge that Abraham would be willing to offer up Isaac when tested (e.g., 1 Macc 2:52). Paul gives a straightforward reading of Scripture that shows that God credited Abraham's

---

[7] Ben Witherington, *Grace in Galatia: A Commentary on Paul's Letter to the Galatians* (Grand Rapids: Eerdmans, 1998), p. 185.

faith as righteousness when he was an idolater and before he was circumcised. That is why Abraham is the prototype of Christian Gentiles and not the prototype of Gentile converts to Judaism. Those who have the same faith as Abraham are sons of Abraham and will be blessed like Abraham.

There are further appeals to Israel's Scripture in Galatians 3:10-14 with a catena of texts cited, including Deuteronomy 27:26, Habakkuk 2:4, Leviticus 18:5 and Deuteronomy 21:23. The logic of the argument can be schematized as follows:[8]

1. Deuteronomy 27:26 threatens a curse to all who do not keep the law.

2. It is evident that no one keeps the law perfectly.

3. Hence, everyone related to the law is under a curse.

4. Habakkuk 2:4 states that the righteous will live by faith.

5. Yet the law is not of faith because it requires dutiful performance of its commands.

6. Hence, no one is justified before God by the law.

7. Leviticus 18:5 promises life to those who keep the law.

8. It is evident that no one keeps the law perfectly.

9. Hence, no one receives life through the law.

Paul then asserts in Galatians 3:13 that Christ has redeemed those under the curse of the law by becoming accursed for them. This is one of the clearest affirmations in the New Testament of penal substitution as Jesus is cursed in the place of others. But please, please, please note the purpose of his cursedness given in Galatians 3:14: "So that the blessing of Abraham might come to the Gentiles in Christ Jesus, in order that we might receive the promise of the Spirit by faith." Paul places his arguments about Scripture, the inability of the law to provide justification, Abraham's call, and Jesus' atoning death within the panoramic horizon of redemptive history concerning God's plan to bring the nations into the family of Abraham when they believe like Abraham. Thus, Galatians 3:6-14 is carefully bracketed with references to the Abrahamic promise. When the Scripture

---

[8]Cf. A. Andrew Das, *Paul, the Law, and the Covenant* (Peabody, Mass.: Hendrickson, 2001), pp. 145-46.

announced the gospel in advance to Abraham, it was with the words "in you all the nations will be blessed" (Gal 3:8), and at the end of this section the Abrahamic promise comes to the Gentiles in Christ Jesus (Gal 3:14). So when you think gospel, think Abrahamic promises. The gospel is about the reception of the Abrahamic promises among Gentiles in the age of deliverance. That means that justification by faith is not the gospel per se, rather, it is the mechanism that describes how the Gentiles can partake of those Abrahamic promises. It is by faith in Christ that Gentiles receive the Holy Spirit and enter into communion with God because their faith in the person and work of Christ puts them in a right relationship with God.

The succeeding argument in Galatians 3:15-29 focuses on how the Abrahamic and Mosaic covenants relate to God's promises. Paul maintains the following: (1) The promises given to Abraham are focused on Jesus Christ as the promised "seed," and the giving of the law 430 years later did not abolish the earlier promises. (2) The law was given to deal with transgression (through the sacrificial system) until the promised seed, that is, Jesus Christ, came. (3) The law is not opposed to the promise, yet the law is limited in the sense that it can bring the conviction of sin but it cannot impart life; only God can do that. (4) The law was a temporary custodian leading people until Christ and leading them to Christ. And (5) the law temporarily cocooned God's promises around Israel until the era of faith was revealed when persons could then be justified by faith in Christ, and so bring fulfillment to the Abrahamic promises. The discussion then ends with Paul's remarks that those promises are now made good through the Gentiles' faith in Christ Jesus. The covenant sign of baptism signifies that they are clothed with Christ, and in Christ the distinctions that the law made between persons have been done away with. That is because it was always God's plan to have one people, not two peoples comprised of Jew and Gentile nor a Jewish class and a Greek/Barbarian subclass, but one people worshipping together in fellowship before their God. The implication is that you are not any closer to the throne of God through circumcision, but by being in Christ believers are part of Abraham's seed and therefore heirs of the promise.

The only other section of Galatians that mentions justification is Galatians 5:2-6. There Paul admonishes his readers that if they seek to be justified by law they will be cut off from Christ and fall from grace. The intruding teachers are forcing them to make a choice between circumcision and Christ or between law and grace. Their choice should be informed by the belief that it is in the Spirit and by faith that believers await the hope of righteousness. Here "righteousness" is not ethical, but refers to the future status of God's people when the verdict of righteousness declared in the present will be fully meted out at the Day of Judgment. Paul can make this statement because circumcision has ceased to have any value for those in Christ since it has been eclipsed by the inauguration of the new creation and by the empowering of faith to produce loving behavior.

In sum, Paul critiques the instruction of the intruders in Galatia through several counterarguments: (1) Paul contests their implicit claim that Christ is merely an add-on to the law. Rather, God sent Christ at the moment of fulfillment to redeem persons from the law and to adopt them into God's family. (2) Paul asserts that the law is not the solution to the problem of sin, but part of the very problem. At the heart of Galatians is the question of what is the problem with humanity that Israel's covenant and its law cannot remedy.[9] The law brings condemnation not justification; it results in curses not blessings; it was temporary not terminal; it was a guide to grace but not the grounds of grace; and it excludes Gentiles rather than includes them. (3) Paul contests the intruders' reading of the Abrahamic story to the effect that Abraham was circumcised and, therefore, so should the Galatians be if they want to be righteous. Instead, Paul claims that Abraham was righteous by faith wholly apart from circumcision. And (4) whereas the teachers see Israel as the locus of God's salvation, hence the necessity of initiation into Israel via *circumcision*, Paul advocates that the church comprising Jews, and Gentiles united in Israel's Messiah is the "Israel of God," hence the necessity of *new creation* for experiencing it.

In a nutshell, we could say that in Galatians the "gospel of justification by faith" is an enumeration of the "gospel of the promise" given to Abraham.

Paul and the Righteousness of God (Romans)

Romans is the literary summit of the Pauline letters. It is theologically intense, socially complex and pastorally rich. The epistle was written from

---

[9]Bruce Longenecker, *The Triumph of Abraham's God: The Transformation of Identity in Galatians* (Nashville: Abingdon, 1998), pp. 120-21.

Corinth in the mid-50s and sent to the church for three primary reasons: (1) Paul prepares to go to Jerusalem and wants to depart knowing that all the Gentile churches are behind him. This letter is also a dress rehearsal of his defense speech when he delivers the collection in Jerusalem. (2) The serenity of Corinth probably afforded Paul some opportunity to reflect on the gospel in light of all the controversies that he had faced (e.g., Antioch, Galatia, Corinth), and Romans functions as a distillation of his thought. (3) He intends to go on to Spain for further missionary work in the far west and solicits the support of the Romans as he goes westward. In order to garner this support Paul has two implied tasks: he must (a) defend himself against rumors that he is anti-law and anti-Israel, and (b) provide some pastoral theology to a cluster of congregations that could potentially fragment along ethnic lines or around contentious beliefs about the law if their bonds of affection are not renewed. Paul writes to the Gentile Christians in Rome (knowing full well that Jewish Christians will probably read it too) in order to gain their support for his gospel mission, and he does that by laying out the panoramic theological vision of his gospel including its content and corollaries.

The central thesis of the letter is set forth in Romans 1:16-17. There Paul states: "I am not ashamed of the gospel, for it is the power of God for the salvation of everyone who believes, first for the Jew then for the Greek. For in it the righteousness of God is revealed from faith to faith, just as it is written, 'The just will live by faith.'" Debate has focused on whether the "righteousness of God" is an objective entity (i.e., a righteousness *from God*) or a subjective entity (i.e., a righteousness that belongs *to God*). I prefer the subjective view for several reasons: (1) It makes sense of the context as Romans 1–3 is pervaded by statements about qualities and activities of God denoted by reference to God's "power" (Rom 1:16), "wrath" (Rom 1:18; 3:5), "judgment" (Rom 2:2-3, 5), "goodness" (Rom 2:4), "truthfulness" (Rom 3:7) and "faithfulness" (Rom 3:3). (2) There are multiple instances in the Old Testament where "righteousness" and "salvation" are effectively synonymous (e.g., Ps 51:14; 71:15-16; Is 46:13; 56:1), and usage here is also analogous to instances where God's righteousness is his mighty actions of deliverance (e.g., Judg 5:11; 1 Sam 12:7). In other words, the "righteousness of God" signifies the uprightness of God's character and how he demonstrates his character as the judge of all the earth and in his faithfulness toward Israel in Jesus Christ. The righteousness of God then is the character of God embodied and enacted in his saving actions, which means vindication for his people and condemnation for the wicked.

It is important to point out what the "righteousness of God" is not. It is *not* the gospel, but is something that is revealed in the gospel. We are back to that apocalyptic framework once more. The dramatic revelation of God's salvation that reaches into the whole world through Israel is unleashed in the good news that the risen Jesus is Lord and Messiah. As Arland Hultgren writes:

> When Paul speaks of the righteousness of God in this instance, and says that it is revealed in the gospel, he does not speak primarily of a righteousness that is imputed to believers. He is speaking of a righteousness revealed in the gospel of God's Son, the saving message of how God has sent his Son for the salvation of sinful humanity. God's righteousness is God's saving activity which is spoken of in the Scriptures of Israel and promises with the coming of the Messiah or the messianic age.[10]

Also, the "righteousness of God" is *not* justification by faith. There is indeed a gift of a righteous status from God (see Rom 5:17; Phil 3:9), but the righteousness of God introduces the entire package of salvation in all of Romans (not just Romans 1–4) including justification, redemption, sacrifice, forgiveness of sins, covenant membership, reconciliation, the gift of the Holy Spirit, power for a new obedience, union with Christ, freedom from sin and eschatological vindication. In the words of James Dunn, "The 'righteousness of God' is nowhere conceived as a single, once-for-all action of God, but as his accepting, sustaining, and finally vindicating grace."[11]

Finally, the righteousness of God is *not* reducible to God's covenant faithfulness. We should acknowledge the link between God's righteousness and faithfulness in the Old Testament (e.g., Deut 7:9; 32:4; Ps 25:10; 26:3; 40:10-11; 89:28, 49; 111:5-10; 143:1; Zech 8:8), yet also observe Mark Seifrid's dictum that all covenant-keeping behavior is righteous, but not all righteousness is covenant keeping.[12] God's righteousness fulfills his

---

[10]Arland J. Hultgren, *Paul's Gospel and Mission* (Philadelphia: Fortress, 1983), p. 31.

[11]James D. G. Dunn, *Romans 1–8* (Dallas: Word, 1988), p. 97; idem, *The Theology of Paul the Apostle* (Grand Rapids: Eerdmans, 1998), p. 386.

[12]Mark A. Seifrid, "Righteousness Language in the Hebrew Scriptures and Early Judaism," in

covenantal promises to Israel and Abraham, but it is also *creational* in that God intends to establish his just reign over all of creation and finally repossess the world for himself (see Ps 98).

In Romans 1:18-32 Paul establishes that the Gentiles in their idolatry and immorality stand condemned under the wrath of God. He then switches in Romans 2:1–3:20 to provocatively establish that the same is true of the Jews. They are equally condemned by God because mere *possession* of the covenant and the law will not acquit them on the final day; that is because what counts is *performance.* In this section Paul is walking a tightrope by simultaneously affirming both God's faithfulness to Israel and the impartiality of God's judgments over Jews and Greeks. Paul shames his imaginary Jewish interlocutor by affirming that when the just desserts are handed out by God without any favoritism, some Greeks might be in a better position than the covenant people.

The statement in Romans 2:13 that the "doers of the law will be justified" has been handled very differently by commentators. This can't mean that salvation is by works since in Romans 3:20 Paul says plain and simple that by works of law no flesh will be justified. But Romans 2:13 can't be a mere hypothetical statement either since Paul doesn't phrase his argument with an "if . . . then" construction or use a rhetorical qualification like "I am using a human argument," as he says elsewhere to signify a "for sake of argument" (see Rom 3:5; 6:19; Gal 3:15). And if the condemnation for the wicked is real, so too the justification for the doers of the law must equally be real. My hunch is that we should read Romans 2:13 in light of Romans 2:14-16, 25-27 about Christian Gentiles who genuinely do the law out of their faith. In line with a great many commentators, I think that the Gentiles described here are not noble pagans or pious God-fearers, but are Christian Gentiles who genuinely do the law through their Spirit-driven behavior (see Rom 3:31; 7:6; 8:4-9; 10:4-11; 13:8; Gal 6:2).[13] That is particularly clear in Romans 2:26, which reads, "If those who are not circumcised keep the law's requirements, will they not be regarded as *[logisthēsetai]* though they were circumcised?" Despite never-ending debates about

---

Justification and Variegated Nomism, vol. 1: *The Complexities of Second-Temple Judaism,* ed. D. A. Carson, Mark A. Seifrid and Peter T. O'Brien (Grand Rapids: Baker, 2001), p. 424.

[13]Cf. N. T. Wright, "Law in Romans 2," in *Paul and the Mosaic Law,* ed. J. D. G. Dunn (Tübingen: Mohr/Siebeck, 1996), p. 136.

imputation, many folks have failed to notice that the first thing imputed to Gentiles in Romans is covenant membership in the people of God!

In Romans 3:21-31 we observe perhaps the most profound description of the salvation of God in Jesus Christ. This salvation has several features: (1) It is both continuous and discontinuous with the dispensation of the law (Rom 3:21). (2) Salvation comes through faith in Christ to all without distinction (Rom 3:22). (3) It is needed because all have sinned and lack God's glory (Rom 3:23). (4) Salvation comes through being declared righteous, by redemption and sacrifice in Christ Jesus (Rom 3:24-25). And (5) this decisively demonstrates that God does not let sin go unpunished while also providing a means of deliverance for all who believe—in other words, God is just and the justifier of those who have faith in Jesus Christ (Rom 3:26). Consequently, all boasting, in either ethnicity or in effort, is excluded (Rom 3:27). Note in particular the alternatives that Paul poses. Is a person justified by faith without works of law? *Or* is God the God of the Jews only (Rom 3:28-29)? That means that justification by faith excludes anything that we might call legalism and anything that is ethnocentric. This is because the law is the Jewish law. It is the law that defines the identity and ethos of Israel. To insist on the law for justification is to engage in both a performance-based means of salvation, but also an equally ethnocentric one. That is why Paul emphasizes that God justifies both the circumcised and the uncircumcised by faith and this upholds the law rather than abolishes it (Rom 3:30-31).

In Romans 4, Paul roots his discussion in the Abraham story as the definitive example of how God brings salvation to Jew and Gentile. The issue is both the means of justification and its scope, as Tom Schreiner writes: "Paul is interested in the inclusion of Gentiles and the basis of their inclusion."[14] Paul's appeal to Abraham in Romans 4:1-8 is illustrative of what he has just said in Romans 3:21-31, that God justifies persons without the law. Paul insists that Abraham, the pagan from Haran, had no works to boast about before God when he was justified. In Romans 4:4-5, Paul lucidly states that Abraham's faith was credited as righteousness without law obedience and given by sheer grace. This is a clear rejection of a work-for-reward view of salvation, as one can imagine, but is also a pen-

---

[14]Thomas R. Schreiner, *Romans,* BECNT (Grand Rapids: Baker, 1998), p. 228.

etrating riposte at those who contend that salvation is tied to Israel's law to the exclusion of Gentiles.

In Romans 4:9-17, Paul picks up the theme of Romans 3:29-30 that righteousness by faith applies equally to Jew and Gentile. Abraham's faith was credited as righteousness *prior* to his circumcision. That is a minor chronological point, but a whole gambit of Paul's theology rides on it. Circumcision was the sign of the promise that was received by faith; circumcision did not establish the promise or mark out who inherits the Abrahamic promises.[15] In this way Abraham became the father of all who believe so that their faith, be they Jew or Gentile, could also be credited as righteousness. Note the mini-climax in Romans 4:13, "For the promise to Abraham and his offspring that he would be heir of the world did not come through the law but through the righteousness of faith." That phrase "righteousness of faith" *(dikaiosynēs pisteōs)* is tantamount to a righteousness gained by means of faith. You cannot then use the law to shut down the promises made to Abraham that were tied to his faith. This justifying faith is directed at the life-giving power of God who raised Jesus from the dead (see Rom 1:4; 4:17, 24; 10:9-10). That is why Paul concludes with the statement that Jesus was handed over to atone for our sins, and raised for our justification (Rom 4:25). Through the redemptive work of the Suffering Servant, God's promises to Abraham were confirmed, and the gospel creates a redeemed and racially diverse people worthy of the name "the children of Abraham."

So much more could be said about justification in Romans (e.g., Rom 6:7; 8:1-32; 9:30–10:12). All I will add is that in Romans we see a clear picture emerging: (1) The righteousness of God bursts into the world through the gospel about the Lord Jesus. This righteousness rectifies idol-worshipping pagans and even Jews overly confident in their status as law-keeping members of Israel. (2) There is no difference *(diastolē)* between Jews and Greeks in condemnation on account of their sins, nor any difference in justification as both are justified by faith in Christ (Rom 3:22; 10:12). (3) Justification is a manifestation of God's gracious gift in putting all believers in a right relationship with himself through faith in Christ

---

[15]The discussion of Romans 4 by Peter T. O'Brien ("Was Paul Converted?" in *Justification and Variegated Nomism*, vol. 2: *The Paradoxes of Paul*, ed. D. A. Carson, Mark A. Seifrid and Peter T. O'Brien [Grand Rapids: Baker, 2004], pp. 376-88) is particularly helpful here.

(Rom 3:24). (4) Justification is indelibly tied to the Abrahamic promises of bringing Gentiles into the family of Abraham, and yet the same promise remains extended to Israel even if they remain in unbelief (Rom 3:30; 4:9; 11:26). (5) Justification is rooted in God's eschatological purposes for the elect (Rom 8:29-30) and secured by the continuing priestly ministry of Jesus Christ (Rom 8:31-34).

IMPUTATION

The standard Reformed view is that Jesus' law obedience is imputed to believers as the grounds of their righteousness. Thus, justification consists of the forgiveness of sins which clears the slate so to speak, while the imputation of Jesus' obedience to the law makes them positively righteous. While this view has "merit," it presses legitimate biblical ideas into an illegitimate framework; it misinterprets some of the language; it is still trapped in medieval categories of merit; and it doesn't adequately grasp the implications of union with Christ.

First, Jesus' obedience matters immensely and without it no one can be saved. But that is not because Jesus was racking up frequent flyer points that could be transferred into our account. Jesus' obedience and faithfulness in his vocation as Son enabled him to execute his role as the second Adam and as the new Israel. Jesus was obedient where Adam and Israel failed to be. Jesus' obedience qualified him to be the sacrifice who could redeem Israel and humanity in their alienation from God. Hence the New Testament emphasizes his *passive* obedience, that is, his obedience to death on the cross (see Rom 5:19; Phil 2:8; Heb 5:8-9).[16]

Second, the language in Romans 4 does not establish the Reformed understanding of imputation. Below I have inserted most of Romans 4 from the ESV. Note in italics the subject and object of what is "counted."

- For what does the Scripture say? "Abraham *believed* God, and *it* was *counted* to him *as righteousness*" (Rom 4:3).

- Now to the one who works, his *wages* are *not counted* as a gift but as his due (Rom 4:4).

- And to the one who does not work but believes in him who justifies the

---

[16]WCF 11.1 deliberately omits reference to the "active" obedience of Jesus Christ. See discussion in J. R. Daniel Kirk, "The Sufficiency of the Cross," *SBET* 24 (2006): 35-39.

ungodly, his *faith* is *counted* as *righteousness* (Rom 4:5).

- Just as David also speaks of the blessing of the one to whom *God counts righteousness* apart from works (Rom 4:6).

- Blessed are those whose lawless deeds are forgiven, and whose sins are covered; blessed is the man against whom the *Lord will not count* his sin (Rom 4:7-8).

- Is this blessing then only for the circumcised, or also for the uncircumcised? We say that *faith* was *counted* to Abraham as *righteousness* (Rom 4:9).

- How then was it counted to him? Was it before or after he had been circumcised? It was not after, but before he was circumcised. He received the sign of circumcision as a seal of the righteousness that he had by faith while he was still uncircumcised. The purpose was to make him the father of all who believe without being circumcised, so that *righteousness* would be *counted* to them as well (Rom 4:10-11).

- That is why his *faith* was "*counted* to him as *righteousness*." But the words "*it* was *counted* to him" were not written for his sake alone, but for ours also. *It* [faith] will be *counted* to us who believe in him who raised from the dead Jesus our Lord (Rom 4:22-24).

There are four types of "counting" statements here:

1. To the one who works his wages are not counted as a gift, but as a reward (Rom 4:4).

2. There is also a non-counting of sins, which is the flip side of forgiveness (Rom 4:7-8).

3. Very prominent is that "faith is counted as righteousness" (Rom 4:3, 5, 9, 22, 24).

4. And "righteousness is counted" to those who believe (Rom 4:6; 11).

So what is it that is actually counted to believers? Is it (3) "faith" or (4) "righteousness"?[17] As we begin, let us heed the warning of D. A. Carson:

---

[17]There is diversity in the Protestant tradition concerning this "counting, crediting, imputing" since the Augsburg Confession (art. iv) refers to the imputation of faith, while the Westminster Confession (art. xi.1) explicitly denies the imputation of faith or evangelical obedience.

"the structure of the crediting or imputing language is not consistent through these verses, so it becomes easy to force the wrong kind of parallelism and miss the train of thought."[18]

Some might want to say that "faith counted for righteousness" means that "faith is the means by which an external righteousness is counted to us."[19] That would be a very convenient solution if it were not for the unfortunate problem that the text just simply does not say that. There is no external source of righteousness identified. What is more, righteousness here is not a property to be transferred, but a status to be conferred. Others suppose that God counted the faith within Abraham to be the equivalent of righteousness.[20] That is admittedly the straightforward reading of the text, but that makes "faith" some kind of moral quality that can stand in lieu of righteous deeds. The wages/work metaphor in Romans 4:4-5 cancels out the idea that God rewarded Abraham's faith by regarding it as a form of righteousness.[21]

My solution is that in Romans 4 Paul is providing an intertextual argument to show how his gospel lines up with Scripture. What he is doing is using the language of Genesis 15:6 to demonstrate the truth of Romans 3:21-31, that God justifies Jews and Gentiles by faith. Let us start with the meaning of "count righteousness":

| For we hold that one | is *justified* by faith | *apart from works* of the law. (Rom 3:28) |
| God | *counts righteousness* | *apart from works*. (Rom 4:6) |

The major difference here is that Paul swaps "justified" in Romans 3:28 for "counts righteousness" in Romans 4:6. Thus, when Paul reports that "God counts righteousness," all he is saying is that "God justifies." Yet Paul never once relates this "righteousness" to the "righteousness of

---

[18]D. A. Carson, "The Vindication of Imputation: On Fields of Discourse and Semantic Fields," in *Justification: What's at Stake in the Current Debates*, ed. Mark Husbands and Daniel J. Treier (Downers Grove, Ill.: InterVarsity Press, 2004), p. 60.

[19]Cf. e.g., John Piper, *Counted Righteous in Christ: Should We Abandon the Imputation of Christ's Righteousness?* (Wheaton, Ill.: Crossway, 2002), pp. 58-63.

[20]Cf. John Ziesler, *The Meaning of Righteousness in Paul: A Linguistic and Theological Enquiry* (Cambridge: Cambridge University Press, 1972), pp. 181-85; Robert Jewett, *Romans*, Hermeneia (Minneapolis: Fortress, 2007), pp. 310-12.

[21]Cf. Philo (*Abraham* 273), "God marveling at Abraham's faith in him repaid him with faithfulness by confirming . . . the gifts which he had promised."

Christ." So he is not providing details about the transfer of a substance or a property from one person to another. Paul is employing the language of Genesis 15:6 to show that God justifies people entirely apart from works of law. Now, coming to "faith counted as righteousness," this means that God only requires faith, and not works, for himself to be in a right covenantal relationship with a human subject. That establishes Paul's next point: Gentiles are justified like Abraham was, by faith, not through performing the works of law. The path to adoption into the Abrahamic family does not run through the Mosaic law and so restrict its recipients to circumcised Jews.

Third, several texts come very close to espousing a theology of imputation, but just fall gloriously short.[22] A classic text is Romans 5:17-19, which is aptly summarized by Piper: "Adam acted sinfully, and because we are connected to him, we are condemned in him. Christ acted righteously, and because we are connected to Christ, we are justified in Christ. Adam's sin is counted as ours. Christ's 'act of righteousness' is counted as ours."[23] But I want to add, first, that "connected" does not necessarily mean "counted." I grant the representative and constitutive force that Adam and Christ exert upon the people identified with them. But the phrase "many will be made righteous" *(dikaioi katastathēsontai hoi polloi)* is not synonymous with "counted righteous" *(logizetai dikaiosynēn),* and the righteousness to which Romans 5:19 refers to is a transformative righteousness (an actual "becoming" righteous) in addition to a forensic righteousness (hence the contrast of condemnation and justification in Rom 5:18).[24]

In addition, Jesus' "one act of righteousness" is probably his obedience in death, not his whole life of obedience.[25] In 1 Corinthians 1:30, Paul says "And because of him [God] you are in Christ Jesus, who became to us wisdom from God, righteousness and sanctification and redemption." Note that these things listed are "from God" and are alien to believers, and yet they are given to believers by sheer grace. The "righteousness" here, while it could be transformative, is most likely a righteous status. But there is no need to infer that righteousness is imputed any more than the holi-

---

[22]Cf. Bird, *Saving Righteousness,* pp. 80-85.
[23]Piper, *Counted Righteous in Christ,* p. 107.
[24]Cf. Schreiner, *Romans,* p. 288.
[25]Cf. Dunn, *Romans 1–8,* p. 238.

ness, redemption and wisdom are imputed. What is said in 1 Corinthians 1:30 is that we receive "righteousness" by being "in Christ Jesus," and the specific means is left undefined. In Philippians 3:7-9 Paul passionately writes: "For his sake I have suffered the loss of all things, and I regard them as human filth, in order that I may gain Messiah and be found in him, not having a righteousness of my own that comes from the law, but one that comes through the faithfulness of the Messiah, the righteousness from God based upon faith." There is clearly a righteousness from God that is given to believers. But we cannot assume that this righteousness is imputed from God any more than we can think that righteousness is imputed from the law. More likely, it is the faithfulness of the Messiah[26] that enables believers to apprehend this righteousness when by faith they trust in him and they are thereby placed *in him*.

Finally, 2 Corinthians 5:21 states: "For our sake he [God] made him [Christ] to be sin who knew no sin, so that in him we might become the righteousness of God." This passage teaches that Christ's participation in human sin enables humans to participate in the righteousness of God through union with Christ. The word *ginomai* ("become") is not a synonym for *logizomai* ("count"). So Paul does not say that "God imputed our sin to the sinless one, and imputed God's righteousness to us." We can say what the text says, no more and no less: Christ was made sin probably in the sense of carrying, bearing and taking sins upon himself, and those who are in Christ share in the "righteousness of God."

When we bundle up these several passages into one heap this is what we get: (a) There is no reference to the righteousness of Christ in any of these passages. (b) Righteousness is not the merits that Jesus accrued in his life of law-keeping, but a quality related to God's character and gift in salvation. (c) The consistent point is that *by faith* and *in Christ* we experience the status of "righteous." This might sound awfully pedantic, but gosh darn it, exegesis should be!

Fourth, let me drop a brick on you that might blow your world apart. God justified Jesus![27] God's verdict against Jesus at the cross is turned into

---

[26]On translating *pistis Christou* this way, see Paul Foster, "Πιστίς Χριστοῦ Terminology in Philippians and Ephesians," in *The Faith of Jesus Christ: Exegetical, Biblical, and Theological Studies*, ed. M. F. Bird and P. M. Sprinkle (Peabody, Mass.: Hendrickson, 2009), pp. 93-100.

[27]See Richard Gaffin, *The Centrality of the Resurrection: A Study in Paul's Soteriology* (Grand Rapids: Baker, 1978), pp. 119-22; Morna D. Hooker, "Raised for Our Acquittal (Rom 4:25),"

his vindication of his Son at the empty tomb. Rome declared Jesus a messianic pretender, but by resurrection God declared him the Son of God (Rom 1:4). In 1 Timothy we read that Jesus was "justified" by the Spirit (1 Tim 3:16), the Spirit that raised him from the dead (Rom 8:11). That is why the forgiveness of sins (1 Cor 15:17) and justification (Rom 4:25) are bound up with the resurrection of Jesus and not only the cross of Jesus (see Rom 3:24-25; 5:9). Viewed this way, union with Christ means that we die to sin and law because we died with Christ. But we are then united to Christ in his resurrection, so that we thereby participate in his justification. Believers are justified because and only because they participate in the justification of the Messiah. The verdict that God the Father executes upon the Son is shared by those who are united to the risen Jesus. They share in the verdict and, I would add, the basis for the verdict, Jesus' obedience to his messianic task of redemptive suffering. So Jesus' obedience does become ours—but not through artificially dividing Jesus' obedience into active and passive varieties,[28] not through a medieval concept of "merit" that is imputed instead of imparted, not because Jesus is the exemplary pelagian who earns salvation when we cannot, not by fulfilling a covenant of works that did not contain grace, not by way of righteousness molecules floating through the air to us—rather, we become "righteous" in Christ when by faith we participate in the vicarious death and resurrection of Jesus Christ. In that sense, an imputation of Jesus' obedience is legitimate, but not within the framework of *most* Reformed theologies that focus on Jesus' law-keeping and a somewhat wooden reliance on an accounting metaphor.[29] Rather than imputation, a better description of the biblical

---

in *Resurrection in the New Testament*, ed. R. Bieringer, V. Koperski and B. Lataire (Leuven: Leuven University Press, 200), pp. 339-40; Mark Seifrid, *Christ, Our Righteousness: Paul's Theology of Justification*, NSBT (Downers Grove, Ill.: InterVarsity Press, 2000), pp. 47, 77, 90-91; Bird, *Saving Righteousness of God*, pp. 40-59; Daniel Kirk, *Unlocking Romans: Resurrection and the Justification of God* (Grand Rapids: Eerdmans, 2008), pp. 78-79; N. T. Wright, *The Resurrection of the Son of God*, COQG 3 (London: SPCK, 2003), pp. 248, 270-71; but note the objections of I. Howard Marshall, *Aspects of the Atonement: Cross and Resurrection in the Reconciling of God and Humanity* (London: Paternoster, 2007), pp. 89-91.

[28]On this point see Carson ("Vindication of Imputation," p. 55) on how the active/passive distinction goes beyond the New Testament and introduces an absolute bifurcation not found in the text.

[29]John Calvin's theology made union with Christ central and is analogous with the paradigm that I am setting forth here. See Craig B. Carpenter, "A Question of Union with Christ? Calvin and Trent on Justification," *WTJ* 64 (2002): 363-86; J. Todd Billings, *Calvin, Participation, and the Gift: The Activity of Believers in Union with Christ* (Oxford: Oxford University

materials is *participation in and incorporation into* the obedience and vindi-cation of Jesus in his death and resurrection.

Where does all of this leave us with imputation then? N. T. Wright goes so far as to say that union with Christ effectively does the job nor-mally attributed to imputation. He writes:

> Paul's doctrine of what is true of those who are in the Messiah does the job, within his scheme of thought, that the traditional Protestant emphasis on the imputation of Christ's righteousness did within that scheme. In other words, that which imputed righteousness was trying to insist upon is, I think, fully taken care of in (for instance) Romans 6, where Paul declares that what is true of the Messiah is true of all his people. Jesus was vindi-cated by God as Messiah after his penal death; I am in Messiah; therefore, I too, have died and been raised. . . . He sees us within the *vindication* of Christ, that is, as having died and risen again with him.[30]

I accept Wright's sketch, but I do think we are still left with the ques-tion, what does union *actually do* that makes us "righteous" before God? This is where a concept like imputation is a necessary *implicate* of the bib-lical materials. If we take all the bits and bobs together, including this language of "counting" from Romans 4, the gift of righteousness in Ro-mans 5:17 and Philippians 3:9, the representative natures of Adam and Christ as federal heads, the forensic nature of *dikaioō* and *dikaiosyne* in several passages (e.g., Rom 3:21-26; 10:10; Gal 2:15-21; 5:4-5), and the indebtedness of salvation to Jesus' faithfulness and obedience in his task as Son, then, something like "imputation" sounds like a logical necessity of describing the application of salvation for those who are "in Christ."[31] But

---

Press, 2007); Mark Garcia, *Life in Christ: Union with Christ and Twofold Grace in Calvin's Theology* (Milton Keynes, U.K.: Paternoster, 2008).

[30]N. T. Wright, "New Perspectives on Paul," in *Justification in Perspective: Historical Develop-ments and Contemporary Challenges,* ed. Bruce L. McCormack (Grand Rapids: Baker, 2006), pp. 260-61. See similarly Don Garlington, "Imputation or Union with Christ? A Response to John Piper," *R&R* 12 (2003): 45-113.

[31]Cf. Bird, *Bird's-Eye View of Paul,* 96-98. See similar Brian Vickers (*Jesus' Blood and Right-eousness: Paul's Theology of Imputation* [Wheaton, Ill.: Crossway, 2006]), who repeatedly sees imputation as resulting from a "synthesis" of Pauline materials. Leon Morris (*The Apostolic Preaching of the Cross,* 3rd ed. [Grand Rapids: Eerdmans, 1984], p. 282) regarded imputation as a "corollary" of the identification of the believers with Jesus. Carson ("Vindication," pp. 72-73) comments: "justification is, in Paul, irrefragably tied to our incorporation into Christ, to our union with Christ . . . imputation is crucial, but it is itself grounded in something more comprehensive."

we have got to be careful. There are different ways of connecting the dots and drawing conclusions about the logic of justification.

The essential element of justification is its forensic nature (i.e., it refers to our divinely declared status and not to our moral state of justness), rather than a precise formulation of the mechanism that explains how justification works. For similar reasons Simon Gathercole suggests that perhaps imputation should not feature in evangelical statements of faith.[32] In any case, the Reformers were correct about an alien and forensic righteousness conferred on believers by faith and the importance of Jesus' obedience for salvation. But where Protestant scholasticism has gone wrong is through an insistence on an active obedience that is needed because forgiveness only clears the slate. It erred in making the accounting metaphor of "credit" the controlling theme in justification. There was often a glossing over Paul's "in Christ" language of justification for a model that looks like an abstract transaction of righteousness[33] and myopically focusing on the sequence of events in personal salvation *(ordo salutis)* without integrating it into the overarching story of salvation history where God brings Jews and Gentiles into the family of the Messiah *(historia salutis)*.[34] Instead, if we locate Paul within a worldview that is properly apocalyptic, then we see how for Paul the event of the gospel is an invasive story that violently intrudes upon the tyrannical despots of evil, sin, and death when the gift of faith brings human subjects to participate in the faithfulness, death and resurrection of the Lord Jesus.

PAUL AND JAMES ON JUSTIFICATION BY WORKS

The purported contradiction between Paul and James on the subject of faith and works is well known. A cursory comparison of Galatians 2:15-21/Romans 3:21–4:25 and James 2:14-26 can leave us scratching our heads

---

[32]Simon Gathercole, "The Doctrine of Justification in Paul and Beyond," in *Justification in Perspective: Historical Developments and Contemporary Challenges,* ed. Bruce L. McCormack (Grand Rapids: Baker, 2006), p. 223.

[33]This is the heart of Seifrid's objection to traditional formulations of justification (*Christ, Our Righteousness,* pp. 171-77). Note Vickers's remark: "Finally it is clear that being righteous before God is intrinsically related to union with Christ. In these texts it is primarily a representative union, with the believer being incorporated into Christ and identified as such by God and so partaking of all Christ's benefits" (*Jesus' Blood,* p. 195).

[34]For an attempt to integrate justification into an *ordo salutis* and a *historia salutis*, see Michael S. Horton, *Covenant and Salvation: Union with Christ* (Louisville: Westminster John Knox, 2007), p. 108.

as to whether or not these views are reconcilable. After all, the only place where the words "faith alone" occurs in the New Testament is in James 2:24, where James explicitly denies that "faith alone" justifies. Moreover, James also cites Genesis 15:6 as Paul does, but to the effect that works actually do matter for acquiring righteousness as it did for Abraham who willingly offered up his son Isaac as a sacrifice. But the purported contradiction between Paul and James disappears if we dig below the surface (and if we perhaps stop reading James through the lens of Paul). Although Paul and James use the same words (faith, works, righteousness), they do not use them in the same sense. See the table below:

	Paul	**James**
Faith	Entrusting oneself to God's act in Jesus Christ for salvation	Assent to certain propositions
Works	Deeds that force Gentiles to become proselytes to Judaism	Expressions of faith in action

When James denies that faith alone justifies, he is talking about faith as mere assent. Simply assenting or acknowledging certain facts to be true is insufficient of itself for justification. Likewise, when Paul talks about faith he means entrusting oneself to God who has acted in Jesus Christ to bring salvation to Jews and Gentiles. Paul's notion of faith involves *passively* trusting and relying on God, yet it *actively* entails a radical transformation of the self and is closely associated with obedience, faithfulness and love. In other words, for Paul, the only justifying faith is that which is characterized by the fruit of righteousness and expressed in deeds of love. It is notable that James and Paul both know of faith as something created by the "word," be that the "implanted word" (Jas 1:21) or the "word of Christ" (Rom 10:17). Again, when James urges the need for works, he is not talking about acts that accrue merit before God. He is talking about loving demonstrations of faith-in-action. That is the very same thing we find Paul talking about in Galatians 5–6 and Romans 7–8. Paul's rejection of "works" and "works of law" is premised on the view that obedience to the precepts of the law is not the basis upon which one will be acquitted at the final judgment, and for Gentiles that meant specifically not having to become proselytes to Judaism. Yet Paul clearly leaves room for the positive role of works in the life of believers (e.g., Gal 6:10; Eph 2:10). In sum, I have no doubt that James and Paul would affirm the words of Calvin: "We are not saved by works, but neither are we saved without them."[35] Or, to put it differently, good works demonstrate the integrity of the faith that we profess.

Let me offer a few final remarks about justification, judgment and works.[36] I confess that I am acutely uncomfortable with how N. T. Wright has sometimes worded justification as God's verdict rendered "on the basis of a life lived" since that would appear to make justification dependent upon performance. I understand why Wright said that; I recognize the cogency of how he got there: he's trying to take certain texts like Romans 2:13 (which often get swept under the carpet) seriously, but his wording is misguided. The basis upon which believers are justified is faith (Phil 3:9). Paul also knows of a distinction between believing and working when it comes to the basis of being put right with God (e.g., Rom 4:4-5; Gal 3:1-5). Nonetheless, justification according to works is entirely biblical (e.g., Rom 14:10; 2 Cor 5:10), and the question is, how do righteousness by faith and judgment according to works relate to each other? The solution I think is to closely observe the prepositions that Paul uses. Paul consistently employs *dia* ("through") and *ek* ("by/from") to indicate that faith is the instrument by which believers are justified (Rom 3:22, 25; 5:1; Gal 2:16). But he uses *kata* ("according to") when it comes to the role of works at the final judgment (Rom 2:6; 2 Cor 11:15). The works, faithfulness, obedience and life of the believer must accord with God's verdict at the final judgment. Thus, justification is on the basis of faith, while judgment is congruent with the life of obedience. That means that we are not justified by mere *assent* nor judged by a criterion of *synergism*.

The basis for our being right with God is faith in Christ Jesus who was handed over for our sins and raised for our justification. Yet we must integrate into that picture the new covenant reality of the indwelling of the Spirit, the organic unity of faith-faithfulness-obedience, the transforming power of union with Christ, and God's continuing work in the life of the confessing community. If so, then the Protestant paranoia against reminding our communities of judgment according to works, lest we become Catholic, misrepresents the biblical witness. Even worse, it has fostered

---

[35]*Institutes* 3.16.1.
[36]See Dane C. Ortlund, "Justified by Faith, Judged According to Works: Another Look at a Pauline Paradox," *JETS* 52 (2009): 323-39.

fans of Jesus rather than followers of Jesus. It has reaped decisions that amounted to little, rather than disciples who finished the race. The antidote to that, I say, is to declare that only a persevering faith is authentic faith. As article twenty-two of the Belgic Confession puts it: "And faith is the instrument that keeps us in communion with him and with all his benefits."

Second, we must highlight that good works really are good and are necessary for salvation. The pew-sitting couch potatoes of our churches need to hear Romans 8:1-3 as well as Romans 8:4-5; 2 Corinthians 5:21; 5:10; John 5:24, as well as John 5:29; Ephesians 2:8-9, as well as Ephesians 2:10! Otherwise it is irresponsible to give a sense of assurance to people who have no right to have it! Third, the relative lack of attention by Reformed theologians to the role of the Holy Spirit in justification is strange given its importance in 1 Corinthians 6:11, Galatians 5:5-6, and Romans 8:1-17.[37] The work of God in salvation does not end at the moment of faith. In Philippians God grants faith (Phil 1:29), but believers work at obedience in their salvation only because God is still at work in them (Phil 2:12-13). Once more, article twenty-four of the Belgic Confession is helpful: "[W]e are indebted to God for the good works we do, and not he to us, since it is he who 'works in us both to will and do according to his good pleasure' [Phil 2:13]," and note also the Tetrapolitan Confession:

> But since they who are the children of God are led by the Spirit of God, rather than that they act themselves (Rom 8:14), and "of him, and through him, and to him, are all things" (Rom 11:36), whatsoever things we do well and holily are to be ascribed to none other than to this one only Spirit, the Giver of all virtues. However it be, he does not compel us, but leads us, being willing, working in us to both will and to do (Phil 2:12-13). Hence Augustine writes wisely that God rewards his own works in us. By this we are so far from rejecting good works that we utterly deny that anyone can be saved unless by Christ's Spirit he be brought thus far, that there be in him no lack of good works, for which God has created in him.[38]

As I see it, God the Father, in Christ Jesus, and by the Holy Spirit, works

---

[37]This is one of N. T. Wright's key concerns; see his *Justification: God's Plan and Paul's Vision* (Downers Grove, Ill.: InterVarsity Press, 2009), pp. 188-89.

[38]N. T. Wright's employment of Phil 2:13 is certainly "confessional" at this juncture as it comports with the citation of the same text in the Belgic and Tetrapolitan Confessions. See his *Paul: Fresh Perspectives* (London: SPCK, 2005), pp. 73-74; *Justification*, pp. 152-53, 189.

his works in us so that we might be blameless and praiseworthy at the final judgment. On that day, God's verdict for us at the cross and resurrection will have parity with God's work in us from the Spirit-driven life of faith.

THE GOD WHO JUSTIFIES AND IS JUSTIFIED

In this study I hope that I have shown that justification is multifaceted. In sum, I think it has five key aspects:

1. Justification is *forensic* as it denotes one's status, not one's moral state.

2. Justification is *eschatological* in that the verdict of the final judgment has been declared in the present, and the verdict is one of acquittal and is assured by the continuing work of Christ and the Spirit.

3. Justification is *covenantal* since it confirms the promises of the Abrahamic covenant and legitimates the identity of Jews, Greeks, Barbarians (and even Americans!) as full and equal members of God's people.

4. Justification is *effective* insofar as moral sanctification cannot be subsumed under justification but neither can they be absolutely separated. Justification and transformation are both rooted in the same reality of union with Christ (i.e., Calvin's "twofold grace").

5. Justification is *trinitarian* because it is "God who justifies" (Rom 8:33). This is seen in the *Father* handing over the Son to the cross and raising him up for our justification (Rom 4:25). Justification only transpires in the sphere of union with *Christ,* and the only one who can condemn believers is at this very moment interceding for them before the Father (Rom 8:34). The *Spirit* activates justification by creating and supplying faith, and the same Spirit that justified Christ (1 Tim 3:16) also justifies believers (1 Cor 6:11).

That supports my contention that justification is the act whereby God creates a new people, with a new status, in a new covenant, as a foretaste of the new age. By faith we are united to Christ in his condemnation on the cross and we are also united to his justification at his resurrection. To expand upon that, God's verdict of condemnation against our sin at the cross is transformed into God's verdict of righteousness issued in the raising of the Son. We are, then, incorporated into the righteousness of Jesus Christ so that his vindication, and his obedient act that was the basis for it, is counted as ours. Justification also has vertical and horizontal elements in declaring the sinner to be right with God and also by bringing Gentiles into the family of Abraham. Thus, when we read about justification in Paul's letters, we must remember that Paul is not only answering the question, "what must I do to be saved?" but also answering the question "who are the people of God?"—the two go together. Moreover, the basis of justification is faith. Yet by the Spirit our lives of faithfulness will prove to be congruent with the verdict of the final judgment. Finally, I close with a quote from one of my favorite New Testament theologians, Markus Barth:

> "Justified by faith" means, accordingly, tried by the faithful God, sentenced conformably to the appearance, death, and rising of the obedient and loving Son, acquitted and set free in a manner identical with new creation and recognizable only with rejoicing and thanksgiving. God's faith, the faith of Jesus Christ, and man's answer in faith are—each in its own way—the means by which righteousness and life are given the community of sinful Jews and Gentiles.[39]

---

[39]Markus Barth, *Justification*, trans. A. M. Woodruff III (Eugene, Ore.: Wipf and Stock, 2006 [1971]), p. 68.

Traditional Reformed Response

Michael S. Horton

I APPRECIATE MICHAEL BIRD'S CONCERN to overcome false choices, especially between forensic and participationist categories in Paul, or between soteriology and ecclesiology. Taking Romans 1:16-17 as the epistle's central thesis, Bird seems to regard Paul's solution to the latter as the deeper solution to the former. Although the problem is deeper and wider than ethnic exclusion (viz., "the curse of the law," Gal 3:10), Bird properly observes that the solution yields an ecclesiological result: "So that the blessing of Abraham might come to the Gentiles in Christ Jesus" (Gal 3:14). "So when you think gospel, think Abrahamic promises," Bird rightly counsels.

Bird properly encourages us to allow a wider range of exegetical possibilities for determining the meaning of the *dikaiosynē tou theou* ("righteousness of God"). I would only add that it also can refer to God's righteous judgment more generally, whether issuing in condemnation or justification. The two-edged sword of the "righteousness of God," evident for example in Isaiah 59 (esp. vv. 15b-20), is as apparent in Romans. God's righteousness revealed through the law brings wrath (Rom 1:18–3:20), while God's righteousness revealed through the gospel brings saving mercy (Rom 3:21-28)—and therefore the realization of the Abrahamic promise for the whole world (Rom 3:22b-23). As both "just and the justifier," God displays his covenant faithfulness precisely in the act of declaring sinners to be righteous for the sake of Christ alone.

For the very reason that Bird rejects a future justification by works (viz., Rom 3:20), I think Paul is talking about an empty set in Romans 2:13. His whole argument is that the whole world is guilty—including Jews, because *keeping* the law, not merely *possessing* it, is the requirement. Furthermore, it would seem uncharacteristic of Paul to say that Gentile *Christians* "do not have the law" yet do "*by nature* [rather than by the Spirit or in Christ] what the law requires" (Rom 2:14). Paul's "Gentiles, who do not have the law" seem to be the same who "in their unrighteousness suppress the truth"

(Rom 1:18). Yet, to borrow Reformation categories, the difference Paul has in mind is civil justice *(coram hominibus)* and justification *coram Deo*. The former is possible because the moral law is inscribed on the conscience and is therefore sufficient to hold Gentiles accountable (Rom 1:19-20). It is even sufficient to curb unrighteous acts, to the point of shaming possessors of the written Torah for their hypocrisy (Rom 2:17-29). Even so, I'm open to Bird's interpretation, and his distinction between a judgment according to *(kata)* works rather than through, much less on account of *(dia/ek)* works is well attested in classic Reformed treatments.

Bird also advances a "mediating position" between objective and subjective genitive constructions of "faith in/of Christ"—"namely, that it refers to entrusting oneself to God's action in Jesus Christ, including in particular Jesus' act of self-giving obedience on the cross (see Gal 1:4; 2:19b-20)." However, I'm not sure how this differs from a standard Reformed (and Lutheran) definition.

More critically still, Bird judges concerning traditional Reformation interpretations of imputation,

> While this view has "merit," it presses legitimate biblical ideas into an illegitimate framework; it misinterprets some of the language; it is still trapped in medieval categories of merit; and it doesn't adequately grasp the implications of union with Christ. . . .
>
> So Jesus' obedience does become ours—but not through artificially dividing Jesus' obedience into active and passive varieties, not through a medieval concept of "merit" that is imputed instead of imparted, not because Jesus is the exemplary pelagian who earns salvation when we cannot, not by fulfilling a covenant of works that did not contain grace, not by way of righteousness molecules floating through the air to us—rather, we become "righteous" in Christ when by faith we participate in the vicarious death and resurrection of Jesus Christ.

Although he fleshes out this complex of charges a bit, they remain rather sweeping and unsupported. Union with Christ is a key motif in Reformed soteriology, encompassing justification and sanctification. Furthermore, the "merit of the fathers" in rabbinical teaching, as well as the transfer/exchange of covenantal status through a substitute, as in Isaiah 53, is hardly medieval in origin. If we can agree that "Jesus was obedient where Adam and Israel failed to be," as Bird states, then the question

arises, "To what purpose?" What is he obeying and how does his fulfillment of covenantal righteousness in the place of Adam and Israel differ in
substance from saying that Christ—the Last Adam—fulfilled the covenant of works, bore its sanctions and rose again triumphantly as the first
fruits of the whole harvest: all so that in him we could inherit his estate,
with his wealth credited or imputed to us?[1]

N. T. Wright caricatures the Reformation view as suggesting the image
of a judge passing his righteousness, like a gas, across the courtroom to
the defendant. Similarly, Bird refers to "righteousness molecules floating
through the air to us." Against this position, Bird suggests, "righteousness
here is not a property to be transferred, but a status to be conferred." Yet
this is the point of asserting *imputation* over against any infused substance
(Rome) or transfer of God's essential righteousness (Osiander). In Wright's
courtroom there is a judge and a defendant, but the mediator is missing. In
the Reformation interpretation, the judge does not transfer his essential
righteousness—whether gas, liquid, steam or solid, but rather declares sinners to be righteous for the sake of his Son. Bird affirms, "There is indeed
a gift of a righteous status from God (see Rom 5:17; Phil 3:9)," so I am not
quite sure why he is so reticent to identify this with the imputation of
Christ's righteousness to believers. Indeed, Paul says that Christ is our
righteousness (1 Cor 1:30b, perhaps glossing Jer 23:6 and Is 53:11b; cf.
Phil 3:9). There are indeed other metaphors for justification than "crediting," but they all point to the same reality: clothed with Christ, cancelled
debts, full inheritance and so on. Paul seems to connect more dots than
Bird suggests here.

Without scruple, the Reformers often spoke of being "justified by
faith" and "faith being counted for righteousness" as shorthand for "justification by Christ's imputed righteousness through faith." It would be
anachronistic to expect Paul or the Reformers to understand *dia/ek* with
the precision of Aristotelian categories of cause that became so important in later refinements due largely to internal controversies.[2] We are

---

[1]In n. 16, Bird asserts that the Westminster Confession (11.1) "deliberately omits reference to
the 'active' obedience of Christ." However, the Confession affirms the covenant of works in 7.2
and adds references to his obedience and satisfaction securing redemption in 8.5 and 11.3. In
fact, by this time, the denial of Christ's active obedience was associated with the Amyraldian
and Arminian schools as a defection from the Reformed system.

[2]In n. 17, Bird says, "There is diversity in the Protestant tradition concerning this 'counting,

justified by faith and faith is counted as righteousness because faith receives Christ.

In my estimation, Romans 5:19 (like 2 Cor 5:21) does not refer to a transformative "becoming," as Bird suggests, any more than Christ's "becoming" sin for us refers to a degenerative process rather than imputation. Here, I think that Paul is thinking about the *historia salutis,* not the *ordo.* Paul has told us how it is that all people "were made sinners" (Rom 5:19a)—namely, that "one trespass led to condemnation for all people" (Rom 5:18a). The opposite of judicial condemnation is justification, not renewal. Although the *transformative impact* of union with Christ is highlighted in chapter 6, here in chapter 5 we are told *how* believers "will be made righteous" (Rom 5:19b)—namely, through "one act of righteousness" (Rom 5:18b). Why not then understand "will be made righteous" *(dikaioi katastathēsontai)* as referring to a new state of affairs—in the future from the perspective of Adam's transgression? Paul was not envisioning the freight that "made righteous" would have in the Reformation debate. He is simply telling us how, in history, the world (Jew and Gentile) became guilty and will be made righteous before God through a forensic verdict. Although 1 Corinthians 1:30 doesn't mention imputation, how else is Christ "our righteousness" in a forensic or legal sense (as Bird agrees)? He grants that in Philippians 3, "There is clearly a righteousness from God that is given to believers." Then why not imputed or credited? In my view, this is a more natural interpretation than "the faithfulness of the Messiah that enables believers to apprehend this righteousness when by faith they trust in him and they are thereby placed *in him.*"

Yet just at this point, Bird challenges Wright's suggestion that "union with Christ" accomplishes everything intended by "imputation."

> I accept Wright's sketch, but I do think we are still left with the question, what does union *actually do* that makes us "righteous" before God? This is where a concept like imputation is a necessary *implicate* of the biblical ma-

---

crediting, imputing' since the Augsburg Confession (art. iv) refers to the imputation of faith, while the Westminster Confession (art. xi.1) explicitly denies the imputation of faith or evangelical obedience." However, again, the diversity is not between traditions but between more general ways of speaking (Reformation-era, illustrated by the Augsburg Confession [1530]) and later refinements (Formula of Concord [1577] and Westminster [1646]) in the face of internal and external challenges, particularly Arminianism, which often made faith the basis (material cause) of justification.

terials. If we take all the bits and bobs together, including this language of "counting" from Romans 4, the gift of righteousness in Romans 5:17 and Philippians 3:9, the representative natures of Adam and Christ as federal heads, the forensic nature of *dikaioō* and *dikaiosynē* in several passages (e.g., Rom 3:21-26; 10:10; Gal 2:15-21; 5:4-5), and the indebtedness of salvation to Jesus' faithfulness and obedience in his task as Son, then, something like "imputation" sounds like a logical necessity of describing the application of salvation for those who are "in Christ."

So the Reformers are vindicated, but blame shifts to Protestant scholasticism's insistence on Christ's active obedience, emphasizing "the accounting metaphor of 'credit,'" and "glossing over Paul's 'in Christ' language of justification for a model that looks like an abstract transaction of righteousness and myopically focusing on the sequence of events in personal salvation *(ordo salutis)* without integrating it into the overarching story of salvation history where God brings Jews and Gentiles into the family of the Messiah *(historia salutis)*."

All I can say is that while I've heard something like this in some evangelistic presentations—including some popular versions of Calvinism, I don't think it is a fair representation of classic Reformed treatments. Besides the fact that all of the elements for active obedience and imputation (crediting) are present in Bird's own helpful and compact summary above, Reformed theology emphasizes union with Christ, and covenantal participation in his active obedience as well as his death and resurrection can hardly be said to detract from "in Christ" language. Nor does Reformed soteriology appear to me to display a myopic focus on the *ordo* over the *historia salutis*. In fact, Bird noted in the introduction that Reformed theologians pioneered biblical theology. Nor, given so many examples that I could cite to the contrary, do I understand the charge of "the relative lack of attention by Reformed theologians to the role of the Holy Spirit in justification." In fact, Bird himself buttresses his salutary point about the importance of the Spirit in salvation—and the fact that "the work of God in salvation does not end at the moment of faith"—by quoting the Belgic and Tetrapolitan Confessions. Having so successfully eschewed false choices, this more polemically charged section exaggerates classic Reformed interpretations and makes his own conclusions seem more radically different than, in my view, they actually are.

■

New Perspective Response

James D. G. Dunn

IN THE CONFUSED DEBATE THAT AROSE around "the new perspective on Paul," Michael Bird's contribution has been a very welcome irenic voice calling for a recognition of the strengths of both sides of the debate and advocating a more balanced assessment of all the Pauline teaching.[1] This essay is a further example of his strategy, and one with which I have very little substantive disagreement.

For example, I echo his warning that "a 'gospel of justification'. . . privileges justification over other equally important images like redemption, reconciliation and adoption," and his critique of "the standard Reformed view" of "imputation." Similarly I warm to his recognition that "justification [by faith] was part of the Jewish Christian tradition from the beginning and not something that Paul invented," and that the gospel of blessing promised to the Gentiles is the thread linking the section Galatians 3:6-14. I warm equally to his reminder that as a forensic metaphor, justification has to do with status and not moral state. I like his treatment of Galatians 3:15-29, and the correlation between Paul and James for which he argues, successfully, I think.

Besides this positive response to Michael's essay, my more negatively critical comments are mostly minor and not very significant.

I question whether he is right to suggest that Paul denounced Peter for trying to compel the Antioch Gentile believers to be *circumcised* (Gal 2:11-14). The issue was rather of Jew/Israelite being required to "separate" from Gentiles/other nations in order to maintain Israel's holiness (the use of the verb "separate" in Galatians 2:12 almost certainly echoes Leviticus 20:24-26). The question of circumcision had been settled in the earlier agreement between James, Peter and Paul in Jerusalem (Gal 2:6-9). And circumcision was not the only "work of the law" that threatened "the truth of the gospel." We don't enhance Paul's argument by over-egging his rebuke

---

[1]I refer particularly to Michael F. Bird, *The Saving Righteousness of God: Studies on Paul, Justification and the New Perspective* (Milton Keynes, U.K.: Paternoster, 2007).

of Peter at this point. Nor do I think Michael is right when he suggests that Paul's Galatian opponents were making the "implicit claim that Christ is merely an add-on to the law." The logic of their appeal to Abraham was presumably that circumcision was an essential corollary to justification by faith, that certain works of the law were a required "add-on" to Paul's gospel.

I wonder if Michael is right to interpret Paul's characterization of himself as a "transgressor" in Galatians 2:18 as indicating one who rejected "the central claim of the gospel." The key seems to me the condemnation (presumably by the group from James) of those who disregarded (in this case) the laws of clean and unclean as "sinners" ("Gentile sinners," Gal 2:15). If those "justified in Christ" were being regarded as "sinners" (because they ignored these laws), that would be tantamount to calling Christ (who justified such "sinners") a "servant of sin" (Gal 2:17; we should not miss the echo of what Jesus was notorious for: Mt 11:19; Mk 2:16-17; Lk 15:2). In contrast, if Paul reverted to a law-determined life, and built again what he had torn down, he would be admitting that in his (previous) failure to observe the law he was an actual law-breaker/"transgressor" (Gal 2:18).

I have another query with regard to Michael's statement that "Leviticus 18:5 promises life to those who keep the law." I am not winning this argument, but I continue to think that Paul understood Leviticus 18:5 as indicating Israel's obligations under the covenant: one would live by doing what the law commanded (the works of the law). That was why he could be so dismissive of the thought of the law as the life-giver (Gal 3:21): only God and his Spirit could "make alive"; in contrast, the law's function was simply to regulate how the covenant people should live (as in Ezek 20:5-26: "by whose observance man shall live").[2]

Michael follows what is probably the main consensus that in Romans 2:13-16 (Gentiles who are "doers of the law" despite not having the law) Paul had in mind only Gentile *believers*. That does make for a consistency in Paul's theology. But I still find myself wondering whether Paul here does not indicate a readiness to acknowledge that there were Gentiles who lived godly lives (equivalent to Second Temple Judaism's recognition of

---

[2]See further my *The New Perspective on Paul,* rev. ed. (Grand Rapids: Eerdmans, 2008), pp. 73-74.

"God-fearers" and rabbinic Judaism's recognition of "righteous Gentiles"). Was this the realization or revelation that came home to Paul, much as Peter's vision in Joppa (according to Acts) brought home to Peter that "in every nation anyone who fears [God] and does what is right is acceptable to him" (Acts 10:35)? A similar question arises with regard to the climax of Paul's exposition in Romans: so confident was Paul that mercy is the baseline of all God's dealings with humankind that he could pose his eventual hope in terms of "all": "in order that he [God] might have mercy on all" (Rom 11:32). There is always a danger of locking up Paul's thought with a strictness of logic that he would not own.

These are small matters that hardly detract from the main thrust of Michael's essay. There are, however, three more important issues or aspects with which I hardly disagree with Michael but I think can be more fully emphasized.

First, in Michael's discussion of Romans, I was slightly disappointed that he reverted simply to the old subjective/objective-genitive debate over the phrase "the righteousness of God." I have always found the relational character of the Hebrew concept of "righteousness" (meeting the obligation that arises from a particular relationship) as a key that unlocks that particular dilemma. As his quotation from Hultgren well states, "God's righteousness is God's saving activity," his vindication and deliverance of the people to whom he had committed himself. We may recall that it was precisely the recognition of this character of God's righteousness, not as punitive but as saving, that came as a great revelation to Luther. When justification is seen not simply in terms of status conferred, but in terms of relation with, so many of the traditional disagreements and controversies are deflated. Apart from anything else it gives a clearer sense of the role of faith in the whole event and process of justification: faith as the total openness to and reliance upon God, on God's promise and enabling, as so vividly demonstrated by Abraham in Romans 4:17-21. Michael passes over this passage without comment, but I think it would help his argument.

Second, one of the strengths of Michael's contribution to the debate on Paul's teaching on justification is his recognition that the forensic metaphor of justification should not be held in opposition to the more participationist categories used by Paul. We should indeed never forget that Paul's "in Christ" language is more pervasive in his writings than his talk of God's (saving) righteousness and justification. It is one of the most frustrating features of the ongoing debate that Paul's interpreters seem to be so unwilling and unable to hold together what Paul himself so clearly held together—both forensic and participationist language—as in passages like 2 Corinthians 5:17-21 and Philippians 3:7-11. The point surely is that Paul recognized that the wonder and profundity of the gospel could not be adequately expressed with only one image, no more than a golfer would go on to the golf course with only one club. So forensic imagery works well when the emphasis is on the event at which someone is declared righteous, her/his status affirmed (whether in conversion-initiation or in final judgment). But it does not work so well to describe the *process* of salvation. And here Michael is quite right: Paul also uses the language of transformation. He cited Romans 5:19 in particular. But we could easily refer also to Romans 12:2, the whole language of becoming like Christ (Rom 8:29; 2 Cor 3:18), being conformed to his death (Phil 3:10) and so forth. Like Michael I have attempted to draw such diverse strands of Paul's theology together,[3] but the need to do so is urgent in current debates, and some more emphasis in Michael's current essay would have been welcome.

Third, probably the most sensitive issue revived by the debate over "the new perspective" has been the question of how Paul's emphasis on judgment "according to works" fits with his emphasis on justification by faith (alone)—I say "revived" since the question was also at the heart of earlier disputes about justification, as is plain from other essays in this volume. Michael is very alert to the issue, but does he present the whole gospel of Paul at this point? Paul's talk of transformation/sanctification has to be linked to his hope of his converts being presented "pure," "blameless," "faultless," "irreproachable" and so on at the coming of Christ (e.g., 1 Cor 1:8; Phil 1:6, 10; Col 1:22; 1 Thess 3:13). But what cannot be neglected here is that Paul does *not* assume that the recipients of his letters would live blameless lives; hence his repeated warnings against moral failure (as in Rom 8:13; 1 Cor 3:17; 9:27; 11:27-29; 2 Cor 13:5; Gal 5:4; 6:7-9). A major weakness in many of the responses to "the new perspective" at this point is what appears to be the assumption that the justification of conversion will assuredly be ratified at the last judgment; that those born of the Spirit will,

---

[3]*The Theology of Paul the Apostle* (Grand Rapids: Eerdmans, 1998), chaps. 13-16, 18; *New Perspective on Paul,* particularly pp. 92-95.

of course, be led by the Spirit and produce the good works which are the (inevitable?) fruit of grace.[4] Paul himself did not make that assumption. His exhortations to perseverance should not be separated from his warnings against failure to persevere. The reassuring words of Philippians 1:6 have to be balanced by the alarm expressed in Galatians 3:3! Any assumption that conversion in effect determines outcome (final salvation) becomes uncomfortably like the similar assumption regarding the elect, so devastatingly exposed by James Hogg's *The Private Memoirs and Confessions of a Justified Sinner!*[5]

So I end with a repetition of my plea: When will we get an irenic and balanced view of the *whole* gospel of Paul?

---

[4]The line of thought was provoked by what is almost Bird's last comment on the point: "Yet by the Spirit our lives of faithfulness will prove to be congruent with the verdict of the final judgment."

[5]James Hogg, *The Private Memoirs and Confessions of a Justified Sinner,* ed. John Carey (New York: Oxford University Press, 1999 [1824]).

■

Deification Response

Veli-Matti Kärkkäinen

ALTHOUGH I APPRECIATE DR. BIRD's careful delineation of what makes him a "progressive" Reformed thinker—and my sympathies lie with him as I also attempt in a small way to offer a "progressive" Lutheran-ecumenical proposal—I also think that one of the criteria he uses in characterizing a progressive thinker may not qualify as such, namely, the refusal "to simply restate the veracity of [one's] tradition in the face of exegetical and theological challenges to it." I don't know any theologian, whether progressive or not, who would be content merely to repeat and restate the views of the past! That observation applies even to Dr. Bird's Reformed colleague Professor Horton, who set out to defend and discuss the "traditional" Reformed view. When it comes to the rest of his definition of what makes one progressive though, I find it useful.

I fear that as an outsider to the Reformed tradition, I must agree with the "in-house" criticism of this Australian theologian: "I think that Reformed theologians in general have read Scripture while wearing a theological straight jacket and have read Paul through the lens of an *ordo salutis* (order of salvation) to the neglect of a *historia salutis* (history of salvation)." My own essay seeks to be a testimony to how much a dogmatic and systematic theologian may—and should!—learn from the guild of biblical scholars. Hence, even though my own way of conceiving a "progressive" Protestant doctrine of justification differs in some respects from that of Dr. Bird, I wholeheartedly welcome his desire first to "go back to the Bible." That said, I also think that merely going back to the Bible, as necessary as it is, is not enough. The formulation of the doctrine of justification, as that of any Christian doctrine, is finally and ultimately a systematic task. Dr. Bird's essay in biblical theology gives a number of useful and thoughtful insights into that kind of task.

An indication of the author's balanced and irenic approach to the topic is that, having chastised his own tradition for the lack of attention to the Bible's historical and social setting as the background for the teaching on justification, he also rightly acknowledges the many gains of the Reformed tradition in relation to the Pauline gospel. I would only like to add one important caveat here, which I also mention in my essay but have developed elsewhere, namely, the thorny issue between the law and gospel. It seems to me that both Calvinistic and Lutheran conceptions of that relation are in need of careful reexamination and redefinition. If that relationship could be rectified in a more "biblical"—and I dare to say, Pauline—way, then some of the ecumenical impasse between Roman Catholics and Protestants, on the one hand, and between the Christian West and East at large may be solved more easily. I believe our task as "Latter Day" Protestants is to seek to do what our Protestants forefathers—and mothers—did, that is, to attempt another fresh reading of the Bible and in light of that reading inform our current understanding. Isn't that what Re-formation is all about? (More that and less Protest-ing!)

Dr. Bird's investigation into key themes in Pauline theology, mainly in Romans and Galatians, including the people of God, covenant, resurrection and eschatology, among others, resonate with my own theological sensibilities. The one theme missing in the author's list of interests—which is crucial in order to formulate the *historia salutis*—is the deeply and thoroughly missionary orientation of Pauline theology. Even the book of Romans is first and foremost a missionary writing and thus dynamic, personal and engaging.

The author's investigation of key Pauline texts such as Galatians 3:10-14 makes the point I have tried to make in my own essay (as well as in my friendly criticism of the other Reformed essay in this collection), namely, that Paul operated with a plethora of metaphors of salvation and soteriology. Even in one short passage he blends materials from various cultic, historical, religious, societal, cultural and other sources. Thus, for example, that passage from Galatians 3 goes back not only to the blessing motif of Genesis 12 with regard to the calling of Abram but also to the cursing of the Deuteronomic law regarding a blasphemous son! Furthermore, earlier in that chapter, Paul complements the predominantly Christological (and patrological) discussion with robust pneumatological materials reminding the Galatians of their powerful Spirit experience, obviously including signs and miracles. Talk about a trinitarian soteriology!

In the treatment of passages in Romans on justification, Dr. Bird rightly highlights various aspects of the Romans 1:17 phrase "the just shall live by faith." I wonder whether it would help him to expand the discussion and make it more inclusive if he would more thoroughly investigate this particular phrase's rich biblical background. I personally find it curious that this phrase occurs in no less than four contexts: Habakkuk 2:4, Romans 1:17, Galatians 3:11 and Hebrews 10:38. The textual and historical contexts alone speak of various facets of what the "living by faith" of the just may mean. Certainly in Habakkuk the accent is on the faithfulness as much as on faith (as of course the Hebrew term *emunah,* fairly similarly to the New Testament equivalent, means). In the book of Hebrews, the context points to the eschatological expectation. And so forth. My point here simply is that not only do biblical writers employ a number of metaphors when it comes to salvation, but that even one and the same metaphor in different contexts and usages may gain different, complementary nuances.

I couldn't agree more with the summative statement of this fine biblical study: "the righteousness of God introduces the entire package of salvation in all of Romans (not just Romans 1–4) including justification, redemption, sacrifice, forgiveness of sins, covenant membership, reconciliation, the gift of the Holy Spirit, power for a new obedience, union with Christ, freedom from sin and eschatological vindication." In keeping with this wider context of the "justification" of God is Paul's statement in Romans 4:25, whose importance Dr. Bird rightly emphasizes later in his essay. In that context, Dr. Bird also speaks of the wider racial reconciliation as the goal of Paul's gospel of justification.

With that "big picture" in view I was both delighted and somewhat surprised by the author's lengthy and somewhat polemical discussion of the role of imputation in the doctrine of justification. As I have mentioned in my essay and in my dialogue with Professor Horton, in my opinion there is no need to debunk the imputation aspect. If not for other reasons, then for the critical role it has played in the history of tradition, that aspect should be preserved, as long as it is not made the defining feature. Even the fact that on the basis of biblical study, the traditional way of using the concept of imputation may be in many instances problematic, it is not illegitimate for dogmatic theology to use concepts in a way that differs somewhat from the biblical usage—as long as that is kept in mind afresh. Any formulation of the doctrine usually means going beyond the Bible, as it were, although one hopes not against it. In that light, Dr. Bird's comment, in another context, that "we can say what the text says, no more and no less," is of course not true. With biblical texts we often say either "more" or "less"; if not, then the whole guild of interpreters would not be needed. One doesn't have to flirt with postmodern hermeneutics to say so! Just think of the number of hermeneutical and exegetical battles, even those in the arena of the doctrine of justification!

I mention in another response in this book that the reviewer has to be cautious when "complaining" about topics not discussed in the essay engaged. There simply is no end to suggestions as to what else could have been included. That said, it seems to me this particular essay would have been significantly strengthened if yet another portion of the book of Romans had been included: chapter 8. Indeed, it seems to me so much of what the author is aiming at would have found resonance in that chapter, which not only speaks of salvation in a robust trinitarian scheme, also highlighting the pneumatological aspects, but also gives due attention to resurrection, eschatological hope, the destiny of creation and so forth. An added reason why I mention that particular chapter in this context is that for some reason neither Protestant Reformers nor Roman Catholic theologians ever really found their way beyond chapter 5 in the book of Romans. Had that happened, perhaps some of the impasse of the past would have been either avoided or at least softened.

As a minor note, let me take up one interpretation of the author with which I would like to take sides on. When it comes to the author's interpretation of Romans 2:13 that "the Gentiles described here are not noble pagans or pious God-fearers, but are Christian Gentiles who genuinely do the law through their Spirit-driven behavior," supported as it is with a great many recent interpreters, it has not (yet!) convinced me. It seems to me the face-value rendering of the text is warranted and also sticks with the context of Paul's reasoning in the beginning part of this epistle.

■

Roman Catholic Response

Gerald O'Collins, S.J.

APROPOS OF WHAT BIRD HAS WRITTEN, I want first to signal seven themes where I found myself warmly agreeing both with the approach he adopts and the positions he expounds.

1. Bird begins by endorsing "the supremacy of Scripture in the life of the church" and the need for theologians "to line up with Scripture." Not only in his opening statement but also throughout his essay, he shows that "love and reverence of Holy Scripture" that the Second Vatican Council admired in "separated" Protestant brothers and sisters.[1] I share with Bird this "high" view of biblical authority; we must do our theological thinking "under the word of God." There remains, of course, the huge question of

---

[1] "Decree on Ecumenism" (*Unitatis Redintegratio*), #21.

what it means "to line up with Scripture," or interpret the meaning(s) of Scripture in our current context(s). But, if we do not join Bird in acknowledging from the start their de jure authority, our exegetical and theological interpretations are sure to go astray.[2]

2. For at least two reasons, Bird's initial description (which he retrieves at the end) appeals to me: "justification is the act whereby God creates a new people, with a new status, in a new covenant, as part of the first installment of the new age." First, as Kärkkäinen rightly stresses, individualism leads us astray when we study justification. Second, Bird's language of "the first installment of the new age" or, as he puts it later, "the apocalyptic revelation of God's saving righteousness" alerts us to Paul's apocalyptic framework of thought. In my chapter I should have mentioned my own debt to Ernst Käsemann for also alerting me years ago to the apostle's apocalyptic worldview.

3. I applaud the way in which Bird, also like Kärkkäinen, presents justification in a firmly Christological and pneumatological (trinitarian) key when expounding it as incorporation into the obedience and vindication of Jesus in his death and resurrection. Basing himself on such texts as Romans 1:4, 1 Timothy 3:16 and Romans 8:11, Bird happily describes justification as *participation in and incorporation* into the obedience and vindication of Jesus in his death and resurrection."

4. As can be seen from my own contribution and my appeal to Gordon Fee and Joseph Fitzmyer, I appreciate Bird's warning against privileging justification "over other images" and his recognition of redemption, reconciliation, adoption and other images as equally important ways for expressing God's saving activity. The "entire package of salvation" includes "justification, redemption, sacrifice, forgiveness of sins, covenant membership, reconciliation, the gift of the Holy Spirit, power for a new obedience, union with Christ, freedom from sin and eschatological vindication." Here Bird once again converges with Kärkkäinen, who insists that, even for Paul, justification is only one way of expressing what God has done for us in Christ and certainly not *the* key to the apostle's thought.

5. At a time when attempts—mostly, one must add, unscholarly ones—

---

[2]See G. O'Collins and D. Kendall, *The Bible for Theology: Ten Principles for the Theological Use of Scripture* (Mahwah, N.J.: Paulist Press, 1997), pp. 7-19.

continue to press the thesis that Paul was the "real" founder of Christianity, it was good to read Bird's firm statement: "the notion that faith and not works of the law is the instrument of justification was part of the Jewish Christian tradition from the beginning and not something that Paul invented." Here and elsewhere, Paul articulated brilliantly what Christians already believed and practiced but did not create and foist on them new and alien doctrines.

6. As readers can see from what I wrote about "the faith of Christ," I side with Bird's "mediating" (perhaps better called an "inclusive") position. The genitive is both objective and subjective; we believe in Christ and can share in the faith/faithfulness exercised by Christ. Perhaps Bird could have adopted a similar approach when treating "the righteousness of God." We catch Paul's thought by speaking of the righteousness that belongs to God (almost a genitive of identity) and so comes from God (a genitive of origin), rather than presupposing alternatives: either righteousness belongs to God or it comes from God.

7. Bird felicitously concluded his discussion of alleged differences between Paul and James by quoting John Calvin: "we are not saved by works, but neither are we saved without them." Bird went on to set out some valuable, final remarks about justification, judgment and works. After citing Augustine in my own contribution, I was delighted to find the Tetrapolitan Confession endorsing the same conviction: "Augustine writes wisely that God rewards his own works in us."

Let me conclude this response by indicating one disagreement. I join Bird in maintaining Christ's "atoning death" but not in talking of "penal substitution." Christian faith should never, of course, forget Jesus' loving obedience and priestly self-sacrifice that expiated human sin. But the Scriptures (even Ps 22; Is 53; Rom 8:3; 2 Cor 5:21; and Gal 3:13) do *not* support the picture of Jesus literally taking upon himself and carrying the sins of others and so being (literally again) "condemned" and "punished" by God.[3] Jesus was condemned by Roman and Jewish authorities. It was they who passed a "verdict" against him, and that (human) verdict was

---

[3]See G. O'Collins, *Jesus Our Redeemer: A Christian Approach to Salvation* (Oxford: Oxford University Press, 2007), pp. 140-60. Far from being a "Protestant" monopoly, this theory of penal substitution has also flourished among Roman Catholics: ibid., pp. 133-40. On Christ's atoning self-sacrifice, see ibid., pp. 161-80.

transformed into "vindication" when God justified and vindicated the crucified Jesus through the resurrection.

What then of Galatians 3:13 ("Christ redeemed us from the curse of the law by becoming a curse for us—for it is written, 'Cursed is everyone who hangs upon a tree'"). Does this mean, as Bird writes, that God passed a "verdict against Jesus on the cross"? Very many Christians, Roman Catholics and others alike, have understood Paul to say that the crucified Christ suffered a divine curse on our behalf. But does the apostle endorse this idea?

In Deuteronomy 21:22-23 a curse was directed against criminals who had been executed and then hung up on a gibbet: "When someone is convicted of a crime punishable by death and is executed, and you hang him on a tree, his corpse must not remain all night upon the tree; you shall bury him that same day, for anyone hung on a tree is cursed *by God*" (emphasis mine). Hanging or impaling the corpse of a criminal on a tree was regarded as the worst disgrace, the ultimate dishonor reserved for criminals under the curse of God. By the time of Jesus, this text had come to be applied to those who suffered the penalty of crucifixion and were hung up alive on a cross to die.[4]

Nevertheless, what has always struck me is how Paul, when quoting in Galatians the text from Deuteronomy, omits the words "by God," and so avoids the suggestion of a divine curse. On the cross Jesus was cursed by the law or at least by those who administered the law, but not by God. By dying on a gibbet, to all appearances like a legally condemned criminal, Jesus delivered us—paradoxically—from the curse involved in the regime of the law and vain human attempts to be justified through keeping that law.

Here one should also mention another text normally cited in support of the penal substitution theory, 2 Corinthians 5:21: "For our sake he [God] made him [Christ] to be sin who knew no sin, so that in him we might become the righteousness of God." This laconic verse leaves much unsaid. Paul does not, for instance, state that Christ is now "no longer sin," since God has raised him from the dead and made him "righteousness," so that we might become righteous by sharing in his righteousness. The connec-

---

[4]See G. O'Collins, "Crucifixion," *ABD*, 1:1207-10, at 1207.

tion between Christ "being made sin" and our becoming "the righteousness of God" is left unexplained. Furthermore, even though the initiative of God is strongly to the fore, nothing is said about the love of God and Christ, unlike such passages as Romans 5:8 and Galatians 2:20. In the context of my response, I need to unpack the first half of Paul's dense and paradoxical or seemingly contradictory statement about Christ who "knew no sin" being "made sin."

Supporters of the penal substitution view understand Paul to state that Christ really became a sinner. Our transgressions were counted against him and he was punished in our place. Such exegesis reads the concrete ("sinner") for the abstract ("sin"). But in what Paul wrote, God is the only one named as an active protagonist. This raises the objection: how could the all-good and just God transform an innocent person into a sinner? What of the possibility of saying that, without doing that, God associated Jesus with all sinful men and women and charged him with their sins? But, as Jean-Noël Aletti remarks, "Paul does not use a judicial vocabulary here. God is not said to accuse, charge, judge, or punish."[5]

We interpret Paul's dense statement better this way: Without literally becoming a sinner, Christ endured the deadly results of sin: he was rejected, condemned and killed. Christ was "made sin," in that he suffered horribly at the hands of sinners and died on a cross between two sinners. God turned this brutal outrage into the means for reconciling sinful human beings and transforming their lives so that they become righteous (2 Cor 5:18-21).

---

[5]Jean-Noël Aletti, "'God Made Christ to Be Sin' (2 Corinthians 5:21): Reflections on a Pauline Paradox," in *The Redemption*, ed. S. T. Davis, D. Kendall and G. O'Collins (Oxford: Oxford University Press, 2004), pp. 101-20, at 111-14.

5

New Perspective View

James D. G. Dunn

The "new perspective" on Paul's teaching on justification by faith is not really "new." It is a perspective that Paul himself defended, as we shall see, an integral part of Paul's own perspective on the subject. It highlights a dimension of Paul's teaching that Paul himself regarded as central to his own understanding of justification. The reason why it has been called "new," then, is not because the aspects and emphases that it highlights have never before been given such attention. Rather it is "new" because the dimension of Paul's teaching that it highlights has been largely lost to sight in more contemporary expositions, even though it was so central to Paul's own formulation of the doctrine. It is "new" because it gives a renewed emphasis to aspects of the historical situation that gave rise to Paul's formulation of the doctrine, which were fundamental to that formulation and which should remain fundamental for our understanding of Paul's gospel for today.

It also follows that the "new perspective" should not be defined or regarded as an alternative to the "old perspective." The "new perspective" does not pretend or think or want to replace all elements of the "old perspective." It does not regard the "new perspective" as hostile or antithetical to the "old perspective." It asks simply whether the ways in which the doctrine of justification has traditionally been expounded have taken full enough account of Paul's theology at this point. It is not necessary for the "new perspective" to call into question what have traditionally been taken to be the central emphases of Paul's doctrine. For the "new perspective" to be "right," or justified, it is not necessary for the "old perspective" to be "wrong." The "new perspective" simply asks whether *all* the factors that made up Paul's doctrine have been adequately appreciated and articulated in the traditional reformulations of the doctrine.

There are four aspects of the new perspective if it is to be properly understood, if Paul's teaching on justification is to be fully grasped in its complete roundedness:

1. The new perspective on Paul arises from a new perspective on Judaism.

2. The significance of Paul's mission is the context for his teaching on justification.

3. Why justification by faith in Christ Jesus and not works of the law?

4. The whole gospel of Paul must be taken into account.

A NEW PERSPECTIVE ON JUDAISM

In the first place, the new perspective calls for a revision in the traditional Christian attitude toward and view of Judaism. The traditional view has a long history and is well rooted. The roots can be traced back to Paul himself.

It is Paul himself who speaks of the way of life he had once/formerly led as "in Judaism" (Gal 1:13).[1] The implication is clear that since his conversion, as a believer in Messiah Jesus, he no longer practiced that way of life, indeed that he counted himself as no longer, in a generally recognized sense, "in Judaism."[2] This is confirmed by the rather negative way Paul now regarded what he had previously counted as of primary importance in his life as a member of the people of Israel and a Pharisee (Phil 3:5-6), as all to be counted "rubbish" in comparison with knowing Christ Jesus as his Lord (Phil 3:7-8).[3] It is generally accepted that for Paul, Christ had now

---

[1]Gal 1:13-14 contains the only two references to "Judaism" in the NT. See also below (n. 7).

[2]See further my "Who Did Paul Think He Was? A Study of Jewish Christian Identity," *NTS* 45 (1999): 174-93.

[3]I deal with Phil 3 fully in "Philippians 3.2-14 and the *New Perspective on Paul*," in *The New Perspective on Paul*, rev. ed. (Grand Rapids: Eerdmans, 2005), chap. 22. Unless otherwise indicated, biblical quotations in this essay are my translation.

replaced Torah as the central focus and motivating factor of his life.[4] The point is nowhere so poignantly expressed as in Galatians 2:19-20:

> I through the law died to the law, in order that I might live for God. I have been crucified with Christ; and it is no longer I that lives, but Christ lives in me. And the life I now live in the flesh, I live by faith[5] which is in the Son of God, who loved me and gave himself for me.

And the consequent contrast Paul drew between old and new is nowhere so sharply expressed as in 2 Corinthians 3, where he sets new covenant over against old covenant, the former characterized by the Spirit and life, a "ministry of righteousness," the latter characterized by the letter (of the law), a "ministry of condemnation" and death, its time past (2 Cor 3:6-11).

This sense of a newness that had superseded the old became central to Christianity's self-understanding. The first known occurrence of the term "Christianity" is in Ignatius, writing in the early second century. In these first instances, "Christianity" was set over against "Judaism," as something distinct and different from "Judaism."[6] There is an interesting sequence here. For the name *Ioudaismos* ("Judaism") was initially introduced to define what it referred to over against and in opposition to *Hellēnismos* ("Hellenism").[7] Ironically, even if understandably in the circumstances, the name "Christianity" was initially introduced in a similar way, to define its referent over against and in opposition to "Judaism." As the Maccabean rebellion in effect defined "Judaism" as "not-Hellenism," so Ignatius in

---

[4]E.g., T. L. Donaldson, *Paul and the Gentiles: Remapping the Apostle's Convictional World* (Minneapolis: Fortress, 1997).

[5]See pp. 195-98 in this essay.

[6]"It is out of place to talk of Jesus Christ and to judaize. For Christianity did not believe in Judaism, but Judaism in Christianity" (Ignatius *To the Magnesians* 10.3). "But if anyone interprets Judaism to you, do not listen to him; for it is better to hear Christianity from a man who is circumcised, than Judaism from one uncircumcised" (Ignatius *To the Philadelphians* 6.1).

[7]The Greek term *Ioudaismos* first appears in literature in 2 Maccabees, in three passages (2 Macc 2:21; 8:1; 14:38), each defining "Judaism" as the religious identity and way of life for which the Maccabean rebels resisted the overlordship of Syria. In 2 Maccabees the term is obviously coined as a counter to *Hellēnismos*, "Hellenism" (2 Macc 4:13) and *allophulismos*, "foreignness" (2 Macc 4:13; 6:25). In other words, for the author of 2 Maccabees, "Judaism" was the summary term for that system embodying national and religious identity that was the rallying point for the violent rejection by the Maccabees of the Syrian attempt to assimilate them by the abolition of their distinctive practices (particularly circumcision and food laws: 1 Macc 1:60-63; so also 4 Macc 4:26).

effect defined "Christianity" as "not-Judaism."[8]

This is the start of the phenomenon of the Christian anti-Judaism and later of Christian anti-Semitism, which has so besmirched the history of Christian Europe. It was not simply that "supersessionism," the belief that Christianity had superseded Judaism, had taken over Israel's status as "the people of God," and had drained all the substance leaving "Judaism" only the husk.[9] It was more that the continuing existence of Judaism was regarded as in effect an anomaly and a threat to Christianity.[10] This was why, even late into the twentieth century, the Judaism of the time of Jesus and Paul was often referred to as *Spätjudentum*, "late Judaism," the logic being that with the coming of Christianity there was no longer need or place for Judaism. First-century Judaism was "late Judaism," because from a Christian perspective, its function within the purpose of God had been completed, Christianity had arrived. It was "late Judaism" because it was the last Judaism. Hence also one of the more troublesome features of the quest of the historical Jesus, that is, the repeated attempt to distance Jesus from Judaism by denigrating Judaism. As Susannah Heschel observes, the liberal theologians of the nineteenth century painted "as negative a picture as possible of first-century Judaism" in order "to elevate Jesus as a unique religious figure who stood in opposition to his Jewish surroundings."[11]

Within this tradition of Christian anti-Jewishness, it is hardly surprising that Paul was regarded, by Jews as well as Christians, as the archetype of this anti-Jewishness, as hostile to the Judaism he had once espoused. Nor is it very surprising that the assumption became more or less given, that Paul opposed Judaism because of its negative and anti-Christian (so un-Christian) character. This became the default perspective of Protestantism, principally because Martin Luther understood Paul's reaction

---

[8]See further K.-W. Niebuhr, "'Judentum' und 'Christentum' bei Paulus und Ignatius von Antiochien," *ZNW* 85 (1994): 218-33, esp. 224-33.

[9]Already in the second century: *Barn.* 4:6-8; Justin Martyr, *Dialogue with Trypho* 11.5; 135.3, 6; Melito of Sardis, *Peri Pascha* 39-45.

[10]See, e.g., A. L. Williams, *Adversus Judaeos* (Cambridge: Cambridge University Press, 1935); H. Maccoby, *Judas Iscariot and the Myth of Jewish Evil* (London: Halban, 1992).

[11]Susannah Heschel, *Abraham Geiger and the Jewish Jesus* (Chicago: University of Chicago Press, 1998), pp. 9, 21; "As Jewishness, Judaism represented a set of qualities associated with everything Christian theologians wished to reject and repudiate: false religiosity, immorality, legalism, hypocrisy" (p. 75).

against Judaism in the light of his own reaction against medieval Catholicism. The degeneracy of a Catholicism that offered forgiveness of sins by the buying of indulgences mirrored for Luther the degeneracy of a Judaism that taught justification by works.[12] In Lutheranism, Paul's distinction between gospel and law became an antithesis between Christianity and Judaism.[13] If "gospel" was the expression of grace, then "law" was the antonym to "grace." In Jewish (mis)understanding, "law" was "a summons to achievement."[14] And "works of the law" were but "man's self-powered striving to undergird his own existence in forgetfulness of his creaturely existence."[15]

What had become an almost instinctive reflex in Christian exposition of Paul, that Paul can be properly appreciated only if the Judaism of his day is treated as the polar negative opposite, is what the new perspective calls in question. The protests of Jewish scholars, that the Judaism thus described was far from Judaism as they understood it, were largely ignored—what C. G. Montefiore called "the imaginary Rabbinic Judaism, created by Christian scholars in order to form a suitably lurid background for the Epistles of St. Paul."[16] It was not until E. P. Sanders challenged this Christian tradition, and did so with blunt polemic, that such protests by Jews and others were finally paid heed to.[17]

Sanders' response was to point to a fundamental dimension of Jewish religion and soteriology that had been largely lost to sight, not least in Christian New Testament scholarship. At its heart was the recognition that Jewish religion was based on the covenant that God had originally made with Abraham and the other patriarchs. This was a divine initiative,

---

[12]See the quotations of E. Lohse, *Paulus* (Munich: C. H. Beck, 1996), p. 285; and Peter Stuhlmacher, *Revisiting Paul's Doctrine of Justification: A Challenge to the New Perspective* (Downers Grove, Ill.: InterVarsity Press, 2001), p. 35, cited in *New Perspective on Paul*, p. 22 n. 89.

[13]See further *New Perspective on Paul*, p. 22 n. 88.

[14]Ernst Käsemann, *Commentary on Romans*, trans. and ed. Geoffrey W. Bromiley (Grand Rapids: Eerdmans, 1980), p. 93.

[15]Rudolf Bultmann, *Theology of the New Testament*, vol. 1 (ET London: SCM, 1952), p. 139.

[16]C. G. Montefiore, *Judaism and St. Paul* (New York: Arno, 1973 [1914]), p. 65. The parallel with Heschel's characterization of the liberal quest for the historical Jesus (n. 11) should not escape notice.

[17]E. P. Sanders, *Paul and Palestinian Judaism* (Minneapolis: Fortress; London: SCM, 1977). See also, e.g., the quotation from G. F. Moore, *Judaism in the First Centuries of the Christian Era: The Age of the Tannaim*, 3 vols. (Cambridge, Mass.: Harvard University Press, 1927-1930), 2:94-95; in *New Perspective on Paul*, p. 6 n. 22.

a promise and an oath given by God, on which Israel's whole sense of identity as a people specially chosen by God rested.[18] The redemption from slavery in Egypt was a further act of divine grace, and the entry into the promised land the fulfillment of the promise given to the patriarchs. The covenant at Sinai both ratified the earlier divine initiatives and spelled out what Israel's response should be, what it must mean to live as the people of God. Sanders summed up the balance or interplay thus embodied in the Sinai covenant and its outworking thereafter in the phrase "covenantal nomism."[19] The point of the phrase is to highlight the interaction or symbiotic relationship implicit in Israel's religion (and Judaism) between divine initiative and human response. Israel's relation with God began with the divine initiative of covenant and fulfilled promise; Israel's part within the covenant thus begun was to maintain the covenant by obeying the law. No document better expresses the double character of "covenantal nomism" than the book of Deuteronomy, with its repeated emphasis both on God's faithfulness to his covenant promises and on the necessity of Israel keeping the commandments given at Sinai.[20]

Sanders also justifiably pointed to the provision of sacrifice for sin and atonement within Israel's cultic system.[21] Jews were not expected to amass good works as though that was the way to compensate for their sins. The covenant made provision for the wiping away of sin. And the cultic act was not simply a superficial routine; repentance was necessary too.[22]

At the same time it began to be taken more seriously than before that central to Paul's gospel as expounded in his letter to Rome was a key Jewish term, "righteousness" (Rom 1:16-17), and that it was understood by Paul in a distinctively Jewish way. In Hebrew thought, "righteousness" was a relational term, denoting the conduct that meets the obligations laid upon the individual by the relationship of which he/she is part.[23] So Israel's righteousness was not so much something to be achieved by their self-

---

[18]Beginning with Gen 12:2-3.

[19]Sanders, *Paul*, pp. 75, 236, 420, 544.

[20]Deut 4:32-40; 6:20-25; 7:6-11; 8:17-20; etc.

[21]Sanders, *Paul*, pp. 157-80, and further in the subject index, p. 617.

[22]Ps 51 is a classic example. See further Sanders, *Paul*, index p. 625. This was one of the features of Paul's teaching that puzzled Jewish scholars: why Paul made so little of repentance, despite its prominence within Judaism.

[23]See further my *The Theology of Paul the Apostle* (Grand Rapids: Eerdmans, 1998), pp. 341-44 and the bibliography there.

effort; rather it was understood and measured in terms of obedience to the law of the covenant, faithfulness to the terms of the covenant. Similarly, God's righteousness was the fulfillment of the obligation that God had taken upon himself in making covenant with Israel. It included or over-lapped with the concept of God's faithfulness to his covenant-determining promise. It was fulfilled when God maintained his covenant despite Isra-el's unfaithfulness,[24] and when he rescued and vindicated his people. That is why the term "righteousness," particularly in the Psalms and Isaiah, is regularly rendered in modern translations as "deliverance" or "vindication."[25] It was *saving* righteousness, not judgmental righteousness.[26] This indeed is precisely what Luther had himself realized, a revelation (or new perspec-tive) that gave rise to the Reformation itself.[27] But it wasn't a new insight for the bulk of Second Temple Judaism; it was rather an axiom that was fundamental to Judaism itself.

Nothing made this clearer in the mid-twentieth century than the dis-covery of the Dead Sea Scrolls, including the hymn at the end of the Com-munity Rule of Qumran (1QS 11.11-15):

> As for me, if I stumble, the mercies of God shall be my eternal salvation. If I stagger because of the sin of flesh, my justification shall be by the right-eousness of God which endures for ever. . . . He will draw me near by his grace, and by his mercy will he bring my justification. He will judge me in the righteousness of his truth and in the greatness of his goodness he will pardon all my sins. Through his righteousness he will cleanse me of the uncleanness of man and of the sins of the children of men.[28]

Here was a text from an intensely nomistic Jewish sect, which spoke sfeelingly of God's grace, mercy and righteousness as the only ground of hope, of the assurance of sins forgiven. The text was so *Pauline* in charac-ter and emphasis! How could this be expressive of the Judaism that was considered to be the opposite of Paul's gospel? Or is the answer rather that the traditional Christian antipathy to Judaism had skewed and distorted

---

[24]Paul reflects briefly on this paradox in Rom 3:3-7.

[25]E.g., Ps 51:14; 65:5; 71:15; Is 46:13; 51:5-8; 62:1-2; Mic 6:5; 7:9.

[26]This is almost explicit in Rom 1:16-17: the gospel is the power of God for *salvation* because in it is revealed the *righteousness* of God.

[27]*LW* 34:336-37, quoted, e.g., in *New Perspective on Paul*, p. 193.

[28]Geza Vermes, *The Complete Dead Sea Scrolls in English* (New York: Penguin Press, 1997), p. 116.

its portrayal of the Judaism against which Paul reacted?

A case can certainly be made that Sanders overreacted in his polemical response to the traditional Christian portrayal of rabbinic Judaism. In asserting a dynamic interaction between covenant and law ("covenantal nomism") he may have focused too closely on the covenant dimension and underplayed the nomisitic dimension (*covenantal* nomism).[29] Second Temple and rabbinic writings may well be less consistent than Sanders argued.[30] The point, however, is that by focusing on the covenant dimension so intensively Sanders was bringing to the foreground a balance that had previously been ignored (*nomism*) or correcting a previous imbalance (covenantal *nomism*). He is certainly not to be countered by retreating back into the older Judaism = law portrayal. Both factors (covenant and law) must be given weight, as well as Paul's own dependence on Israel's understanding of divine righteousness. The dynamic between the two is different between different Jewish writings—as it is between different Christian writings. But that there is such a dynamic cannot and should not be disputed.[31]

This then is the first aspect of the new perspective on Paul—the claim that Paul's gospel is rooted in the priorities and emphases that Judaism also inherited, particularly in the conception of "God's righteousness," and that this dimension of Paul's teaching on justification has not been given sufficient weight.

FOR ALL WHO BELIEVE, JEW AND GREEK

One of the consequences of Christianity's tradition of anti-Judaism was that the character of earliest Christianity and the significance of Paul's emphasis, the gospel for Gentile as well as Jew, were obscured. For a Christianity that continued to define itself over against Judaism it was something of an embarrassment not only that Jesus had been a Jew, but

---

[29]D. A. Carson et al., eds., *Justification and Variegated Nomism*, vol. 1: *The Complexities of Second Temple Judaism*, WUNT 2.140 (Tübingen: Mohr Siebeck, 2001); S. J. Gathercole, *Where Is Boasting? Early Jewish Soteriology and Paul's Response in Romans 1–5* (Grand Rapids: Eerdmans, 2002).

[30]So particularly the critique of Friedrich Avemarie, *Tora und Leben: Untersuchungen zur Heilsbedeutung der Tora in der frühen rabbinischen Literatur* (Tübingen: Mohr Siebeck, 1996).

[31]See, e.g., Avemarie's positive assessment of Sanders published in the same year as his *Tora und Leben*, cited in *New Perspective on Paul*, pp. 63-64 n. 252; also on the volume edited by Carson et al., *Justification and Variegated Nomism*, see *New Perspective on Paul*, pp. 61-62 n. 242.

also that his first and leading disciples, that is, the earliest Christians, were all Jews. The first modern critical history of Christianity, by F. C. Baur, faced up to the challenge but also posed the issue afresh. In Baur's perspective, Christianity brought a universal religious "idea" to realization, within the bounds of national Judaism, but essentially different from "all the national peculiarities of Judaism."[32] And it was Paul who was "the first to lay down expressly and distinctly the principle of Christian universalism as a thing essentially opposed to Jewish particularism."[33] Baur's consequent analysis of early Christianity as a long-running conflict between Gentile Christianity (Paul party) and Jewish Christianity (Peter party) was itself a reflection of the Lutheran gospel/law antithesis (Paul → gospel → Reformation; Judaism → law → Peter → Catholic Church) and is open to the same criticism as unjustly denigrating Judaism—and Catholicism!

Baur's focus on Christianity's emergence from its Jewish matrix was an important step in the ongoing study of Christianity's beginnings. So too his recognition that the national character of Judaism[34] was deemed by Paul to be a restriction on the gospel, was on the right lines, as we shall see. But to pose the contrast in terms of universalism versus particularism failed to recognize both the universal claims and appeal of Judaism and that Christianity has its own particularism.[35] Baur's tendentious rejection of all but four of the Pauline epistles as inauthentic and late dating of other New Testament writings have made little or no lasting impact.[36] Typical, however, of the influence he continues to have is his characterization of Paul's opponents as "Judaizers," denoting Jewish believers who insisted that Gentile believers must be circumcised, even though in historical usage a "judaizer" (one who judaizes) denoted a Gentile living like a Jew (as in Gal 2:14).[37]

Baur's categorization of Paul's gospel in terms of "universalism" also

---

[32]F. C. Baur, *Paul: The Apostle of Jesus Christ* (ET London: Williams & Norgate, 1873), 1:3.

[33]F. C. Baur, *The Church History of the First Three Centuries,* 2 vols. (ET London: Williams & Norgate 1878-1879), 1:47.

[34]See above n. 7.

[35]See further my "Was Judaism Particularist or Universalist?" in *Judaism in Late Antiquity,* part 3: *Where We Stand: Issues and Debates in Ancient Judaism,* vol. 2, ed. J. Neusner and A. J. Avery-Peck, Handbuch der Orientalisk (Leiden: Brill, 1999), pp. 57-73.

[36]See e.g., Scott J. Hafemann, "Baur, F. C.," in *Dictionary of Major Biblical Interpreters,* ed. Donald K. McKim (Downers Grove, Ill.: InterVarsity Press, 2007), pp. 177-81.

[37]For full detail see my *Beginning from Jerusalem* (Grand Rapids: Eerdmans, 2009), pp. 473-74.

allowed the issue of race, ethnicity and nationalism to be put to one side. In the individualism of nineteenth-century liberalism and twentieth-century existentialism, Paul's "all" could be read as every single individual troubled by guilty conscience or *Angst*, irrespective of race and ethnicity. And the gospel could be readily presented as an offer to the sinful individual of peace with God.[38] No matter how much truth there was in all this, as there is, what had been neglected was also important—what might be called the social or racial dimension of Paul's gospel.

Today we take Paul's title, "apostle to Gentiles" (Rom 11:13), more or less for granted. As we know well, it is above all (humanly speaking) to Paul that we owe the opening to Gentiles of what became known as "Christianity." But we too easily forget what a major, unprecedented and controversial step this was. From a Jewish perspective, the "Jews-Gentiles" distinction denoted one of the great divisions of human society—similar to the other major division of the Mediterranean world, from a Greek perspective, between "Greeks" and "barbarians."[39] "Gentiles," we should not forget, is simply another way of translating "the nations." From an internal Jewish perspective, there was Israel and there was all the rest, the nations, Gentiles. Of course, Israel was itself a nation *(ethnos)*, but even so it could simply distinguish itself from "the nations." And Israel was not alone in using the term *ethnē* as equivalent to "foreigners."[40] But in Hebrew usage Israel preferred to think of itself as a "people" *(ʿam)* rather than a "nation" *(goy)*. And the plural, *goyim* ("nations"), attracted to itself a negative overtone, similar to the English "heathens," the *goyim* being regarded as distant from God, outside the covenant and hostile to God and his people.[41]

What has been inadequately appreciated is that this attitude to "the nations/Gentiles" was carried over into the first century and was widespread among the first Christians. This essentially Jewish perspective is reflected

---

[38]In NT scholarship, particularly Bultmann; in popular evangelism, typically the rallies of Billy Graham. As Nils Dahl shrewdly noted, "a certain narrowing occurred. . . . The focus of the doctrine became the individual's relationship to God" ("The Doctrine of Justification: Its Social Function and Implications" [1964], *Studies in Paul* [Minneapolis: Augsburg, 1977], pp. 95-120, at p. 118).

[39]See LSJ, p. 306.

[40]BDAG, p. 276.

[41]E.g., Deut 7:1-6; 2 Kings 17:8-15; Ps 2:1-3; Ezek 20:32. See further R. E. Clements, *"goy,"* *TDOT* 2:431-43; also, e.g., N. Walter, *"ethnos,"* *EDNT* 1:382.

nowhere more clearly than in the letter to the Ephesians:

> Remember that at one time you were the nations/Gentiles by birth, called
> "the uncircumcision" by those who are called "the circumcision" in the
> flesh, made by hands, that you were at that time without Christ, aliens
> from the community of Israel, and strangers to the covenants of promise,
> having no hope and without God in the world. (Eph 2:11-12)

In this perspective, Gentiles were not merely disadvantaged, but equivalent to law-breakers, the disobedient. By virtue of being outside God's covenant, they were without the law, literally "law-less," "out-laws"; they could be referred to simply as "sinners."[42] It is a rather uncomfortable fact that this usage, Gentiles = sinners, as a given, still appears in the New Testament.[43] Even with Paul, the dismissive note in Galatians 2:15 ("Gentile sinners") is hard to miss.

All this helps to make clear how astonishing was the step that some of the first Christians (Jews) took in preaching the gospel to Gentiles (non-Jews). In turning to this point, we should not forget or play down the fact that Israel was very concerned for the welfare of the non-Israelite in their midst (the resident aliens),[44] or that Second Temple Judaism was very open to Gentile God-fearers who were attracted to Judaism (who "judaized") and welcoming to Gentile proselytes who wished to become Jews,[45] or that there was a widespread hope and expectation that together with the restoration of the tribes dispersed among the nations, there would be many Gentile proselytes who made pilgrimage to Zion in the last days.[46] But none of this made Jews anxious to become evangelists or to engage in missionary effort to convert non-Jews. Judaism was not missionary minded.[47] Why should it? Judaism was primarily an ethnic religion, the religion of the residents of Judea, that is, Judeans.[48] So it was natural for Second Temple Jews to think of Judaism as only for Jews,

---

[42]Ps 9:17; Tob 13:6; *Jub.* 23.23-24; *Pss. Sol.* 1.1; 2.1-2.

[43]Mt 5:47 = Lk 6:33; Mk 14:41 pars.; Gal 2:15.

[44]See, e.g., Ex 12:48-49; Num 9:14; Deut 31:12.

[45]See *Beginning from Jerusalem*, pp. 560-63.

[46]References and bibliography in my *Jesus Remembered* (Grand Rapids: Eerdmans, 2003), p. 395 n. 71.

[47]Bibliography in *Beginning from Jerusalem*, p. 299 n. 247.

[48]BDAG indeed elects to translate *Ioudaios* primarily as "Judean," and not as "Jew" (pp. 478-79).

and for non-Jews who became Jews.[49]

This was where Christianity, initially a Jewish sect, broke the established mold. It became an evangelistic sect, a missionary movement, something untoward, unheard of within Judaism. We can still get a real sense of the shock this must have caused. For example, in the insistence in Matthew's Gospel that Jesus' mission was only for "the lost sheep of the house of Israel" (Mt 10:5-6; 15:24). And in the shock experienced by the believing Jews when they realized that God was giving his Spirit to Gentiles, without their becoming proselytes: "the uncircumcised believers . . . were astounded that the gift of the Spirit had been poured out even on the Gentiles" (Acts 10:45). Paul too attributed the Gentile mission breakthrough to the Spirit being given so freely to Gentiles and could record that the Jerusalem leadership had fully acknowledged this manifest grace of God in his mission to Gentiles (Gal 2:7-9; 3:2-5). It would have taken such unmistakable revelation of divine approval for such a huge shift in Jews' perception of God's will to be accepted to the extent that it was within earliest Christianity.

However, such a shattering of the mold was not so widely accepted, certainly not among Jews who had not acknowledged Jesus to be Messiah, but also not even among believing Jews. Given Israel's centuries-old conviction that it was a people specially chosen by God, such a reaction can be easily understood. And it was Paul's lot to make the case that God was now doing something unexpectedly new, that the initiative of the Spirit should be followed wholeheartedly. Once again it is in Ephesians that the full significance of what Paul was about is expressed.

> Surely you have already heard of the commission of God's grace that was given me for you, and how the mystery was made known to me by revelation. . . . In former generations this mystery was not made known to humankind, as it has now been revealed to his holy apostles and prophets by the Spirit: that is, the Gentiles have become fellow heirs, members of the same body, and sharers in the promise in Christ Jesus through the gospel. (Eph 3:2-6 NRSV)

This was the same mystery that Paul had unveiled in Romans 11:25,

---

[49]Here Baur was correct, in what he referred to as Jewish particularism, although he went off at a tangent at this point.

the mystery that had been unveiled to him as he wrestled with the problem of why Israel remained so obdurate to the gospel, when so many Gentiles were accepting it. The mystery was precisely God's purpose to bring salvation to Gentiles, as a means of bringing salvation also to Israel, that is, to all (Rom 11:11-14, 25-26, 32).

The point is that the "all" for Paul meant not just everyone or anyone. The "all" meant specifically Gentile as well as Jew, Jew as well as Gentile. This is why Paul emphasizes repeatedly in his letter to Rome that the good news and its ramifications have in view precisely "Jews and Greeks," "Jews and Gentiles,"[50] "circumcision and uncircumcision."[51] To be more precise, for Paul the mystery unveiled in the gospel was God's purpose to bring Jew and Gentile together in shared worship of the one God. Here the climax of Romans is too often neglected. In Romans 15:8-12, Paul sums up his whole gospel outlined in the earlier chapters by quoting from all three parts of Scripture[52] to affirm that in his mission to the Gentiles the hopes of lawgiver, psalmist and prophet were being fulfilled: Gentiles were being fully caught up in praise of Israel's God.

Here again it is Ephesians that makes the point most explicit.

> Now in Christ Jesus you who were once far off have been brought near by the blood of Christ. For he is our peace; he has made both [Jews and Gentiles] one, and in his flesh has broken down the dividing wall, the enmity [which separated them]. He has annulled the law with its rules and regulations, in order that he might create in him one new humanity out of the two, thus making peace, and might reconcile both to God in one body, through the cross, thereby killing the enmity in it/him. (Eph 2:13-16)

Here it could hardly be plainer. The Paul of Ephesians, like the Paul of Romans, saw the purpose of the gospel not only in terms of the vertical relation between individual humans and God, but also in terms of the horizontal relation between nations and peoples, here, between Jews and Gentiles. For Paul, evidently, "the dividing wall" that prevented Gentiles from fully entering the presence of God had been broken down.[53] The

---

[50]Rom 1:16; 2:9-10; 3:9, 29; 9:24; 10:12; also 1 Cor 1:23-24; 10:32; 12:13; Gal 3:28; Col 3:11.

[51]Rom 2:25-27; 3:30; 4:10-12; also 1 Cor 7:18-19; Gal 2:7; 5:6; 6:15; Col 3:11.

[52]Rom 15:9 from Ps 18:49; Rom 15:10 from Deut 32:43; Rom 15:11 from Ps 117:1; Rom 15:12 from Is 11:10.

[53]"The dividing wall" may be a reference to the balustrade that in the Jerusalem Temple separated the Court of Gentiles from the inner courts and beyond which non-Jews could only pass

"enmity" between Jew and Gentile, which had been in effect a consequence of Israel's election, had been brought to an end, killed off. This too was the mystery of God's purpose, long hidden but now revealed and enacted in Paul's ministry.

This is the second feature of Paul's significance and teaching that has been too much neglected and that the new perspective wants to bring back into sharper focus—and for the very relevant reason that Paul's teaching on justification grew out of the context of this ministry and of Paul's understanding of his mission.[54] This is why it should occasion so little surprise that Paul's doctrine of justification by faith is so heavily focused in his letters to Rome and Galatia. For it is precisely in these letters above all that Paul expounds and defends his gospel as the gospel for all who believe, Greeks as well as Jews, Gentiles as well as Israel. And it was gospel, good news, precisely because it made possible the breaking down of the old barrier between Jew and Gentile, because it made the worship of Gentile with Jew, in one body, a reality at last. The social dimension of the doctrine of justification was as integral to its initial formulation as any other. It was not a corollary that Paul drew from his primary emphasis at a later date; as an apostle he was never anything other than apostle to the Gentiles. This emphasis was at the heart of his gospel, why he felt so committed to it and why he defended it so resolutely. A doctrine of justification by faith that does not give prominence to Paul's concern to bring Jew and Gentile together is not true to Paul's doctrine.

JUSTIFICATION BY FAITH AND NOT BY WORKS OF THE LAW

The recognition of these two aspects of the background and context for Paul's teaching on justification has been the starting point for the new

---

on pain of death. Some wonder whether such an allusion would have been recognized in Asia Minor, though the very strongly Jewish perspective expressed in Eph 2:11-12 suggests an expectation of readers' familiarity with such Jewish distinctives. An alternative, as indicated in the following clauses, may be the law itself, the Torah as itself a fence around Israel. See, e.g., discussion in A. T. Lincoln, *Ephesians*, WBC 42 (Dallas: Word, 1990), p. 141; E. Best, *Ephesians*, ICC (Edinburgh: T & T Clark, 1998), pp. 253-57.

[54]The point had been made more than once in the twentieth century, but it was K. Stendahl that gave it fresh life in the later decades ("The Apostle Paul and the Introspective Conscience of the West," *HTR* 56 [1963]: 199-215 = *Paul Among Jews and Gentiles* [London: SCM, 1977], pp. 78-96).

perspective: (1) that to characterize the Judaism of Paul's day as thoroughly legalistic, as assuming that God's righteousness was purely punitive, as thinking that acceptance by God could be achieved only by good works, was a grave distortion of the historical reality and completely ignored the dimension of God's initiative and covenant made gratuitously with Israel, which remained fundamental to that Judaism; (2) that Paul's teaching on justification must have reflected and may even have been a reflection of the commitment that dominated his life and ministry as apostle to the Gentiles and made him stand out from his fellow Jewish believers, that the gospel of Messiah Jesus was for all who believe, not just for Jews, but for Gentiles too, without their having to become Jews.

In view of this I found myself asking with more and more intensity a simple question: Why then does Paul articulate key expressions of his understanding of justification in a polemical form—"by faith in Jesus Christ and not by works of the law"? If he was not objecting to, but rather drawing on Israel's understanding of God's *saving* righteousness, then what was he objecting to when he spoke of "works of the law"? As I reflected on these questions, four points became clear to me, four interlocked aspects of the whole picture. I have developed these points in some detail in several earlier contributions, so here I will treat them only briefly.

1. There was a function of the law/Torah that had been largely ignored in the discussion of Paul's attitude to the law—another missing dimension, if you like. This was the role of the law as *marking out Israel from the other nations*, as a people of the law[55]—which is why, as we saw above, Gentiles were by definition outside the law, out-laws, that is, "sinners." In this role the law served as a kind of bulwark, protecting Israel's holiness, that is, its set-apartness to God, from the corruption and defilement that would otherwise be the consequence of being too close to the other nations. The image of the law as a protective palisade around Israel is nowhere so clearly expressed as in the *Letter of Aristeas*, written probably in the second century B.C.E., and in effect trying to explain the relation between Jews and non-Jews.

---

[55]I first developed this point in the introduction to my commentary on *Romans*, WBC 38 (Dallas: Word, 1988), pp. lxiv-lxxii, reprinted in K. P. Donfried, ed., *The Romans Debate* (Peabody, Mass.: Hendrickson, 1991), pp. 299-308, and *New Perspective on Paul*, chap. 4 (particularly pp. 146-49).

> In his wisdom the legislator [i.e., Moses] . . . surrounded us with unbroken
> palisades and iron walls to prevent our mixing with any of the other peoples
> in any matter, being thus kept pure in body and soul. . . . To prevent our
> being perverted by contact with others or by mixing with bad influences, he
> hedged us in on all sides with strict observances connected with meat and
> drink and touch and hearing and sight, after the manner of the Law.[56]

"Holiness" is the key term in denoting this set-apartness to God.[57] The
point here is that separateness *to God* also meant separateness *from the nations* that would otherwise defile and render unclean.

2. There were various *boundary markers,* particular ritual practices
that expressed Israel's set-apartness with particular clarity.[58] One was
circumcision. Although circumcision was more widely practiced, it was
already generally regarded as a distinguishing feature of the Jewish male.
As the Roman historian Tacitus was to put it: "They adopted circumcision to distinguish themselves from other peoples by this difference"
(*Historiae* 5.5.2). So much so that Paul could reexpress the Jew/Gentile
distinction not as "circumcised/uncircumcised" but as "circumcision/
uncircumcision."[59]

A second boundary marker was the *laws of clean and unclean.* That the
fundamental distinction between clean and unclean animals reflected and
reinforced the separation between Israel and the nations is nowhere so
clear as in Leviticus 20:23-26:

> You shall not follow the practices of the nation that I am driving out before
> you. Because they did all these things, I abhorred them. . . . I am the LORD
> your God; *I have separated you from the peoples.* You shall *therefore* make a
> distinction between the clean animal and the unclean, and between the
> unclean bird and the clean; you shall not bring abomination on yourselves
> by animal or by bird or by anything with which the ground teems, which I

---

[56]*Letter of Aristeas* 139-42, in James H. Charlesworth, ed, *The Old Testament Pseudepigrapha,*
2 vols. (Garden City, N.Y.: Doubleday, 1983-1985), 2:22. The imagery is significant, since
Aristeas itself is devoid of an aggressive zeal for the Law.

[57]E.g., Ex 19:6; Lev 11:44-45; 19:2; 20:7, 26.

[58]I drew attention to the social function of the law and "boundary markers" in "Works of the
Law and the Curse of the Law (Gal 3:10-14)," *NTS* 31 (1985): 523-42, reprinted in *Jesus, Paul
and the Law: Studies in Mark and Galatians* (London: SPCK, 1990), pp. 215-41, and again in
New Perspective on Paul, chap. 3 (here particularly pp. 122-25).

[59]Rom 2:26; 3:30; Gal 2:7; Col 3:11. See further *Beginning from Jerusalem,* pp. 439-42, where I
also reflect on why the crisis over circumcision of Gentile believers did not arise earlier (pp.
442-46).

have set apart for you to hold unclean. *You shall be holy to me; for I the LORD am holy, and I have separated you from the other peoples to be mine.* (NRSV, emphasis added)

A third boundary marker was Israel's observation of the *sabbath*, a regular day of rest and worship that marked Jews off from other religions with more diverse festivals. The Roman satirist Juvenal well indicates how the judaizing Gentile would approach Judaism by surmounting each of these boundary markers:

> Some who have had a father who reveres the Sabbath, worship nothing but the clouds, and the divinity of the heavens, and see no difference between eating swine's flesh, from which their father abstained, and that of man; and in time they take to circumcision. Having been wont to flout the laws of Rome, they learn and practice and revere the Jewish law, and all that Moses handed down in his secret tome. (*Satires* 14.96-102)[60]

These, it should perhaps be stressed, were not necessarily the most important commandments of the law, but they were often the make or break issues, the most defining issues because they were so distinctive of Judaism. Hence the sensitivity shown in Paul's letters precisely on these issues.[61]

3. The reason why Saul/Paul persecuted "the church of God." There were probably several factors involved here, but Paul himself gives the reason for it as *"zeal"*: his persecution was an expression of and testimony to his zeal (Phil 3:6). This factor is often ignored, even though it is the only reason that Paul himself gives for his former conduct. Alternatively it is assumed that his zeal was simply a more general "zeal for the law" or for "the traditions of [his] fathers" (Gal 1:14) that motivated the real reason, namely, denial that Jesus was Messiah or outrage at the claims made by the earliest believers for Jesus. What has almost always been missed in this is the link between Israel's tradition of "zeal" and its set-apartness to God. What needs to be taken more note of here, however, is that the zeal of which Paul spoke was probably understood by Saul the persecutor as re-

---

[60]See *GLAJJ* 2.102-7.

[61]Circumcision: Galatians, Romans; laws of clean and unclean: Rom 14:1–15:6; Gal 2:11-14; Col 2:16; sabbath: Rom 14:5-6; Gal 4:10; Col 2:16. In questioning the appropriateness of recognizing a boundary function of the law to have been in play in Galatians 2, D. A. Campbell, *The Deliverance of God: An Apocalyptic Rereading of Justification in Paul* (Grand Rapids: Eerdmans, 2009), pp. 449-50, completely ignores passages like Lev 20:22-26 and *Letter of Aristeas* 139-42.

flecting God's own "zeal." It was Yahweh's own "zeal" or "jealousy" (the same word) that insisted that Israel must not worship other gods but remain dedicated to him alone, "for I the LORD your God am a jealous God."[62]

The classic model of zeal in Israel's history was Phinehas, who, when an Israelite brought a Midianite woman into his tent killed them both, "because he was zealous for God," a zeal that reflected God's jealousy/zeal (Num 25:6-13). Other heroes of zeal in Israel's history displayed the same determination to defend Israel's separateness from other nations, and regularly with the same readiness to use violence against fellow Israelites/Jews. The fact that Paul gave the reason for his persecution of fellow Jews as "zeal," and that he was willing to use such violence ("I persecuted the church of God in excessive measure and tried to destroy it," Gal 1:13), strongly suggests that his zeal was motivated by God's zealous insistence that Israel keep itself apart from other nations and their gods.[63]

4. Against all this background, Paul's reference to "works of the law" and his antithesis between "works of the law" and faith in Christ Jesus (Gal 2:16) gains fresh illumination. By "works of the law," of course he means what the law requires.[64] But it is also clear from Galatians 2:1-16 that when he wrote these words (Gal 2:16), he had in mind the events that led up to this key statement of the (for Paul) fundamental gospel truth. The "works of the law" that he had in mind would certainly include the circumcision that the "false brothers" tried to "compel" the Gentile believer Titus to undergo and that Paul resisted, with the support of the Jerusalem leadership (Gal 2:3-6). The "works of the law" (Gal 2:16) would certainly also focus on the laws of clean and unclean that Peter in effect tried to "compel" the Gentile believers in Antioch to observe (Gal 2:14). It was Peter who had in effect insisted that in addition to believing, the Gentile Christians had to observe certain "works of the law."[65] Peter, we can

[62]Ex 20:5; 34:14; Deut 4:23-24; 5:9; 6:14-15; 32:21; 11QTemple 1.12-13.
[63]I have argued the case in detail in "Paul's Conversion: A Light to Twentieth Century Disputes," in *Evangelium—Schriftauslegung—Kirche*, ed. J. Ådna et al., P. Stuhlmacher FS (Göttingen: Vandenhoeck & Ruprecht, 1997), pp. 77-93, reprinted in *New Perspective on Paul*, chap. 15; more briefly in *Beginning from Jerusalem*, pp. 341-46.
[64]I emphasize the point, since my early formulation of the point in "The *New Perspective on Paul*," *BJRL* 65 (1983): 95-122, reprinted in *Jesus, Paul and the Law*, pp. 183-214, and in *New Perspective on Paul*, chap. 2, caused some misunderstanding or confusion on the point.
[65]Campbell seems strangely unwilling to acknowledge the obvious train of thought linking the

safely infer was motivated by the theology of Leviticus 20:23-26: he had "separated" from the Gentiles (Gal 2:12), fellow believers though they were, in order to preserve Israel's holiness. As Paul says, Peter had in effect insisted that the Gentiles "live like Jews," he had tried to "compel them to judaize" (Gal 2:14). The "works of the law" to which Paul objected (as a requirement in addition to believing in Jesus Christ) were in this case the boundary markers, the laws that marked out Jews in their distinctiveness/ separation from other nations. In this case "works of the law" and "living like a Jew" overlap and are almost synonymous.

To repeat, "works of the law" is a more general phrase, which refers to the principle of keeping the law in all its requirements. But when the phrase comes in the context of Paul's mission to Gentiles, and particularly of Jewish believers trying to compel Gentile believers to live like Jews, then its most obvious reference is to, or should we say, particularly to the law in its role as a wall dividing Jew from Gentile, the boundary markers that define who is "inside" and who is "outside," that is, inside the law/ covenant and outside the law/covenant people. Of course Galatians 2:16 is a restatement of the fundamental principle that Paul cites from Psalm 143:2 (as again Rom 3:20). Of course there is a restatement of the founda- tional principle of Israel's theology, that Israel's own status as a people chosen by God and made covenant with was solely by divine initiative, and so did not presuppose any prior merit of Israel as precondition. But here what occasions and motivates that restatement is the particular attempts made in Jerusalem and Antioch to "compel" the Gentile believers to accept certain works of the law, and thereby either to live like Jews or to become Jews. "The truth of the gospel" that Paul insisted on in both situations (Gal 2:5, 14) was that the gospel was free to all who believe without taking on any further obligation, as a gospel requirement, any "work of the law" that implied that the gospel was not free to Gentiles as Gentiles.

If these four points can be seen as expressive of the new perspective, or

---

issues in Jerusalem and Antioch (Gal 2:1-14) to Gal 2:16 (*Deliverance of God*, pp. 449-50), despite the fact that Gal 2:15-16 is presented as a continuation of Paul's rebuke to Peter (Gal 2:14), and the obvious deduction that 2:16 is Paul's statement of "the truth of the gospel" that he was defending in Gal 2:5 and 14. The reason why Paul was so "flexible" on "boundary" is- sues in Rom 14–15 (*Deliverance of God*, p. 453) is presumably because in the latter case it was a Gentile majority threatening Jewish liberty, whereas in Gal 2:1-14 it was a Jewish majority threatening Gentile liberty.

at least my version of it, then the case made by the new perspective itself is clear. It affirms that Paul taught and defended the principle of justification by faith (alone) because he saw that fundamental gospel principle to be threatened by Jewish believers maintaining that as believers in Messiah Jesus they had a continuing obligation to maintain that separateness to God, a holiness that depended on their being distinct from other nations, an obligation, in other words, to maintain the law's requirement of separation from non-Jews. This "gospel truth" was of a piece with Israel's own election, that God's saving purpose is an act of grace from beginning to end, that God's acceptance of individuals or a people is not premised on how good or great they were. But this principle, this gospel truth, was confronted with its initial test in the history of Christianity when Jewish believers thought it necessary to require more of Gentile believers as essential than the faith through which they had already received God's grace and Spirit—the insistence (compulsion) that believing Gentiles had to become proselyte Jews or live like Jews. For Paul, the truth of the gospel was demonstrated by the breaking down of the boundary markers and the wall that divided Jew from Gentile, a conviction that remained the central part of his mission precisely because it was such a fundamental expression of and test case for the gospel. This is the missing dimension of Paul's doctrine of justification that the new perspective has brought back to the center of the stage where Paul himself placed it.

THE WHOLE GOSPEL OF PAUL

The new perspective has given a fresh emphasis to several features of Paul's theology and gospel, and it suggests that more work is necessary if still other dimensions of Paul's gospel are to be properly seen as part of his soteriology.

1. Justification by Faith in Jesus Christ

Paul takes it for granted that the faith through which Abraham was counted righteous (Gen 15:6) now comes to expression as faith in Jesus Christ. Abraham's trust in God's promise of a son, in God as the one "who gives life to the dead and calls into existence the things that do not exist" (Rom 4:17 NRSV), was the prototype of Christian faith "in him who raised Jesus our Lord from the dead" (Rom 4:24 NRSV). In the same way, God's promise to Abraham, that "in you all the Gentiles shall be blessed" (Gen

12:3; 18:18), was already the gospel (Gal 3:8), since the gospel was that in the gift of the Spirit received through faith, the blessing of Abraham came also to Gentiles (Gal 3:14). It was because the gospel was fully experienced through believing in Jesus Christ that Paul could and did insist that Gentiles who had received the gospel through faith in Christ were fully part of the church of God, and why for Paul any further requirement to do works of the law as a precondition of God's acceptance was so offensive to the truth of the gospel.

This basic aspect of the gospel for Paul has been somewhat obscured in recent years by the renewed popularity that by the phrase cited above as "faith in Christ" *(pistis Christou)*, Paul actually meant "the faith(fulness) of Christ." The argument is that the phrase is a summary reference to the story of Jesus, particularly his faithfulness to death on the cross. What Paul puts in contrast to "works of the law" is not another human action or attitude (faith) but *Christ's* faith or faithfulness.[66] The issue is not integral to the new perspective and is somewhat peripheral to it. But because it relates to the key phrase, "justification by faith," and because it is posed in antithesis to "works of the law," the debate should be addressed, even if briefly.

From my perspective, the value of the "faith of Christ" interpretation of *pistis Christou* is that it has brought to the fore the underlying narrative element that undergirds Paul's thought—Jesus' life and death alluded to more explicitly in such passages as Galatians 2:20; 4:4 and Romans 15:3, 8. Since Paul is ready to refer to Christ's death as "obedience" (Rom 5:19; Phil 2:8), it is certainly arguable that Paul would have found it equally natural to speak of Jesus' "faith," even though he never mentions Jesus believing or trusting. As we shall also note shortly, to focus the phrase *pistis Christou* on the believer's dependence on what Jesus has done also highlights another dimension of Paul's soteriology which has also suffered some neglect.

---

[66]Most influentially by Richard B. Hays, *The Faith of Jesus Christ: The Narrative Substructure of Galatians 3:1–4:11*, 2nd. ed. (Grand Rapids: Eerdmans, 2002). The interpretation has won strong support: e.g., Morna D. Hooker, *"PISTIS CHRISTOU," NTS* 35 (1989); J. L. Martyn, *Galatians*, AB 33A (New York: Doubleday, 1997), e.g., p. 276; L. E. Keck, *Romans*, ANTC (Nashville: Abingdon, 2005), pp. 104-5. See now M. F. Bird and P. M. Sprinkle, eds., *The Faith of Jesus Christ: Exegetical, Biblical and Theological Studies* (Milton Keynes, U.K.: Paternoster, 2009).

The main problems with the "faith of Christ" interpretation are that it involves questionable and even poor exegesis, and that it diminishes or sidetracks the importance of Paul's emphasis on "justification by faith in Christ." The clue as to what Paul was referring in the phrase *pistis Christou,* for me, is his more regular use of the phrase *ek pisteōs.*[67] His earliest and most intensive usage is in Galatians 3:7-12, 22, 24 (seven times). This is the passage in which he shows most clearly what he had in mind by using the phrase. The key is that Galatians 3:7-9 is Paul's exposition of or line of argument arising from Genesis 15:6, where Paul was evidently explaining the significance of the Galatians' acceptance of the gospel and reception of the Spirit (Gal 3:2-5): "Just as 'Abraham believed God, and it was reckoned to him for righteousness' [Gen 15:6]. Know then that those *ek pisteōs,* they are Abraham's sons" (Gal 3:6-7). The claim being made, obviously, is that those who believed as Abraham did are Abraham's sons. Those who are *ek pisteōs* are those who shared Abraham's faith. The *pistis* in Galatians 3:7 could hardly have been intended as other than "belief/ faith," as Abraham believed. It seems highly unlikely that Paul would vary the reference of *pistis* in the rest of the chapter (where it occurs thirteen times) without some explicit indication that he was now referring to Christ's faith and no longer to faith like Abraham's believing. And by the same logic, it is very unlikely that Paul would have used *pistis* with a different referent elsewhere in the letter (notably Gal 2:16). The same considerations apply to Romans, where Paul mounts the same argument that Abraham's believing (Gen 15:6) is the prototype of Christian faith (particularly Rom 4:16).[68]

The other problem is that to take so many *pistis* references, perhaps even all for consistency, as referring to *Christ's* faith cuts more seriously at the root of justification by faith than is usually appreciated. The faith that Paul's gospel sought to engender was the complete reliance on God so fully exemplified by Abraham (Rom 4:17-22).[69] It is the absence of such trustful

---

[67]Paul uses the phrase 21 times, all in Romans and Galatians. The phrase *pistis Christou* (with variations) appears 7 times, in Romans and Galatians, but also Phil 3:9.

[68]I argue the case in detail in *"EK PISTEŌS:* A Key to the Meaning of *PISTIS CHRISTOU,"* in *The Word Leaps the Gap: Essays on Scripture and Theology in Honor of Richard B. Hays,* ed. J. R. Wagner et al. (Grand Rapids: Eerdmans, 2008), pp. 351-66.

[69]It is a grievous mistake, even calumny, to suggest that setting human faith as the alternative to works of the law in effect makes faith something humanly achieved or contrived.

reliance on God that Paul describes as the basic human failing (Rom 1:21), the failure to act out of that faith that he regards as sin (Rom 14:23), the acting out of that faith in love as the only thing that counts (Gal 5:6). In contrast, it is much less clear what Paul could have meant if he had characterized his Christian life as living "by the faithfulness of the Son of God" (Gal 2:20). Of course, justification by believing (the verb) in Christ would still be sufficiently well rooted in Paul's letters,[70] but not really justification by faith (the noun).

2. Paul's Attitude to the Law

An important corollary to the new perspective is that it undermines the strong gospel/law antithesis that has so characterized Lutheran appropriation of Paul. It is true, of course, that Paul speaks very negatively of the (Jewish) law on several occasions. I referred to some of the most negative passages early on.[71] And it is certainly the case that Paul believed that the role of the law as protector of Israel had come to an end (Gal 3:19–4:7). And, as already noted, it can be said with confidence that for Paul, Christ had replaced the law as the referent point for daily living. However, it is equally clear that a sharp gospel/law antithesis fails to recognize the nuances of Paul's attitude to the law, and the degree to which he still regarded the law as a measure of what God demands of his human creatures.

For example, as in Galatians 3 Paul addressed the question of the reason why the law was given (Gal 3:19), so in Romans 7 Paul meets the challenge that he himself has posed by referring to the law so disparagingly: "Is the law sin?" (Rom 7:7). And the main thrust in what follows is a defense of the law; the real blame lies with sin and with the weakness of human flesh. So it should be hardly surprising that Paul begins the next chapter by asserting that the purpose of Christ's coming was "that the requirement of the law might be fulfilled in us who walk not in accordance with the flesh but in accordance with the Spirit" (Rom 8:3-4). Again, it is too little noted that Paul could say, "Circumcision is nothing, and uncircumcision is nothing; what matters is keeping the commandments of God" (1 Cor 7:19). Of course Paul would have been well aware that circumcision is one of the commandments (Gen 17:9-14). The point is that only someone who

---

[70]Though Paul only occasionally speaks of believing in Christ (Rom 9:33; 10:11, 14; Gal 2:16).
[71]Gal 2:19; 2 Cor 3; also Rom 7:5.

differentiated between commandments (works of the law) could make such an assertion. This obviously provides an explanation of how Paul could set aside or devalue commandments like circumcision and the laws of clean and unclean, while, at the same time, strongly reasserting the commandments against idolatry and sexual license. Moreover, the fact that Paul could follow Jesus not in rejecting the law, but in summing it up in the love command (Rom 13:8-10; Gal 5:14) indicates a similar readiness of Paul's part to cut through the surface reference of the law (the letter) to the underlying principles of the relation with God (faith) that should determine conduct (cf. Rom 2:28-29; Phil 3:3).

3. Judgment According to Works

One of the most disturbing features of the new perspective for many is that it has drawn fresh attention to Paul's teaching on final judgment.[72] It has always been a problem to reconcile Paul's teaching on justification by faith and *not works* with his teaching that judgment will be *according to works*, that the works done by humankind, including Christians, will be the ground on which they are judged. "All of us must appear before the judgment seat of Christ, so that each may receive recompense for what has been done in the body, whether good or bad" (2 Cor 5:10).[73] Here we see one of the most important continuing functions of the law for Paul, that it will serve as the measure of God's judgment. Again, it will not be a matter of simply the surface reference of the law, for Paul envisages a more deeply rooted doing of God's will, and judgment in accord with his gospel, when God will judge the secrets of humankind (Jew and Gentile) through Jesus Christ (Rom 2:9-16).

The tension point between new and older perspectives on justification is that Paul's thinking on this issue seems too like Judaism's for the comfort of those who define Christianity over against Judaism. For Paul in effect seems to put forward a variation on covenantal nomism![74] As Israel's status before God was rooted in God's covenant initiative, so for Paul

---

[72]I draw here from *New Perspective on Paul*, particularly pp. 80-89.

[73]See also Rom 2:5-11; 14:10; 1 Cor 3:10-15; 2 Cor 11:15; Col 3:25.

[74]As Morna D. Hooker noted in her review of Sanders's *Paul*, "Paul and 'Covenantal Nomism'" (1982), reprinted in *From Adam to Christ: Essays on Paul* (Cambridge: Cambridge University Press, 1990), pp. 155-64: "In many ways, the pattern which Sanders insists is the basis of Palestinian Judaism fits exactly the Pauline pattern of Christian experience: God's saving grace evokes man's answering obedience" (p. 157).

Christians' status before God is rooted in the grace manifested in and through Christ. And as Israel's continuation within that covenant relationship depended in substantial measure on Israel's obedience of the covenant law, so for Paul the Christians' continuation to the end depends on their continuing in faith and on living out their faith through love. Wording and suggested correlation are certainly open to revision, but the basic point is surely beyond dispute: that Paul wanted his converts to produce "good works" (2 Cor 9:8; Col 1:10), that he used the imagery of reward for such good deeds,[75] that for Paul full/final salvation is in some degree conditional on faithfulness,[76] and that accordingly Paul had to warn his converts again and again of the perils of moral failure.[77]

The new perspective does not offer a neat solution to these paradoxes and tensions. What it does call for is that expositions of Paul's teaching should be faithful to the *whole* of Paul's teaching, "warts and all," as it were. Perhaps we simply have to accept that the whole of Paul's teaching on these subjects cannot be fitted neatly into a single package or confessional statement. Perhaps we simply have to accept that there are tensions that can never be resolved and that to do so would inevitably lose something important in Paul's theology. What we should not do, however, is push the uncomfortable parts of Paul's teaching on justification and judgment into the long grass, to be lost to sight. It is part of the new perspective's remit, as it were, to ensure that this will not happen and that we will continue to wrestle with the whole Paul.

4. Participation in Christ

One of the annoying and frustrating features of older arguments about Paul's theology is that the different dimensions of his theology are too easily treated as inconsistent. The tensions, like those just mentioned, are allowed to pull Paul's theology apart. One of the major tensions has been between the forensic imagery of justification and the relation-focused imagery of participation in Christ ("in Christ," "in the Lord"). Some who have overreacted against the traditional Reformation focus on justification have sought instead to replace it with a focus on participation.[78]

---

[75]1 Cor 3:14; 9:24-25; Phil 3:14; Col 3:24.
[76]Rom 8:13; 1 Cor 15:2; Gal 6:8; Col 1:23.
[77]1 Cor 3:17; 10:12; 11:27-29; 2 Cor 12:21; 13:5; Gal 5:4; 6:7-8; Col 1:22-23.
[78]Particularly Albert Schweitzer, *The Mysticism of Paul the Apostle* (London: Black, 1931); Sand-

Now it is quite true that Paul's understanding of individual believers as "in Christ" is much more prevalent throughout his writings than the imagery of justification.[79] The church as the body of Christ is the corporate expression of the same point (particularly Rom 12:4-8; 1 Cor 12). And salvation can be readily conceived in terms of the individual believer becoming like Christ, being conformed to his death in the hope of sharing his resurrection,[80] and the corporate body of believers growing "to maturity, to the measure of the full stature of Christ" (Eph 4:13). In most cases, however, what has been too quickly passed over is the fact that Paul held *together* these two ways of conceptualizing the process of salvation. "There is therefore now no condemnation for those who are in Christ Jesus" (Rom 8:1). "For our sake [God] made him to be sin who knew no sin, so that in him we might become the righteousness of God" (2 Cor 5:21). Paul's hope is "that I may gain Christ and be found in him, not having a righteousness of my own that comes from the law, but a righteousness that comes through faith in Christ, the righteousness from God to faith" (Phil 3:9).

What we need once again is to hold the whole Paul together. We might not be able to understand how he did so, but we should hardly think that we can do a better job by downgrading or dispensing with aspects of Paul's thought that were clearly integral to his theology. If the new perspective sparks off a renewed attempt to do justice to the whole Paul, it will have been a worthwhile blip in the ongoing process of receiving what Paul has still to say about the gospel for today.

---

ers, *Paul,* pp. 502-8. Campbell maintains that there are "two very different soteriologies" in Rom 1-4 and 5-8, and sets himself to "eliminate" what he calls "justification theory" (*Deliverance of God,* pp. 94, 217).

[79]Full documentation in *Theology of Paul the Apostle,* §15. Note also the equal emphasis Paul places on the gift of the Spirit (§16).

[80]Rom 6:5; 8:29; 13:14; 1 Cor 15:49; 2 Cor 3:18; Phil 3:21; Col 3:10.

Traditional Reformed Response

Michael S. Horton

ALTHOUGH THE NEW PERSPECTIVE OFTEN defines itself over against the Reformation, Professor Dunn (n. 38) helpfully identifies a more specific (and quite different!) target: namely, the narrowing of the gospel to "individual peace with God": "In NT scholarship, particularly Bultmann; in popular evangelism, typically the rallies of Billy Graham."

Although I read Sanders' *Paul and Palestinian Judaism* years ago, prepared to be properly chastened, I became even more convinced of the striking parallels with medieval theology—and Sanders' own implied agreement with both on key points, summarized as "covenantal nomism."[1] Sanders' own theological convictions were everywhere apparent in his assumption that any element of leniency or divine assistance militated against any attribution of "works-righteousness." By the end of the book, I was convinced that at least the streams of Judaism he described (election based on foreseen obedience, the "merit of the fathers," the "weighing of merits," even repentance—resembling the elements of penance—making up for sins, etc.) bore striking resemblances to the "covenantal nomism" of late medieval (especially nominalist) theology. Yet where Sanders saw in Paul a different "pattern of religion" (participationist vs. covenantal nomism), James Dunn and N. T. Wright see these more as integrated tensions in Paul.

Of course, we must avoid anachronism, not to mention caricature. Nevertheless, whatever one calls it—synergism, covenantal nomism, future justification based on an entire life lived, or congruent merit, the basic

---

[1] E. P. Sanders, *Paul and Palestinian Judaism* (Minneapolis: Fortress, 1977); for "getting in by grace, staying in by obedience," see pp. 93, 178, 371, and for his definition of "covenantal nomism," see pp. 75, 543-56.

problem from a classic Reformed perspective is a confusion of law and gospel.

Given the prominence of Abraham in the covenant of grace, Reformed theology has never drawn a sharp distinction between Old and New Testaments or Israel and the church. In this respect, its emphasis is *promise and fulfillment*. At the same time, it has recognized a distinction between two different kinds of covenantal arrangements—namely law and promise. However, in its zeal to overcome ancient and more recent Christian caricatures of Judaism, the new perspective elides important considerations of the distinctions *within the Hebrew Scriptures themselves* between different types of covenants. From Moshe Weinfeld to Jon Levenson, Jewish scholars have recognized parallels between biblical covenants and political treaties of the ancient Near East.[2] The new perspective has found a rich quarry in Second Temple Judaism, but surprisingly little attention has been drawn to these sources, which I engage elsewhere especially in relation to the new perspective.[3]

In Second Temple Judaism, it seems that these distinct covenants had become assimilated into a general tendency that Sanders properly identifies as covenantal nomism. I couldn't agree more with Sanders' evaluation: "No document better expresses the double character of 'covenantal nomism' than the book of Deuteronomy." It is certainly true also that there

---

[2]Moshe Weinfeld, "The Covenant of Grant in the Old Testament and the Ancient Near East," *Journal of the American Oriental Society* 90 (1970): 185-86; cf. Suzanne Booer, *The Promise of the Land as an Oath* (Berlin: W. de Gruyter, 1992), for a more recent and extended treatment. See also G. E. Mendenhall, *Law and Covenant in Israel and the Ancient Near East* (Pittsburgh: The Biblical Colloquium, 1955); Delbert Hillers, *Covenant: The History of a Biblical Idea* (Baltimore: Johns Hopkins University Press, 1969); Dennis J. McCarthy, S.J., *Treaty and Covenant: A Study in the Ancient Oriental Documents and in the Old Testament* (Rome: Biblical Institute Press, 1963); Steven L. McKenzie, *Covenant* (St Louis: Chalice Press, 2000), especially p. 66; Jon D. Levenson, *Sinai and Zion: An Entry into the Jewish Bible* (San Francisco: HarperSanFrancisco, 1985), pp. 24-45, 75-100, 165-83. See also David Noel Freedman, "Divine Commitment and Human Obligation," *Interpretation* 18 (1964): 419-31. The Reformers and their heirs recognized the differences between law-covenants and covenants of gracious promise long before recent comparisons with Hittite treaties. This reminds us that the distinction itself does not depend on any direct correlation between biblical and secular treaties that can be drawn by contemporary scholarship. Weinfeld's typology (viz., suzerainty treaties vs. royal grants) has been challenged (esp. Gary N. Knoppers, "ANE Royal Grants and the Davidic Covenant," *Journal of the American Oriental Society* 116, no. 4 [October-December 1996]: 670-97). However, the obvious distinction in content between Abrahamic/Davidic/New covenants and the Sinai covenant remains well-established in current scholarship.
[3]Michael Horton, *Covenant and Salvation* (Louisville: Westminster John Knox), chaps. 1-5.

was "a provision for sin and atonement within Israel's cultic system." The whole purpose of the covenant of law (Sinai) was to direct Israel to its coming Savior; in that sense, it was *in service to* the covenant of grace. However, the terms laid down especially in Deuteronomy make it clear enough that the Sinai covenant *itself* is not the same in form or content as the Abrahamic covenant, or the new covenant that Jeremiah prophesies, which is "not like the covenant" at Sinai (Jer 31:32). Paul especially labors to draw out the differences between Sinai and Zion, earthly and heavenly Jerusalem, law and promise, and even designates them explicitly as "two covenants" (Gal 4:24). The earlier (Abrahamic) covenant cannot be annulled by a later (Sinaitic) covenant (Gal 3:15-18). Like Adam, Israel was given a commission to fulfill in the land. "But like Adam, they transgressed the covenant" (Hos 6:7). "In Adam," Israel stands condemned along with the Gentiles (Rom 3:9-20; 5:12-14), yet "in Christ" Jew and Gentile are justified together through faith (Rom 3:21-26; 5:15-21).

So while covenantal nomism is a good way of capturing the dynamics of Sinai, the Abrahamic-Davidic-New covenant (i.e., the covenant of grace) is qualitatively distinct. Assimilating law and promise into a single covenant leads to attempts (strained, in my view) to reconcile the obvious conditionality of Sinai to the new covenant. For example, Dunn writes, "So Israel's righteousness was not so much something to be achieved by their self-effort; rather it was understood and measured in terms of obedience to the law of the covenant, faithfulness to the terms of the covenant." "Achieved by their self-effort" may be the wrong way of putting it, but "measured in terms of obedience to the law of the covenant" barely softens that idea! We can both grant that everlasting life was never "achieved by self-effort": Abraham believed the same gospel (Rom 4:22-25; Gal 3:8), as did Moses and other Jewish luminaries (Heb 11:1-40). However, the terms for the national covenant (Sinai) contrast sharply with this Abrahamic covenant.

Dunn allows that Sanders may have "overreacted," focusing "too closely on the covenant dimension and underplayed the nomistic dimension (*covenantal* nomism). Second Temple and rabbinic writings may well be less consistent than Sanders argued." Nevertheless, I suggest that we need something more than a mere tinkering with the definition of "covenantal nomism." In short, where the new perspective sees "covenantal" as a gracious modifier of "nomism" (with a dynamic tension between law and grace), classic Reformed theology sees *two distinct types of covenants*. After the Fall, every divine-human relationship is predicated on grace in some sense, so not even the Sinai covenant is "Pelagian." The land grant is a gift, based on the Abrahamic promise (Deut 7:6; 8:17-18; 9:4-12), but a gift to keep or lose. "Get in by grace, stay in by obedience" is a good way of summarizing the Sinai treaty, but not the covenant of grace. There is indeed "law" in the new covenant as well. However, it functions as the "reasonable service" in view of God's mercies, not as the basis for covenantal blessing. Only in Christ do we have "every spiritual blessing in heavenly places" (Eph 1:3). So here I am closer to Sanders in seeing Paul as advancing not only a different emphasis, but a completely different paradigm from covenantal nomism.

Dunn helpfully highlights the significance of boundary markers like circumcision, but in my view the new perspective fails to account adequately for the deeper problem.[4] In the Abrahamic covenant, circumcision was a sign and seal of a gracious covenant. As G. E. Mendenhall observes,

> It is not often enough seen that no obligations are imposed upon Abraham. Circumcision is not originally an obligation, but a sign of the covenant, like the rainbow in Gen 9. It serves to identify the recipient(s) of the covenant, as well as to give a concrete indication that a covenant exists. It is for the protection of the promisee, perhaps, like the mark on Cain of Gen 4. The covenant of Moses, on the other hand is almost the exact opposite. It imposes specific obligations upon the tribes or clans without binding Yahweh to specific obligations, though it goes without saying that the covenant relationship itself presupposed the protection and support of Yahweh to Israel.[5]

However, interpreted as the sign and seal of the *Sinai* covenant, circumcision could only render one personally liable to the law's sanctions rather than identify heirs of promise. By itself, circumcision is now indifferent (Gal 5:6), but not if one requires (or undergoes) circumcision in order to be a rightful heir of the promise. In that case, one is "cut off" from Christ

---

[4]By the way, in commenting on the relevant passages, Calvin was busily engaged in refuting his opponents' argument that "works of the law" referred exclusively to the boundary markers, again raising the question as to the novelty of the new perspective.

[5]G. E. Mendenhall, *Law and Covenant*, p. 36

(Gal 5:2-4). Why? Because "every man who accepts circumcision is obligated to keep the whole law" (Gal 5:3). The "circumcision party" is faulted not merely for ethnic exclusion: "For even those who are circumcised *do not themselves keep the law*" (Gal 6:13, emphasis added). Circumcision has become for them not a sign and seal of the covenant of grace, as it was for Abraham (Rom 4:11), but as a sign and seal of their "All this we will do" in a covenant (Sinai) that was never intended to yield participation in the everlasting inheritance. Paul's agitators had collapsed Zion into Sinai, the promise-covenant into the law-covenant. As "a Pharisee of Pharisees," Paul says that he had trusted in "a righteousness of my own" (Phil 3:9), and the problem he addresses in the Galatian church is not merely ethnocentricity but legalism (Gal 2:21, etc.). The contrast is between covenants of law and promise, not between some works and others (Gal 3:10-29; 4:21-31). Consequently, I disagree with Dunn's conclusion that Paul sees "Israel's status before God" and "Christians' status before God" as equivalent. Not even the individual Jew's status before God in the Old Testament was equivalent to the nation's status in the typological land.

I found important areas of agreement as well, especially on the controversial *pistis Christou* question, his concern to "hold Paul together" on justification and participation, and his critique of Baur's contrast between Judaism and Christianity in terms of "universalism versus particularism." I also agree with his concern that the law-gospel distinction can be turned into an abstract antithesis, as if the law itself were intrinsically opposed to the promise. After all, justification provides the legal basis on which the new creation can finally dawn, with the law written on the heart rather than merely on tables of stone.[6] This is why Paul can observe the irony that "Gentiles who did not pursue righteousness have attained it, that is, a righteousness that is by faith; but that Israel who pursued a law that would lead to righteousness did not succeed in reaching that law" (Rom 9:30-31). The indicative grounds the imperative (Rom 6; 12:1-2; 13:8-14; Gal 5:16-26). I also appreciate Dunn's emphasis on Paul's gospel answering the horizontal as well as vertical relationships. However, the question remains: What is the *content* of that inheritance that creates one family? It is not

---

[6]For the record, whatever the Baurs and Bultmanns of modernity have said otherwise, the Lutheran Book of Concord also affirms the third use of the law (i.e., as God's rule for Christian living).

enough that Jews and Gentiles are reconciled in Christ as one body, if the source of that unity in Christ (viz., election, redemption, effectual calling, justification, sanctification and glorification) is the back-page rather than front-page story.

■

Progressive Reformed Response

Michael F. Bird

I TREMENDOUSLY ENJOYED READING Jimmy Dunn's essay on justification. I confess that I had a wry smile on my face as I worked through it. I wondered to myself, "If Dunn had written this in 1983 when he published his well-known article "The New Perspective on Paul,"[1] would we have had half of the fuss that we've had since then about Paul and justification?" Only heaven knows!

Anyway, I shall begin by affirming with Dunn that the old perspective and the new perspective are not antithetical. Indeed, the new perspective has appeared among old commentators many times before. John Chrysostom in his homilies on Romans recognized that Paul advocated salvation by faith and not by works, but Chrysostom also engaged the topic of Gentiles becoming heirs with Israel. The Greek presbyter stated: "For these two things were what confused the Jews; one, if it were possible for men, who with works were not saved, to be saved without them, and another, if it were just for the uncircumcised to enjoy the same blessings with those, who had during so long a period been nurtured in the Law."[2]

Augustine regarded Romans as a commentary on 2 Corinthians 3:6, "For the letter kills, but the Spirit gives life." The letter to the Romans was Augustine's key weapon to beat the absolute snot out of the works-salvation scheme of Pelagius. However, Augustine also knew the big picture of

---

[1] J. D. G. Dunn, "The New Perspective on Paul," *BJRL* 65 (1983): 95-122.
[2] John Chrysostom, *Homiliae in epistulum ad Romanos* 7.

Romans and its redemptive-historical context about the gospel coming to
Gentiles:

> The Letter of Paul to the Romans, in so far as one can understand its literal
> content, poses a question like this: whether the Gospel of our Lord Jesus
> Christ came to Jews alone because of their merits through the works of the
> law, or whether the justification of faith that is in Christ Jesus came to all
> nations, without any preceding merits for works. In this last instance, peo-
> ple would believe not because they were just, but justified through belief;
> they would then begin to live justly. This then is what the apostle intended
> to teach: that the grace of the Gospel of our Lord Jesus Christ came to all
> people. He thereby shows why one calls this "grace," for it was given freely,
> and not as a repayment of a debt of righteousness.[3]

The British philosopher John Locke in his paraphrase and notes on
Paul's letters made this comment on Romans 3:26: "God rejected them
[i.e., the Jews] for being his people, and took the Gentiles into his church,
and made them his people jointly and equally with the few believing Jews.
This is plainly the sense of the apostle here, where he is discoursing the
nation of the Jews and their state in comparison with the Gentiles; not of
the state of private persons. Let anyone without prepossession attentatively
read the context, and he will find it to be so."[4] Chrysostom, Augustine,
and Locke (as mere examples) show that it is possible to see a letter like
Romans addressing an anthropological issue of human sin and divine redemption without divorcing it from the wider redemptive-historical theme
of how the promises given to Israel result in the salvation of the Gentiles.

I can also affirm the new perspective on Judaism since it is simply impossible to reduce all of Second Temple Judaism into one scheme and to
regard that scheme as essentially legalistic. This became apparent to me
when I read a passage from the Alexandrian Jewish philosopher Philo who
referred to contemporary debates about whether God's blessings were
earned or freely bestowed:

> For though they confess that the supreme Ruler is the cause of the good

---

[3]Cited in Paula Fredriksen Landes, *Unfinished Commentary on the Epistle to the Romans* I.1, Text
and Translations 23, Early Christian Literature, series 6, ed. Robert L. Wilken and William
R. Schoedel (Chico, Calif.: Scholars Press, 1982), p. 53.
[4]John Locke, *A Paraphrase and Notes on the Epistles of St Paul to the Galatians, First and Second
Corinthians, Romans, and Ephesians* (Cambridge: Brown, Shattuck, 1832), p. 277.

that has befallen them, they still say that they deserved to receive it, for that they are prudent, and courageous, and temperate, and just, so that they may well on these accounts be esteemed by God and be worthy of his favors . . . and Moses reproves the man who looks upon himself as the cause of the good things that have befallen him in this manner, "Say not" says he, "my own might, or the strength of my right hand has acquired me all this power, but remember always the Lord thy God, who gives thee the might to acquire power" [Deut 8:17]. And he who conceives that he was deserving to receive the possession and enjoyment of good things, may be taught to change his opinion by the oracle which says, "You do not enter into this land to possess it because of your righteousness, or because of the holiness of your heart; but, in the first place because of the iniquity of the nations, since God has brought on them the destruction of wickedness; and in the second place that he may establish the covenant which he swore to our fathers" [Deut 9:5].[5]

Judaism it seems was theologically variegated and different authors had diverse views about what God required of people and what it meant to be saved or blessed by God. Not every Jewish scheme was legalistic. Dunn urges us to remember that the dynamic between covenant and law was common to Judaism and inherited by Paul. I think that is correct, but what we need to add is that Paul confronted a Jewish theology that had shifted the accent from covenant to nomism. What Paul confronted in debates in Antioch and Galatia is something that I call "ethnocentric nomism," that is, eschatological salvation is tied to performance of the Jewish law.[6] I do not like the terms "legalism" and "synergism" because they are freighted and anachronistic. Yet there is clearly a nomistic element to what Paul critiques explicitly in Galatians and implicitly in Romans. Paul reacts against the view that outside of Israel and its law there is no salvation.

Despite the diversity of perceptions about salvation in ancient Judaism, the performance of the law could be regarded as determinative for salvation under certain sociological conditions or in conjunction with particular theological emphases: (1) In some eschatological schemes the role of works becomes more acute when one considers the grounds for entrance into the

---

[5]Philo, *Sacrifices* 54-57, in *The Works of Philo*, trans. C. D. Yonge (Peabody, Mass.: Hendrickson, 1993).
[6]Cf. Michael F. Bird, *The Saving Righteousness of God*, Paternoster Biblical Monographs (Carlisle, U.K.: Paternoster, 2007), pp. 116-18.

future age, that is, who inherits the world to come and on what basis. (2) Amidst intra-Jewish sectarian debates about *which* and *whose* interpretation of the law is valid, the necessity for particularized law observance is heightened. And (3) in debates within a community about the rite of entry for new members, works play a determinative role for the status of persons entering the group because the community is viewed the exclusive locus of God's salvation. I submit that all three conditions are arguably present in Galatians and more obliquely in Romans! In which case, the laws that emblemize the covenant people and defined the identity of Israel still took on a nomistic substance in contrast to Paul's contention that Gentiles are saved by faith in Christ.[7]

So Dunn is right to point out that E. P. Sanders was on to something when he noted the preponderance of covenant in ideas of salvation in Palestinian Judaism. My point is—and I think Dunn might well agree here—that in the situations that Paul faced, he reacted negatively against Jewish Christians who demanded a nomistic basis for the salvation and inclusion of Gentiles in the church.

Concerning the nature of Paul's gospel, I would like to tweak Dunn's remarks in several areas. First, I concur that the *pistis Christou* constructions should generally be taken as an objective genitive, that is, faith in Christ. However, I don't think that we have to make an absolute distinction between "faith in Christ" and the "faithfulness of Christ." When we believe in Christ, we are entrusting ourselves to what God did in Christ, which encompasses his faithfulness and obedience in his life and death. So the faithfulness of Christ is implied not in the noun *pistis,* but in the reference to the revelation of God's salvation in the *Christos.*

Second, I agree with Dunn that Paul's critique of the law should not be pressed into a violent law versus gospel antithesis. The law is not a bad thing that has been done away with, rather it is a good thing that has been fulfilled. Yet Dunn could have said a lot more about the anthropological problem of the law. What Paul finds wrong with the law is three things: (1) Because of sin, noone can actually perform it satisfactorily (Rom 3:20; Gal 3:11-14); (2) The law was temporary, not terminal and not the instru-

---

[7]Michael F. Bird, "What if Martin Luther Had Read the Dead Sea Scrolls? Historical Particularity and Theological Interpretation in Pauline Theology: Galatians as a Test Case," *JTI* 3 (2009): 118.

ment by which the Abrahamic promises would be fulfilled (Gal 3; Rom 4); and (3) The law is indelibly linked to the old age of sin, condemnation, and death that is replaced by the ministry of the new covenant that brings righteousness and life (Rom 8:2; 1 Cor 15:56; 2 Cor 3:6-13).

Third, Dunn acknowledges the tension in Paul's thought about justification by faith and judgment according to deeds. I concur that Paul believes that salvation is conditional on faithfulness and Paul also expects his congregations to produce good deeds. Something that Dunn missed out and what might be the vital ingredient here is the role of the Holy Spirit and the power of the new creation for enabling believers to fulfill the law in their deeds and way of life. In fact, I think that is precisely what Paul says in Romans 8:4, Galatians 5:5-6, 16 and Philippians 2:12-13.

Fourth, Dunn wrestles with the forensic and participatory imagery in Paul and how to integrate them together. He is completely right that Paul held these in concert without any apparent concern for contradiction. On the back of that, I want to suggest that if we regard participation in Christ as union with the justified and exalted Messiah, then union with Christ will always be in some sense forensic.

■

Deification Response

Veli-Matti Kärkkäinen

HAVING BEEN INVITED AS A SYSTEMATIC theologian to make remarks on this learned essay in biblical theology by the leading international authority, the master of the art of New Testament studies, is not only a humbling experience but also an opportunity to mention in public how very much I have learned from Professor Dunn's writings in general and in particular on the topic under discussion. As early as during my doctoral student days at the University of Helsinki when the "new interpretation" of Luther's theology of justification was being developed by my Lutheran

Doktorvater and his school, I was struck by the similarity between many of the motifs in the "new perspective" and the "new interpretation." Unfortunately, little work has been done in coordinating these two lines of inquiry; much more attention is needed to reap the full harvest.

The opening sentence of the essay, "The 'new perspective' on Paul's teaching on justification by faith is not really 'new,'" means to me two things. First of all, it means what the author himself is saying: that what is now called the "new perspective" is indeed as old as the view of St. Paul himself! The other meaning of the sentence to me is that the "new perspective" on Paul and New Testament studies has already been in circulation long enough to generate ever new "new perspectives." Indeed, when Professor Dunn was giving a guest lecture at my school, Fuller Theological Seminary, Pasadena, California, some time ago, he fittingly titled it "New Perspective on the 'New Perspective.'"

One of the many things I greatly appreciate about Professor Dunn's discussion is that with his approach to Paul and New Testament theology—unlike some other new perspective advocates—he is not wanting to replace the older paradigm but rather offer a complementary view. And I would add: hopefully this new way of looking at the doctrine of justification may also help those who align themselves with the "old perspective" to interpret the doctrine of justification in a more coherent way and in keeping with Pauline theology.

What also strikes me very positively about the essay is that the author is constantly seeking for a more balanced and also more self-critical account of the issue. Particularly in the beginning stages of the new perspective it was customary for some advocates to debunk the "old perspective," especially the Reformation-based traditional doctrine, and for the sake of argumentation, one-sidedly highlight the radical differences between the two paradigms. Nothing like that can be discerned in the current essay. That is yet another reason why it is of such great value to biblical, historical, systematic and ecumenical studies in the topic of justification.

Among the four "aspects," as the author names them, in need of revisiting in order for us to gain a proper understanding of the doctrine of justification, I would like to highlight one in particular: the missionary orientation of Pauline theology. The robustly missionary background and intent of the book of Romans (and much of the rest of Pauline theology) is something the New Perspective has rediscovered. Even though in contemporary New Testament scholarship it is a commonplace to consider Pauline epistles as "occasional" and thus "contextual" responses rather than formal doctrinal treatises, the implications of this foundational hermeneutical insight have not often been brought to bear on the topic of justification. Such reading of Pauline letters would also help us better understand and develop soteriology with a view to global and intercultural diversity. What Paul is up to in the book of Romans, the magna carta of the Protestant understanding of justification, is the defense of his apostolic ministry as he is envisioning extending his missionary enterprise to the other side of the world! As part of that defense and in order to secure proper support for the trip, he presents the outline of his gospel of salvation—and he does that on the basis of his Bible, namely the Old Testament. This kind of "contextual" reading of Paul's major epistle, as summarized at the end of the section on "For All Who Believe, Jew and Greek," helps bring the issues of reconciliation and liberation into the discussion of justification. Many Lutherans as well as other Protestants, most prominently the Reformed Jürgen Moltmann, have already for years spoken of the importance of finding an integral link between justification and justice, or justification and reconciliation of not only human beings in relation to God but also, as in Pauline theology, reconciliation between people groups.

Having mentioned above the fact that early in my scholarly career in Helsinki I came to the tentative conclusion that in many ways the "new perspective" in biblical studies and the "new interpretation" of Luther's own theology of justification strike many similar notes, let me highlight two of the most prominent issues on the basis of Professor Dunn's discussion. First, I am thinking of the groundbreaking insight into the centrality of the idea of "saving righteousness" in Second Temple Judaism. Professor Dunn rightly notes that this same idea was so central to Luther himself that the whole program of the Reformation emerged out of this finding. This is indeed one of the most, if not the most critical issues in the assessment of the continuing validity of the Reformation doctrine of justification for later generations. Although the diversity of metaphors for salvation in the New Testament prevents any denying the importance of legal and forensic accounts of justification that have played such an important role in post-Reformation traditions, it is also of highest importance to see the wider, more inclusive, and perhaps even more appropriate framework of justification. The dominance of forensic, imputative hermeneutics in the Lutheran confessional writings and in the post-Reformation Protestant traditions at large came to blur the meaning of "saving righteousness," which is part of the covenant framework that speaks of faithfulness, love and relationality. The Lutheran systematician Wolfhart Pannenberg has rightly spoken of the influence of the late medieval and Reformation eras' penitential mentality, judicial understanding of law and similar cultural aspects, which helped marginalize the view of saving justification. "Going back to the Bible" has served here as the needed self-criticism of dogmatic and systematic theology.

Second, there is the widely debated and often misconstrued negotiation between "faith" and "works." Dunn's careful and nuanced discussion of the meaning(s) of "works of the law" helps resolve many misunderstandings in the tradition and also comes up with a more nuanced view. Of course, I cannot develop any of these issues in any detail here, so suffice it to mention them briefly and so invite my colleagues for further dialogue. Granted what Dunn says about the primary meaning of the Pauline phrase "works of the law" (namely, the desire to require the Gentiles to become Jews, to follow Jewish customs and "markers" in order to be justified)—which I myself believe is basically the correct view— it doesn't have to mean that the later reinterpretation in Christian tradition has to be all wrong. In other words, the interpretation of the "works of law" in terms of self-justification ("works-righteousness"), which came to culmination in the Catholic-Protestant debates at the time of Reformation, may be a valid "contextualization" of the original Pauline meaning. That said, while continuing with this contextualization we should keep in mind the fact that this may not have been the original meaning and that, even if basically valid, it has to be relativized and "tested" against the original intention. It simply is the case that after the break with Judaism in the early centuries of the church, most missionary encounters have happened between Christians and other Gentiles rather than with Jews. In those contexts, Paul's original meaning was not at issue, yet the materially similar way of trying to get around the faith-based/God-driven way of justification was in view. If my argumentation is acceptable, then that would also facilitate a more creative contextualization of the justification message in relation to people among other living faiths, say the Buddhists and Hindus who live more in a shame-based rather than guilt-based culture. In those contexts, "works of law" may mean yet something else.

Dunn's revisiting and sympathetic, balanced critique of the currently popular reinterpretation of "faith in Christ/Christ's faith(fulness)" is a most welcome note in my book. I have elsewhere expressed my concern about the somewhat unnuanced acceptance of the interpretation that makes faith a matter of Christ's act rather than total human surrender (trust and assent) to God. I am often reminded of the importance for Luther of the idea of faith as trust that also means—using the Lutheran Pannenberg's favorite term—the "ecstactic" nature of the Christian's existence. By placing his or her trust fully on Christ, the Christian ek-sists ("stands outside") himself/herself in Christ.

Other issues discussed in Professor Dunn's essay important to the systematic and constructive work in the theology of justification include a more nuanced and less antagonistic interpretation of the Reformation era law-gospel relationship. As I explain in my essay, particularly Pannenberg—in active dialogue with several authors in the new perspective, among others—has done groundbreaking work in redefining this formative issue.

■

Roman Catholic Response

Gerald O'Collins, S.J.

IN EXPOUNDING THE "NEW PERSPECTIVE" on justification by faith, James Dunn helps to clarify further what he understands the whole new perspective on Paul to involve. It does not, for instance, pretend to "replace all elements of the 'old perspective.'" But it rightly presses the need, when treating justification by faith or any other major theme, to take full account of Paul's theology and all the factors involved in shaping the apostle's thought.

This entails, in particular, attending to Paul's distinctively Jewish mindset and refusing to indulge the notion of the apostle turning hostile to the Judaism he once espoused and embodied. Dunn's warnings here are as timely as ever. Witness a book published in 2008 by a reputable publishing house that (ignoring Romans!) presented Paul as disowning his Jewish heritage, turning anti-Semitic and playing his role in downplaying the Jewishness of Jesus.[1]

Paul, as Dunn insists, understood righteousness in a specifically Jewish way—within the matrix of the gracious initiative of God who made a covenant with Abraham and then, in "a further act of divine grace," redeemed his people from slavery in Egypt and brought them into the promised land. Paul never lost sight of the covenant originally made with Abraham and Sarah and of the "relationship implicit in Israel's religion (and Judaism) between divine initiative and human response." The double character of "covenantal nomism," so forcefully expressed in the book of Deuteronomy, formed the background for Paul's distinctively Jewish interpretation of God's righteousness in fulfilling the obligations assumed in "making covenant with Israel." (One might add here Bird's remarks about the divine righteousness being *also* creational, "in that God intends to establish his just reign over all of creation and finally repossess the world for himself.")

The hymn Dunn cites from the Community Rule of Qumran, which declares "God's grace, mercy and righteousness" to be "the only ground of hope," shows how Paul's gospel, and not least his concept of God's righteousness, is rooted in "the priorities and emphases" of his inherited Judaism.

Dunn sets out powerfully how "astonishing" was the step taken by Paul and some of the other first (Jewish) Christians when they preached the good news to Gentiles. This missionary movement was something "unheard of within Judaism," which was "not missionary minded."

Unquestionably, by giving the Holy Spirit to the Gentiles, God revealed a *universal* divine benevolence. Yet we already find some remarkable wit-

---

[1]Barrie Wilson, *How Jesus Became Christian* (London: Weidenfeld & Nicholson, 2008); see my review in *The Tablet*, May 3, 2008, p. 22

ness to this benevolence in the Hebrew Scriptures themselves: for instance, in First Isaiah. Wedged into oracles against the nations, several verses foretell a coming relationship of Egypt and Assyria with YHWH. The prophet announces that "there will be an altar to the LORD in the center of the land of Egypt, and a pillar to the LORD at its border" (Is 19:19). The Egyptians will experience deliverance from oppression through the power of God just as Israel did. Without going to Jerusalem, "the Egyptians will know the LORD on that day, and will worship with sacrifice and burnt offering, and they will make vows to the LORD and perform them" (Is 19:21). At that time "the Egyptians will worship with the Assyrians" and Israel will be a blessing to the nations: "Israel will be the third with Egypt and Assyria, a blessing in the midst of the earth, whom the LORD of hosts has blessed, saying: 'Blessed be Egypt my people, and Assyria the work of my hands, and Israel my heritage'" (Is 19:23-25).

These last three verses form a remarkable statement of universal divine benevolence. They put Egypt and Assyria (both denounced elsewhere in Isaiah and other biblical texts for cruelly oppressing Israel) on a par with Israel, as "my people" and "the work of my hands." Such expressions are elsewhere reserved for Israel itself (e.g., Is 60:21; 64:8). Yet there is no question here of Egypt and Assyria joining themselves or being assimilated to Israel. The passage at the end of Isaiah 19 looks like a corrective inserted into a polemic against Egypt and Assyria. The positive view about the future of these "others" inevitably recalls the universal, divine promise to Abraham and to his people that in them "all the nations of the earth shall be blessed" (Gen 12:3).[2]

Like Bird, Dunn emphasizes "the social dimension of the doctrine of justification." But, even more than Bird, Dunn understands the doctrine of justification by faith as emerging from Paul's "concern to bring Jew and Gentile together." Hence Paul objected to the "works of the law . . . (as a requirement in addition to believing in Jesus Christ)" as "boundary markers" or a wall separating Jew from Gentile. He would not accept "the law's requirement of separation" that defined who was "inside" and who was "outside."

Apropos of the possibility of "the faith of Christ" (or its equivalent) being understood as a subjective genitive, Dunn argues that this issue is not

---

[2]On the universal divine benevolence that the Hebrew Scriptures witness, see G. O'Collins, *Salvation for All: God's Other Peoples* (Oxford: Oxford University Press, 2008), pp. 1-78.

"integral" to "the new perspective" approach to Paul and the question of justification. Yet he moves on to state his (exegetical) objections to the subjective genitive view defended by Richard Hays and others. With differing nuances, various exegetes now understand the language about the faith of Christ to point to his faithful obedience to God and our participating in Christ and his faithfulness to God and the divine purposes.

As I explained in my initial essay, I shifted to the position of Hays and others after first agreeing with Dunn. The two arguments he produces against Hays and those others do not, however, convince me to renounce my change. First, beyond question Paul has much to say about believing as Abraham did and becoming justified *ek pisteōs*. But it seems to me that, by specifying "the faith of Christ" (or the equivalent) the text does supply what Dunn requires: namely, some "explicit indication" that Paul in places is now referring to Christ's own faith/faithfulness. That specification indicates that the reference is to Christ's faith and not to Abraham's faith. Second, Dunn finds it "much less clear what Paul could have meant if he had characterized his Christian life as living 'by the faithfulness of the Son of God.'" Here Romans 5:12-21 (not to mention Phil 2:8) could supply an answer: living by the faithfulness of Christ is sharing in his obedience. Dunn writes of believers depending on what Jesus has done. In this context I would suggest that they depend on what he has done in and through his own obedient faith/faithfulness.

I was glad to find Dunn facing the difficult question of reconciling Paul's teaching on justification by faith *and not by works* with what the apostle teaches when he states that judgment will be *according to works*. Here Bird usefully reminds readers that it is "through" *(dia)* faith and "by/from" *(ek)* faith that believers are first justified, whereas Paul uses "according to" *(kata)* when "it comes to the role of works at the final judgment." Dunn quotes the key texts about Paul wanting his converts to produce good works and living out their faith through love. All of this means that full/final salvation is "in some degree conditional on faithfulness."

Finally, Dunn happily remarks that being "in Christ" and "the imagery of justification" are "two ways of conceptualizing the process of salvation." Yet, of course, as Bird and I myself have pointed out, there are also other Pauline ways of conceptualizing salvation, not least through the language of reconciliation.

6

Deification View

Veli-Matti Kärkkäinen

INTRODUCTION: TOWARD A NEW INTERPRETATION OF JUSTIFICATION

> Until recently, there has been a predominant opinion that the Lutheran and Orthodox doctrines of salvation greatly differ from each other. In the conversations, however, it has become evident that both of these important aspects of salvation [namely, justification and deification] discussed in the conversations have a strong New Testament basis and there is great unanimity with regard to them both.[1]

As early as 1977, the Finnish-Lutheran and Russian Orthodox dialogue produced a highly influential soteriological document titled "Salvation as Justification and Deification," from which the above quotation comes. That statement illustrates well the new emerging interpretation of Luther's soteriology and Lutheran doctrine of justification that attempts to overcome the centuries-long impasse between the churches of the Christian West and East as well as between two Western traditions, Roman Catholic and Lutheran. According to the typical textbook wisdom, the main dividing issue between Roman Catholics and Lutherans is the differing interpretation of the doctrine of justification by faith, and the issue between Western and Eastern churches is the irreconcilable breach between understanding salvation in terms of justification and *theosis*, respec-

---

[1]Cited in Hannu Kamppuri, ed., *Dialogue Between Neighbours: The Theological Conversations Between the Evangelical-Lutheran Church of Finland and the Russian Orthodox Church, 1970-1986* (Helsinki: Luther-Agricola Society, 1986), p. 73.

tively. Historically, especially Eastern and Western traditions have been considered to be diametrically opposed to each other.[2] With regard to the first conflict, it is claimed that whereas for Lutherans justification is a forensic action, God declaring the sinner righteous in God's sight, for Catholics it is making the person righteous. Regarding the latter dispute, it is usually argued that for the Lutheran tradition the concept of *theosis* is almost blasphemous for several reasons: first, it smacks of the "theology of glory"; second, it seems to enforce the highly problematic view of human-divine synergy; and finally, it champions the idea of freedom of the will. If true, these anathemas seem to build an insurmountable obstacle between the Lutheran and Orthodox understanding of salvation. For the Roman Catholics, traditionally, the concept of *theosis* has been more acceptable for the simple reason that their understanding of salvation includes the idea of making righteous rather than merely pronouncing just in the eyes of God. Furthermore, Roman Catholic tradition has never eschewed talk about good works as an integral part of salvation. Yet the language of *theosis* has been marginally used even in the Roman Church.[3]

Recently, a new paradigm has emerged in ecumenical Luther studies. The New Interpretation of Luther's theology, as advanced by the so-called Mannermaa school at the University of Helsinki, has challenged the prevailing German Old School approach, as it were.[4] Beginning in the late

---

[2]See, e.g., Georg Kretschmar, "Die Rezeption der orthodoxen Vergöttlichungslehre in der protestantischen Theologie," in *Luther und Theosis: Vergöttlichung als Thema der abendländischen Theologie*, ed. Simo Peura and Antti Raunio, Schriften der Luther-Agricola-Gesellschaft 25 (Helsinki and Erlangen: Martin-Luther Verlag, 1990), pp. 61-80. While it is only in recent times that Orthodox and Lutheran traditions have come to a better understanding of each other, we should not forget the very early historical contacts between the two churches. The bilateral relations go back to the latter part of the sixteenth century to the correspondence between Patriarch Jeremiah II of Constantinople and some Tübingen theologians from 1573 and 1581. For the standard work, see D. Wendebourg, *Reformation und Oikonomia: Der ökumenische Briefwechsel zwischen der Leitung der Württembergischen Kirche und Patriarch Jeremias II. Von Konstantinopel in den Jahren 1573-1581* (Göttingen: Vandenhoeck & Ruprecht, 1986).

[3]That said, I find the comment by a Catholic theologian an overstatement, namely, that "the Roman Catholic Church has always taught the deification of man through God's grace." Miguel Garijo-Guembe, "Schwesterkirchen im Dialog," *Catholica* (1994): 285. For an important Roman Catholic appropriation of the idea of *theosis*, see Hans Urs von Balthasar, *Theologik*, vol. 3: *Der Geist der Wahrheit* (Basel: Johannes Verlag, 1987), pp. 169-71 especially.

[4]Globally considered, German Luther scholarship has been either hostile to or at its best ignorant of the Finnish School's interpretation. This attitude is well illustrated in the recent major work on Luther's theology by the leading German scholar Bernhard Lohse (*Martin Luther's Theology: Its Historical and Systematic Development* [Minneapolis: Fortress, 1999], p. 221) who virtually dismisses the Mannermaa school's insight altogether. In general, American Lutheran

1970s, under the leadership of Tuomo Mannermaa, now emeritus professor of ecumenics at the University of Helsinki, the Mannermaa school has offered an alternative reading of Luther's theology.[5] Significantly, the impetus for this new reading of Luther's theology came as a result of the dialogue between the Lutheran and Eastern Orthodox churches[6] and, to be more precise, between the Russian Orthodox Church and the Lutheran Church of Finland. This new paradigm has also been influential in the long-standing Roman Catholic-Lutheran conversations on justification.

The basic theses and claims of the new interpretation can be summarized as follows:

1. Luther's understanding of salvation can be expressed not only in terms of the doctrine of justification, but also—occasionally—in terms of *theosis*. Thus, while there are differences between the Eastern and Lutheran understandings of soteriology, over questions such as free will and understandings of the effects of the Fall, Luther's own theology should not be set in opposition to the ancient Eastern idea of deification.

2. For Luther, the main idea of justification is Christ present in faith *(in*

scholarship, in contrast, has appreciated the new interpretation, and several American Lutheran scholars, such as Ted Peters, Robert W. Jenson and Carl Braaten, have actively engaged the conversation. Only the conservative American Lutheranism of the Missouri Synod has been reserved about the Mannermaa school (as well as the Catholic-Lutheran "Joint Declaration"). Robert Kolb and Charles P. Arand (*The Genius of Luther's Theology: A Wittenberg Way of Thinking for the Contemporary Church* [Grand Rapids: Baker Academic, 2008], p. 48) levels the fancy charge of "Osianderism" against this view. (On a careful engagement with Osiander, see Simo Peura, "Gott und Mensch in der Unio: Die Unterschiede im Rechtfertigungsverständnis bei Osiander und Luther," in *Unio: Gott und Mensch in der nachreformatorischen Theologie*, ed. Matti Repo and Rainer Vinke [Helsinki: Luther-Agricola-Gesellschaft 35, 1996], pp. 33-61.)
[5]The publications of the Mannermaa school are written mainly in German (and Scandinavian languages). Not until 1998 was the first English monograph, a collection of essays by Finnish Luther scholars edited by two leading American Lutheran experts, offered to the English-speaking world, entitled *Union with Christ: The New Finnish Interpretation of Luther*, ed. Carl E. Braaten and Robert W. Jenson (Grand Rapids: Eerdmans, 1998). Only recently was the English translation of the groundbreaking work by Tuomo Mannermaa published: *Christ Present in Faith: Luther's View of Justification*, ed. Kirsi Stjerna (Minneapolis: Augsburg Fortress, 2005; orig. 1979). A succinct introduction to the methodological orientations and the main results of the Mannermaa school can be found in Tuomo Mannermaa's essay, "Why Is Luther So Fascinating? Modern Finnish Luther Research," in Braaten and Jenson, *Union with Christ*, pp. 1-20.
[6]A meticulous study on the ecumenical dialogues between Lutherans and Orthodox is offered by Risto Saarinen, *Faith and Holiness: Lutheran-Orthodox Dialogue 1959-1994* (Göttingen: Vandenhoeck & Ruprecht, 1997).

ipsa fide Christus adest). Justification for Luther means a "real-ontic" (a somewhat controversial term we will discuss below) participation in God through the indwelling of Christ in the heart of the believer through the Spirit.

3. In contrast to the theology of the Lutheran confessions, Luther does not make a distinction between forensic and effective justification, but rather argues that justification includes both.[7] In other words, in line with Catholic theology, justification means both declaring righteous and making righteous.

4. Therefore, justification means not only sanctification, but also good works, since Christ present in faith makes the Christian a "christ" to the neighbor.

The purpose of this essay is to consider the ecumenical and systematic potential of the emerging convergence between the Protestant idea of salvation as justification and the Eastern Church's notion of salvation as *theosis* and the relation of those developments to the emerging rapprochement between Protestant and Roman Catholic views. My aim is neither to try to convince my audience of the supremacy of the new interpretation, nor naively believe that the Christian West and East (or even the Western churches, Protestant and Catholic) could too easily move beyond the centuries-long doctrinal and cultural differences in their understanding of salvation. Rather, in a questioning and learning spirit, I would like to remind my colleagues of the need to maintain an open mind to new ways of viewing ancient questions as well as of the complexity of the issues under consideration.

I will first discuss the attempt by some Lutheran theologians to understand justification in relation to *theosis*. Second, I will highlight the implications of this new interpretation by linking it with the Catholic-Lutheran joint agreement on justification. The third part of the essay seeks to set

---

[7]For the Mannermaa school, the distinction between "Luther's theology" (denoting the theology of the Reformer himself) and "Lutheran theology" (the subsequent theology of the Confessional Documents of the Lutheran Church, as drafted under the leadership of Philipp Melanchthon) is vital. Finnish scholars argue that one of the weaknesses of the older Luther research, as conducted mainly in the German academy, is the neglect of this vital distinction. Indeed, one of the main motifs of the new perspective is to dig into core themes of Martin Luther's own theology and not hasten to read Luther in light of his later interpreters or vice versa.

this ecumenical convergence in the wider theological perspective by looking at reasons and resources for such a revised understanding of justification. The last part engages a critical dialogue with the new interpretation
by raising several questions and challenges as a way to foster continuing
dialogue and exchange of ideas.[8]

JUSTIFICATION AS PARTICIPATION IN GOD AND *THEOSIS*

The Mannermaa school has claimed that *Luther's* view of justification differs in a significant way from the official *Lutheran* doctrine as expounded
in the Confessional Books of the Evangelical Lutheran Churches.[9] In
contrast to the confessional writings,[10] for Luther the main idea of justification is Christ present in faith *(in ipsa fide Christus adest)*. Consequently,
The Mannermaa school rejects the distinction between justification and
sanctification as foreign to Luther's thought.

Justification can be described in at least three interrelated ways: participation in God, the presence of Christ in the believer through the Holy
Spirit, or *theosis*. Luther also occasionally uses other images such as "union
with God," *perichoresis,* the famous Eastern term, and others. Christ's real
presence in a believer is the leading motif in Luther's soteriology. In other

---

[8]For various aspects of the discussion, see Veli-Matti Kärkkäinen, *One with God: Salvation
as Deification and Justification,* Unitas Books (Collegeville, Minn.: Liturgical Press, 2004),
which contains detailed discussion and documentation of various aspects of the new interpretation by the Mannermaa school. For my other contributions on various aspects of the
topics, see my "Justification as Forgiveness of Sins and Making Righteous: The Ecumenical
Promise of a New Interpretation of Luther," *One in Christ* 37, no. 2 (April 2002): 32-45; "The
Ecumenical Potential of Theosis: Emerging Convergences Between Eastern Orthodox, Protestant, and Pentecostal Soteriologies," *Sobornost/Eastern Churches Review* 23, no. 2 (2002): 45-
77; "The Holy Spirit and Justification: The Ecumenical Significance of Luther's Doctrine of
Justification," *Pneuma: The Journal of the Society for Pentecostal Studies* 24, no. 1 (2002): 26-39;
"Salvation as Justification and Deification: The Ecumenical Potential of a New Perspective
on Luther," in *Theology Between West and East: Honoring the Radical Legacy of Professor Dr. Jan
M. Lochman,* ed. Frank Macchia and Paul Chung (Lanham, Md.: University Press of America,
2002), pp. 59-76.

[9]As mentioned above, the term "Lutheran" has two meanings: it can denote either Martin
Luther's theology as it is expressed in his own writings or the theology/theologies of Lutheran
confessions and subsequent Lutheran formulations. During the course of the discussion I will
show that these two have to be distinguished from each other.

[10]I am of course aware of the fact that even in the confessions justification is at times talked
about in terms of the change of life—or at least such an implication is there. However, in
the main they insist, and often, in contradistinction to the Roman position, on the forensic
interpretation.

words, Luther saw justification as the union between Christ and the believer as Christ through faith abides in the Christian through the Spirit. In fact, Luther says, Christ is "one with us,"[11] and "Christ lives in us through faith."[12] A classic formulation can be found, for example, in his *Lectures on Galatians* (1535). Speaking about "true faith," Luther says, "it takes hold of Christ in such a way that Christ is the object of faith, or rather not the object, but so to speak, the One who is present in the faith itself. . . . Therefore faith justifies because it takes hold of and possesses this treasure, the present Christ."[13] In other words, Christ in both his person and his work is present in faith and is through this presence identical with the righteousness of faith. The advocates of the new interpretation claim that for Luther the doctrine of justification is not primarily a forensic term but rather a matter of Christ abiding in the heart of the believer in a "real-ontic" way.[14]

Luther's view of justification can also be called *theosis,* according to the ancient doctrine of the Fathers with whom Luther agreed. Justification and deification, then, mean the "participation" of the believer in Christ, which, because Christ is God, is also a participation in God himself. This participation is the result of God's love,[15] human beings cannot participate

---

[11]*HDT* 26; *LW* 31:56.

[12]*HDT* 27; *LW* 31:56.

[13]*WA* 40, 228-29; *LW* 26:129-30. Ted Peters ("The Heart of the Reformation Faith," *Dialog: A Journal of Theology* 44, no. 1 [Spring 2005]: 6-14) offers a helpful comparison between three models of faith, namely, faith as believing, faith as trusting, and faith as the real presence of Christ. When discussing the third model (pp. 10-12), he dialogues with the Finnish interpretation and its emphasis on Christ's presence as the heart of the Reformer's understanding of justification; Peters quotes the passage from *LW* 26:129-30.

[14]This somewhat ambiguous and contested term "real-ontic" is used by the Mannermaa school to combat the neo-Protestant, neo-Kantian distinction between God's "essence" and "effects" according to which we do not have any means of knowing anything about God; we only can know the effects of God in our lives. This older paradigm has argued that Luther was moving beyond the old scholastic metaphysics with its idea of "essence" toward a more relational view of knowledge. Similarly, the Mannermaa school rejects the existentially oriented notions of God's presence in the believer in favor of a "real" presence. The methodological basis is offered by Risto Saarinen, *Gottes Wirken auf uns: Die transzendentale Deutung des Gegenwart-Christi-Motivs in der Lutherforschung* (Stuttgart: Franz Steiner, 1989).

[15]Mannermaa argues that for Luther the structuring principle of theology is not justification as is routinely assumed but rather a creative juxtaposition between the theology of the cross and love. This comes to culmination in the 1518 Heidelberg Disputation, the last thesis of which (#28) contrasts the love of God and human love. See further, V.-M. Kärkkäinen, "'Evil, Love and the Left Hand of God': The Contribution of Luther's Theology of the Cross to Evangelical Theology of Evil," *Evangelical Quarterly* 79, no. 4 (2002): 215-34.

in God on the basis of their own love; rather, God's love effects their deification. Christian participation in Christ thus is the result of the divine presence in the believer as love. This participation, following Athanasius and others, is a participation in the very *ousia* of God. Luther, unlike the Orthodox tradition, does not know the distinction between God's energies and God's essence; yet the distinction between God and the human being is not negated. God still remains God and the human being the human.

There is, then, what the Mannermaa school calls a "real-ontic" unity between Christ and the Christian though the substances themselves do not change into something else. What makes the claim of this new paradigm unique—and controversial, especially with regard to the established canons of German Luther interpretation—is that the idea of Christ's presence is "real-ontic," not just a subjective experience or God's "effect" on the believer, as the neo-Protestant school has exclusively held.

The Finnish scholar Simo Peura, now bishop, who has written a full-scale monograph on *theosis* in Luther, shows that the idea of deification is an integral motif of Luther's theology. The most explicit passage comes from Luther's *Sermon on the Day of St. Peter and St. Paul* (1519): "For it is true that a man helped by grace is more than a man; indeed, the grace of God gives him the form of God and deifies him, so that even the Scriptures call him 'God' and 'God's son.'"[16] Another example comes from Luther's Christmas sermon of 1514:

> Just as the Word of God became flesh, so it is certainly also necessary that the flesh become Word. For the Word becomes flesh precisely so that the flesh may become Word. In other words: God becomes man so that man may become God. Thus power becomes powerless so that weakness may become powerful. The Logos puts on our form and manner.[17]

Another way to look at the doctrine of justification in Luther and its parallels with the Eastern doctrine of *theosis* is to focus on Luther's doctrine of God. What is highly significant here is the fact that for Luther the divinity of the triune God consists in that "God gives" himself. The essence of God, then, is identical with the essential divine properties in

---

[16] *WA* 2, 247-48; *LW* 51:58.
[17] *WA* 1, 28, 25-32, quoted in Tuomo Mannermaa, "Theosis as a Subject of Finnish Luther Research," *Pro Ecclesia* 4, no. 1 (1995): 43.

which he gives of himself, called the "names" of God: Word, justice, truth, wisdom, love, goodness, eternal life and so forth. "The *theosis* of the believer is initiated when God bestows on the believer God's essential properties; that is, what God gives of himself to humans is nothing separate from God himself."[18] A Christian is saved when the "spiritual goods" or the names of God are given to her or him. God is, as Luther says, the whole beatitude of his saints; the name of God donates God's goodness, God himself, to the Christian; the spiritual goods are God's gifts in the Christian. Not only is the human being saved when God gives himself to the Christian; in that very same act, God proves to be the real God when he donates his own being to humanity. "Thus, God realizes himself and his own nature when he gives his wisdom, goodness, virtue, beatitude, and all of his riches to the Christian, and when a Christian receives all that he gives."[19] Participation in God means putting down those human traits that are contrary to the righteousness of God, and on the other hand, participating in the goodness, wisdom, truthfulness and other characteristics of God. Luther also expresses this truth by saying that God in fact becomes truthful, good and just in the person when God himself makes the person truthful, good and just. Never is there reason to boast, though, since even the presence of Christ and its consequences are always hidden in the Christian.

As mentioned, consequently, the Mannermaa school posits a radical difference between Luther's own theology and the theology of subsequent Lutheranism; their thesis is that Luther's own theology has the potential of creating a common foundation in relation to both Catholicism and Eastern Orthodoxy. The conclusion of the Mannermaa school with regard to the differences between Luther's theology and the theology of the Lutheran confessions and subsequent Lutheranism is well worth hearing because of its profound ecumenical implications. According to Peura, for Luther, "Justification is not a change of self-understanding, a new relation to God, or a new ethos of love. God changes the sinner ontologically in the sense that he or she participates in God and in his divine nature, being made righteous and 'a god.'"[20]

---

[18]Mannermaa, "Why Is Luther So Fascinating?" p. 10.
[19]Simo Peura, "Christ as Favor and Gift," in Braaten and Jenson, *Union with Christ*, p. 50.
[20]Ibid., p. 48.

The relationship between effective and forensic justification comes to light also in Luther's theology in his usage of two classic concepts: "grace" (*gratia,* favor) and "gift" *(donum).* The former denotes that the sinner is declared righteous (the forensic aspect) and the latter that the person is made righteous (the effective aspect). As early as in the beginning of his career, in his Lectures on Romans (1515/16), following tradition Luther expresses an opinion that is totally in line with the mainline Catholic teaching, but that later Lutheranism has lost sight of: "But 'the grace of God' and the 'gift' are the same thing, namely, the very righteousness which is freely given to us through Christ."[21] In other words, Luther found it most important already in those early years to relate grace and gift closely to each other, and to understand them both as given to the Christian through Christ. Thus we can see that grace and gift together constitute the donated righteousness of a Christian.

For Luther, then, a distinction between effective and forensic right-eousness is not an issue as it has been in subsequent Lutheran doctrine. What is crucial to Luther's own doctrine of justification is the distinction between two kinds of righteousness, namely, the righteousness of Christ and the righteousness of the human being. The first type Luther defines as the alien righteousness that is being infused to us from outside; it is that kind of righteousness that Christ is in himself and is the righteousness of faith. It is this righteousness of Christ that makes the human being just.[22] Furthermore, Luther states that this first type of righteousness is given without our own works solely on the basis of grace.[23] This is the famous *sola gratia.* Human activity is totally excluded in this process. The infusion of this first kind of righteousness is more than mere forensic imputation, though; it also means the realization of the righteousness of Christ in the believer.

The other kind of righteousness is given righteousness, in this sense human righteousness. Luther calls it "our" righteousness.[24] It is a result of the first kind of righteousness and makes it effective, "perfects" it.[25] Even though it is called "our" righteousness, its origin and source is out-

---

[21]*WA* 56, 318, 28-29; *LW* 25:36.
[22]*WA* 2, 145, 9-14; *LW* 31:297 ("Two Kinds of Righteousness").
[23]*WA* 2, 146, 29-30; *LW* 31:299.
[24]*WA* 2, 146, 36; *LW* 31:299.
[25]*WA* 2, 147, 12-13; *LW* 31:300.

side the human being, in the righteousness of Christ. Christ's righteousness is the foundation, cause and origin of human righteousness.[26] Christ present in faith "absorbs all sin in a moment," since the righteousness of Christ infused into the human heart is "infinite"; at the same time, the power of sin and death is deteriorating day by day but is not fully destroyed until death.[27] The infusion of Christ's righteousness into the heart of the believer marks the beginning of the process of nullifying the power of sin and transforming the fallen nature. The emerging good deeds have nothing to do with salvation because the believer is already justified and the only purpose of the good deeds now is the good of fellow people.[28]

What then, if any, is the role of good works in Luther? This has been, again, a major dispute between not only Lutherans and Catholics but also Lutherans and Orthodox. In line with *sola gratia,* Luther insists we can certainly do nothing for our salvation. On the contrary, God makes the sinner *nihil,* "nothing" to help him or her to open up to the righteousness of God. Yet good works spring from the union—*theosis,* if you may—between Christ and the believer and, thus, from Christ's real presence in the believer. The Christian becomes a "work of Christ," and even more a "christ" to the neighbor; the Christian does what Christ does.[29] The Christian identifies with the suffering of his or her neighbor. Christ is the subject of good works. This is what Christ present in faith effects in the believer.

In other words, the presence of Christ for Luther is not only "spiritual" or *extra nos* (outside of us) but rather *in nobis* ([with]in us), in the language of the Mannermaa school, in a "real-ontic" way. According to Luther, "since Christ lives in us through faith . . . he arouses us to do good works through that living faith in his work, for the works which he does are the fulfillment of the commands of God given us through faith."[30] As *donum* (gift) Christ gives himself in a real way to the Christian to make him or her participate in the divine nature.

---

[26]*WA* 2, 146, 16-17; *LW* 31:298.

[27]*WA* 2, 146, 12-16, 32-35; *LW* 31:298-99.

[28]*WA* 2, 146, 36-147; *LW* 31:299-300.

[29]See further, V.-M. Kärkkäinen, "Christian as Christ to the Neighbor," *International Journal of Systematic Theology* 6, no. 2 (April 2004): 101-17.

[30]*HDT* 27; *LW* 31:57.

JUSTIFICATION AS DECLARING AND
MAKING RIGHTEOUS

An ecumenically and systematically fruitful way to highlight the significance of Lutheran-Orthodox convergence is to take a brief look at the
historic breakthrough between Catholics and Lutherans in the shared understanding of some key themes of the doctrine of salvation. On October
31, 1999, the Roman Catholic Church and the Lutheran World Federation[31] signed an ecumenically groundbreaking "Joint Declaration on the
Doctrine of Justification." This agreement is the result of decades of mutual talks going back to the closing of the Second Vatican Council.[32] While
mutual condemnations of the Reformation era are still valid today[33]—and
this conversation only deals with some aspects of the doctrine of justification leaving aside a number of other dividing issues—the ecumenical significance of this agreement should not be ignored. A convergence document, it first lists the common agreements and then highlights the
particular Catholic and Lutheran emphases. It therefore does not aim at a
total agreement but rather a shared common basis in the midst of continuing and legitimate—but not church-dividing—differences.

The starting point for the joint declaration between Catholics and Lutherans is the common reading of the Bible: In line with the new developments in biblical studies, it is acknowledged that the New Testament testifies to a diversity of meanings attached to the terms *righteousness* and
justification. For example, various Evangelists approach the terminology
for their own specific contexts (#9).[34] The manifold biblical witness to the
doctrine of justification is encapsulated succinctly in the following summary (#11): "Justification is the forgiveness of sins (cf. Rom 3:23-25; Acts
13:39; Lk 18:14), liberation from the dominating power of sin and death
(Rom 5:12-21) and from the curse of the law (Gal 3:10-14). It is acceptance

---

[31]There are of course some Lutheran churches that are not part of the agreement, such as the
Missouri Synod in the United States.

[32]Significantly, the Roman Catholic Church has not offered an official definition of her doctrine of justification after the Council of Trent when in its sixth session on January 13, 1547,
as a response to the Reformation, the main outline of the Catholic view was articulated. For a
theological analysis of Trent's formulation, see Kärkkäinen, *One with God*, pp. 100-103.

[33]This was noted in the preamble to the "Joint Declaration on the Doctrine of Justification:
Lutheran World Federation and the Catholic Church," #1 (*Joint Declaration on the Doctrine of
Justification* [Grand Rapids: Eerdmans, 2000]).

[34]Paragraph numbers (#) in the following refer to the "Joint Declaration."

into communion with God: already now, but then fully in God's coming kingdom (Rom 5:1-2). It unites with Christ and with his death and resurrection (Rom 6:5)."

What is noteworthy here is the acknowledgment of the fact that justification not only means forgiveness of sins but also "communion with God" and union with Christ. On the basis of these biblical delineations and insights from recent ecumenical developments, a remarkable common statement is put forth between Catholics and Lutherans: "Justification thus means that Christ himself is our righteousness, in which we share through the Holy Spirit in accord with the will of the Father" (#15). The affirmation that Christ is our justification forms a common foundation between two opposing interpretations, namely, the Lutheran confessions' forensic and the Catholic effective views of justification. This is in fact mentioned directly in the title of section 4.2, "Justification as Forgiveness of Sins and Making Righteous," the issue that has historically been the main point of contention: "These two aspects of God's gracious action are not to be separated, for persons are by faith united with Christ, who in his person is our righteousness (1 Cor 1:30): both the forgiveness of sin and the saving presence of God himself" (#22).

Clearly, the Lutheran side has taken a significant ecumenical step in agreeing that justification is not only forgiveness of sins but also internal change, even effecting love through the Spirit. The focal point is the union with Christ. The Lutheran qualification to this clause underlines the fact that it is only by virtue of "union with Christ" that one's life is renewed, even though for Lutherans this life-renewing effect is not a necessary condition for justification (#23). The union language is quite evident in the joint declaration. For example: "We confess together that in baptism the Holy Spirit unites one with Christ, justifies, and truly renews the person" (#28).

Having agreed about this common affirmation, both parties wanted to add explanations on this crucial topic. Lutherans say that in the doctrine of "'justification by faith,' a distinction but not a separation is made between justification itself and the renewal of one's way of life that necessarily follows from justification and without which faith does not exist" (#26). This is a very carefully drafted explanation that also shows the real struggle the Lutheran confessions bring to the question of forgiveness and renewal. This statement attempts to steer a middle course between the one-sided forensic view and the sanative view of Luther himself. The continuation of the Lutheran comment is interesting in that it dares to use the Catholic language of "impartation" of God's love: "Thereby the basis is indicated from which the renewal of life proceeds, for it comes forth from the love of God imparted to the person in justification" (#26). The Catholic counterpart statement reiterates the standard Catholic position according to which justifying grace is always sanative, effective grace, or it is no real justification at all (#27).

Roman Catholics confess with Lutherans that even as justified persons, Christians are still sinners in need of constant renewal (#28). This is the core of the Lutheran insistence on *simul iustus et peccator* ("just and sinner simultaneously"). Lutherans also believe that even though sin in the justified person is "real sin," it is sin "ruled" by Christ and does not bring about separation from God (#29). Catholics for their part talk about "concupiscence," an inclination to sin that is not counted as a "real sin," since the personal element (which in Catholic theology makes sin sin) is lacking. Only if the person voluntarily separates herself from God does separation happen (#30). It has been one of the disputes in the past to argue whether or not concupiscence is sin (Lutherans have tended to say *yes;* Catholics insist *no).*

In several places the joint declaration talks about the human cooperation that has been another major point of contention. It was mutually agreed that salvation comes "by grace alone" (e.g., #19). "By grace alone" means that human beings are unable to save themselves because of sin (#19). However, it is important for Catholics to underline the role of human "cooperation" in the preparation for and acceptance of justification. Even Lutherans are ready to acknowledge that persons may reject the offer of grace (#20-21). When it comes to the role of good works, here also some significant ecumenical steps have been taken: "We confess together that good works—a Christian life lived in faith, hope, and love—follow justification and are its fruits. When the justified live in Christ and act in the grace they receive, they bring forth, in biblical terms, good fruit. Since Christians struggle against sin their entire lives, this consequence of justification is also for them an obligation they must fulfill" (#37). The confessional difference lies in determining the relation of good works to justification. In Catholic tradition, good works contribute to growth in grace (#38), while for Lutherans it is important also to emphasize the nonmeritorious nature of salvation and the completeness of justification (#39).

In sum, several significant affirmations and insights can be found in this document which both form links with the Lutheran-Orthodox convergence and also anticipate themes to be taken up in the rest of my essay. Let me mention them here both as a summary and also an anticipation:

1. Justification is one of the many metaphors of salvation, making room and calling for other metaphors. In other words, the Bible employs a number of legitimate metaphors.

2. Justification can also be expressed in terms of union and participation, even theosis.[35]

3. Justification is more than a forensic declaration; it is an act and process of making righteous.

4. Good deeds, thus, are a natural "fruit" of making righteous.

5. Justification, while a Christologically based doctrine, is best expressed in trinitarian and pneumatological terms as well.

6. Thus, a particular formulation of the doctrine of justification, such as that of Luther's, does not have to be church-dividing nor exclusive of other formulae. Convergence-method helps to both affirm the emerging consensus between traditions and maintain each church's own particular foci.

REASONS AND RESOURCES FOR A REVISED UNDERSTANDING OF JUSTIFICATION

So far, I have concentrated on discussing as carefully as I can the meaning of the emerging ecumenical consensus concerning the shared understand-

---

[35]Ecumenically it is highly significant that in recent years the idea of union, participation and even deification has been found in Anglican and several Protestant traditions such as that of John Calvin, John Wesley and Methodism, Anabaptism, and even Pentecostalism (Edmund J. Rybarczyk, *Beyond Salvation: Eastern Orthodoxy and Classical Pentecostalism on Becoming Like Christ*, Paternoster Theological Monographs [Waynesboro, Ga.: Paternoster, 2004]). See further Veli-Matti Kärkkäinen, "*Theosis:* Western Theology and Ecumenical Developments," in *The Encyclopedia of Christianity*, vol. 5, ed. Erwin Fahlbusch et al., trans. and English-language ed., David B. Barrett, statistical ed. (Grand Rapids: Eerdmans, 2008).

ing of salvation in terms of justification and *theosis* and its implications for Protestant, Orthodox and Roman Catholic relations. The question of "Why such a revised interpretation?" has not yet been raised; addressing that question alongside the kinds of resources and insights that might best help in that endeavor will occupy this current section. In other words, here my aim is to place the significant and groundbreaking work done by ecumenical Lutheran scholarship and bi-lateral ecumenical dialogues between Lutherans and Orthodox as well as Lutherans and Catholics in a wider theological perspective.

It seems to me the impetus for a revised understanding of justification has been inspired by several current developments and also echoes many of them—to my knowledge, quite independently from each other:

1. The new perspective in Pauline and biblical theological studies, with a changed/changing view of what key terms such as "law," "gospel," "justice" and "righteousness" may mean.

2. The criticism and revision of the Lutheran doctrine of salvation by some leading Lutheran scholars, particularly by Wolfhart Pannenberg.

3. Constructive theological efforts to make the doctrine of justification more authentically pneumatological-trinitarian and so complement the predominantly Christological orientation. This orientation also helps bring in the communal and participatory aspects of soteriology.

4. Emerging attempts to link (the doctrine of) "justification" with (the practice of) "justice," in other words, linking the traditional view of changed status with a changed life and behavior.

Before discussing these themes in more detail, it is important to note that—as far as I know—neither Lutheran-Orthodox nor Lutheran-Catholic ecumenical scholars and dialogues have made any extensive use of the insights listed above. Therefore, I thought it appropriate to engage these insights only after I had an occasion to look at the ecumenical convergence first. In other words, I am not arguing that the emerging convergence between the three traditions would be a function of the emergence of new perspectives in biblical and systematic studies. Rather, I believe it is a matter of parallel developments taking place more or less independently from each other.

The New Testament scholar James D. G. Dunn speaks for many of his colleagues as he voices criticism against the traditional way of framing the doctrine of justification in light of the new perspective:

> Luther's conversion experience and the insight which it gave him also began a tradition in Biblical interpretation, which has resulted for many in the loss or neglect of other crucial Biblical insights related to the same theme of divine justice. And particularly in the case of Paul, Luther's discovery of "justification by faith" and the theological impetus it gave especially to Lutheran theology has involved a significant misunderstanding of Paul, not least in relation to "justification by faith" itself.[36]

Dunn is not of course naively debunking the traditional doctrine of justification; rather, his desire is to continue conversation about the potential misinterpretations and loci of focus—or lack thereof—in the traditional understanding of justification in light of biblical studies. What, then, are the typical complaints against the traditional view? Biblical scholars maintain that the traditional view has made the doctrine too much a function of a personal, at times even existential, experience rather than looking at the biblical perspective of the need to "justify" God.[37] Second, Lutheran doctrine is too individualistic and thus misses the communal ramifications of justification. Third, the traditional doctrine sets Paul and Judaism in antithesis, making the religion of Israel virtually a degenerate religion. Furthermore, faith and good works, or declarative and effective righteousness, are not only separated (as in the Protestant distinction between justification and sanctification) but also set in opposition to each other (allegedly, to protect the gratuitous nature of justification by faith). And so forth.

Learning from biblical scholars, a growing number of systematicians are convinced that the metaphor of justification is just that, *a metaphor,*

---

[36]James D. G. Dunn, "The Justice of God: A Renewed Perspective on Justification by Faith," *Journal of Theological Studies* NS 43 (1992): 2. I am using the term "new perspective" in a loose, nontechnical sense, not only referring to the (original) new perspective on Paul heralded by E. P. Sanders, Bishop Tom Wright and Dunn (all of whom of course do not speak with one voice!) but rather in a more inclusive sense that denotes various attempts to revisit the whole biblical teaching about salvation, faith, justification, law, covenant and so forth. Illustrative of the rapid pace of changes is the title given by Professor Dunn to his recent talk at Fuller Theological Seminary: "New Perspective on the 'New Perspective'"!

[37]The alleged reason for this is to follow the ancient reading (going back to Augustine) of Romans 7 through the lens of an inward spiritual struggle related to one's pre-conversion time.

and therefore cannot be considered the normative symbol of salvation. It simply is not true that in the Pauline soteriology, let alone in the midst of the diversity of New Testament interpretations, justification or any other one single metaphor should be considered as the normative one. As Pannenberg rightly notes, "The doctrine of justification is but one of many ways of expounding the theme [of the salvation of God in Christ]." He reminds us that, for example, the Johannine traditions speak of salvation in very different ways. "Even for Paul himself," Pannenberg adds, the doctrine of justification "is not the only center of his theology that controls all else."[38] The conclusion thus is inevitable:

> The many early Christian approaches to a theological explanation of the salvation that is accessible to faith by and in Jesus Christ help us to grasp the various ways of understanding salvation in the history of Christianity right up to our present ecumenical situation, and this fact should warn us not to single out any one form of understanding, even the doctrine of justification, as the only legitimate one, as though, were this lacking, no authentic Christian faith could be present. Instead, the various ways of understanding salvation are calculated to correct the one-sidedness that can arise with each one of them.[39]

At the same time, biblical scholarship makes us reconsider the meaning and context of the terms "justification" and "righteousness." This means moving away from the predominantly forensic understanding toward an understanding of "saving righteousness" with a view to setting things right for the whole creation and between creation and God.[40] This redemptive justice, while not totally lacking forensic aspects, is more about "justifying" God's saving deeds with the world in a way that is in keeping with his faithfulness, holiness, love and integrity.[41] Righteousness is thus a relational concept: it speaks of the way Yahweh, the Father of Jesus Christ, relates to creation and humanity, and how humanity, redeemed in Christ,

---

[38]Wolfhart Pannenberg, *Systematic Theology*, vol. 3 (Grand Rapids: Eerdmans, 1997), p. 213.

[39]Ibid., 3:214.

[40]For a helpful brief discussion, see Frank Macchia, "Justification Through New Creation: The Holy Spirit and the Doctrine by which the Church Stands or Falls," *ThTo* 58, no. 2 (July 2001): 207-11. Macchia fittingly titles this section "Justification as Redemptive Justice in Christ and New Creation."

[41]See, e.g., Karl Barth, *Church Dogmatics* 4/2, ed. Geoffrey Bromiley and Thomas F. Torrance (Edinburgh: T & T Clark, 1958), p. 562.

should relate to God and other people. Consequently, this terminology is more communal than individualistic. Being relational and communal, the talk about justice and righteousness is focused on the covenant and covenant faithfulness. The forensic, court-driven mentality of the times of the Reformation has a hard time envisioning the justice of God through the lens of his merciful and holy covenantal faithfulness. Yet a focus on covenant and on God's own faithfulness and justice also helps rediscover the key biblical insight of the integral relation of justification to justice. In the words of Kathryn Tanner, "a modification promoted by biblical theology has to do with the way mercy and justice are woven together in Christian theologies of justification. Mercy and justice will no longer be merely juxtaposed but will instead be brought to bear on one another to produce a radically altered sense of both but especially a radically altered sense of justice."[42]

To summarize a vast amount of scholarship and insights, let me cite a summary of my earlier writing:

> First, justification is one of the many legitimate images of salvation in the Bible; it cannot be made *the* hermeneutical key. Second, in line with Old Testament usage, the term *dikaiosyne* primarily means the *justice* of God. Even when Paul uses the terminology of "imputation," he is not suggesting that the essence of the doctrine of justification is "legal imputation"; Paul uses this legal image as *one* of the ways to illustrate *one* side of his doctrine. Third, justification and sanctification cannot be distinguished from each other in the way the Reformation theology—in contrast to both the Roman Catholic and Orthodox theologies—has done. Justification means primarily making just, setting a person in a right relationship with God and with others. Fourth, the standard Christian interpretation of Jewish religion and law has to be reassessed in light of Jesus' and Paul's teaching. Even though the question of whether God intended the law to be a means of salvation in any sense has to be left open for further investigation, the emphasis of Jesus was on the inbreaking of the kingdom in his own person. For Paul, Christ meant the end and goal of the law in that the covenant requirement had been met in Christ's cross, and that opens a possibility for a response of faith. Apart from that, membership even in the Jewish covenant community does not bring about salvation. Fifth, justification is a new status and

---

[42]Kathryn Tanner, "Justification and Justice in a Theology of Grace," *ThTo* 55, no. 4 (1999): 513.

relationship to God by faith in Christ through the Spirit. It means union between the human person and her Creator. Sixth, even when justification requires individual response, it is not merely individualistic: it is integrally related to God's saving purposes for the covenant community and to the coming of the kingdom of God. Righteousness is thus also a relational concept, being right with God and other people.[43]

The quotation reminds us of the need to reinterpret the traditional Lutheran understanding of the relationship between law and gospel. As Pannenberg has convincingly shown, the Reformers mistakenly "viewed the law as an expression of God's demand in antithesis to the gospel as promise and pronouncement of the forgiveness of sins." Whereas for Paul, "we have in the law on the one side, and faith in Christ, on the other, two realities in salvation history that belong to two different epochs in what God does in history. The coming of Christ ended the epoch of the law (Gal 3:24–25; Rom 10:4)."[44] While it is understandable that Luther, against the penitential mentality of his times, mistakenly contrasted with each other the law as the demand of God (telling us what to do and what not) and the gospel as the forgiveness of sins, that distinction cannot be maintained anymore. Among other problems, that kind of distinction blurs the wider context of the biblical idea of forgiveness of sins that "has its basis in the proximity of the divine rule" of God and thus links together forgiveness and God's righteous demands.[45] In other words, we should understand the integral relationship between forgiveness of sins and the desire of the forgiven person to submit one's life under the demands of the rule of God. Thus there is also the eschatological orientation: Since the turn from the law to grace has happened definitively in Christ, this turn "must always be related to the broad context of world history in its movement by divine world rule toward the future of God."[46]

Alongside a changed understanding of the biblical notion of justification in terms of relationships and community as well as living rightly and justly, in personal life and community, recent scholarship also aims at a proper trinitarian account of salvation. That would help highlight the

---

[43]Kärkkäinen, *One with God*, p. 16.
[44]Pannenberg, *Systematic Theology*, 3:61; for the whole discussion, including a careful engagement of biblical scholarship and tracing of historical developments, see pp. 58-96.
[45]Ibid., 3:82-83 (82).
[46]Ibid., 3:87.

pneumatological resources in a more integral way. As is well known, one of the main differences between Eastern and Western theologies has been the prominence of a pneumatological/trinitarian outlook in the East. Somewhat ironically, the Protestant *ordo salutis*, while usually under pneumatology, has tended to be one-sidedly built on Christological categories in the sense that the Holy Spirit has to do only with the "subjective" reception of the "objective" work wrought about by Christ. This is, however, "soteriological subordinationism." While in no way diminishing the work of the Son, the Spirit's work cannot only be considered "subjective," in other words, secondary in the accomplishment of salvation. It was through the Spirit that the Father raised Jesus from the dead (Rom 1:4), the act that led to our justification (Rom 4:25). Christ's cross requires the Spirit's resurrection and vice versa.

The Pentecostal theologian Frank Macchia states bluntly: "If justification is to offer a liberating word in an increasingly graceless world, the doctrine must be reworked precisely at this point of neglect, namely, at the relationship between justification and the work of the Spirit as the giver of new life." Therefore, he suggests, an attempt has to be made to open "the doctrine to the full breadth of the Spirit's work in and through Christ to make all things new."[47] What Macchia is rightly aiming at is a vision of justification that—in a properly trinitarian framework[48]—would empower and energize the justified and renewed person to work in fulfillment of the demands of the kingdom in all areas of life, with a view toward final consummation. I would add one more important task for such a constructive work: justification should be framed in a way that would help link the individual person's union with Christ with the fellowship of believers, thus including communal aspects as well.

Thus, the doctrine of salvation cannot be expressed in Christological terms alone but requires pneumatological grounding as well. This is what Pannenberg is doing: he places the talk about soteriology under the telling heading "The Basic Saving Works of the Spirit in Individual Christians"

---

[47]Macchia, "Justification Through New Creation," pp. 202-3.

[48]Robert Jenson makes the interesting observation that whereas the "Pauline" understanding of justification is focused on God the Father and the maintenance of divine righteousness in the act of redemption, the "Protestant" view is focused on the grace of Christ, and the "Catholic" understanding centers on the Spirit's transformative work. Robert Jenson, "Justification as a Triune Event," *Modern Theology* 11 (1995): 422-23.

in his discussion of pneumatology and ecclesiology.[49] Moltmann similarly has criticized the traditional Reformation/Lutheran view for not paying due attention to the role of the Spirit in salvation. Referring to passages such as Titus 3:5-7, which speaks about the "washing of regeneration and renewal in the Holy Spirit, which he poured out upon us richly," Moltmann emphasizes that "'regeneration' as 'renewal' comes about through the Holy Spirit" when the "Spirit is 'poured out.'"[50] By making further reference to John 4:14, the metaphor of the divine "wellspring of life," which begins to flow in a human being, he contends that "through this experience of the Spirit, who comes upon us from the Father through the Son, we become 'justified through grace.'"[51] This is what Macchia is looking toward with his vision of framing justification in a way that links it with the gift of the Spirit as the giver of new life.

Paul's soteriological argumentation in Romans, which often has been interpreted as the magna charta of the traditional Protestant view of justification, yields a different picture when looked at in trinitarian, pneumatological, communal, and cosmic perspectives. It was through the resurrection by his Father in the power of the Spirit that Jesus Christ was "designated Son of God in power" (Rom 1:4).[52] From the point of view of our salvation, he "who was put to death for our trespasses" was "raised for our justification" (Rom 4:25). Consequently, God not only "justifies him who has faith in Jesus" but also, importantly, "prove[s] at the present time that he himself is righteous" (Rom 3:26). The saving act of the righteous and just God is not only about the salvation of individuals by faith such as Abraham (chap. 4) but harks back to the very beginnings and whole history of humankind, to Adam (chap. 5). In Jesus, there is a New Counterpart to the failing first Adam. Indeed, the saving act of God in Christ through the Holy Spirit is meant to be hope for the whole cosmos, "the whole creation [that] has been groaning in travail together until now" (Rom 8:22). "We ourselves, who have the first fruits of the Spirit" (Rom

---

[49]The heading is on p. 135 of Pannenberg, *Systematic Theology*, vol. 3.

[50]Jürgen Moltmann, *The Spirit of Life: A Universal Affirmation*, trans. Margaret Kohl (Minneapolis: Fortress, 1992), p. 146.

[51]Moltmann, *Spirit of Life*, p. 146. See also Kenneth L. Bakken, "Holy Spirit and Theosis: Toward a Lutheran Theology of Healing," *St. Vladimir's Theological Quarterly* 38, no. 4 (1994): 410-11.

[52]Biblical quotations in this essay are taken from the RSV.

8:23) join in these "groans of hope" as we look forward to the consummation of eschatological *shalom*.

CRITICAL REMARKS AND TASKS FOR THE FUTURE

Having introduced the new interpretation of Luther's doctrine of justification in the context of the Eastern Orthodox understanding of *theosis* and
the relation of that convergence to the rapprochement between Protestant
and Catholic soteriologies, I wish to facilitate further study and dialogue
by pointing to several critical issues and challenges in the new interpretation. Before listing the critical questions, let me mention that, unlike some
other voices, I do not consider justification and *theosis* to be in principle a
"problematic synthesis"[53]—if not for other reasons then for the fact that
there are a number of different metaphors of salvation available in the
biblical canon and that those metaphors are complementary.

A major critical question and challenge I wish to raise with regard to
the new Luther interpretation has to do with theological, especially theo-
logico-anthropological ramifications, of the doctrine of salvation in Lutheran, Orthodox and Catholic traditions.[54] Notwithstanding the emerging consensus concerning some key aspects of the doctrine of salvation,
the highly complex set of issues remains unclarified with regard to topics
such as Luther's anthropology, doctrine of sin and the Fall, and understanding of grace, especially when it comes to the role of human will with
regard to God's gracious offer of salvation. Theological anthropology is of
course integrally related to the question of the nature-versus-grace relationship. While Catholic theology, based on Thomistic tradition, operates
with the principle of continuity—in many ways similarly to the Orthodox
tradition (which, however, does not utilize such Western terminological
apparatus!)—the Protestant tradition in general, and the Lutheran in particular, leans toward the idea of discontinuity. A corollary issue, closely
related to all of this, has to do with the notion of faith and how that affects
soteriological categories. While the advocates of the new Lutheran inter-

---

[53]For a somewhat skeptical view, see George Vandervelde, "Justification and Deification—
Problematic Synthesis: A Response to Lucian Turcescu," *Journal of Ecumenical Studies* 37, no.
2 (Winter 2001): 73-78.

[54]Some helpful insights are offered in Paul R. Hinlicky, "Theological Anthropology: Toward
Integrating *Theosis* and Justification by Faith," *Journal of Ecumenical Studies* 34, no. 1 (1997):
44-47.

pretation have not engaged these topics in any extensive ways, fortunately the Roman Catholic-Lutheran dialogue process has devoted considerable time to some of these issues.

My second query has to do with the quite liberal use of the concepts of *theosis* and union among the Helsinki scholars in explaining Luther's doctrine of salvation. The term *theosis* itself only occurs a little more than thirty times in the whole extensive Luther corpus.[55] That is not much indeed. Yet, in fairness—and this is of course a major point in the Mannermaa school's line of argumentation—it has to be acknowledged that the idea of deification may be much more extensive than the term itself. The occasional use of the term *unio* is then invoked by the new interpretation supporters as another key here. Basically that is a correct observation. Yet they fail to deal with the obvious question, how close does Luther's idea of *unio* come to the Eastern understanding of union? The term *union* is quite widely used in Christian theology—say, for example, in the theology of John Calvin and in theologies as far removed from Lutheranism and Eastern Orthodoxy as Anabaptism or Methodism.[56] It is quite another thing to say that all traditions intend the same meaning with the common word.

I would also like to engage some methodological issues, particularly with regard to the term "real-ontic" union. While I affirm the Mannermaa school's desire to critique the neo-Kantian view that tends to blur completely the meaning of the real presence of Christ—similarly to the existentially oriented paradigm that makes the presence merely a matter of subjective experience—I also applaud the attempt by Helsinki scholars to let Luther speak in the context of late-medieval and Protestant "realistic" ontology. That said, I also wonder if the alternative offered is viable. On the one hand, the exact meaning of the term "real-ontic" is left open. Some friendly critics[57] have made the obvious observation that there are a number of ways to understand this elusive concept. On the other hand, the term "real-ontic" to me sounds almost tantamount to the old charge—

---

[55]Simo Peura, "Vergöttlichungsgedanke in Luthers Theologie 1518-1519," in *Thesaurus Lutheri*, ed. Tuomo Mannermaa et al. (Helsinki: Luther-Agricola-Society, 1987), pp. 171-72.

[56]See further, Kärkkäinen, *Union with God*, chap. 5.

[57]Dennis Bielfeldt speaks of various "ontic/ontological" models that could explain what the Mannermaa school argues ("The Ontology of Deification," in *Caritas Dei: Beiträge zum Verständnis Luthers und der gegenwärtigen Ökumene*, Festschrift für Tuomo Mannermaa zum 60. Geburtstag, ed. Oswald Bayer, Robert W. Jenson and Simo Knuuttila [Helsinki: Luther-Agricola-Gesellschaft, 1997], pp. 90-113).

mistaken I believe—against the "physicalist" understanding of *theosis* in the Christian East; even if it is not, the view is subject to misunderstanding. My point here is that while the Mannermaa school has been quite successful in offering a critical response to the canons of the German research, the constructive task still lies ahead.

Yet another major task for ecumenical Luther scholarship is to critically dialogue with and glean from the developments in the new perspective on Pauline and New Testament studies briefly discussed above. As mentioned, to my knowledge the advocates of the new Luther interpretation have failed to consider carefully the obvious connections here and their potential significance to a more adequate understanding of Luther.

Other tasks await ecumenical reflection, such as the relationship between the passivity of faith in Lutheranism and the Eastern Orthodox idea of *synergia*. While I believe Luther's own theology—especially the idea of the Christian as "christ" by virtue of the "real presence" of Christ in the believer—may have resources to tackle this thorny issue, I also acknowledge how curiously little this question has occupied scholars.

To put the topic under discussion in a wider ecumenical context, let me also once again clarify my approach here. I am not saying that Catholic, Lutheran and Orthodox soteriologies have given up—or should give up—their distinctive features. What I am saying is that much of the problematic attached to traditional positions, mostly going back to the time of the Reformation and Counter Reformation, is historically conditioned and no longer necessarily forms an irreconcilable obstacle to dialogue and joint ventures. That said, I am not naive about what ecumenism is. Ecumenical thinking does not mean collecting pieces from here and there and putting them together to make a more appealing mixture. Sometimes ecumenical work may lead to a more precise and explicit acknowledgment of differences between various Christian traditions or to acknowledgment of convergence despite legitimate differing emphases. The approach taken by the joint declaration is to be commended: "[The] Joint Declaration has this intention: namely, to show that on the basis of their dialogue the subscribing Lutheran churches and the Roman Catholic Church are now able to articulate a common understanding of our justification by God's grace through faith in Christ." Then it adds that this "does not cover all that either church teaches about justification; it does encompass a consensus on basic truths of the doctrine of justification and shows that the remaining differences in its explication are no longer the occasion for doctrinal condemnations" (#5). This is a fruitful way to proceed, I suggest, in the ecumenical discussions between Eastern Orthodox and Lutheran theologies as well.

As a footnote, let me suggest that the ecumenical discussion of the doctrine of salvation is not only urgent for the sake of Christian unity, but also in light of the relation of Christian faith to other religions. The theology-of-religions question may open up new vistas for reconsidering ancient Christian doctrines and help us move beyond the ecumenical impasse. What if the doctrine of divinization were a viable candidate for all Christians to talk about salvation in relation to other religions such as Hinduism and Buddhism and, say, African spiritualities?[58] In addition to other religions, the relevance and accuracy of soteriological discourse should also be studied in relation to other cultures where the questions of "salvation" come yet from another angle.[59] Little work, if any, has been done in these areas specifically—this is a call for all of us, regardless of our respective traditions.

---

[58]See Kärkkäinen, *One with God*, pp. 1-4, 133-37.
[59]See further Wolfgang Grieve, ed., *Justification in the World's Context*, Documentation 45 (Geneva: LWF, 2000). See further Veli-Matti Kärkkäinen, "The Lutheran Doctrine of Justification in the Global Context," *International Journal of Systematic Theology* (2010, forthcoming).

■

Traditional Reformed Response

Michael S. Horton

I SHARE KÄRKKÄINEN'S INTEREST IN Orthodox-Protestant dialogue.[1] However, I do not share Kärkkäinen's enthusiasm for the New Finnish interpretation of Luther. There is a difference between saying that Luther's understanding of justification *does not exclude* deification and understanding his view of justification *as* deification. In my view, Kärkkäinen, following the Mannermaa school, supports the latter (stronger—and, in my view, untenable) claim.[2]

There is indeed more in Luther concerning union with Christ (influenced in part by Bernard of Clairvaux) than is often acknowledged—so much so that Andreas Osiander (1498-1552) thought that he was merely extending Luther's logic when he argued that, in Christ, the believer participates in the deity of God. Melanchthon, Flacius and Calvin piled on in criticism of this view.[3] Besides indulging in "speculation," Calvin faulted Osiander for "something bordering on Manichaeism, in his desire to transfuse the essence of God into men." Osiander's theory is based on a series of fatal conflations, says Calvin: human into divine essence; the Spirit's person and work into the deity of the essentially-indwelling Christ, and justification (imputation) into sanctification (infusion).[4] Calvin also objected to Osiander's notion that "faith is Christ," rather than understanding faith as the empty vessel that receives Christ.[5] While observing that "the mystical union is accorded by us the highest degree of importance," Calvin complains that Osiander has demanded a false choice between forensic justifi-

---

[1]I devote more than a chapter to deification in *Covenant and Salvation: Union with Christ* (Louisville: Westminster John Knox, 2007), first in dialogue with New Finnish proposals, pp. 174-80, 209, 214-15, 306, and then in conversation with the Orthodox doctrine of theosis in chap. 14.

[2]On this point, see Carl Trueman, "Is the Finnish Line a New Beginning?" *WTJ* 65, no. 2 (Fall 2003): 231-44. See also the response of Robert W. Jenson to Trueman's essay in the same volume.

[3]Calvin added a lengthy refutation of Osiander to his 1559 edition of the *Institutes*.

[4]*Institutes*, 3.11.5-6.

[5]Ibid., 3.11.7.

cation and participation in Christ and has virtually eliminated the need for the Spirit's person and work in salvation.[6] On at least these points, I think that Calvin is refuting a position that is pretty close to the New Finnish interpretation.[7] In any case, I doubt that the Luther of Helsinki would have been excommunicated, or that Trent's well-informed condemnations would have reached their target.

But there is another reason for wondering if the Finnish school is the best conversation partner with Orthodoxy. Crucial to Orthodoxy is the distinction between God's essence and energies. The West has tradition-ally acknowledged only uncreated essence (God) and created essence (crea-tures), so that union with God would mean union with God's essence. Yet for the East, there is only union with the energies—which are God, but in God's activity rather than in God's being.[8] This marks the crucial differ-ence between pagan Greek *henōsis* (absorption into deity) and *theōsis*.

Kärkkäinen notes in passing, "Luther, unlike the Orthodox tradition, does not know the distinction between God's energies and God's essence." However, this is not as serious a problem if Luther did not teach a "real-ontic unity" in the way that the Finnish interpreters do. Despite the dis-claimer that "the substances themselves do not change into something else," I wonder what the Russian interlocutors made of Mannermaa's point, quoted by Kärkkäinen: "The *theosis* of the believer is initiated when God bestows on the believer God's essential properties." Or Simo Peura's state-ment that "God realizes himself and his own nature" in deifying the Christian?

Though critical of synergism (much less collapsing justification into deification), Calvin and the Reformed tradition bear strong and well-documented influences from the Christian East on many topics that bear on this subject.

First, often referring to theologians of the Christian East, Calvin as-sumes something like the essence-energies distinction throughout the *In-*

[6]Ibid., 3.11.11.

[7]Kärkkäinen notes in n. 4 that conservative American Lutherans have described the Manner-maa school as "Osiandrian," citing Robert Kolb and Charles P. Arand, *The Genius of Luther's Theology: A Wittenberg Way of Thinking for the Contemporary Church* (Grand Rapids: Baker Aca-demic, 2008), p. 48.

[8]Vladimir Lossky, *The Mystical Theology of the Eastern Church* (Crestwood, N.Y.: St. Vladimir's Seminary Press, 1976), pp. 65-89.

stitutes: We know God not in his essence, but according to his works; God's being is incomprehensible, but his energies are revealed to creatures analogically.[9] Breezes from the Christian East are suffused throughout Calvin's treatment of the Trinity and Christology, and especially in his understanding of the Eucharist.[10] Calvin is not unique; similar statements can be culled from Reformed colleagues such as Peter Martyr Vermigli and their successors.

Second, there are convergences in Trinitarian theology. Upbraiding Augustine and Jerome for misunderstanding the East, particularly the meaning and significance of *hypostasis,* Calvin sought a mediating position. Emphasizing the distinctness and reality of the persons (each with his own incommunicable properties), Calvin drew explicitly on Gregory of Nazianzus (see, for instance, *Institutes,* 1.13.17). Following Basil, he wrote, "To the Father is attributed the effective principle of what is done, and the fountain and wellspring of all things; to the Son, wisdom, counsel, and the ordered arrangement of what is done; but to the Spirit is assigned the power and efficacy of the action."[11] All of God's energies come from the Father, in the Son, through the Spirit.

Third, classic Reformed theology affirmed theosis in principle, understood in terms of the essence-energies qualifier. Calvin writes, "Let us mark that the end of the gospel is to render us eventually conformable to God, and, if we may so speak, to deify us." Nevertheless, he immediately adds,

> But the word nature [in 2 Pet 1:4] is not here *essence* but *quality.* The Manichaeans formerly dreamt that we are a part of God, and that after having run the race of life we shall at length return to our original. There are also at this day fanatics who imagine that we thus pass over into the nature of God, so that he swallows up our nature. . . . But such a delirium never entered the minds of the holy Apostles; they only intended to say that when divested of all the vices of the flesh, we shall be partakers of divine and blessed immortality and glory, so as to be as it were one with God *as far as our capacities will allow.* (emphasis added)[12]

---

[9]See, for example, *Commentary on Paul's Epistle to the Romans* (Edinburgh: Calvin Translation Society, 1844; repr., Grand Rapids: Baker, 1993), on Rom 1:19; *Institutes* 1.2.2; 1.10.2.

[10]I point this out at length in *People and Place: A Covenantal Ecclesiology* (Louisville: Westminster John Knox, 2008), pp. 124-52.

[11]Calvin, *Institutes,* 1.13.18.

[12]John Calvin, *Commentaries on the Catholic Epistles,* trans. and ed. John Owen (repr., Grand Rapids: Baker, 1996), p. 371.

"Plato recognized man's highest nature as union with God," yet even he "'could not even dimly sense its nature' apart from Christ." Far from raising our minds away from the body to incorporeal universals, Calvin says that "they alone receive the fruit of Christ's benefits who raise their minds *to the resurrection*" (emphasis added).[13] As Philip Walker Butin points out, "Calvin's most complete definition of the *imago Dei* in the *Institutes* is based on the assumption that 'the true nature of the image of God is to be derived from what scripture says of its renewal through Christ.'"[14]

Resurrection and deification converge in the Reformed doctrine of *glorification,* which received far more attention in sixteenth- and seventeenth-century theologies than it has more recently. William Ames can say that glorification "is actually nothing but the carrying out of the sentence of justification. . . . In glorification the life that results from the pronouncement and award given to us: We have it in actual possession."[15] Francis Turretin adds that it is nothing less than the uncreated glory that "effloresces" from God that causes the bodies of the saints to shine forever. The result, he says, is that love begun will be consummated; faith will be turned to sight; hope will yield to complete joy.[16] Yet this deification/glorification never allows the creature to merge with the divine essence, Turretin observes, quoting John of Damascus.[17] Turretin's view may be contrasted with that of Aquinas, when the latter wrote, "When . . . a created intellect sees God in his essence, the divine essence becomes the intelligible form of that intellect."[18] Reflecting Calvin's exegesis, Turretin adds that in the consummation, "There is nothing else than a certain effusion and emanation *[aporroē]* of the deity upon the souls of the saints, communicating to them the image of all his perfections, *as much as they can belong to a creature*" (emphasis added).[19]

---

[13]Calvin, *Institutes* 3.25.2.

[14]Philip Walker Butin, *Revelation, Redemption, and Response: Calvin's Trinitarian Understanding of the Divine-Human Relationship* (New York: Oxford University Press, 1995), p. 68.

[15]William Ames, *The Marrow of Theology,* trans. John D. Eusden (1968; repr., Durham, N.C.: Labyrinth, 1983), p. 172.

[16]Francis Turretin, *Institutes of Elenctic Theology,* ed. J. T. Dennison Jr., trans. G. M. Giger (Phillipsburg, N.J.: Presbyterian & Reformed, 1992), 3:209.

[17]Ibid., 3:611.

[18]Thomas Aquinas, *Summa theologiae,* Blackfriars ed. (New York: McGraw Hill, 1964), 1.12.5.

[19]Turretin, *Institutes of Elenctic Theology,* 3:612.

As I have said, in Reformed approaches the beatific vision (glorification) centers on the resurrection: not an ascent of mind, but a bodily, cosmic, eschatological event in which the new creation will be consummated. It is "the glorious view of Christ exalted in his kingdom and it will be nothing else than the irradiation of God's glory, from which the bodies will be made to shine."[20] In his commentary on the Westminster Confession, Thomas Watson rhapsodizes concerning the soul's reunion with its flesh, concluding, "The dust of a believer is part of Christ's mystic body."[21]

With respect to the "Joint Declaration," Kärkkäinen says, "Clearly, the Lutheran side has taken a significant ecumenical step in agreeing that justification is not only forgiveness of sins but also internal change, even effecting love through the Spirit. The focal point is the union with Christ." However, in my view, this merely surrenders the Reformation position. As Kärkkäinen observes, "The Catholic counterpart statement reiterates the standard Catholic position according to which justifying grace is always sanative, effective grace, or it is no real justification at all (#27)." For his own part, Kärkkäinen celebrates the following consensus: (1) justification as one metaphor among many, (2) justification as "union and participation, even *theosis*"; (3) justification as "more than a forensic declaration," but "an act and process of making righteous." Furthermore, "As Pannenberg has convincingly shown, the Reformers mistakenly 'viewed the law as an expression of God's demand in antithesis to the gospel as promise and pronouncement of the forgiveness of sins.'" Apparently, as a result of Pannenberg's critique, "that distinction cannot be maintained anymore."

Finally, Kärkkäinen wonders, "What if the doctrine of divinization were a viable candidate for all Christians to talk about salvation in relation to other religions such as Hinduism and Buddhism and, say, African spiritualities?" I grant that divinization is more congenial to other religions than justification but doubt that this is a good test of Christian confession and proclamation.

While forensic justification dissolves into theosis or sanctification in Orthodox and Roman Catholic perspectives, the Reformed affirm justification, sanctification and glorification as distinct and inseparable elements of union with Christ. If death is the curse for transgressing the law, then

---

[20]Ibid., 3:619.
[21]Thomas Watson, *A Body of Divinity* (repr. Edinburgh: Banner of Truth Trust, 1986), p. 309.

even the gift of immortality depends on forensic justification (1 Cor 15:56-57; 2 Tim 1:10). Even Christ's victory over the powers is predicated on "cancelling the record of debt that stood against us with its legal demands" (Col 2:14-15). Precisely because of the forensic ground that justification secures, so much more than justification is obtained in the bargain—nothing less than Christ with all of his gifts.

■

Progressive Reformed Response

Michael Bird

THE ESSAY BY VELI-MATTI KÄRKKÄINEN forces me to think about an area that I have for a long time been very interested in, but not had much time to actually study, namely, theosis. Theosis has of course been a staple diet in the soteriology of Eastern Orthodoxy. The Eastern Orthodox Church and the Reformed churches have not always been natural dialogue partners. In fact, when His Beatitude Jonah, Metropolitan of All America and Canada, leader of the Orthodox Church of America, addressed the Anglican Communion of North America in June of 2009, he said that for intercommunion to occur between Anglicans and the Orthodox, Anglicans would have to reject the heresies of the Reformation such as Calvinism. Not a good thing to hear if you're a Calvinist.

Yet it might not be all that bad between the Reformed and the Eastern Orthodox. For instance, Michael Horton has presented what I think is a compelling case that Calvin's theology of the Lord's Supper was influenced by patristic writings from the eastern church whereby the Spirit communicates the energies of Christ's life-giving flesh in the elements thus accounting for the real presence of Christ in the bread and wine.[1]

---

[1]Michael S. Horton, *People and Place: A Covenant Ecclesiology* (Louisville: Westminster John Knox, 2008), pp. 124-52.

Also, Cyril Lucaris (1572-1638) came into contact with Reformed theology while ministering in Poland before he became the Patriarch of Constantinople. He purportedly wrote a confession of faith that attempted to express Calvinism in the categories of Eastern Orthodoxy.[2] A recent surge of scholarly interest in theosis means that perhaps the time is indeed ripe to see how theosis relates to traditional Protestant understandings of salvation.[3]

There are a number of areas that I would like to engage Kärkkäinen on: the distinction between justification and sanctification in Luther and in the New Testament, the Trinitarian nature of justification, Catholic and Lutheran dialogue on justification, and the ontology of union with Christ. However, space does not permit me to do so. Instead I will focus on one claim in his essay, namely, that "justification can also be expressed in terms of union and participation, even theosis" and what that means in light of the New Testament and Calvin.[4]

First, I have to say that I found it odd that Kärkkäinen nowhere in his essay defines what he actually means by theosis or deification. Ideas of theosis are notoriously varied among ancient and modern theologians. Some treat theosis as the absorption of the divine nature, while others regard theosis as conformity to the image of Christ. In other writings Kärkkäinen appears to identify theosis as union with God and attaining Godlikeness.[5] In search of a fuller description, the *Orthodox Study Bible* says this about deification:

This does not mean we become divine by nature. If we participated in

---

[2]*The Confession of Cyril Lucaris,* ed. Dennis Bratcher (copyright 2006), on the CRI/Voice, Institute website. <www.crivoice.org/creedcyril.html>

[3]Cf. recently Michael J. Christensen and Jeffery A. Wittung, eds., *Partakers of the Divine Nature: The History and Development of Deification in the Christian Traditions* (Grand Rapids: Baker, 2007); Stephen Finlan and Vladimir Kharlamov, eds., *Theōsis: Deification in Christian Theology* (Eugene, Ore.: Pickwick, 2006); Michael J. Gorman, *Inhabiting the Cruciform God: Kenosis, Justification, and Theosis in Paul's Narrative Soteriology* (Grand Rapids: Eerdmans, 2009).

[4]Kärkkäinen wants to move justification and righteousness away from the "forensics court-driven mentality" of the Reformation and supplant it with relational and covenantal conceptions instead. I have two things to say: (1) We cannot eliminate the forensic element of justification/righteousness as long as we have Greek lexicons and commentaries on the Greek text of the NT. (2) The relational and covenantal aspects of justification/righteousness undergird rather than compete with their forensic meaning.

[5]Veli-Matti Kärkkäinen, *One with God: Salvation as Deification and Justification* (Collegeville, Minn.: Liturgical Press, 2004); idem, "Theosis," in *The Encyclopedia of Christianity,* 5 vols. (Grand Rapids: Eerdmans, 2008), 5:452-55.

God's essence, the distinction between God and man would be abolished. What this *does* mean is that we participate in God's energy, described by a number of terms in scripture such as glory, love, virtue, and power. We are to become like God by His grace, and truly be His adopted children, but never become like God by nature. . . . When we are joined to Christ, our humanity is interpenetrated with the energies of God through Christ's glorified flesh. Nourished by the Blood and Body of Christ, we partake of the grace of God—His strength, His righteousness, His love—and are enabled to serve Him and glorify Him. Thus we, being human, are being deified.[6]

There is some scriptural basis for theosis. We read in 2 Peter, "he has granted to us his precious and very great promises, so that through them you may become *partakers of the divine nature (theias koinōnoi phuseōs),* having escaped from the corruption of the world because of sinful desire" (2 Pet 1:4). In Romans, Paul states that the purpose of divine predestination is so that believers will be "conformed to the image of his Son" (Rom 8:29). A further destiny of believers is that they will be "glorified" (Rom 8:30), presumably with divine glory. Paul also wrote, "And we all, who with unveiled faces contemplate the Lord's glory, are being transformed into his image with ever-increasing glory, which comes from the Lord, who is the Spirit" (2 Cor 3:18). Here are certainly the biblical ingredients for a doctrine of theosis or something like it.

Undoubtedly the biblical texts cited above refer to a transformation of believers that brings them into ontological conformity, in some mysterious sense, with God. Yet I am unsure if we should call this deification. In fact, the concept of theosis/deification is rather slippery when you think about it. Athanasius wrote that the Word "was made man so that we might be made God."[7] Yet what Athanasius meant by "made God" was unclear. According to Jaroslav Pelikan, "The church could not specify what it meant to promise that man would become divine until it had specified what it meant to confess that Christ had always been divine," and he adds later, "The idea of deification in the Greek fathers had run the danger of obscuring the distinction between Creator and creature."[8]

---

[6]*The Orthodox Study Bible: Ancient Christianity Speaks to Today's World* (Nashville: Thomas Nelson, 2008), pp. 1691-92.
[7]Athanasius, *The Incarnation* 54.3.
[8]Jaroslav Pelikan, *The Christian Tradition* (Chicago: University of Chicago Press, 1977), 1:155, 345.

Union with Christ is, through the Holy Spirit, union with God—that much seems obvious. Yet rather than speak in terms of theosis/deification, I think that *participation* and *transformation* are the more appropriate categories to describe how believers enter into the messianic story of salvation. Because believers are united with Christ, co-crucified and co-resurrected with him, they participate in the benefits of his life as the faithful one, his death as the crucified one, his resurrection as the vindicated one raised immortal, and his ascension as the exalted one reigning in his heavenly session. That involves a participation in Jesus' humanity transforming them into the body of Christ, a participation in the benefits of Jesus' death transferring them from alienation to reconciliation, a participation in Jesus' divine life, which transmutes their state from death to immortality. In sum, it is participation in the person and work of the Messiah that transforms believers' status from condemnation to righteousness and transforms their state from human death to divine life. I am happy to use the term theosis/deification, but only as a shorthand summary for describing how, through Christ's mediation, believers are transformed to *share in the divine life that God has* and conformed to the pattern of Christ in order to *imitate the righteousness that God is*. Anything beyond that is going to raise more problems than it solves.

Second, how does theosis shed light on justification?[9] According to Kärkkäinen, justification refers to the presence of Christ in the believer and Christ "is through this presence identical with the righteousness of faith." He cites Tuomo Mannermaa to the effect that the believer receives God's "essential properties," presumably including divine righteousness. Yet as I think about this take on justification and theosis, I constantly hear a voice at the back of my mind: beware the error of Andreas Osiander! Osiander's view was that justification meant the impartation of the essential righteousness of Christ's deity to the believer. Calvin was right to reject Osiander's position because Osiander's rejection of the forensic character of justification was a denial of the necessity of the work of the cross for the forgiveness of sins. Calvin also argued that the substance of our bond with Christ is not an infusion of divine essence, but is communicated through the Holy Spirit.[10] So union is a spiritual union that brings us into

---

[9]Cf. Gorman, *Inhabiting the Cruciform God*, pp. 40-104.
[10]Calvin, *Institutes* 3.9.5-12.

the life of God. I think Kärkkäinen's position is Osianderian insofar that it emphasizes union with divinity at the expense of the communication of the benefits of Jesus' redeeming work that must be given to us.

I teach my students, in line with many Eastern Church fathers, that God's plan has always been to unite himself to creation through the Logos. Yet due to the Fall God cannot unite himself to sinful and fallen creatures unless those creatures experience his saving love. Unless the Logos is a redeemer who rectifies their status and state, there can be no communion between God and humanity. There can be no meeting between humanity and God's essential righteousness until the Logos rectifies the unrighteousness of humanity through sharing the righteousness of his Adamic task with them.[11]

Third, what did Calvin think about theosis?[12] There are several texts from Calvin that might be said to support theosis: "[T]he flesh of Christ is like a rich and inexhaustible fountain that pours into us the life springing forth from the Godhead into itself. Now who does not see that communion with Christ's flesh and blood is necessary for all who aspire to heavenly life?"[13] And, in their union with Christ, believers are "participants not only in all his benefits but also in himself."[14] Calvin can be regarded as theosic if by that one accounts Calvin's view of participation in Christ, which envisages the incorporation of believers into the triune life, as a legitimate form of theosis. However, if one holds up Calvin to a Byzantine standard, I think that he fails.[15]

Bruce McCormack rejects the notion that Calvin's idea of union with Christ can be seriously integrated with the Eastern Orthodox notion of theosis. McCormack notes that Calvin's Christology will not actually al-

---

[11]I am not suggesting that Kärkkäinen denies the work of Christ; instead I fear that Kärkkäinen's view of Christ's divinity implies the human work of Christ is almost superfluous. If Osiander (and I fear Kärkkäinen) is right, it is the divinity and not the humanity of Christ that is redemptive. In which case we are left asking with Anselm, *Cur Deus Homo* (Why did God become Man)? This scheme needs no incarnation, only a conduit for the impartation of divinity such as the Spirit.

[12]Cf. J. Todd Billings, *Calvin, Participation, and the Gift* (Oxford: Oxford University Press, 2007), pp. 13-14, 51-61, 193; Mark A. Garcia, *Life in Christ: Union with Christ and Twofold Grace in Calvin's Theology* (Carlisle, U.K.: Paternoster, 2008), pp. 209, 257-58.

[13]Calvin, *Institutes* 4.17.9.

[14]Ibid., 3.2.24.

[15]Billings, *Calvin*, p. 54.

low God's essential life to be communicated to believers.[16] McCormack
argues that Calvin has dispensed with that which made divinization theo-
ries possible, namely, the idea of an interpenetration of the natures. For
Calvin, the believer participates only in the human nature of Christ.
Moreover, since there can be no interpenetration of the natures in Christ,
participation in the human nature of Christ cannot result in a participation in the divine nature. The upshot is that one simply cannot find the
ontological currency needed for a divinization theory in Calvin's Christology. In my mind, Calvin is at best an advocate of a soft form of deification
(i.e., participation), but not in the fully orbed Eastern sense.

---

[16]Bruce McCormack, "Participation in God, Yes, Deification, No: Two Modern Protestant
Responses to an Ancient Question," in *Denkwürdiges Geheimnis: Beiträge zur Gotteslehre. Festschrift für Eberhard Jüngel zum 70. Geburtstag,* ed. Ingolf U. Dalferth, Johannes Fischer and
Has-Peter Großhans (Tübingen: Mohr/Siebeck, 2004), pp. 347-74; idem, "Union with Christ
in Calvin's Theology: Grounds for a Divinisation Theory?" in *Tributes to John Calvin,* ed. David W. Hall (Phillipsburg, N.J.: Presbyterian & Reformed, 2010), pp. 504-29.

■

New Perspective Response

James D. G. Dunn

THIS IS ONE OF THE MOST INTERESTING contributions to the current
debate about justification. Finland being itself part of the boundary between East and West, the resultant dialogue between Orthodoxy and Lutheranism has opened up a whole new and highly significant dimension to
the debate. The reminder that *theosis* is another way of describing Christian soteriology—and of ancient pedigree—brings home the extent to
which even the fruitful rapprochement between Catholic and Lutheran/
Reformed and "the new perspective" have been limited in their scope and
probably too restricted in even their positive outcomes. I am grateful to be
thus introduced to the Mannermaa school's contribution to the debate in
systematic theology, and rather excited by it, although I had better remain

within my own New Testament and biblical field of expertise since I am only partially tuned in to the systematic and historical theology dimensions of the debate.

I begin, however, with an initial cautionary note. From a New Testament perspective I find myself hesitant about making too much of the *theosis* theme. It is rather limited as a theme in the New Testament itself, and I hesitate to build so much on a single verse within the New Testament document nearest to the edge of the New Testament canon: 2 Peter 1:4. The verse certainly holds out the prospect of believers becoming "sharers *[koinōnoi]* of divine nature," but is that best described as "deification" or "divinization"? Richard Bauckham, for example, justifiably cautions us on the point:

> Not participation in *God,* but in the nature of heavenly, immortal beings, is meant. Such beings, in the concepts of Hellenistic Judaism, are *like* God, in that by his grace, they reflect his glorious, immortal being, but they are "divine" only in the loose sense, inherited from Hellenistic religion, of being god*like* and belonging to the eternal world of "the gods." To share in divine nature is to become immortal and incorruptible.[1]

Other verses can be summoned to support the *theosis* theme (particularly Eph 3:19; 2 Cor 8:9; Jn 1:16; 17:23), but there is something forced about finding "deification" even in these passages. And the more familiar motifs of union with Christ, the indwelling Christ and Christians as God's "sons," to which Veli-Matti refers, also as indicating ontological change, can be drawn upon if "deification" is already established as a prime soteriological category, but hardly otherwise. I suppose it is the concern that the infinite distinction between Creator and creation is endangered which makes me so uneasy. Perhaps I am too Western in my theology—*koinōnia* is a more important motif than *koinōnos*—but I welcome the ongoing dialogue between East and West on this as on other theological issues and hope to learn further from it.

I also very much welcome Veli-Matti's attempt to move beyond a too narrow conception of justification. But I am far from sure that the way forward is to broaden the concept itself: "effective justification"; "justification not only means forgiveness of sins but also 'communion with God'

---

[1]Richard Bauckham, *Jude, 2 Peter,* WBC 50 (Waco, Tex.: Word, 1983), p. 181.

and union with Christ"; justification "means union between the human person and her Creator." The problem may be with the word "means"; if for "means" we could say "involves" or "is closely allied to," then all that makes good sense. But justification does not "mean" these things. To "justify" *means* to "declare innocent or guiltless," to "absolve or acquit," to "acknowledge to be right." The Reformers were right to emphasize the forensic context that the term evokes and that provides its basic meaning. Justification as such is primarily about change of status than about change of state or person.

I much prefer the way Veli-Matti puts the point, with the support of Pannenberg: "Justification is one of the many metaphors of salvation, making room and calling for other metaphors"; "'The doctrine of justification is but one of many ways of expounding the theme [of the salvation of God in Christ].' . . . 'Even for Paul himself' . . . the doctrine of justification 'is not the only center of his theology that controls all else'" (quoting Pannenberg); "justification is one of the many legitimate images of salvation in the Bible; it cannot be made *the* hermeneutical key. . . . Paul uses this legal image as *one* of the ways to illustrate one side of his doctrine." That is surely the point, and the way to respond to those who pile everything on to and into "justification" as though that was the only legitimate way of describing the grace of God in and through the gospel. Justification does not "mean" forgiveness; but the gospel does offer forgiveness. Justification does not "mean" "union with Christ"; but the gospel does promise union with Christ to those who commit themselves in trust to Christ.

The realization that for Paul God's righteousness means "saving righteousness" and the relational aspect of "righteousness" (which Veli-Matti also recognizes) do begin to point beyond the limitations of the forensic imagery. But the way to respond to a too narrow focus on the legal terminology is to highlight the *other* images and metaphors and dimensions of Paul's soteriology, not to expand (and in effect burst) the legal metaphor by heaping nonlegal imagery into it. Justification does not mean "sanctification" or even include sanctification. But alongside the forensic imagery Paul speaks of believers as "in Christ," of salvation as a process to be worked out throughout a life of committed trust and obedience, as a process of being transformed into the image of Christ, of being made mature or perfect. The criticism of scholastic Lutheranism is not that it emphasized the doctrine of justification, but that in doing so it either neglected other images and metaphors or forced them to conform to the only privileged way (justification by faith) of speaking about the operation of grace to humankind. And here, like Veli-Matti, I would want to bring the gift of the Spirit much more into the picture, whether in conjunction with justification or in its own right, as Paul so often does.[2]

The suggestion that the degree of rapprochement being recently achieved between Lutheran and Orthodox and Lutheran and Catholic parallels the development of "the new perspective on Paul" is also very stimulating. His characterization of "the new perspective" as protesting against a too narrowly individualistic reading of Paul, as unfairly denigrating the religion of Israel, as setting faith and good works (declarative and effective righteousness) too much in opposition to each other is quite a good summary of key emphases in "the new perspective." But I would have liked to see a bit more interaction with these themes.

First, the "communal ramifications of justification" are not just about the "fellowship of believers." It is much more about breaking down the barrier (law) that separated Jew from Gentile and in effect debarred Gentiles from participation in the covenant grace of God. This denial of an ethnic or national priority and prerogative in divine grace still needs to be heard (and heeded), as well as the offer to the individual sinner of peace with God. The exposition of Ephesians 2–3 on this subject too often stops at Ephesians 2:9 and ignores the powerful exposition (so central to the letter) of Ephesians 2:11–3:13.

Second, in the dialogue between Western Christianity and Orthodoxy, the former has already acknowledged its history of anti-Judaism and anti-Semitism. That was the product of a recovery of a full biblical (not just New Testament) theology, as well as a reaction against the horrors of the Holocaust.[3] But Orthodoxy has still to come to that point, being too much determined by the attitudes of the Fathers when Christianity was trying to define itself by distancing itself from rabbinic Judaism. Orthodoxy needs its Vatican II moment on this issue. Lutherans have long ago disowned Luther for his polemical tract, *On the Jews and Their Lies*, but so far as I am

---

[2]I refer again to my *The Theology of Paul the Apostle* (Grand Rapids: Eerdmans, 1998), chap. 16.
[3]The Lutheran antithesis between law and gospel too easily transmuted into an antithesis between Judaism and Christianity.

aware, the Orthodox have still to disown Chrysostom for his diatribes *Against the Jews.*

Third, the emphasis on "effective justification," and on "the infusion of righteousness" is an understandable, and, in the historical context, an acceptable way of bringing out the "sanctification" side of the gospel's outworking, the "good deeds" that Paul expected of believers. But I would like to have seen more reflection on Paul's teaching on judgment according to works and his warnings that if believers lived according to the flesh they would reap corruption and death. It is all very well to recognize that a believer's sin might be "real sin" and to insist that even so it "does not bring about separation from God." But is that what Paul says? Are his warnings so easily softened, the "provided that's" of passages like Romans 8:17; 11:22; 1 Corinthians 10:12; 15:2; and Colossians 1:22-23 so easily set to one side? I think not.

So, as much as has been gained by developing an open dialogue between East and West, between Catholic and Reformed—and much has already been gained—all sides are probably still too entrenched in their own tradition and need to have the grip of their tradition's interpretation of Scripture slackened lest it suffocate the dialogue and fail to be sufficiently open to the God-given insights of the others—not to mention the full range of the insights that God gave to and through Paul.

■

Roman Catholic Response

Oliver P. Rafferty, S.J.

KÄRKKÄINEN'S APPROACH TRIES TO TAKE us beyond the polemical certainties that have too often and for too long characterized Protestant and Roman Catholic approaches to the question of justification. He does so by setting the Western discussions against the background of Eastern Orthodox ideas of deification. On that basis alone his essay is of great value. Writing from a convinced ecumenical perspective he is concerned to stress that the historical conditioning of debate and counterdebate of the Reformation era should not still be allowed to act as an impediment to ecumenical dialogue. In this context the "Joint Declaration on Justification" is a healing balm on wounds that have lacerated interchurch relations since the sixteenth century. All this is welcome and praiseworthy. But questions do arise. What of Kärkkäinen's central thesis that justification is materially equivalent to deification? How true is this as an assertion about Luther's views on this crucial "Reformation discovery"?

A major component in Kärkkäinen's analysis is the conviction that the Finnish Mannermaa school provides more authentic paradigms for interpreting Luther's thought than those that have prevailed in the older German viewpoint. The Finnish view was given immense stimulus by contact with the Russian Orthodox Church and this dialogue has in turn influenced Roman Catholic-Lutheran discussions. At the heart of the Finnish approach is the conviction that Luther has no distinction between forensic and effective justification and that the process of justification in the life of the individual involves both a "making righteous" and well as a "declaring righteousness." This process of sanctification also has important implications for the Roman Catholic-Lutheran discussions on justification.

Without doubt Kärkkäinen is trying to put the debates about justification into a new context and to show that genuine convergence is possible. At the same time one wonders if it is rather like Newman in Tract XC showing that the theology of the 39 Articles was indeed compatible with that of the Council of Trent. He is anxious to demonstrate that Luther's views on justification are not primarily concerned with a forensic declaration but with a transformation by Christ of the heart of the believer, in which the leitmotif becomes one of participation by the believer in God's own life. The "ontic unity" thus brought about is not only strikingly similar to Orthodox views of deification but also enables us to see that Luther's own theology is potentially closer to Catholic understanding than that preserved in historic Lutheranism. Furthermore, Kärkkäinen is not alone in drawing this to our attention. Even Alister McGrath thinks that there is some affinity between Luther's "theology of justification" as seen in ideas propagated in *The Freedom of a Christian* (1520), "and the eastern notion of divinisation."[1] McGrath also offers supporting evidence for Kärk-käinen's position when he makes the point that for Luther justification

> is an all-embracing process, subsuming the beginning, development and subsequent perfection of the Christian life. This is one of the clearest *differentiae* between Luther and later Protestantism, and places Luther closer to the position of the Council of Trent than is generally realised.[2]

All this is highly stimulating, but one has to ask: is it actually true to the historic Luther? Because there is a sense in which it proves too much. No one can take issue with the fact that on certain issues we can point to divergence between Luther and Lutheranism; even in his own day Melanchthon had begun to formulate ideas not entirely to Luther's liking. Further, if Luther's stated views can be seen to be compatible with sixteenth-century Catholic theology, why did the Council of Trent so vehemently resist Luther's views concerning justification and spend so much time debating those views? It is also clear in our own day that the official Catholic response to the "Joint Declaration" highlights the fact that fundamental differences do remain in the respective theologies of justification, not least in regard to the idea of "The Justified Sinner."[3]

Kärkkäinen is anxious to stress the new insights coming from the rich biblical exegesis over the last fifty years and their importance for our interpreting of what justification meant in the Pauline writings. Indeed some scholars such as Mark A. Seifrid have argued that Luther, in some crucial and fundamental respects, misses the point of Paul's reasoning in Romans. Hence: "Paul's thought . . . unlike that of Luther, is not based on the individual, but on *Heilsgeschichte*, and particularly on the turning point of the ages in the death and resurrection of Christ."[4] While this is a good and important approach in ecumenical theology, it does not of itself help us in determining Luther's view, nor that of historic Lutheranism, except per-

---

[1]Alister E. McGrath, *Iustitia Dei: A History of the Christian Doctrine of Justification*, 3rd ed. (Cambridge: Cambridge University Press, 2005), p. 226.
[2]Ibid., p. 233.
[3]*Response of the Catholic Church to the Joint Declaration of the Catholic Church and the Lutheran World Federation on the Doctrine of Justification*, "Clarifications," 1998, p. 1. Cf. www.vatican .va/roman_curia/pontifical_councils/chrstuni/documents/rc_pc_chrstuni_doc_01081998_ off-answer-catholic_en.html.
[4]Mark A. Seifrid, *Justification by Faith: The Origin and Development of a Central Pauline Theme* (Leiden: Brill, 1992), p. 9.

haps to say that neither Luther nor his successors fully understood what St. Paul was concerned with.

Equally, our quest for Luther's understanding, while it is interesting as a historical exercise, cannot of itself help us in the present. Our circumstances are not those of the sixteenth century. As Markus Wriedt has commented, "Luther can only be understood through his time and in his time. Thanks be to God, time has changed."[5] And that is precisely why the "Joint Declaration" is of such decisive importance for the context in which we live. Kärkkäinen is therefore correct to see a major development in thinking about justification as represented by the "Joint Declaration." In particular the Lutherans who signed the "Joint Declaration" seem to have made a considerable concession on the question of sanctification. Justification produces an internal change in the believer. It is true of course that Luther, at some points in his theology, argues that justification and sanctification are part of the same process. The question then is: what exactly takes place in sanctification? I am less happy, and I hope I have not misunderstood him, when Kärkkäinen appears to argue that in this matter the "Joint Declaration" is being true to Luther's own view and spirit. For Luther, surely, God envelops the individual with "alien righteousness" in a process that is dependent on faith, not of course in any sense a human work, and in which the human person remains entirely passive. As that nuanced and careful exponent of Luther's theology, Alister McGrath, comments: the change brought about by justification in the status of the individual is not in his or her nature and hence the justified has the status of *simul iustus et peccator.*[6] And as we have seen above this issue is still one on which the Catholic Church feels deeply its divergence from Luther and the Lutheran tradition.

We are all aware of the centrality of justification for Luther's whole theology and life. As he himself was to say "without this article the world is nothing but death and darkness."[7] Furthermore, as Peter Toon remarks, Luther's view represented a major development in theological thinking about justification and on this basis Luther broke with historic Catholi-

---

[5]Markus Wriedt, "Luther's Theology," in *The Cambridge Companion to Martin Luther,* ed. Donald K. McKim (Cambridge: Cambridge University Press, 2003), pp. 86-119 at p. 114.
[6]Alister E. McGrath, *Justification by Faith* (Grand Rapids: Academies Books, 1990), p. 52.
[7]*WA* 39/1, 205, 5.

cism. Toon also draws attention to Luther's famous declaration in the Schmalkaldic Articles of 1537 that on his doctrine of justification

> rests all that we teach and practice against the pope, and the devil and the world. Therefore we must be quite certain and have no doubts about it. Otherwise all is lost and the pope, the devil and all our adversaries will gain the victory.[8]

And while it is true, as Kärkkäinen says, that justification is only one of the metaphors for salvation that the Scriptures employ, it is nevertheless for Luther the central metaphor. Indeed as Eberhard Jüngel points out, Luther insisted that nothing in the justification article could be given up or compromised.[9] For it was on this basis that Luther believed himself to be breaking with the distortions of medieval Catholicism that had parted from the true gospel. As John Brewer points out in his introduction to Jüngel's book, for Jüngel justification is the center around which other theological material on salvation can be arranged.[10] There is a sense in which the same can be said of Luther. It seems to me that in this way Jüngel is being faithful to Luther in a way that perhaps the "Joint Declaration" is not, at least not in its entirety.

Although sensitive to the issues of theological anthropology, Kärkkäinen does not fully engage with the question of the freedom of the will. That we are free to accept or reject God, despite concupiscence as a result of the Fall, is a conviction with which the Roman Catholic Church will not easily part. Historically in Catholic theology that freedom enables the individual to embrace the justifying grace given by God, and at some level that movement of the will is also part of the justifying process. For Luther our will is in a state of slavery by the very nature of our creatureliness. In addition, Luther's insistence on double predestination not only goes beyond Augustine's theology but is something incompatible with Roman Catholic understanding, and makes it difficult to mesh easily Lutheran and Catholic views on the process of justification.

An important point remains in terms of developments within Luther-

---

[8]Peter Toon, *Justification and Sanctification* (Westchester, Ill.: Marshall, Morgan & Scott, 1983), p. 57.
[9]Eberhard Jüngel, *Justification: The Heart of the Christian Faith*, ET (New York: T & T Clark, 2001), p. 17.
[10]Ibid., p. xv.

anism in the sixteenth century. Did those who came after Luther and who insisted, for example, on "forensic justification" go too far and somehow distort Luther's own theological mindset? Once again, although highly sensitive to the historical development within Lutheranism and quite prepared to concede that there were radical modifications in some of Luther's most cherished ideas,[11] Alister McGrath penetrates to the heart of the matter when he observes that with regard to "imputed righteousness," the origins of the idea may "legitimately be considered to lie with Luther."[12]

Some years ago the late British scholar of the Reformation, Francis Clark, in the course of a lecture characterized the differences in Catholic and Lutheran approaches to justification in the following manner. He drew an analogy with the manner in which cats and monkeys rescue their young in moments of danger. The cat saves its young from danger by lifting its young in its mouth by the scruff of the neck and yanking it from calamity. The monkey by contrast reaches down from the tree to the upraised hand of its young and snatches it from danger. In a certain sense this does mark the difference historically between Catholic and Lutheran approaches. Of course as Catholics we want to maintain that the ability to reach up is something God given and therefore dependent on grace, so that all is grace. Nevertheless we do, in God's providence, have our role which is not simply passive.

Kärkkäinen's closing observations about the implications of divinization for interfaith issues are, it seems to me, among his most controversial speculations. Certainly from a Roman Catholic perspective his views are, at the very least, incompatible with the pronouncement of the then Cardinal Joseph Ratzinger in his Vatican document of the year 2000: *Dominus Iesus.*

It would, however, be inappropriate to end on a negative note. Kärkkäinen, building on important dialogue between Lutheran and Orthodox theologians and following hermeneutical developments in relation to Luther's theology in the Mannermaa school, has shown us how central the "Joint Declaration" is for a contemporary understanding of justification. He has also demonstrated how this document opens us to a more comprehensive understanding of salvation as seen through the theological device

[11]McGrath, *Iustitia Dei,* p. 248.
[12]Ibid., p. 229.

of divinization. In particular he has indicated how divinization as a theological paradigm is quite compatible with Luther's own understanding of justification. That is as it should be. Despite the centrality of the idea of justification for Luther and historical Lutheranism, and without trying to detract from it, Kärkkäinen has reminded us that, in approaching the God in whom we believe, our ultimate goal is communion with the ineffable mystery that God is. We are, however, enabled to speak in a meaningful way of him, and to love him, by his self-revelation in Christ Jesus. And yet God remains mystery, and that mystery we cannot fully comprehend.

7

Roman Catholic View

Gerald O'Collins, S.J., and Oliver P. Rafferty, S.J.

CATHOLIC VIEWS OF JUSTIFICATION (OLIVER P. RAFFERTY)

Introduction

Perhaps the clearest and most systematic exposition of the Catholic theology of justification is that provided by the Council of Trent in its sixth session and approved on January 13, 1547.[1] Such, however, were the complexities involved in arriving at what the church meant by justification that it took almost seven months to complete the debates and to work through the various draft documents presented to the conciliar fathers. Jaroslav Pelikan has remarked that no other decree at Trent "and few decrees of any Council before or since, received such meticulous care."[2] It is also clear that Trent had a limited intention in framing the decree on justification. It wanted to draw a clear distinction between Roman Catholic and Protestant teaching on the question, but was determined to avoid contentious

---

[1] In the first part of this chapter, Oliver Rafferty sets out the historical development of the Roman Catholic teaching on justification that was normatively expressed in the 1547 decree of the Council of Trent. In the second part of the chapter, Gerald O'Collins offers an account of how one Roman Catholic theologian has thought about justification, down to the 1999 "Joint Declaration" and beyond into the twenty-first century.

[2] Jaroslav Pelikan, *The Christian Tradition: A History of the Development of Doctrine*, vol. 4: *Reformation Church and Dogma (1330-1700)* (Chicago: Chicago University Press, 1984), p. 281. The Council itself was well aware of the importance of the decree. The presidents wrote to Rome from Trent on June 21, 1546: "The significance of the Council in the theological sphere lies chiefly in the article on justification; in fact, this is the most important item the Council has to deal with." Quoted by Hubert Jedin, *A History of the Council of Trent*, trans. Ernest Graff (Edinburgh: Nelson, 1961), 2:171.

adjudication on issues of divine grace and human freedom of the will that had formed the basis for disputed questions between the various theological schools of the Catholic Middle Ages.[3] Moreover, some commentators have warned that it is a mistake to think that Trent presented only a single view of justification, or that we might in a univocal way speak of "the Tridentine doctrine of justification."[4]

Trent's teaching has historically not satisfied all Protestant scholars. Karl Barth famously declared that the teaching had about it "no light from above."[5] Adolf von Harnack, on the other hand, speculated that, had the decree been passed at Lateran V (1512-1517), the history of the Reformation might have been very different.[6] On the Catholic side, Hans Küng has tried to show that in effect the Catholic and Lutheran understandings are materially equivalent.[7] Such an approach would, on the surface, seem to have received authoritative affirmation in the joint declaration on the subject between the Lutherans and the Roman Catholic Church at Augsburg in 1999.[8] Problems remain, however, and Eberhard Jüngel has gone to great lengths to show that the supposed agreement in the declaration is chimerical.[9]

At Trent the fathers tapped into a rich and variegated vein of theological speculation on justification that had been set in train by St. Augustine of Hippo (354-430) and in particular by the post-Augustinian history of the church in its horror of Pelagianism. Martin Luther would, in time, charge medieval Catholicism with being vitiated with Pelagian errors, as he asserted his "rediscovery" of the true heart of the gospel, justification by

---

[3]Jedin, *Council of Trent*, p. 304.

[4]Alister McGrath, *Iustitia Dei: A History of the Christian Doctrine of Justification*, 3rd ed. (Cambridge: Cambridge University Press, 2005), p. 195.

[5]Karl Barth, *Church Dogmatics* 4/1, trans. G. W. Bromiley (Edinburgh: T & T Clark, 1956), p. 626.

[6]Adolf von Harnack, *History of Dogma*, vol. 7, trans. William McGilchrist (London: Williams & Norgate, 1899), p. 57.

[7]Hans Küng, *Justification: The Doctrine of Karl Barth and a Catholic Reflection*, trans. T. Collins, E. E. Tolk and D. Grandskou, 2nd ed. (London: Burns & Oates, 1981).

[8]Walter Kasper, although affirming the basic point that full consensus exists about the fundamental issue, introduces the caveat that "we are dealing with differentiated consensus rather than a total agreement." He also points out that in Catholic catechesis we tend to speak of salvation, forgiveness and reconciliation rather than justification. Walter Kasper, "The Joint Declaration on the Doctrine of Justification: A Roman Catholic Perspective," in *Justification and the Future of the Ecumenical Movement: The Joint Declaration on the Doctrine of Justification*, ed. William G. Rusch (Collegeville, Minn.: Liturgical Press, 2003), pp. 18, 20.

[9]Eberhard Jüngel, *Justification: The Heart of the Catholic Faith*, trans. Jeffrey F. Cayzer (New York: T & T Clark, 2001).

faith alone. The only theologian to completely escape Luther's indictment was Gregory of Rimini (d. 1358), although Luther also treats sympathetically the general approach of St. Bernard of Clairvaux (1090-1153). In contrast to Luther, Heiko Oberman maintained that, taken as a whole, none of the medieval theologians and doctors can be convicted of Pelagianism per se.[10]

It is perhaps worth saying that the doctrine of justification and the debates on the issue as we know them historically are almost entirely a concern of the Latin and Western church,[11] and even here the meaning of justification could and would change over time. At the core of the debate lies a distinction between the idea of God's own justice and the idea of the justice with which God justifies the sinner. For most of the Catholic Western tradition, these are two distinct things. That by which God is in himself just is theologically distinct from that by which God makes a sinner just. Equally, if we take the propositions "Augustine is just" and "God is just," although they may be related analogously, they clearly involve two different theoretical concepts of justice. At least some of the problems in the Augustinian and post-Augustinian age were a function of the definition of justice, as derived from Cicero and which was in widespread use in antiquity. Here justice meant to render to each one that to which he is entitled, and this was used virtually indiscriminately of both human and divine justice.

At an intellectual level, the Catholic tradition has, of course, profoundly accepted and maintained that no one can stand in the sight of God without blame. "All have sinned and fall short of the glory of God" (Rom 3:23).[12] We cannot make ourselves sinless. It is God alone who justifies the sinner through the merits of Jesus Christ. At the same time, the tradition, in general, affords the conviction that all was not lost by the sin of Adam and Eve. There was not an utter corruption of the human person, and although the image of God was severely occluded, it was not obliterated and was certainly

---

[10]Heiko Oberman, *Forerunners of the Reformation: The Shape of Late Medieval Thought Illustrated by Key Documents,* new ed. (Philadelphia: Fortress, 1981), p. 125.

[11]The Eastern church was more concerned with the process of divinization. Equally, Finbarr Clancy has shown that divinization was also an aspect of Augustine's soteriology, although he rarely refers to it. See Clancy, "Redemption," in *Augustine Through the Ages: An Encyclopedia,* ed. Allan D. Fitzgerald (Grand Rapids: Eerdmans, 1999), p. 703.

[12]Biblical quotations in this essay are taken from the RSV.

not replaced by the "image of the devil," as Luther, in a perhaps unguarded outburst, maintained.[13] Most importantly of all, human beings retained, despite concupiscence, an essential freedom of the will, which, under the right conditions and stimulus, could move toward God.[14]

In conjunction with the basic conviction that only God justifies the sinner, Catholic teaching preserved two essential features: (1) an explication of the fact that the believer can fulfill the moral imperative to live righteously, knowing that Christ will come again to judge all according to their deeds, and (2) the capacity of men and women in freedom to cooperate with God's grace. As Albrecht Ritschl observed long ago, Catholic thinking on justification can be seen as God giving to humanity "the ability to perform the moral offices toward men which make up the task of the kingdom of heaven."[15] This then brings us immediately to the essential questions: Can we in some way contribute to our own justification? Do we in fact have a disposition toward God as demonstrated in right actions? If so, what is to be made of the idea of God's absolute sovereignty over man and the human will? If we veer too closely to a positive anthropomorphic account of these questions, do we run the risk of making the incarnation and redemption redundant? At the same time, if we are wholly negative in our estimation of human capacity, founded on and aided by grace as it must be, do we not fall foul of St. Bernard's stricture, "take away free will and there is nothing that needs to be saved."[16] It is to the unfolding of these and related issues in the history of the Roman Catholic tradition that we must now turn our attention.

---

[13]Luther, *WA* 24, 50, 8-9. For his part, Philipp Melanchthon, with Luther's approval, could speak of God as the origin of both good and evil—a view entirely repudiated by Trent: see *Decretum de iustificatione*, can. 6., D 798.

[14]One aspect of the issue that Luther seems to ignore but which does find expression in the Catholic tradition is the question of God's assessment of the human nature of Christ. The uniqueness of Christ from the human perspective is that he is sinless. Here at least is one instance in which human nature does not share Adam's condition and cannot in Lutheran terms be utterly corrupt. And precisely because of this, the atonement is brought about by one like us, although free from sin. If justification is God's movement toward humanity, Christ in his human nature is humanity's movement toward God.

[15]Albrecht Ritschl, *The Christian Doctrine of Justification and Reconciliation*, trans. H. R. MacKintosh and A .B. Macaulay, 3rd ed. (Edinburgh: T & T Clark, 1900), p. 35.

[16]Bernard also immediately adds, "take away grace and there is nothing that can save it" (i.e., the will); quoted in Pelikan, *Christian Tradition*, 4:144. This echoes an observation of Augustine himself: "If there is no grace of God, how does he save the world? And if there is no free will, how does he judge the world?" (Epistle 214).

Augustine's Contribution

Before the time of Augustine, the fathers of the church seem to have had little interest in the subject of justification. It is also clear that even Augustine underwent a sharp change of mind in his thinking. Prior to his dispute with Julian of Eclanum (around 386-454), he seems to have thought of God's justice according to the then received sense that God gives to each one what is his due.[17] Furthermore, he may well have held to the conviction that it is possible for us to take the first step in the process of being made righteous and that God rewards such initiative. By the time of his polemic against the Pelagians, Augustine could assert that without grace, that is to say, without God's specific gift to the individual,[18] the will was free to do evil but never free to do anything good.[19] In that sense merit and reward for meritorious acts, having their origin in human will, were impossible.

The human being's inability to rise above evil inclinations, the person's rootedness in sin, is in virtue of the fact that every person not only inherits original sin but is in fact guilty of it. Since all have sinned in Adam, everyone bears the guilt of Adam's sin. In Augustine's mature theology he concludes that on the basis of the Fall man simply does not have the freedom to choose the good or to engage in good acts.[20] It is impossible therefore for us to will or perform good actions that would merit the reward of justification from God. Human beings have no power to resist sin and cannot rise above their sinful state. It is also clear from Augustine's treatise *De gratia et libero arbitrio* that he repudiates any idea that we are capable of a free choice for the good independently of God. Indeed had any capacity for good remained in us in our post-lapsarian state, then Christ's death would have been in vain.

Nevertheless, there is a sense in which justification is indeed a reward for merit, but that merit is itself pure gift owing to the saving activity of Christ, and more importantly in a strict sense such merit belongs to Christ and not to humanity.[21] Merit is, however, given to us and comes through grace. The meritorious in us is something God himself does: "God there-

---

[17]Henry Chadwick, "Justification by Faith: A Perspective," *One in Christ* 20 (1984): 209.

[18]This is also clearly articulated in *De gratia et libero arbitrio* 4.7-9.

[19]*Contra duas epistulas Pelagianorum ad Bonifatium* 1.7.

[20]McGrath, *Iustitia Dei*, p. 42.

[21]Ibid., p. 44.

fore crowns his own work, and not human merits."[22] Indeed left to ourselves we are incapable of either deserving or achieving justification. Once we are justified, however, it is our duty to keep the commandments, and we cannot claim that God's precepts are impossible to observe.[23]

In the face of this grace and this capacity for good, based and founded on God's gift, in what sense can it be said that we have freedom with relation to grace? Is God's grace in us irresistible? Augustine would appear to argue that grace cannot be separated from free will or vice versa. In a sense it is grace that facilitates and brings about the freedom of the will. But it is also clear that God prepares the will by the gift of grace. God's mercy and his call are not given in vain in such a way that the person can accept or reject them. God calls to justification "those whom he pities . . . in the way he knows suits them."[24] This must clearly imply that the human response is indeed free, even though that which "suits them" is already given by God and certainly foreknown by him. Nevertheless, the idea that the will is prepared by God to respond to his call to justifying grace is something Augustine repeats in a number of places,[25] and it would become a fixed principle in medieval theological speculation.

This leads to the related and vexed question: Is God's call indiscriminate? Is his will that all should be saved and come to the knowledge of the truth? Augustine was clearly overwhelmed with the consideration in Romans 9:10-29 that God had accepted Jacob and rejected Esau. God did not treat Esau justly. Why not? Because God's justice is not the same as human justice. This is given further confirmation for Augustine by the parable of the laborers in the vineyard. Not only does God's justice differ from human justice, but also God's choice—his election of Jacob and the rejection of his elder brother—is based in the inscrutable and mysterious will of God. Augustine also argues that the number of the elect is fixed and will not be added to or subtracted from. God in his eternal wisdom has determined to prepare the will of a limited number to receive the gift of justification.[26]

The call to justification is manifested in the individual by the gift of faith. The gift of faith is given only to the elect. As J. Patout Burns ob-

---

[22]*De gratia et libero arbitrio* 6.15.

[23]*De natura et gratia* 43.50.

[24]*De diversis quaestionibus ad Simplicianum* 2.13.

[25]See for example *Contra Julianum* 4.3.14 and *Retractationes* 9.2.

[26]*De praedestinatione sanctorum* 10.21, 10.16-18.

serves, with reference to the elect, "Without reference to their prior, contemporary, or subsequent merits, God separates those who become the Christian faithful from others who will die in their sins."[27] At the same time, Henry Chadwick has warned against too rigid an interpretation of Augustine's view on predestination.[28] Peter Brown in his magisterial work has also introduced a note of caution. He has suggested that in the vicissitudes of the world inhabited by Augustine with its uncertainties, persecutions, apostasies and wars, predestination had only one meaning for the great theologian: "it was a doctrine of survival, a fierce insistence that God alone could provide men with an irreducible inner core."[29]

The main ingredients of Augustine's thought are then readily discernible: the central themes of justification by faith, divine election, the corruption of human nature by original sin for which all are responsible, the impossibility of human merit and the necessity of grace to condition the will and give it freedom. These would form the dynamics for Luther's theological protest in the sixteenth century. One aspect, however, that would not give Luther comfort, was the fact that for Augustine justification was something not simply imputed to us, but rather righteousness becomes intrinsic and inherent in humanity.[30] But in the intervening centuries what was Augustine's influence on theological speculation concerning justification?

The Early Middle Ages

To say the least, Augustine constructed a formidable theoretical account of justification and its dependent theological cognates. But did his views actually condition theological speculation on justification in the centuries immediately after his death? Even in his own lifetime Augustine was aware of resistance to his ideas on justification on the part of many religious individuals, especially monks.[31] Similarly, later in the fifth century, reaction to Augustine became more widespread, especially in Southern Gaul and in the writings of those such as Faustus of Riez (d. around 490). He could assert that, although we are incapacitated by sin, "at least we may

---

[27]J. Patout Burns, "Grace," in Fitzgerald, *Augustine Through the Ages*, p. 397.
[28]Chadwick, "Justification by Faith," p. 209.
[29]Peter Brown, *Augustine of Hippo: A Biography* (London: Faber & Faber, 1967), p. 407.
[30]See McGrath, *Iustitia Dei*, pp. 47-51.
[31]*De dono perseverantiae ad Prosperum et Hilarium* 15.38.

placate [God] through the importunity of our searching."[32] We have then
the beginnings of the emergence of the idea of man's preparation for grace,
as something inherent, and brought to fruition by human desiring. Such
an idea has clear patristic roots. By the High Middle Ages this will have
evolved into the principle *facienti quod in se est Deus non denegat gratiam*
("To the one who does all he can, God does not deny grace").

James J. O'Donnell is of the opinion that the more "extreme" aspects of
Augustine's thought on justification, grace and predestination were simply
jettisoned in the history of Catholic theology until the Protestant Reformation.[33] On the other hand, the Second Council of Orange (529), under
the influence of Prosper of Aquitaine and Caesarius of Arles, not only
rejected the idea that the person can take the initiative in the process of
justification but also repudiated any understanding that somehow the will
remained unaffected by the Fall.[34] Furthermore, our inability to fulfill
God's commands on the basis of free will without the aid of grace was
condemned as heretical. The views of Orange received the approbation of
no less a figure than Pope Boniface II (pope 530-532).[35]

Although one can see a strong Augustinian streak in the thinking of
some Carolingian theologians—Hincmar of Reims (around 806-882) and
Gottschalk (around 804-around 869) among them—after the tenth century and before the sixteenth, the theological climate shifts and the teaching of the Council of Orange appears to fall from view. Furthermore, before the later schoolmen, there is no real attempt in the medieval tradition
to give "justification" a precise theological definition. It is true, however,
that some medieval commentaries on Paul's letter to the Romans,—that
attributed to St. Bruno (around 925-965) is a case in point—can say that
justification is brought about neither by human merit nor by works of the
law.[36] Moreover, there is no real attempt before the sixteenth century to
work out a strong distinction between justification and sanctification.

What does emerge more emphatically is a relationship between justi-

---

[32]*De gratia Dei et libero arbitrio* 2.10.
[33]James J. O'Donnell, *Augustine: A New Biography* (New York: HarperCollins, 2005), pp. 270-
    71.
[34]Canons 5-7 of the Second Council of Orange. D 375-77.
[35]George Tavard, *Justification: An Ecumenical Study* (New York: Paulist Press, 1983), p. 24.
[36]Charles P. Carlson Jr., *Justification in Early Medieval Theology* (The Hague: Nijhoff, 1975),
    p. 46.

fication and the evolving sacrament of penance. There are indirect indications of such an idea even in the work of Ambrosiaster (an anonymous fourth-century writer),[37] at least with relation to baptism and public penance. But it is with the emergence of penance as practiced in Celtic monasticism that the relation between penance and justification, with strong undercurrents of making satisfaction, come to the fore.[38] These ideas are taken up and expounded with some force by Alcuin (around 740-804), who uses the term *justification* in relation to penance and indeed in conjunction with confession to a priest, but not in such a way as to indicate a systematic theology of justification.[39] Still a link is thereby established between justification on the one hand and the sacraments on the other. This would eventually have some implications later in the Middle Ages for the question of faith and the *ex opere operato* nature of the sacraments, to the extent that the sacrament of penance is made to produce justification and sacramental penance takes the place of merit in the process of justification.[40]

In general then, justification became at times no more than another term for the remission of sins. The stimulus for such a conceptual ambiguity was provided by St. Paul himself, who at times seems to use the terms virtually interchangeably.[41] A further complication was intruded into thinking on justification by speculation on the relationship between divine and human justice, but also on justice in relation to the devil. Because of the Fall, the devil had acquired rights over humanity.[42] This idea is completely rejected by Anselm,[43] who offers in *Cur Deus Homo* a reflection on the fact that the only justice that is acceptable to God is that which comes from God himself. The idea and process of justice are that which God himself offers and brings about.[44] Although Anselm uses the term *justificatio* in a perfectly conventional way, by the standards of the Middle Ages, to signify simply justification from sin,[45] he does

[37]Ibid., p. 9.
[38]McGrath, *Iustitia Dei*, p. 91.
[39]Alcuin, PL 101, col. 621.
[40]Carlson, *Justification in Early Medieval Theology*, p. 125.
[41]Ritschl, *The Christian Doctrine of Justification*, p. 38.
[42]Gregory the Great, *Moralium libri* 33.15.31.
[43]*Cur Deus Homo* 1, 7.
[44]Ibid., pp. 1, 9.
[45]Carlson, *Justification in Early Medieval Theology*, p. 91.

add considerably to the theological understanding of redemption in terms of God's righteousness. God always acts in conformity with his nature: this is what assures the "rightness" of salvation in Christ. His love and mercy are both operative in ensuring a just balance to divine mercy after the offence of sin.[46] It is the self-offering of Christ that ensures that the divine justice as an attribute of God is completely operative in the divine mercy. God always acts in a way that is fully just and at the same time fully merciful.[47] This notion of the relationship between mercy and justice was to have considerable influence on the Tridentine teaching on justification, as was Anselm's view of the satisfaction for sin brought about by Christ's sacrifice.[48]

Hugh of St. Victor (d. 1142) draws on the idea of satisfaction to say that the sacraments are an indication of God's promise of mercy and it is by this "remedy" that people are saved. He further argues that God acts justly whether he punishes or justifies a sinner. The justification of the sinner is by grace and not human merit, and this justification of the sinner is on the basis of faith.[49] By contrast, Peter Lombard (around 1100-1160) argued in book four of the *Sentences* that the sacrament of penance was in fact our part in justification. Later in the twelfth century there was a concern for what became known as the *processus justificationis*, especially associated with Peter of Poitiers (around 1130-1215), again related to penance, which had a profound effect on subsequent scholastic theology. At the same time, this interest was also connected to the notion that individuals could prepare themselves for the gift of justification. This idea would be taken up by both the early Dominican and Franciscan schools.

One of the frustrations in surveying the medieval period is that it yields contradictory results. The Council of Sens (1141) could, for example, condemn Abelard's view that "free will as such suffices to perform something good." At the opposite end, the Council of Reims (1148) could condemn the proposition that "apart from Christ there is no meritorious human action."[50]

---

[46]Anselm had already argued in his *Proslogion* that God is merciful because he is just (no. 7).

[47]*Cur Deus Homo* 1, 19 and 2, 4-5. I would like to thank my colleague Fr. John McDade for a stimulating discussion on this aspect of Anselm's theology.

[48]*Decretum de iustificatione*, chap. 7.

[49]Hugh of St. Victor, *De Sacramentis Christianae fidei* 1.8.11.

[50]Oberman, *Forerunners of the Reformation*, p. 130.

It would be impossible here to give more than a fleeting sense of early medieval teaching on justification. We can, however, see that in general justification is treated in relation to the sacraments of baptism and penance. Although Lombard and Bernard offer some refinements, we cannot speak of a doctrine of justification in any strict sense and certainly not in the way that this was to emerge in the sixteenth century.

The Later Middle Ages

Charles Carlson makes a telling and pertinent observation to the effect that medieval theologians never quite understood Paul's idea of the primacy of faith, and that as the Middle Ages progressed the idea of faith was subsumed under the idea of grace. Grace became the primary theological category to which all other concepts were related. This was as true for justification as for everything else.[51] There was a widely held view that God's initial gift of grace, which was the foundation for justification, was given *ex puris naturalibus*. In other words, from the very condition of humanity there could be a reaching out to God. Such an idea was a central part of the theology of Gabriel Biel (around 1420-1495), and was taught right up to the eve of the Reformation.[52]

This was very much part of a preoccupation with the respective roles of God and the person in the process of justification. Augustine had bequeathed to medieval theology the idea that God crowns his own gifts, as an explanation for the way in which God rewards human effort. By the time of the Augustinian revival of the fourteenth century, associated with such figures as Gregory of Rimini and Thomas Bradwardine, this view prevailed, and it was emphasized that man was justified by faith alone without prior merit on his part, a view that Duns Scotus (around 1265-1308) had also maintained.[53]

An earlier theological revival in the eleventh and twelfth centuries had attempted to protect the idea of rewards and merits by the idea of *meritum de congruo*. God rewards human acts, which have no value in themselves, on the basis of his loving disposition toward humanity. In other words, he

---

[51]Carlson, *Justification in the Early Middle Ages*, pp. 137-39.
[52]Heiko Oberman, *The Harvest of Medieval Theology* (Cambridge, Mass.: Harvard University Press, 1963), p. 175.
[53]See for example Thomas Bradwardine, *De causa Dei* 1.43. Gregory of Rimini's views are a departure from the general tenor of nominalism.

treats human works as if they had some value. This pastoral approach
would become especially associated with the Franciscans. By contrast, the
idea also emerged of *meritum de condigno,* whereby God had established a
covenant, *pactum,* with humanity, in which he obliged himself to accept
good works performed in a state of grace and to reward these with eternal
life. But here the important element, as asserted by Scotus and developed
by Biel, was the divine acceptance and estimation of such acts, and the
priority of the divine will over issues of what is right or wrong.[54] Human
actions of themselves were worthless, but God having entered into this
covenant relationship with humanity gives to human acts a much more
exalted value than they actually possess. At the same time in a tradition
from John of La Rochelle (around 1200-1245) to Biel, it was stressed that
even in these circumstances there is no external compulsion involved in
this process so far as God is concerned.[55] Thomas Aquinas (around 1225-
1274), however, taught that neither type of merit represented a true claim
on our part in relation to God's justice.[56] There is then in the scholastic
tradition a certain reserve with relation to humanity's rights, even for the
justified. We do not have proprietary rights to righteousness; by God's gift
we do, however, in a sense, truly *possess* righteousness as our own.[57]

Already in the early Middle Ages there was some understanding that
the process of justification involved three elements: the infusion of grace,
contrition, and the remission of sins.[58] Aquinas elaborates this scheme,
doubtless under Aristotelian influence,[59] into a fourfold process: the infusion of grace, the movement of the will directed toward God, the movement of the will away from sin, and finally the remission of sins.[60] It is also
important to keep in mind that for Thomas one cannot have the infusion
of grace without simultaneously having the remission of sins. That at least
is from God's perspective, while from the human point of view these two

---

[54]Duns Scotus, *Opus Oxoniense* 3 dist. 19 q. 1 n. 7.

[55]McGrath, *Iustitia Dei,* p. 88.

[56]*Summa Theologiae,* 1a 2ae, q. 114, a 1.

[57]Karl Rahner, "Gnade: IV Systematisch," in *Lexikon für Theologie und Kirche,* vol. 4 (Freiburg:
    Herder, 1960), p. 994.

[58]See Philip S. More, *The Works of Peter of Poitiers: Master in Theology and Chancellor of Paris
    1193-1205* (Notre Dame, Ind.: University of Notre Dame Press, 1936), pp. 41-43.

[59]See A. E. McGrath, "The Influence of Aristotelian Physics upon St. Thomas Aquinas's Dis-
    cussion of the 'Processus Iustificationis,'" *Recherches de théologie ancienne et médiévale* 51 (1984):
    223-29.

[60]*Summa Theologiae* 1a 2ae, q. 113, a. 8.

things appear to take place in succession. For Aquinas, as McGrath observes, justification involves humanity being translated "from a state of corrupt nature to one of habitual grace; from a state of sin to a state of justice, with the remission of sin."[61] Sanctifying grace, which brings about justification, creates a habit of virtue in the soul, which is the fruit of sanctification, an idea that Trent would subsequently be anxious to uphold against the Lutherans.

For St. Bonaventure (1217-1274) and the Franciscan school, the three operations of grace in justification were purification, illumination, and the perfection of the soul. But Bonaventure also emphasized that the soul was incapable of receiving sanctifying grace unless it had been first prepared by God. Although the Dominicans tended to argue that this disposition was a natural property of every individual, Aquinas had taught that, of themselves, men and women are not naturally disposed to receive grace and must be moved to do so by an act of the divine will. Thus human preparation for justification is God's work,[62] even if this preparation is brought about by the somewhat confusing quality of "created grace."

The symbol by which justification was conveyed to the sinner was baptism. The sacrament not only removed sin but also made us good and enabled the soul to be conformed to God's will. Justification in baptism entailed regeneration; it produced real change intrinsically in the individual.[63] Sin of course remained, even the marks of original sin, but materially and not formally.[64] Actual sins could blot out sanctifying grace but not faith, which was the presupposition for justification. Sanctifying grace could be restored by repentance and the sacrament of penance. For some currents in the Franciscan school, justification could be regained by simple attrition, outside of sacramental confession.

The scholastic tradition also took up Anselm's idea of the intimate relation between God's justice and his mercy.[65] This was rejected by Scotus, for whom justification of the sinner can only be the result of God's mercy and not of his justice. The problem was resolved in nominalism by the argument that the differences in the divine attributes lay in human per-

---

[61]McGrath, *Iustitia Dei*, p. 65.
[62]*Summa contra Gentiles* 3, 149, 8.
[63]*Summa Theologiae* 3a, q. 69, art. 4.
[64]Pelikan, *Christian Tradition*, 4:278.
[65]*Summa Theologiae* 1a 2ae, q. 3, art. 2.

ception and not in God, who is supremely simple.

Faith was, as we have seen, the foundation for justification, the essential presupposition either in the individual or, for babies at baptism, in the church. Equally, Aquinas held that love toward God is the highest good and is the essential characteristic of faith.[66] Thomas also maintained that love for God is inextricably linked to love of others. Indeed the love of God and one's neighbor are one and the same act, but with two extensions.[67] Faith implies love and cannot be separated from it. In the Reformation debates this would become one of the hotly contested issues in the fragmentation of the Western church.

The Council of Trent

The Council of Trent had two aims in view when formulating its teaching on justification: to present what the Catholic Church understands of the nature and process of justification and to refute what it took to be Lutheran errors. Above all Trent wanted to uphold the view that justification involved not only the remission of sins but also the sanctification of the individual. While justification was God's work in us, we too have our part to play in the willing acceptance of the grace that God imparts to human beings. It would be wrong, however, to think that the sophisticated and subtle theology expounded by Trent can easily be summarized. Some Protestant critics have suggested that given the history of the decree its contents are riddled with compromises and ambiguities. As Friedrich Loofs argued, the *Decretum de iustificatione* is unclear "because of its sheer cleverness."[68] Although the interpretation of the decree was to give rise to serious dispute within Catholic theology in the post-Tridentine period, we can, nevertheless, delineate the lines along which the Council fathers enunciated Catholic views on the subject of justification. One of the problems here, however, is that, although free will and the necessity for grace are both affirmed, the connection between the two is not precisely worked out.[69]

Discussion about justification followed on from the decree on baptism.

---

[66]Ibid. 2a, q. 4, art. 3.
[67]Ibid. q. 25, art. 1.
[68]As quoted in Jüngel, *Justification*, p. 186.
[69]Jean Delumeau, *Catholicism Between Luther and Voltaire: A New View of The Counter-Reformation*, trans. Jeremy Moiser (London: Burns & Oates, 1977), p. 100.

We have seen how in the Middle Ages the issue had been linked with the question of the sacraments. And indeed until Trent the only authoritative pronouncement on Luther from the Catholic Church had been Pope Leo X's bull *Exsurge Domine* (1520), which continued to link justification with baptism.[70] Now Luther had forced the Church to look at the matter as a central theological issue in its own right. There was no absolute consensus about the veracity of Luther's position; Cardinal Reginald Pole warned, for example, that not everything Luther said was to be rejected just because he had said it.

In the discussions between June 22 and 28, 1546, a consensus emerged that the process of justification involved more than simply forgiveness of sin or the non-imputation of guilt. In justification something positive was established that made the person pleasing to God. In some way or at some level the person had to cooperate with God's grace, although a minority of theologians argued for the idea that in justification the will was purely passive.[71] The superior general of the Augustinians, Luther's own former order, Cardinal Girolamo Seripando, argued in favor of the idea of *duplex justitia*, a view that Luther himself had advanced at an early stage in the Reformation and that had already found expression in the early Franciscan school in the writings of Alexander of Hales (1186-1245).[72] The main point here was that justification involved both imputed and inherent righteousness in order to facilitate salvation. This formulation may have gone some way to placate Lutheran opinion, and although not condemned by Trent, neither was it incorporated into the text of the decree. The Jesuit theologians in particular spoke strongly against it, including the second general of the order, Diego Lainez, on the grounds that imputed righteousness undermined the idea of heavenly reward appropriate to the sanctity of the individual. Imputed righteousness was in any case incompatible with the doctrine of purgatory.[73]

The decree of Trent in its final form, with its attached canons and

---

[70]See *Exsurge Domine* 2 (1) in B. J. Kidd, *Documents Illustrative of the Continental Reformation* (Oxford: Clarendon, 1911), p. 76.

[71]Jedin, *Trent*, 2:177.

[72]*WA* 2, 145-52.

[73]Some of the details are touched on by Edward Yarnold, *"Duplex iustitia:* The Sixteenth Century and the Twentieth," in *Christian Authority: Essays in Honour of Henry Chadwick,* ed. G. R. Evans (Oxford: Oxford University Press, 1988), pp. 205-22.

anathemas, is a robust refutation of the Lutheran position. Although the will is prepared by God's grace for justification,[74] nevertheless, the consent of human free will in cooperation with the process is essential.[75] While faith is necessary, it is not sufficient for justification, since faith must be united to love.[76] Chapter eight confronts head on the idea that justification comes as a free gift from God, and does so following the perennial teaching of the Catholic Church, on the basis of faith, "without which 'it is impossible to please God'" (Heb 11:6).

Chapter sixteen of the decree deals with the thorny issue of merit. It argues that on the basis of inherent righteousness we can be said to have "truly deserved eternal life" given our good deeds. But such reward is, as with Augustine, God's crowning of his own gifts in us, so that no one might "glory in himself."

Although justification is "intrinsic," the chapter does go some way toward Luther's view that justification is in some sense "alien" to us. Our personal justice "is not established in us as something coming from us," but it is God's justice in us having been imparted by the merits of Christ. Chapter seven had made clear that God's justice in us is not that by which "God himself is just, but that by which he makes us just." The justice thus imparted is the "one formal cause" of justification in us. The other causes of justification are set out in a systematic way: final, efficient and meritorious, which originate in God. The instrumental cause, also a gift of God through Christ, is baptism, "the sacrament of faith, without which no one can be justified."

For the most part the decree avoids the language of the medieval schools with the varying interpretations of grace and justification and is instead heavily biblical in its exposition of "this Catholic teaching about justification."[77] One thing it does not have, however, is a sustained treatment of predestination or election.[78] Even so, it does reject the doctrine of double predestination (canon 17). At the same time the decree makes clear (chapter 9) that no one can know with certainty that he has been saved, and further, unless by a special revelation, no can claim that he has the gift

---

[74]*Decretum de iustificatione*, chap. 6.
[75]Ibid., can. 4 and 9.
[76]Ibid., can. 11 and 12.
[77]*Decretum de iustificatione*, chap. 16.
[78]Chadwick, "Justification by Faith," p. 205.

of final perseverance (canon 16). With the publication of the decree on justification, a major milestone had been reached in the Catholic Church's thinking, and yet as Jedin has observed, the initial reaction to this theological tour de force was both feeble and patchy.[79]

A PERSONAL JOURNEY (GERALD O'COLLINS)

Looking back at over forty years of publishing articles and books in theology, I feel a little embarrassed to find that I have written only sporadically and briefly on justification. In retrospect that seems odd for several reasons. First, my maternal grandfather, who helped to write the Australian constitution and was a member of the federal parliament, represented for nearly twenty years an electorate that was heavily and devoutly Lutheran. Then, he left in our family library many volumes by John Henry Newman (1801-1890), including an early copy of his *Lectures on Justification* (1838). Years later, study in Germany and contact with such great Lutheran scholars as Gerhard Ebeling (1912-2001) and Ernst Käsemann (1906-1998) could well have drawn from me work on justification.

In the spirit of "better late than never," let me now face some of the many questions that "justification" brings up. It may be more illuminating to tell the story of my own modest engagement with this theme as an individual Roman Catholic. Hence what follows is more *a* rather than *the* Roman Catholic version of justification.

My Point of Departure

During my seminary days spent in Sydney, Australia (1960-1964), our major professor in systematic theology and two professors of Sacred Scripture expounded justification as the faithful and saving action of God or the covenant faithfulness and liberating presence of God in making repentant sinners righteous through the merits of Jesus Christ appropriated in faith. Being justified by faith meant God making ungodly sinners righteous (Rom 4:5) and their entering the life-giving and "gracious" dominion of God (Rom 5:21). Justification came through the obedience of Jesus Christ in shedding his blood on the cross (Rom 5:9-11, 19, 21).[80]

---

[79]Jedin, *Trent*, 2:312.

[80]The Feast of the Most Precious Blood, celebrated on July 1 and eventually ranked as a "double of the first class," reinforced a sense of being justified through the blood of Christ. In the aftermath of the Second Vatican Council (1962-1965), this feast was combined with the Feast

This new life of grace was not primarily some created "thing" that was "infused" in our souls. Rather it was the personal indwelling of the Holy Spirit, being incorporated in Christ, and so sharing, as far as possible, in the inner life of the Blessed Trinity. In other words, we were encouraged to follow Eastern Christians, who have always cherished the notion of divine grace as sharing in the life of God (see 2 Pet 1:4).

Our professors understood that justification involved a call to righteous living; faith should bear fruit. Hence we could reconcile the teaching of Paul with James's stress on good works. Nevertheless, righteousness should not be construed as "wages" paid for anything we did (Rom 6:23). We were warned against following (through any modern equivalents) those at the time of Paul who made sabbath observance, dietary practices, and other "works of the law" the path toward righteousness. Yes, we could follow Matthew (e.g., Mt 6:19-21; 24:45-51), Luke (e.g., Lk 14:12-14), other biblical witnesses, and behind them Jesus himself and maintain the language of "merits." Jesus' call to action included a promise that God will faithfully reward those who are faithful to the divine covenant—a promise expressed not least in the Beatitudes special to Matthew (Mt 5:3-12).[81] But it was made perfectly clear to us that God's freely and lovingly given grace "precedes" any human act that might be construed as claiming righteousness before God (Rom 3:27; 5:6). In season and out of season, our major professor of systematic theology appealed to St. Augustine of Hippo when stating that "when God crowns our merits, he does nothing else but crown his gifts."[82]

Our professors did not attend to everything about justification by faith to be found in Paul's letters. For instance, they had little or nothing to say about Abraham (and Sarah) as prototypes of faith (Rom 4:1-25). In any case, in the one Eucharistic Prayer used in those days before the changes in the liturgy, we heard Abraham named every day as our "patriarch" (translated in the 1969 *Roman Missal* as "our father in faith"). My profes-

---

of Corpus Christi as the Solemnity of the Most Holy Body and Blood of Christ, celebrated shortly after Pentecost. Both before and after the Council another Roman Catholic liturgical feast recalled and recalls the blood (and water) that came from the pierced side of Christ on the cross (John 19:34): the solemn feast of the Most Sacred Heart of Jesus.

[81]See J. P. Meier, *A Marginal Jew: Rethinking the Historical Jesus*, vol. 2 (New York: Doubleday, 1994), pp. 334-36.

[82]See n. 22 in Oliver Rafferty's section in this chapter.

sors had little to say about Martin Luther's account of justification, except to insist that *dikaioō* primarily meant to *make* righteous interiorly and so to transform repentant sinners rather than (merely?) impute righteousness exteriorly to them. But that did not disallow, secondarily and externally, the "forensic" or legal meaning of "declaring" sinners to be now, through the merits of Christ, forgiven and righteous.

My two professors of Scripture, who belonged to an ecumenical group that met regularly at the University of Sydney, took the initiative of inviting me to join as a junior member. Other Christians in the group repeatedly endorsed a view of redemption that they called "penal substitution": burdened with the guilt of human sin, Jesus was treated like a sinner on the cross and through his suffering and death propitiated the anger of God. I cannot remember that we ever discussed justification as such. But this initial contact with the penal substitution theory troubled me and set me reflecting for a lifetime on the nature of redemption and, in particular, on whether certain passages in Paul's letters (Rom 8:3, 32; 2 Cor 5:21; Gal 3:13) offer any support for this view. All of this study was eventually drawn together in my *Jesus Our Redeemer: A Christian Approach to Salvation.*[83]

Cambridge and Tübingen

Graduate studies in theology at the University of Cambridge (1965-1968), three summer semesters at the University of Tübingen (1966-1968) and their aftermath took me further in my thinking about justification. In Tübingen I shared in a superb seminar on Christ's resurrection led by Ebeling and attended a large and crowded lecture theater to hear Käsemann's powerful lectures on Romans. I knew and had welcomed what he had done a decade earlier in breaking away from his former teacher Rudolf Bultmann. The latter had argued that our historical knowledge of Jesus (in particular, the knowledge derived from the Synoptic Gospels) was almost entirely irrelevant for Christian faith, and had championed his own version of realized eschatology or doctrine of "the final things," as if eschatology concerns what is here and now in "final" importance rather than what will finally come at the end of time. Käsemann led the way in maintaining that what we know historically about Jesus plays its role in faith; he also insisted that a genuinely future eschatology, or hope for a final end to

---

[83]Oxford: Oxford University Press, 2007.

come, shapes Christian theology and, in particular, that of Paul himself.

When expounding Romans—for instance, Romans 3:24—Käsemann recognized that we faced a creative divine act that made sinners righteous and added that this did not exclude a further, "forensic" meaning being involved. In his subsequent commentary he stated: "Mankind's justification is the actuality of God's right to his creation as this reveals itself as saving power."[84] This converged with what my seminary professors had taught about justification as the saving action of God who forgives sinners and makes them righteous. Käsemann troubled me, however, by claiming that justification is *the* key to understanding Paul's message. In his commentary he was to write: "the doctrine of justification forms the center of his [Paul's] theology."[85]

Some have pushed this view further and made justification *the* key for understanding the message of the entire Bible. This entails claiming too much for one metaphor among many biblical metaphors of salvation. It also entails proposing a wide-ranging understanding of the language for justification (and righteousness) that leaves behind any precise profile and takes justification to be broadly equivalent with healing, liberating, reestablishing communion, and so forth.[86]

In the years that followed my enriching contact with Käsemann in Tübingen, it gradually became clear to me that, for all its importance, justification is only one of the ten or so metaphors that Paul uses for salvation—a metaphor that, apart from Philippians 3:2-11, is limited to Romans and Galatians. This started to come home to me when I wrote the entry "Salvation" for the *Anchor Bible Dictionary*.[87] Then some New Testament scholars made it obvious that one should not continue to support Käsemann's position. In various publications Joseph Fitzmyer points to the other metaphors Paul employs to illuminate "the Christ-event": salvation, reconciliation, expiation, redemption, freedom (liberation), sanctification,

---

[84]Ernst Käsemann, *Commentary on Romans*, trans. G. W. Bromiley (London: SCM Press, 1980), p. 93.

[85]Ibid., p. 92. Some (but certainly not all) Lutheran systematic theologians have pushed this even further by proposing that the doctrine of justification is *the* criterion or even the *one and only* criterion for theological statements.

[86]See W. Klaiber, *Justified by God: A Contemporary Theology* (Nashville: Abingdon, 2006).

[87]"Salvation," in *Anchor Bible Dictionary*, ed. D. N. Freedman (New York: Doubleday, 1992), 5:907-14.

transformation, new creation, and glorification.[88] In a symposium on redemption I co-chaired in New York in 2003, Gordon Fee had much the same to say: justification is only one among many Pauline metaphors and should not be highlighted in a one-sided way.[89]

During my studies at the University of Cambridge, I initiated a lifelong friendship with James Dunn and his wife Meta. For a time the work of this great Pauline scholar persuaded me not to join Richard Hays, Morna Hooker and others in moving beyond Luther's translation of a phrase that recurs eight times in the apostle's letters: "the faith of Jesus (Christ)" (e.g., Gal 2:16). For centuries Luther was followed by many, seemingly the overwhelming majority of translators and commentators, in understanding the genitive to be an "objective" genitive and so to mean our "faith *in* Christ." Hence being justified "by the faith of Christ" signifies trusting and believing *in* Christ (or trusting *in* Christ) and the saving impact of his obedience toward God that culminated in his death on the cross and that makes our righteousness possible.

Even though for years I argued, on the basis of the Synoptic Gospels and Hebrews 12:2, that during his earthly existence Jesus lived by faith and not by sight, I refused to appeal to the Pauline phrase "the faith of Jesus (Christ)." The limited biblical expertise of those who did so failed to persuade me.[90] But then I kept pondering on what was implied by Paul's reflections on Christ's "obedience" and its consequences (Rom 5:12-21). In the apostle's understanding "obedience" and "faith" coincide (Rom 1:5; 16:19). I thought more about Morna Hooker's account of "the faith of Christ" as "a *concentric* expression, which begins, always, from the faith of Christ himself, but which includes, necessarily, the answering faith of believers, who claim that faith as their own."[91] Finally, thanks to discussions with Thomas Stegman about passages in 2 Corinthians (e.g., 2 Cor 4:13),[92]

---

[88]See Joseph A. Fitzmyer, "Pauline Theology," in *New Jerome Biblical Commentary*, ed. Raymond E. Brown, Joseph A. Fitzmyer, Roland E. Murphy (London: Geoffrey Chapman, 1990), pp. 1382-1416, at 1397-1402.

[89]Gordon D. Fee, "Paul and the Metaphors of Salvation: Some Reflections on Pauline Soteriology," in *The Redemption: An Interdisciplinary Symposium on Christ as Redeemer*, ed. Stephen T. Davis, Daniel Kendall and Gerald O'Collins (Oxford: Oxford University Press, 2004), pp. 43-67.

[90]See Gerald O'Collins, *Christology: A Biblical, Historical, and Systematic Study of Jesus* (Oxford: Oxford University Press, 1995), pp. 257-58.

[91]Morna D. Hooker, "Pistis Christou," *New Testament Studies* 35 (1989): 321-42, at 341.

[92]Thomas D. Stegman, *The Character of Jesus: The Linchpin of Paul's Argument in 2 Corinthians*

I was ready to accept that Paul's phrase would be more accurately rendered as "the faith exercised by Christ" or "the faithfulness of Christ" and our participation in his faithfulness to God and the divine purposes.[93] This means that the justification of the ungodly brings them to share in the faithfulness of Christ himself and all the benefits that the exercise of his faith has brought them.

I leave to the specialists what this different translation of "the faith of Christ" might do to Luther's and subsequent Lutheran theologies of justification. But the new way of interpreting the genitive in Paul's phrase, "the faith of Jesus (Christ)," could and should, I hope, support an even more Christ-centered view of what is involved when the ungodly are justified.

From the time of attending Ebeling's seminar on Christ's resurrection (which involved reading authors from Thomas Aquinas to Wolfhart Pannenberg), I have been constantly concerned to follow Paul by putting the resurrection of Christ at the center of my theological thinking and writing. This has involved respecting the distinct but inseparable contribution of Good Friday and Easter Sunday: "he [Jesus] was handed over for our sins and was raised for our justification" (Rom 4:25). Innumerable theologians, not to mention rank and file believers, have long neglected the resurrection in their versions of redemption in general and of justification in particular.

Finally, on the biblical front I must confess to struggling for years to appropriate the role of the Holy Spirit in my thinking about salvation and justification. The best that I have managed to do has come very recently in a chapter of *Salvation for All*: "The Universal Presence of Christ and the Spirit."[94] Sin, as Paul teaches in Romans, is universal and makes human life an experience of slavery. Without the new life brought by Christ and his Holy Spirit, we remain enslaved.

At this point I may be permitted an attempt at summarizing Paul's teaching on justification. I would call justification God's faithful activity of human and cosmic restoration effected through the inseparable work of Christ and the Holy Spirit, a restoration vividly manifested in the worship

---

(Rome: Pontificio Istituto Biblico, 2005).

[93]See my rather tentative endorsement of the Hays-Hooker-Stegman view in *Salvation for All: God's Other Peoples* (Oxford: Oxford University Press, 2008), p. 137. My full agreement came in *Christology*, 2nd ed. (Oxford: Oxford University Press, 2009), pp. 270-71.

[94]O'Collins, *Salvation for All*, pp. 207-29, see also pp. 242-47.

of Christian communities formed and nourished through the proclamation of the gospel and the administration of the sacraments.

Rome, Milwaukee and London

The pilgrimage toward an even fuller understanding of justification continued during my years of teaching theology at the Gregorian University in Rome (1973-2006). The pontificate of John Paul II (1978-2005) formed the heart of those years. I rejoiced in his bridge-building with Lutherans through his visits to Germany and the Scandinavian countries and through his being the first pope to preach in a Lutheran church, as he did in Rome itself on the occasion of the five-hundredth anniversary of the birth of Martin Luther (1983). From a theological point of view, that bridge-building reached its highpoint on October 31, 1999, when in the city of Augsburg representatives of the Lutheran World Federation and the Roman Catholic Church signed a "Joint Declaration on the Doctrine of Justification," which contains forty-four common statements covering basic truths regarding justification.

Cardinal Edward Cassidy, the president of the Pontifical Council for the Promotion of Christian Unity, who represented John Paul II at the signing ceremony in Augsburg, summed up in a very personal way the momentous nature of that achievement. He remarked that when asked on the day of judgment to give an account of himself, he would simply say that he had signed the "Joint Declaration."

After four hundred years of division, the "Joint Declaration" is a remarkable achievement. Both sides agree on the basics: it is entirely from God that salvation comes; it is pure grace, available through the life, death and resurrection of Jesus Christ; the saving gift of righteousness that makes human beings acceptable to God comes through faith in Jesus Christ. They also agree that the mutual condemnations of the sixteenth century no longer apply to the churches of the twenty-first century. Where Lutherans have traditionally stressed the justifying verdict of God passed by God on those who have sinned, Catholics (and Orthodox) have highlighted the grace received, which actually transforms sinners through the Holy Spirit. Many of these and other differences can be seen as complementary approaches rather than mutually exclusive positions. Both sides also have recognized how recent scholarly studies of Paul, in particular, the so-called new perspective on Paul, coming from Protestant and Anglican exegetes (e.g., E. P. Sanders, J. D. G. Dunn, N. T. Wright and others), have seriously put into question some aspects of Luther's and subsequent Lutheran readings of Paul.[95]

Of course, some sticking points remain. Catholics have reservations about the Lutheran doctrine of *simul justus et peccator,* which maintains that, while believers are "right" with God, they continue to be at the same time sinners, since the concupiscence that remains after baptism is actually sin. Catholics agree that the inherited concupiscence remains in the baptized as an inclination that comes from sin and presses toward sin, without understanding concupiscence to be sin in the proper sense, since sin always involves a personal decision. Lutherans have reservations about the way Catholics speak of "merit": God rewards believers for their actions, even though these actions come entirely from God's grace and may not be boasted about.

I was delighted that many paragraphs were excerpted from the "Joint Declaration" to form nine sections on justification (nos. 2000k-s) for the seventh edition of the classic collection of Roman Catholic doctrines: *The Christian Faith,* edited by Josef Neuner and Jacques Dupuis.[96] In producing this edition, I collaborated with Dupuis (1923-2004), who after many years of teaching in India had become a colleague at the Gregorian University. Neuner, who played an essential role in producing the first edition of *The Christian Faith* (1973), had many years before ceased being an active coeditor of the work. Dupuis himself, especially in the last years of his life, helped to develop my thinking about the salvation of those who are not baptized. With gratitude I dedicated to him *Salvation for All: God's Other Peoples.* But it was another colleague at the Gregorian who was more directly important on the doctrine of justification.

To guide my understanding and interpretation of justification, I enjoyed for twenty-five years of my life in Rome the constant company of Jared Wicks, S.J. It was in Münster (Germany) that we first met in 1964 when he was pursuing his doctorate on the spirituality of the young Luther. Subsequently Wicks played a major role in the Lutheran-Roman

---

[95]See David E. Aune, ed., *Rereading Paul Together: Protestant and Catholic Perspectives on Justification* (Grand Rapids: Baker Academic, 2006).

[96]Bangalore/New York: Theological Publications in India/Alba House, 2001.

Catholic official dialogues in the United States and also at the international level. He was one of the principal drafters of the 1999 "Joint Declaration." At the Gregorian University he proved a key figure over the years when we welcomed groups of Lutherans and individual Lutheran professors who came for six weeks or more as visiting professors. By listening to exchanges between Wicks and visiting Lutherans, I learned to deepen my understanding and appreciation of Luther and his teaching. After we had both retired from the Gregorian, I invited him to a symposium held in London in March 2008 on the theological legacy of John Paul II. Wicks's paper, "John Paul II and Lutherans: Actions and Reactions," forms a central chapter in the book that emerged from that meeting.[97] Wicks threw much light on the movement toward the "Joint Declaration on the Doctrine of Justification" of 1999 and on subsequent assessments by individual Lutherans and Roman Catholics.[98]

In the 1990s I was able to spend three semesters as a visiting professor at Marquette University, Milwaukee, where I enjoyed regular and fruitful contacts with Lutheran and Calvinist professors and students of Marquette's theology department. That Marquette experience every now and then alerted me to some differences between Lutheran and Calvinist readings of Paul. They concern, among other things, the status of the law, the value of human actions, and the place within theology of the doctrine of justification by faith.

Questions about God's justification and human righteousness came up again at the start of the twenty-first century, when I collaborated with two other scholars in producing two books. In *Catholicism: The Story of Catholic Christianity*, Mario Farrugia and I dedicated pages to the theme of grace and justification and tried our best to set out fairly the views of the Reformers and the Council of Trent.[99] At the end of my years in Rome and during a three-year appointment as research professor at St. Mary's University College, Twickenham (London) (2006-2009), I engaged in work

---

[97]In G. O'Collins and M. Hayes, eds., *The Legacy of John Paul II* (London: Continuum, 2008), pp. 139-202.

[98]To the items Wicks mentions, one should add C. Stephen Evans, "Catholic-Protestant Views of Justification: How Should Christians View Theological Disagreements?" in *The Redemption*, ed. Stephen T. Davis, Daniel Kendall and Gerald O'Collins (Oxford: Oxford University Press, 2006), pp. 255-73.

[99](Oxford: Oxford University Press, 2003), pp. 200-15. See also my own *Catholicism: A Very Short Introduction* (Oxford: Oxford University Press, 2008), pp. 37-39, 64-66.

on the priesthood of Christ with Michael Keenan Jones. In early 2010 it was published as *Jesus Our Priest: A Christian Approach to the Priesthood of Christ*.[100] This book contains a whole chapter about the interpretation of Christ's priesthood by Luther and Calvin, as well as a long section in a subsequent chapter on Tom Torrance's understanding of Christ's priesthood. An informed grasp of what Christ's triple role as priest, prophet and king and, in particular, of his role as priest affects seriously any understanding of the justification of the ungodly. Whenever such justification takes place, this occurs through the priestly intercession of Christ that continues forever at "the right hand" of God (Rom 8:34; Heb 7:25; 9:24).

To conclude, looking back at my long but modest engagement with the doctrine of justification, I can see the two great milestones in that journey. It was a great blessing to hear Ernst Käsemann at the height of his powers lecture on Paul's Letter to the Romans. It was also a great blessing to experience more than thirty years later the signing of the "Joint Declaration on the Doctrine of Justification," the fruit of so many years of patient dialogue involving John Reumann, Jared Wicks and other outstanding exegetes and theologians. That document has already entered history as one of the truly great achievements of the ecumenical movement.

---

[100]Oxford: Oxford University Press, 2010.

■

Traditional Reformed Response

Michael Horton

As a beneficiary of Gerald O'Collins's writings, I appreciate the opportunity to interact with his deeply well-informed summary of developments regarding justification. It is helpful to be reminded that the Council of Trent was not only an answer to the Reformation, but a "committee document," consolidating a position that would assuage rather than provoke fresh controversies between medieval schools.

While denying that we can make ourselves sinless, the authors note that a chief concern of Roman Catholic theology is to highlight that believers "can fulfill the moral imperative to live righteously" and human beings can "cooperate with God's grace." This is stated over against Luther's view of the near-dissolution of the *imago Dei* due to the Fall.

It should be noted that Reformed theology has always differed somewhat from Luther and Lutheranism on this point. For example, Calvin argues in various places that it is not nature, but the corruption of nature, that is the problem; sin, he says, is "accidental" rather than "essential" to human nature and it would be a "Manichaean" error to identify sin with a creaturely faculty.[1] He points out that even after the Fall there are remnants of original dignity that make it possible for unbelievers to achieve a civil justice between human beings even though they have no righteousness before God. Total depravity, for Calvin, does not mean that human beings are as bad as they could be, but that original sin has corrupted every good gift. Although we are fallen in the totality of our being (not just in our will, sensual appetite or body), no faculty has been destroyed. It is not that we cannot reason, but that we use our reason to "suppress the truth in unrighteousness" (Rom 1:18). We have not lost any of our senses, but employ these good gifts in mutiny against the good Creator. No power of will has been lost, but only the moral power of choosing that which our hearts should love but do not. Rays of God's glorious creation still break out in the physical beauty, design and strength of our bodies. The Reformed

---

[1]Calvin, *Institutes* 2.13.4.

scholastics distinguished between *natural* and *moral* ability. We have lost nothing of our natural ability as God's image-bearers, but are morally incapable of fulfilling this charge.

In fact, Reformed theology has often faulted Roman Catholic theology for substituting a sin-and-grace problematic for a nature-and-grace dualism, with Platonism's ladder of being descending from a higher to a lower realm. The *donum superadditum* presupposes that nature as God created it is already in need of being supplemented by grace.

This is a cursory sketch of typical Reformed criticisms, whose accuracy Roman Catholic theologians may dispute at various points, but at least it underscores the concern to guard the integrity of nature as God's creation. Reformed churches would endorse wholeheartedly the author's argument in footnote 14, that our Lord's sinlessness demonstrates that there is no necessary connection between sin and human nature. Indeed, our emphasis on Christ's fulfillment of the covenant of works (i.e., "active obedience") presupposes agreement with Rafferty's statement: "If justification is God's movement toward humanity, Christ in his human nature is humanity's movement toward God." Indeed, Christ could say of himself, "I have glorified you on earth, having accomplished the work that you gave me to do" (Jn 17:4). He therefore had the right to ask, "And now, Father, glorify me in your own presence with the glory that I had with you before the world existed" (Jn 17:5). In his ascension, he had the right to command the mighty gates to open for him, not only as the Covenant Lord but also as the faithful Covenant Servant.

I found the survey of medieval treatments illuminating, attesting to the variety of positions and emphases that were tolerated in the church (until, I would add, the condemnations of Trent). (A number of years ago, before mentioning the source, I read the canons of the Council of Orange to a group of students at an evangelical college and asked whether they thought this could be an acceptable evangelical creed. No, the consensus returned, it was too Calvinistic! They were more than a little surprised when I mentioned the source.) Especially enlightening was the way in which penance came to occupy a prominent role in the theology of justification.

The discussion of the later Middle Ages reminds us of how unoriginal the Reformers were in complaining of "Pelagianism." Such unimpeachable fourteenth-century authorities as Archbishop Thomas Bradwardine and Gregory of Rimini could warn of "the new Pelagians," and theologians in the next century like Gabriel Biel seemed to justify such fears.

On one hand, Protestants sometimes need to be reminded that the Council of Trent offered no quarter to Pelagians; nominalists like Biel could not have been much happier than Luther with the Council's canons. On the other hand, Trent captured well the Reformation's central theses and condemned them. "Above all Trent wanted to uphold the view that justification involved not only the remission of sins but also the sanctification of the individual," the authors remind us. This remains the heart of the issue. The question I've often asked my Roman Catholic friends on this issue is this: "Why does justification have to be subsumed under sanctification in order for us to affirm both?"

Like our differences with Orthodoxy, the divergence between Roman Catholics and churches of the Reformation over justification cannot be addressed simply by focusing on this doctrine by itself. Behind this doctrine stand different views of grace, for example. Is grace a divine substance infused into the soul, enabling cooperation with God toward the goal of final justification? Or is grace God's mercy and favor toward sinners in Jesus Christ—in fact, the gift of Christ himself (a person, not a substance), who makes all of his riches ours by imputation (justification) and impartation (sanctification and glorification)? Is grace a principle that elevates nature toward the supernatural, so that it may ascend to a higher realm of existence, or is grace the Father's action in Christ through the Spirit, liberating nature to fulfill its proper created telos?

Finally, it would be interesting to know what Professor O'Collins would make of the claim by Roman Catholic scholars such as Karl Rahner, Joseph Fitzmeyer and Raymond Brown, that *dikaioō* and its cognates belong to the law court as exclusively forensic in character and that this is a settled consensus in New Testament scholarship? Did the Vulgate erroneously translate *dikaioō* ("to declare righteous") as *iustificare* ("to make righteous"), and if so, what is the impact on the medieval development of the doctrine?

Pope Benedict XVI also acknowledges the exegetical implications of the Ancient Near Eastern research to which I have referred in response to Professor Dunn—specifically, the distinction between law-covenants and promissory covenants.[2] The New Testament "sees the covenant made with Abraham as the real, fundamental, and abiding covenant; according to Paul, the covenant made with Moses was interposed (Rom 5:20) 430 years after the Abrahamic covenant (Gal 3:17); it could not abrogate the covenant with Abraham but constituted only an intermediary stage in God's providential plan."[3] Benedict's exegesis leads him to conclude that "Paul distinguishes very sharply between two kinds of covenant that we find in the Old Testament": "a covenant that consists of legal prescriptions and the covenant that is essentially a promise, the gift of friendship, bestowed without conditions." In fact, *"Whereas the covenant imposing obligations is patterned on the vassal contract, the covenant of promise has the royal grant as its model.* To that extent Paul, with his contrast between the covenant with Abraham and the covenant with Moses, has rightly interpreted the biblical text" (emphasis added).[4] "The conditional covenant, which depended on man's faithful observance of the law, is replaced by the unconditional covenant in which God binds himself irrevocably. We are unmistakably here in the same conceptual milieu as we found earlier in 2 Corinthians, with its contrast between two covenants."[5] In fact, Benedict adds, the conditionality of the law-covenant "draws man's changeable will into the very essence of the covenant itself and thus makes it a provisional covenant. By contrast, the covenant sealed in the Last Supper, in its inner essence, seems 'new' in the sense of the prophetic promise: it is not a contract with conditions but the gift of friendship, irrevocably bestowed. Instead of law we have grace."[6]

Remarkably, Benedict even acknowledges,

> The rediscovery of Pauline theology at the Reformation laid special emphasis on this point: not works, but faith; not man's achievement, but the free bestowal of God's goodness. It emphatically underlined, therefore, that what was involved was . . . a "testament," a pure decision and act on God's part. This is the context in which we must understand the teaching that it

---

[2]Joseph Cardinal Ratzinger, *Many Religions—One Covenant: Israel, the Church and the World* (San Francisco: Ignatius Press, 1999), pp. 36-47
[3]Ibid., p. 55.
[4]Ibid., pp. 56-57.
[5]Ibid., p. 64.
[6]Ibid., p. 66.

is God alone who does everything. (All the *solus* terms—*solus Deus, solus Christus*—must be understood in this context.)[7]

Therefore, "With regard to the Sinai covenant, we must again draw a distinction."[8]

Nevertheless, Pope Benedict finally backs away from the exegetical conclusions he has drawn, returning to the central dogma of "covenantal nomism." Yet my point in citing him is to show that the exegetical path that led to the Reformation remains very much alive, including the distinction between law and gospel.

Finally, Professor O'Collins offers a valuable personal narrative of his own development on this and related themes. I agree when he says, "Innumerable theologians, not to mention rank and file believers, have long neglected the resurrection in their versions of redemption in general and of justification in particular." Since Christ was "raised for our justification" (Rom 4:25), this eschatological connection deserves prominence. Much like Herman Ridderbos, Richard B. Gaffin Jr., provides a sustained treatment of this in his book *Resurrection and Redemption*.[9] The resurrection brings together the themes not only of justification and sanctification, but also of glorification, with Christ as the first fruits of the new creation.

O'Collins concludes, "I would call justification God's faithful activity of human and cosmic restoration effected through the inseparable work of Christ and the Holy Spirit, a restoration vividly manifested in the worship of Christian communities formed and nourished through the proclamation of the gospel and the administration of the sacraments." This is a lot of freight for justification to carry! I would argue that precisely because it is the exclusively forensic ground of our salvation, justification brings all of the things that O'Collins mentions in its wake. In short, what he refers to as "justification," I would refer to "salvation" more broadly.

---

[7]Ibid., p. 67. However, the Reformers (certainly the covenant theology that arose in the Reformed tradition) did not contrast *covenant* and *testament*, as the writer suggests, but recognized that the specific type of *berith* that was the Abrahamic-Davidic-new covenant was a promised inheritance (testament) rather than a mutual contract, and so could only be served by the Greek *diathēkē* rather than *synthēkē*. On this point, see Geerhardus Vos, "Hebrews: The Epistle of the Diatheke," *Princeton Theological Review* 13 (1915): 587-632 and 14 (1916): 1-61, included in Richard B. Gaffin Jr., ed., *Redemptive History and Biblical Interpretation: The Shorter Writings of Geerhardus Vos* (Phillipsburg, N.J.: Presbyterian & Reformed, 1980), pp. 161-233.

[8]Ratzinger, *Many Religions—One Covenant*, pp. 67-68.

[9]Phillipsburg, N.J.: Presbyterian & Reformed, 1987.

Sticking points remain, even after the "Joint Declaration," which O'Collins regards as "a remarkable achievement." He mentions "reservations about the Lutheran doctrine of *simul iustus et peccator*" and differences over concupiscence. He adds, "Lutherans have reservations about the way Catholics speak of 'merit.'" Although the "Joint Declaration" does not resolve these issues—and by implication, reduces their importance, I agree that these remain "sticking points," and my earnest prayer is that we can return together to the Scriptures and wrestle with the texts in dependence on the Spirit of truth.

■

Progressive Reformed Response

Michael Bird

IF I EVER HAD DINNER WITH POPE Benedict XVI, I would earnestly beseech him to have a "do-over" concerning the Council of Trent. It was Trent that condemned the Protestant view of justification by faith with anathemas. Despite that, in terms of a reconciliation between the Protestant and Catholic churches, some good progress has already been made. Hans Küng did his best to line up Karl Barth and the Catholic Church on justification. The 1999 "Joint Declaration on Justification" by Lutherans and Catholics was a step in the right direction, though there is clearly a long way to go before the disagreements and concerns of both sides are assuaged. I am also encouraged by the fact that many Catholic commentators are peculiarly Protestant in their exegesis. I have no idea how any Catholic bishop on earth could give an imprimatur to Father Joseph A. Fitzmyer for his Romans commentary when he says things that are so Protestantesque. For instance:

> This Pauline message of judgment is what the Christian needs to hear first, and in the light of that message the message of justification by grace through faith takes on new meaning. It is only in light of divine judgment according

to human deeds that the justification of the sinner by grace through faith is rightly seen. Hence there is no real inconsistency in Paul's teaching about justification by faith and judgment according to deeds.[1]

I doubt that Calvin could have put it better! It is in light of that hope— "Rethink Trent" (perhaps we need an official Facebook page)—that I read the essay by Father Oliver Rafferty and Father Gerald O'Collins.

Rafferty does a good job of presenting the diversity in the patristic and medieval tradition on justification. His section shows that while the Reformers were in many ways innovative in their formulation of justification, there are a number of precedents and precursors in medieval Christian thought to Luther, especially Augustine. To that I would add that there was also a great diversity in Protestant teaching on justification. Luther and Melanchthon applied their Augustinianism differently. Martin Bucer believed in a double justification, the first by faith, the second by works, and left room for the Holy Spirit. Richard Hooker linked justification more closely with regeneration than others did, and Ulrich Zwingli connected justification with election in an original way. The Augsburg Confession and many puritans like Richard Baxter held to an imputation of faith.[2] I think there is enough breadth in the medieval and Reformation traditions to enable us to at least attempt to bridge the gap between Catholic and Protestant understandings.

In fact, I really do wonder if Girolamo Seripando's notion of a *duplex iustitia* (twofold justice) could be combined with John Calvin's notion of a *duplex gratia* (twofold grace) so that we could agree that righteousness in the Scriptures is forensic and transformative. It could be said that we receive a grace in Christ to be declared righteous and we also receive a grace to actually become righteous. The declaration of "righteous" is distinguishable from but not separated from the transforming righteousness wrought in us by the Holy Spirit as both righteousnesses originate in one saving act of God and share the same conduit of union with Christ. Christ is the source of our righteous status and the power for righteous living. Could we all sign off on that? I could!

---

[1]Joseph A. Fitzmyer, *Romans: A New Translation with Introduction and Commentary*, AB (New York: Doubleday, 1993), p. 307.
[2]Cf. James R. Payton, *Getting the Reformation Wrong: Correcting Some Misunderstandings* (Downers Grove, Ill.: InterVarsity Press, 2010), pp. 116-31.

Yet I fear that when all of that is said and done, the core differences will probably remain. Catholic teaching, as Rafferty expresses it, affirms that the believers can fulfill requisite moral imperatives and cooperate with God's grace and thus contribute to their own justification. To that the Reformers say "no," and I think they are right. In my reading of the New Testament, the bondage of the will, slavery in sin and the efficacious nature of God's grace rule out cooperation as a soteriological option. The Bible does not give us a God who says he wants to help us help ourselves. The God of Abraham, Jesus and Paul brings life to death, acquittal to the guilty, justification to the ungodly, and calls things that are not as though they are (see Rom 4). The association of justification with a particular sacramental theology of penance and baptism also serves to widen the divide since justification becomes bound up with a particular sacramentalism that the Reformed churches cannot accept. At the end of the day, the Reformed churches will continue to reject the idea that justification is an analytic verdict rendered on the basis of what God works into a person and instead regard justification as a synthetic verdict rendered on the basis of the righteousness that God adds to the believer by union with Christ.

It was also a pleasure to read Gerald O'Collins biographical treatment of the subject, not only because he is a fellow Australian, but because he looks back on the subject from a career as a Doctor of the Church and as an ecumenist.

O'Collins makes several references to the German scholar Ernst Käsemann, who argued that justification is both forensic and transformative. That certainly works in some passages like Romans 6:7, where Paul refers to being "justified from sin" in the sense of liberation from sin's mastery. In other contexts, however, I think righteousness/justification is straightforwardly and strictly forensic (e.g., Rom 5:1; 8:34, etc.). The transformative notion of righteousness, if parsed properly, can work, as long as justification is not identified with this transformation.[3]

Otherwise, I can affirm a lot of what O'Collins says in regards to what his professors taught him and how he defines justification himself.

[J]ustification as the faithful and saving action of God or the covenant

---

[3]On "righteousness" in the New Testament, see Michael F. Bird, *The Saving Righteousness of God: Studies on Paul, Justification, and the New Perspective* (Milton Keynes, U.K.: Paternoster, 2007), pp. 6-39.

faithfulness and liberating presence of God in making repentant sinners righteous through the merits of Jesus Christ appropriated in faith. . . .

This new life of grace was not primarily some created "thing" that was "infused" in our souls. Rather it was the personal indwelling of the Holy Spirit, being incorporated in Christ, and so sharing as far as possible in the inner life of the Blessed Trinity. . . .

I would call justification God's faithful activity of human and cosmic restoration effected through the inseparable work of Christ and the Holy Spirit, a restoration vividly manifested in the worship of Christian communities formed and nourished through the proclamation of the gospel and the administration of the sacraments.

I think that scheme is, for the most part, accurate, except that I would not call it justification. For me this is what we call more broadly salvation, of which justification is merely one part. While Reformed theologians can have a narrow view of justification as restricted to a system of imputation of Jesus' merits, I fear that O'Collins is making his definition as broad as the English Channel! Given that justification is, as O'Collins rightly notes, one metaphor among many, he should not freight it with the weight of the entire doctrine of salvation.

I must unfortunately nit-pick at three other elements of O'Collins's essay as well. First, I do not share his antipathy toward penal substitution. This doctrine can get caricatured and misrepresented, but as long as Jesus suffers the penalty of our sins in our place, then a doctrine of substitution is clearly biblical.[4] Second, I have referred to the "faith(fullness) of Christ" in my response to Jimmy Dunn. Now theologically I find the concept very attractive, Jesus' representative faithfulness is biblically sound and theologically warranted, but I simply do not think the Greek genitive will fly with the theological payload that theologians and exegetes want to mount upon it. With perhaps the exception of Philippians 3:9 and Ephesians 3:12, I doubt that Paul intended the *pistis Christou* constructions to be read as subjective genitives of "Christ's faith."[5] Third, the Reformed maxim

---

[4]Cf. Simon Gathercole, "The Cross and Substitutionary Atonement," *SBET* 21 (2003): 152-63; D. A. Carson, "Atonement in Romans 3:21-26," in *The Glory of the Atonement: Biblical, Theological, and Practical Perspectives*, ed. Charles E. Hill and Frank A. James (Downers Grove, Ill.: InterVarsity Press, 2004), pp. 119-39; N. T. Wright, *Justification: God's Plan and Paul's Vision* (Downers Grove, Ill.: InterVarsity Press, 2009), pp. 105-6.
[5]Cf. Michael F. Bird and Preston M. Sprinkle, eds., *The Faith of Jesus Christ: Exegetical, Biblical, and Theological Studies* (Milton Keynes, U.K.: Paternoster, 2009).

simul iustus et peccator (at the same time both righteous and sinner) really does reflect the point of contention. How can God declare a sinful person to be just? In my Reformed reading of Paul, the answer is, because believers are incorporated into the righteousness of Christ, his messianic task, his messianic death, his messianic vindication. That is why (to use the language of Romans) believers are justified freely by grace through the redemption that avails itself in Christ Jesus, why God justifies the ungodly, why there is now no condemnation for those in Christ. Justification means that God regards me as something that I am not, because of what Christ has done for me and, one day, in me.

To conclude, unless the Roman Catholic Church is prepared to rethink the Tridentine formulations that are so polemically anti-Lutheran, there isn't much hope for a reconciliation with the Protestant churches. That is sad, because Jesus calls us to pursue a visible unity as part of our witness to the world. I think the 1999 "Joint Declaration" was a good start to the kind of conversations that we need to have. We should explore and exploit the diversity of the Catholic and Reformed traditions and find as much common ground as we can therein. Commentators such as Ernst Käsemann, Markus Barth, Joseph Fitzmyer and N. T. Wright are good dialogue partners to help facilitate the conversation as to what "righteousness" means and how God's declaration of acquittal relates to God's work of renewal. In the end, however, I leave readers with the words of Martin Luther:

> If the Pope will grant unto us that God alone by His mere grace through Christ does justify the sinners, we will not only carry him in our hands, but will also kiss his feet. But since we cannot obtain this, we in God's will give no place, no, not one hair's breadth, to all the angels in heaven, not to Peter, not to Paul, not to a hundred emperors, nor to a thousand popes, nor to the whole world. Let this be then the conclusion: that we will suffer our goods to be taken away, our name, our life, and all that we have; but the gospel, our faith, Jesus Christ, we will never suffer to be wrested from us.[6]

---

[6]Martin Luther, *Commentary on Galatians* (Grand Rapids: Revell, 1988), p. 75.

■

New Perspective Response

James D. G. Dunn

OLIVER RAFFERTY'S ACCOUNT OF THE history of Christian discussion about justification is very informative and helps clarify the context out of which Luther's reformulation of the doctrine emerged. And Gerry O'Collins's biographical account of his own personal engagement with the subject is both fascinating and instructive (and provokes a number of very good personal memories). It is quite hard for a *Neutestamentler* to find much leverage in both accounts, beyond expressing my gratitude. But there is some.

As a New Testament specialist, and given that the subject being debated is so identified with the mission and teaching of the apostle Paul, I naturally looked for indications of the stimulus from Paul and engagement with Pauline texts in the history of the discussion. Such stimulus and engagement is certainly present with Gerry's personal story, and has evidently been a key factor in the development of his own insights into the subject. And it is no doubt unfair to lament the lack of such clear engagement with Paul in Oliver's account. But it did strike me that, so far as Rafferty's account is concerned, the debate among medieval theologians in particular seems characteristically to have been quite far removed from the biblical terms and theologizing of Paul within the context of his mission. The terms of reference seem to have been much more the interpretations of the biblical text which then became more influential than the biblical text itself—such factors as the Augustinian concept of original sin, freedom of the will, merit, penance, purgatory. No mention, it would appear, of Paul's principal motivating issue: whether Gentiles were equally acceptable to God (the God of Israel) as were Jews (the chosen people), how that acceptance was evidenced and on what terms. That concern for Paul was certainly rooted in the conviction that "no one living shall be justified before you [God]" (Ps 143:2). But it is sufficiently clear that his formulation and application of that conviction was conditioned by his calling as apostle to the Gentiles and the hostility which that mission aroused among more traditionalist Jewish believers. When that context is left behind or ignored, something of first importance for Paul himself is left behind.

A similar point relates to what Oliver refers to as "the core of the debate" for the Catholic tradition—namely, "a distinction between the idea of God's own justice and the idea of the justice with which God justifies the sinner. For most of the Catholic Western tradition, these are two distinct things. That by which God is in himself just is theologically distinct from that by which God makes a sinner just." That some distinction has to be made is self-evident, since the phrases "God is just" and "God justifies" are not simply synonyms. But when the key phrase in Paul's letter to the Romans is "the righteousness of God" (Rom 1:17), it is much less clear that a theological distinction should be made or is justified. For if the revelation of "the righteousness of God" "from faith to faith" is "the power of God for salvation for all who believe" (Rom 1:16-17) then God's justice/righteousness is for Paul his saving action on behalf of human beings. This follows directly from the fact that verse 17 explains verse 16, as Luther saw. But it also follows from an appreciation of the Hebrew understanding of righteousness, which Paul was able to take for granted (he didn't think it necessary to explain what the phrase "the righteousness of God" meant). It is the concern to understand that biblical background so central Pauline conceptions, and thus to understand Paul better, which I find lacking, at least in Rafferty's account. The richness of the Hebrew understanding of righteousness has been lost behind the rather different Greek and Latin understandings of righteousness and justice.

Equally disturbing is Rafferty's observation "that medieval theologians never quite understood Paul's idea of the primacy of faith, and that as the Middle Ages progressed the idea of faith was subsumed under the idea of grace." Here I confess to some disappointment that Gerry has jumped on the bandwagon that reads Paul's phrase *pistis Christou* as a reference to "the faith(fulness) of Christ," rather than "faith in Christ." It is not that I have any misgivings as to the legitimacy and importance of recognizing that Paul attributes so much to what Christ did, as expressed particularly in his talk of the obedience of Christ (Rom 5:19; Phil 2:8). It is simply that, in my view, to take the phrase in the sense "the faith of Christ" is poor exegesis in most of the cases where that sense is now being found. It is almost impossible to detach the phrase in Galatians 2:16 and Galatians 3:22 from the frequent *ek pisteōs* phrases that pepper Galatians 2:16–3:26 (Gal 3:22 is one such). And Paul's understanding of the latter phrase is the focus of Galatians 3:6-14, where it is surely clear beyond much doubt that the "faith" being talked about is the equivalent of Abraham's believing.[1]

This leads me to my second reaction to Gerry's conversion to the "faith of Christ" interpretation of the *pistis Christou* phrase: that so to take the phrase in effect diminishes and diverts the thrust of the phrase from its role in expressing and reinforcing Paul's argument that the gospel is effective because it works "from faith, to faith" and "through faith." For Paul, Abraham is the model of how God reckons someone righteous, because he simply believed in God's promise, hoping against hope (Rom 4:18), and so is the father of those who believe as he did, who had faith as he did. Which provokes a further sense of regret that Paul's powerful exposition of what believing means (Rom 4:16-22) seems to receive so little attention in all this. Justification *by faith* is important in Reformed theology simply because it was so important to Paul. Regrettably the "faith of Christ" rendition of *pistis Christou*, whatever its strengths, has obscured that central theme of Paul. On this point, it is rather significant, and should probably serve as some kind of warning, that Gerry's summary of "Paul's teaching on justification" omits any reference to believing or faith! Come back, Martin; all is forgiven!

The value of an attentive listening to Catholic doctrine on the subject is severalfold: not least, of course, the Catholic attempt to link sanctification more closely to justification, whether in terms of God giving the believer the ability to live a moral life, or the infusion of righteousness. Whether it is the best way to include sanctification within justification ("Above all Trent wanted to uphold the view that justification involved not only the remission of sins but also the sanctification of the individual") is a fair question. But Paul himself was quite ready to describe the event of becoming a Christian as being both sanctified and justified (1 Cor 6:11), just as he could express his gospel in terms of forgiveness of sins equally as in terms of justification (Rom 4:6-9). And elsewhere he did not hesitate to speak of believers' righteousness in terms of moral and caring action that he expected of his converts—the harvest of their righteousness (2 Cor

---

[1]See further my contribution to the festschrift for Richard Hays referred to in n. 68 of my own essay in this volume.

9:10-11). So hopefully further open dialogue between Catholic and Protestant will be able to build on the elements of each's traditional emphases which are there in Paul but which one or the other has glossed over or fitted awkwardly into the principal emphases of their own theology.

Not least, attention to Catholic tradition should provide a reminder that justification is not the sole or only central feature in Paul's soteriology. I remember the not unpleasant surprise when I first learned years ago that "justification" was not a particularly Catholic doctrine. The point was made to me in similar terms to Walter Kasper's observation that "in Catholic catechesis we tend to speak of salvation, forgiveness, reconciliation rather than justification" (n. 8). My experience was somewhat paralleled by Gerry's in his reaction to Ernst Käsemann, when "it gradually became clear to me that, for all its importance, justification is only one of the ten or so metaphors that Paul uses for salvation—a metaphor that, apart from Philippians 3:2-11, is limited to Romans and Galatians." Käsemann indeed exemplifies the danger of a Lutheran narrowing of Paul's soteriology to "justification by faith" ("the article by which the church stands or falls"), since he regarded "justification by faith" as the "canon within the canon" by which all theology should be judged. But if Paul could express his apostolic and evangelistic concern by a variety of metaphors, metaphors that do not all fit easily together or integrate into a single metaphor, like regeneration or justification, then to insist that all metaphors should be so fitted or so integrated will simply diminish the richness of Paul's theology and the effectiveness of the evangelistic preaching that it embodies.[2] This is one of the chief reasons why I welcome Gerry's shift of focus to give more prominence to the resurrection of Jesus (in a sequence of publications) and to the Holy Spirit. When the Catholic-Protestant dialogue on justification embraces also the Pentecostal focus on the gift of the Spirit, we may find ourselves much closer to Paul than we had imagined possible.

---

[2]I have attempted to make these points elsewhere, particularly in *The Unity and Diversity of the New Testament* (London: SCM, 1977, 2006³), chaps. 2 and 15; *The Theology of Paul the Apostle* (Grand Rapids: Eerdmans, 1998), pp. 328-33.

■

Deification Response

Veli-Matti Kärkkäinen

IT IS DELIGHTFUL TO ENGAGE AN ESSAY that offers the reviewer a surprise. The current essay by two leading Roman Catholic theologians certainly did so—in more than one way. Having Professor O'Collins, himself a leading international authority in systematic and dogmatic theology, to share a personal "testimony" rather than a tightly argued essay was an unexpected move, to say the least! Over many years I have benefited so much from his scholarship on key dogmatic issues from the Trinity to Christology to sacraments and beyond. To have an opportunity to follow his autobiographical theological journey on three different continents and various theological environments was an eye-opening experience. Another surprise was the choice by Professor Rafferty to focus solely on the Tridentian formulation and its pre-history in the dogmatic presentation of the doctrine of justification from a Roman Catholic perspective. The first sentence of the essay immediately points to that choice: "Perhaps the clearest and most systematic exposition of the Catholic theology of justification is that provided by the Council of Trent." The choice of Trent as the defining point of the Roman Catholic understanding of the doctrine of justification is of course a legitimate decision. Nevertheless, it would have been exciting to hear from these two experts in what ways later theological tradition has engaged, interpreted and perhaps expanded or even relativized the doctrine. As a non-Catholic, I have never understood why the Roman Catholic Church has not seen it necessary since Trent to revisit the doctrine of justification—not even at Vatican II!

Although it is not fair to "complain" about what is missing in an essay that in itself is full of invaluable, carefully argued and clearly presented insights, I wished that some (more) attention would have been paid to the meaning of the 1999 "Joint Declaration" with the Lutherans. I was of course delighted to read the last sentence of the essay: "That document has already entered history as one of the truly great achievements of the ecumenical movement." To know what those great achievements are in the contemporary Roman Catholic understanding, however, would be a useful lesson to all of us! For an outsider, it looks like some significant changes and shifts were taken by both parties in the understanding of many aspects of the doctrine of justification.

Professor Rafferty rightly warns us that even in the presentation of the "official" doctrine, one has to be mindful of various interpretations within that tradition. That, however, is the case with other ecclesiastical traditions as well, say, with Lutherans. In my essay I argue that to discern Lutheran views (in the plural) of justification, a distinction has to be made between Luther's own theology and that of the confessional writings. (As a side note, let me add here: Isn't it interesting that in this compilation of essays there is no defining Lutheran presentation. My essay presents one interpretation of the Lutheran view of justification but less from the perspective of confessional writings and more from an ecumenical perspective—and I am not a Lutheran theologian myself.)

Professor Rafferty's careful and meticulous tracing of the history and developments of the doctrine of grace and justification culminating with the Council of Trent is a storehouse in itself. I will make sure my (mainly) Protestant students both in Pasadena, California, and Helsinki will read those pages carefully. As a Protestant theologian I would just like to add the self-evident fact that this history of traditions is also as much my own theological history. As the author rightly reminds us, it is only Eastern Orthodox theology that was never interested in the debates on justification, as they went about soteriology with the idea of *theosis*. All Western churches owe their soteriology to the history accounted so eloquently by the first part of the essay. Professor Rafferty also makes the important observation that prior to Augustine, not much debate about the doctrine of justification took place—the term itself does not even occur often! I wonder if this familiar observation not only helps Protestants to put the doctrine of justification in perspective—as one of the many legitimate metaphors of salvation—but also opens an ecumenical avenue for the Western and Eastern churches to continue searching for a more appropriate convergence in the understanding of salvation.

Reflecting on the personal sharing of Professor O'Collins—deceitfully easy reading at first glance, but backed up with careful, insightful reasoning between the lines—I was moved by the number of themes familiar to the new interpretation of Luther's understanding of justification that I attempt to develop in my essay. In O'Collins's Catholic understanding, going back to his student days in Australia, justification is

> the faithful and saving action of God or the covenant faithfulness and liberating presence of God in making repentant sinners righteous through the merits of Jesus Christ appropriated in faith. Being justified by faith meant God making ungodly sinners righteous (Rom 4:5) and their entering the life-giving and "gracious" dominion of God (Rom 5:21). Justification came through the obedience of Jesus Christ in shedding his blood on the cross (Rom 5:9-11, 19, 21).

> This new life of grace was not primarily some created "thing" that was "infused" in our souls. Rather it was the personal indwelling of the Holy Spirit, being incorporated in Christ, and so sharing, as far as possible, in the inner life of the Blessed Trinity. In other words, we were encouraged to follow Eastern Christians, who have always cherished the notion of divine grace as sharing in the life of God (see 2 Pet 1:4).

There is very little here that the advocate of the new interpretation of Luther's theology of justification would want to take away—and so much to affirm. Coupled with this is the fact that, again in the words of O'Collins, "justification involved a call to righteous living; faith should bear fruit. Hence we could reconcile the teaching of Paul with James's stress on good works. Nevertheless, righteousness should not be construed as 'wages' paid for anything we did (Rom 6:23)." Even the way this profound Jesuit theologian continues reminiscing about the Roman Catholic teaching on justification a few decades ago in his own context, namely, in relation to "merits"—against my typical Protestant sensibilities—I found appealing. I may not be willing to say everything O'Collins says, but I am delighted to hear him say what he says as a Catholic believer.

Reflecting further on Professor O'Collins's account of developing thinking on justification, this time in relation to the great Protestant New Testament scholar Ernst Käsemann, I couldn't agree more with the way he negotiates the mutual roles of the "saving" and "forensic" natures of justification:

> Käsemann recognized that we faced a creative divine act that made sinners righteous and added that this did not exclude a further, "forensic" meaning

being involved. In his subsequent commentary he stated: "Mankind's justification is the actuality of God's right to his creation as this reveals itself as saving power." This converged with what my seminary professors had taught about justification as the saving action of God who forgives sinners and makes them righteous.

I also fully agree with O'Collins's criticism of Käsemann's claim that justification would be the key to understanding Paul's message. In my own essay I show evidence that currently even some leading Lutheran theologians such as Pannenberg maintain that there is no basis—nor need—to insist on the exclusive role of justification either in Pauline theology or in the dogmatic understanding of salvation.

From the great Lutheran dogmatician Gerhard Ebeling, this Jesuit theologian learned a lesson that has come to play an important role in my own developing thinking about justification and the work of Christ in more general terms, namely resurrection. Differently from the Eastern Christians, we Westerners, particularly Protestants, cherish the all-importance of the cross. Good Friday—which, interestingly enough in my home language (Finnish) means literally "Long Friday," signifying an extended period of suffering—rather than resurrection Sunday is our focus. By doing so, we are in danger of missing the wider context of justification, which is not about us but rather about God, who "justifies" himself by raising to new life in the power of the Spirit the Son who willingly surrendered himself "for us." God thereby shows himself to be faithful to his creation and to his promises. Resurrection also properly opens the way to post-Easter events, culminating in Pentecost and the presence and power of the Spirit, another emphasis of the Eastern Church. In my essay, I attempt to highlight in a new and fresh way the importance of resurrection and the work of the Spirit in justification—always, of course, in the framework of a proper Trinitarian grammar. Following the Reformed Karl Barth, we should also highlight more robustly the importance of the Ascension of Christ, the event that lies between Easter and Pentecost and that speaks of the cosmic rule of Christ at the right hand of his Father.

Contributors

James K. Beilby is professor of systematic and philosophical theology at Bethel University, St. Paul, Minnesota. He has coedited several Spectrum multiview books (with Paul Eddy), most recently *The Historical Jesus: Five Views* (2009). He is also the author of *Epistemology as Theology* (2006) and *Thinking About Christian Apologetics* (2011).

Michael F. Bird is lecturer in theology and Bible at Crossway College in Queensland, Australia. Among his books in New Testament studies are *The Saving Righteousness of God* (2007) and the edited volume, *The Faith of Jesus Christ: Exegetical, Biblical, and Theological Studies* (2009).

James D. G. Dunn is emeritus Lightfoot Professor of Divinity at Durham University, Durham, England. He has widely published on Jesus, Paul and early Christianity, and he is one of the leading figures in the new perspective on Paul.

Paul Rhodes Eddy is professor of biblical and theological studies at Bethel University, St. Paul, Minnesota. He has edited several Spectrum multiview books (with James K. Beilby), and has authored a number of other books including *John Hick's Pluralist Philosophy of World Religions* (2002) and *The Jesus Legend* (2007).

Steven E. Enderlein is associate professor of New Testament studies at Bethel University, St. Paul, Minnesota. He specializes in New Testament Greek and Pauline studies.

Michael S. Horton is J. Gresham Machen Professor of Systematic Theology at Westminster Seminary California, president of White Horse Inn and editor-in-chief of *Modern Reformation* magazine. His publications include *The Christian Faith* (2011).

Veli-Matti Kärkkäinen is professor of systematic theology at Fuller Theological Seminary and docent of ecumenics at the University of Helsinki. He is the author of numerous theological studies, including *One with God: Salvation as Deification and Justification* (2005).

Gerald O'Collins, S.J., is emeritus professor of theology at the Gregorian University (Rome) and adjunct professor of the Australian Catholic University (Melbourne). He has authored or coauthored fifty-seven published books, the latest including *Jesus Our Redeemer* (2007), *Jesus: A Portrait* (2008) and *Jesus Our Priest* (2010).

Oliver P. Rafferty, S.J., teaches church history at Heythrop College, University of London. His recent publications include: *The Catholic Church and the Protestant State: Nineteenth Century Irish Realities* (2008) and the edited collection *George Tyrrell and Catholic Modernism* (2010).

Author and Subject Index

Scripture Index

Spectrum Multiview Books

From IVP Academic

Baptism: Three Views, edited by David F. Wright

Christian Spirituality: Five Views of Sanctification, edited by Donald L. Alexander

Church, State and Public Justice: Five Views, edited by P. C. Kemeny

Divine Foreknowledge: Four Views, edited by James K. Beilby and Paul R. Eddy

Divorce and Remarriage: Four Christian Views, edited by H. Wayne House

God & Time: Four Views, edited by Gregory E. Ganssle

The Historical Jesus: Five Views, edited by James K. Beilby and Paul Rhodes Eddy

Justification: Five Views, edited by James K. Beilby and Paul Rhodes Eddy

The Lord's Supper: Five Views, edited by Gordon T. Smith

The Meaning of the Millennium: Four Views, edited by Robert G. Clouse

The Nature of the Atonement: Four Views, edited by James Beilby and Paul R. Eddy

Predestination & Free Will: Four Views of Divine Sovereignty and Human Freedom,
    edited by David Basinger and Randall Basinger

Psychology & Christianity: Five Views, edited by Eric L. Johnson

Science & Christianity: Four Views, edited by Richard F. Carlson

Two Views of Hell: A Biblical and Theological Dialogue, by Edward William Fudge and
    Robert A. Peterson

What About Those Who Have Never Heard? Three Views on the Destiny of the Unevangelized,
    edited by John Sanders

Women in Ministry: Four Views, edited by Bonnidell Clouse and Robert G. Clouse

IVP Academic
Evangelically Rooted. Critically Engaged.